# CASE STUDIES IN SOCIAL WORK PRACTICE

517

# CASE STUDIES IN SOCIAL WORK PRACTICE

**CRAIG WINSTON LeCROY**

*Arizona State University*

**Brooks/Cole Publishing Company**

Pacific Grove, California    A Division of International Thomson Publishing, Inc.

Social Welfare Editor: Peggy Adams
Development Editor: John Bergez
Editorial Assistant: Tammy Goldfeld
Print Buyer: Randy Hurst
Designer: Wendy Calmenson
Copy Editor: Melissa Andrews
Cover: Donna Davis
Cover Photograph: Plaza, Milan (Viesti Associates, Inc.)
Compositor: Bi-Comp
Printer: Malloy Lithographing

This book is printed on acid-free paper that meets
Environmental Protection Agency standards for
recycled paper.

2  3  4  5  6  7  8  9  10

**Library of Congress Cataloging in Publication Data**

Case studies in social work practice / Craig
Winston LeCroy.
    p.    cm.
   Includes bibliographical references.
   ISBN 0-534-15138-8 (alk. paper). —
ISBN (invalid) 0-534-00000-0
   1. Social service—United States—Case
studies.  I. LeCroy, Craig W.
  HV91.C36  1992
  361.3′2′0973—dc20       91-30613
                              CIP

ISBN 0-534-00000-0

*To Kerry B Milligan*

# CONTENTS

*Preface   xi*
*Contributors   xv*

## 1

## CASE STUDIES IN INTEGRATING THEORY AND PRACTICE   1

*Overview   1*

1-1   Ecologically Oriented, Competence-Centered Social Work Practice   5
*Anthony N. Maluccio, Shelley Washitz, and Mary Frances Libassi*

1-2   Social Learning Theory in the Treatment of Phobic Disorders   14
*Bruce A. Thyer*

1-3   Object Relations Marital Therapy: Engaging the Couple   22
*Judith Siegel*

1-4   Toward a Multiple Perspective in Family Theory and Practice: Social
Exchange, Symbolic Interactionism, and Conflict Theory   28
*Craig Winston LeCroy and Mark R. Rank*

## 2

## CASE STUDIES IN CHILD AND FAMILY WELFARE   35

*Overview   35*

2-1   Family Therapy and Child Welfare   39
*Rita DeMaria*

2-2   Challenging the Tradition: In Some Families Violence Is a Way of Life   45
*Steven Krugman*

2-3   Clinical Social Work in a Multidisciplinary Team: An Adolescent Inpatient
Psychiatry Case   50
*Catherine Sammons*

2-4   Treatment of Denial in Families Where There Is Child Sex Abuse   57
*Mary Jo Barrett and Terry S. Trepper*

## 3

## CASE STUDIES IN FAMILY THERAPY 69

*Overview 69*

3-1 Completing Brad's Dreams 71
*David Eddy*

3-2 Homebuilders: Helping Families Stay Together 74
*Nancy Wells Gladow and Peter J. Pecora*

3-3 Solution-Focused Therapy 87
*Steve de Shazer*

3-4 A Family Systems Approach to the Treatment of Codependency 92
*Christine Curry*

## 4

## CASE STUDIES IN TREATING ADULT DYSFUNCTIONS 97

*Overview 97*

4-1 Individual Treatment of Depression Utilizing Cognitive Therapy 99
*Brent B. Geary*

4-2 Brief Treatment of Anxiety 106
*Michael Liebman*

4-3 The Win-Win Bind 112
*Richard G. Whiteside*

4-4 Forensic Social Work: A Case of Infidelity, Intoxication, and Homicide 115
*José B. Ashford and Larry Whirl*

## 5

## CASE STUDIES IN PREVENTING PROBLEMS AND DEVELOPING RESOURCEFULNESS 125

*Overview 125*

5-1 The Shelter: Every Day Is a Struggle to Keep the Faith 127
*Lascelles W. Black*

5-2 The Multimethod Approach to Stress Management 136
*Randy Magen and Sheldon D. Rose*

5-3 Friends Don't Really Understand: The Therapeutic Benefit of Social Group Work for Caregivers of Older Persons 147
*Terry Peak and Ronald W. Toseland*

5-4 Divorce Mediation: An Application of Social Work Skills and Techniques 154
*Ann L. Milne*

5-5  Yonkers: A New Tale of Two Cities  161
*Jacqueline B. Mondros and Neil McGuffin*

# 6

# CASE STUDIES IN GROUP WORK  171

*Overview  171*

6-1  A Short-Term Single-Parents' Group  175
*Lawrence Shulman*

6-2  A Group for Relatives and Friends of Institutionalized Aged  186
*Tony Berman-Rossi and Alex Gitterman*

6-3  A Social Skills Group for Children  198
*Craig Winston LeCroy*

6-4  Group Work with Men Who Batter  206
*Richard M. Tolman and Larry Bennett*

# 7

# CASE STUDIES IN CROSS-CULTURAL SOCIAL WORK  215

*Overview  215*

7-1  AIDS and the Gay Couple  219
*John Patten*

7-2  Counseling an Interracial Couple  224
*Man-Keung Ho*

7-3  Dropping Out: A Feminist Approach  228
*Sophie Freud*

7-4  Working with the Urban Poor  235
*Myrtle Parnell and Jo VanderKloot*

7-5  Couple Counseling with Lesbian Women  243
*Natalie Jane Woodman*

# 8

# CASE STUDIES IN USING PRACTICE EVALUATION  251

*Overview  251*

8-1  Evaluating the Treatment of a Sexually Assaulted Child  255
*Betty J. Blythe*

8-2  Doing Family Therapy with an Acting-Out Adolescent: Applying the
Empirical Clinical Practice Model  262
*Kevin Corcoran*

**8-3**   Practice Evaluation Methods: Practical Variations on a Theme   268
         *Paula S. Nurius*

**8-4**   An Intensive Case Analysis: Application of the Quasi-Judicial Method   278
         *Craig Winston LeCroy and Bian Ismail*

**8-5**   Preventing Substance Abuse Among Native American Youth   287
         *Steve P. Schinke, Michael S. Moncher, Gary Holden, Mario A. Orlandi, and
         Gilbert J. Botvin*

# PREFACE

THIS BOOK PROVIDES A DIFFERENT FORMAT to learn about social work practice than is currently available in traditional social work textbooks. My intent is to provide students with a different educational experience. That experience results from reading and thinking about case studies.

Case studies are an action-oriented educational tool because they provide students with an opportunity to vicariously participate in the process of doing social work practice. It is critical to provide an interesting educational atmosphere for effective adult education.

In order to achieve this goal I have asked a number of different people, primarily teachers and social workers, to write case studies that reflect their experiences. Indeed, over 45 people helped to contribute to this book. The people chosen to write case studies reflect the diversity of social work practice. As a result, each case study is unique in approach, content, and writing style.

I have always told my students that doing social work is much more exciting and gratifying than reading about social work practice. Because the case study method of teaching allows students to participate in social work, there is a corresponding increase in interest and motivation for learning.

The objective of *Case Studies in Social Work Practice* is teaching students about the process of doing social work. The book is appropriate to a number of classes at the undergraduate and graduate levels. At the undergraduate level it may be used to teach students about the range and diversity of the social work profession. In this context the emphasis is on the various fields of practice, the organizational setting, and the variety of roles that social workers embrace. At the graduate level it may be used as the primary text or as a supplement to a more theoretical textbook with the emphasis on understanding the complex variables involved in delivering social work services.

*Case Studies in Social Work Practice* is also designed to be useful as a textbook for field seminars. Here the focus is to help students learn to discuss cases within a social work frame of reference. The instructor can use the case material and emphasize the practice principles relevant for the particular class and level of the student.

## TO THE STUDENT

This book was designed to make learning about social work interesting and exciting. In it you will find fascinating experiences that social work practitioners have shared about their work. The focus is on what social workers actually do as professionals, a picture of their day-to-day lives. As you read these case studies think about being confronted with each situation yourself. How would you feel? What do you notice? What would you do? By doing this you can vicariously participate in social work practice. This will give you important clues about whether this is the profession for you and where your interests are in the various fields of practice.

The purpose of this book is to help you learn to integrate theory and practice by studying how practitioners have applied general social work principles to particular case situations in the real world. In order to facilitate learning, each case study begins with a series of questions. These questions are designed to stimulate critical thinking and promote class discussion.

Classroom discussions about the case studies will investigate judgments made by the practitioners, answer questions you have about social work practice, and reveal the limitations of textbook generalizations. In many instances information in the case studies may be incomplete and opinions divided about the manner in which to intervene.

## FOR INSTRUCTORS—HOW TO USE THIS BOOK

This book can be used in a variety of ways to teach students about social work practice. The book is designed to be used in a flexible manner—depending on your needs and the objectives of the particular course. Some suggestions for how this book might be used include:

1. Having students think about what they might have done differently and why;
2. Having students write out treatment plans based on the information presented;
3. Using the case studies to discuss the range of roles and skills needed by social workers in a variety of settings;
4. Having students describe and analyze policies, organizational factors, and community implications inherent in the case studies;
5. Having students gather theoretical and empirical studies that could have been useful to the social worker in the different case situations.

With this kind of book it is important for you to decide how you can best use the case material. In my own experience, I have found some of the following ways of using case studies helpful.

The case studies can be used to get students to think like social workers. By reading the cases, students learn about the different environments that social workers must perform in, the decisions that social workers must make, and the importance of complex and competing factors in making those decisions. By vicariously participating in the practice of social work, students develop an understanding of how social work is performed, the social work environment, and human behavior in the social environment.

Use the case studies to help students develop a social work frame of reference. Each chapter is an opportunity for students to explore the various aspects and roles of social work: advocacy, case management, community organization, clinical counseling, referral, resource development, mediation, evaluation, and so on. As a result of reading the case studies, students will develop skills in approaching various social work problems and an understanding of the function social workers perform.

In order to stimulate student thinking and class discussions, each case study is preceded with a series of questions. The questions are designed to promote critical thinking and act as a catalyst for class discussion.

The case studies can be used for class discussion with many positive benefits. With a group of students a number of perspectives about the case will develop. Within this context the instructor can examine with students their underlying theories and assumptions about human behavior and social work practice. The natural interaction and exchange of ideas and information will promote an atmosphere for critical discussion. Too often, students accept any approach to a case without critique and analysis. Group discussion of the cases can be a safe environment to teach students more critical problem-solving skills.

Teach students to examine the facts and opinions in a case. Encourage students to take on the case situation and decide what they would do in some of the practice situations. Stimulate students to develop alternatives and choose the most effective course of action. Although each case contains its own particular approach to resolving a practice problem, each case also contains new problems to be addressed and new decision points that can be brought out in a class discussion.

You may also wish to use the case material to conduct role plays with the students. Students can be selected to act out the characters involved in the case study. As they take turns playing the social work practitioner, they will grapple with the real situations that social workers face in a variety of circumstances. You can provide students with feedback on skills and alternative courses of action. With experimentation you will find *Case Studies in Social Work Practice* an effective format for teaching social work practice.

The case studies will stimulate students to think critically, analytically, and objectively about social work practice. Clear thinking skills are a necessity in social work, and the cases should be used to promote such skills. As students move from one case to the next they will begin to develop an accumulation of experience in thinking and reasoning as applied to the very different problem configurations presented.

## ACKNOWLEDGMENTS

This book is the result of the many authors who agreed to graciously contribute a case study. Without them there would be no book, and I sincerely appreciate their efforts. Many people helped to make this a successful project. Arizona State University, School of Social Work provided the needed institutional support. Special appreciation goes to my colleague at the school, José Ashford, who has provided support, encouragement, and advice. Kerry Milligan, who observed my ritual of getting up early every morning to work on this book, was helpful regardless of what I needed at the moment—sympathy, support, guidance, or counsel. The staff and editors at Wadsworth are to be thanked for their work in turning this into a publishable book. In particular, Peggy Adams was critical in all phases of the book's development. I also acknowledge with thanks Richard Simon, editor of the *Family Therapy Networker,* for allowing me to reprint several of the case studies that appeared in the *Networker.*

I would like to acknowledge the following people for reviewing this book: Gemma Beckley, Grambling State University; Ernestine Brittingham-Brown, Delaware State College; Grafton H. Hull, Jr., University of Wisconsin—Eau Claire; Samuel Indelicato, Delaware State College; Karen K. Kirst-Ashman, University of Wisconsin—Whitewater; Dr. Alexander Szabo, Southern Illinois University.

# CONTRIBUTORS

*José B. Ashford, Ph.D.*
Associate Professor
Arizona State University
School of Social Work
Tempe, AZ

*Mary Jo Barrett, M.S.W.*
Director, Midwest Family Resources
Chicago, IL

*Larry Bennett, M.S.W.*
Visiting Lecturer
Jane Adams College of Social Work
Chicago, IL

*Toby Berman-Rossi, D.S.W.*
Assistant Professor
School of Social Work
Columbia University
New York, NY

*Lascelles W. Black*
Senior Case Manager
Volunteers of America
Wards Island, NY

*Betty J. Blythe, Ph.D.*
Associate Professor
School of Social Work
Florida International University
Miami, Florida

*Gilbert J. Botvin, Ph.D.*
Professor
Department of Public Health
Cornell University Medical College
New York, NY

*Kevin Corcoran, Ph.D.*
Associate Professor
University of Houston
Graduate School of Social Work
Houston, TX

*Christine Curry, M.A.*
Consultants on Family Addiction
Atlanta, GA

*Rita M. DeMaria, M.S.*
Executive Director
Center for Family Development
Ambler, PA

*Steve de Shazer, M.S.W.*
Director
The Brief Family Therapy Center
Milwaukee, WI

*David Eddy, Ph.D.*
Executive Director
Family Therapy Institute of Washington, DC
Rockville, MD

*Sophie Freud, Ph.D.*
Professor
School of Social Work
Simmons College
Boston, MA

*Brent Geary, M.S.*
Private Practice
Scottsdale, AZ

*Alex Gitterman, Ph.D.*
Professor
School of Social Work
Columbia University
New York, NY

*Nancy Wells Gladow, M.A.*
Formerly with Homebuilders
    Behavioral Science Institute
Washington D.C. and currently
Social Worker
King County Department of Public Health
Seattle, WA

*Man-Keung Ho, Ph.D.*
Professor
School of Social Work
University of Oklahoma
Norman, OK

*Gary Holden, Ph.D.*
School of Social Work
Columbia University
New York, NY

*Bian Ismail, M.S.W.*
Social Worker
New Foundation
Scottsdale, AZ

*Steven Krugman, Ph.D.*
Private Practitioner and
Co-Director, Trauma Clinic
Massachusetts Mental Health Center
Newton, MA

*Craig Winston LeCroy, Ph.D.*
Associate Professor
School of Social Work
Arizona State University
Tempe, AZ

*Mary Frances Libassi, M.S.W.*
Associate Professor
University of Connecticut
West Hartford, CT

*Michael Liebman, M.S.*
Private Practice
Phoenix, AZ

*Anthony Maluccio, D.S.W.*
Professor
University of Connecticut
School of Social Work
West Hartford, CT

*Neil McGuffin, M.S.*
Executive Director
Yonkers Interfaith Education and Leadership
    Development
Yonkers, NY

*Randy Magen, M.S.W.*
Doctoral Student
University of Wisconsin–Madison
School of Social Work
Madison, WI

*Ann L. Milne, M.S.W.*
Executive Director
Association of Family and Conciliation
    Courts
Madison, WI

*Michael S. Moncher, Ph.D.*
School of Social Work
Columbia University
New York, NY

*Jacqueline B. Mondros, D.S.W.*
Associate Professor
School of Social Work
Columbia University
New York, NY

*Paula Nurius, Ph.D.*
Associate Professor
University of Washington
School of Social Work
Seattle, WA

Mario A. Orlandi, Ph.D.
American Health Foundation
New York, NY

Myrtle Parnell, M.S.W.
Parnell & VanderKloot
New York, NY

John Patten, M.D.
Co-Director, AIDS Project
Ackerman Institute for Family Therapy and
Assistant Professor of Psychiatry
Cornell Medical School
New York, NY

Peter J. Pecora, Ph.D.
Associate Professor
University of Washington
Seattle, WA
and The Casey Foundation

Terry Peak, M.S.W.
Doctoral Student
School of Social Welfare
Rockefeller College of Public Affairs and
    Policy
State University at Albany
Albany, NY

Mark R. Rank, Ph.D.
Associate Professor
School of Social Work
Washington University
St. Louis, MO

Sheldon Rose, Ph.D.
Professor
University of Wisconsin–Madison
School of Social Work
Madison, WI

Catherine Sammons, Ph.D.
Social Worker
Neuropsychiatric Institute
University of California, Los Angeles
Los Angeles, CA

Steve Schinke, Ph.D.
Professor
Columbia University
School of Social Work
New York, NY

Lawrence Shulman, Ph.D.
Professor
School of Social Work
Boston University
Boston, MA

Judith Siegel, Ph.D.
Associate Professor
New York University
New York, NY

Bruce Thyer, Ph.D.
Associate Professor
University of Georgia
Athens, GA

Richard M. Tolman, Ph.D.
Associate Professor
University of Illinois at Chicago Circle
Jane Adams School of Social Work
Chicago, IL

Ronald W. Toseland, Ph.D.
Professor
School of Social Welfare
Rockefeller College of Public Affairs and
    Policy
State University of New York at Albany
Albany, NY

Terry S. Trepper, Ph.D.
Director, Family Studies Center and
Associate Professor
Department of Psychology
Purdue University Calumet
Hammond, IN

Jo VanderKloot, M.S.W.
Parnell & VanderKloot
New York, NY

Shelley Washitz, M.S.W.
Court Clinic Coordinator
Central District Courts of Northern Essex
Haverhill, MA

*Larry Whirl, A.C.S.W.*
Executive Director
Court Diagnostic and Treatment Center
and Private Practice
Toledo, OH

*Richard Whiteside, M.S.W., L.C.S.W.*
Senior Staff Member
Family Therapy Institute
Rockville, MD

*Natalie Jane Woodman, M.S.W.*
Associate Professor
School of Social Work
Arizona State University
Tempe, AZ

# CASE STUDIES IN SOCIAL WORK PRACTICE

# 1

## CASE STUDIES

# IN INTEGRATING THEORY AND PRACTICE

THE PROFESSION OF SOCIAL WORK IS BUILT on the assumption that social workers will use theory to guide their practice. A well-known hallmark of being recognized as a profession is that there is a body of knowledge that is organized into a consistent framework of theory. Thus an important professional skill is the application of theory to practice.

In what ways does the application of theory enhance the practice of social work? Theory provides a lens through which a practitioner can obtain a better perspective and understanding of a practice situation. If we can understand a situation better, we are more likely to find the best solution to that situation. In fact, practice theory should suggest the effects of a social worker's intervention. A school social worker might decide if she can identify children at risk she can prevent the likelihood of more serious problems developing later in life. Because of this theory she begins the process of developing such a program.

All the case studies presented in this chapter represent a different theory that guides practice. The approach to each case is quite different depending on the theory being used. Of course, the obvious question becomes, How do I know which theory to use? There are two general guidelines for the answer to this question: (1) the extent to which the theory is considered valid and (2) the degree of fit or appropriateness given the particular case.

A theory is considered valid if enough consistent scientific findings support its propositions. A well-supported theory in social work is the proposition that an empathic relationship will provide a basis to begin to help someone change. Without an empathic relationship the prospect for individual change is less likely. This theory has undergone much scientific study. Most social work scientists consider it valid.

Although a theory may be valid or true, it may not necessarily fit the case situation. For

1

example, good eye contact has been shown to enhance a person's ability to be perceived as empathic; however, this may not be the case with certain clients like Native Americans. Here a valid theory does not have a good fit with the particular client. Too often social workers attempt to extend theories that they are familiar with to case situations that do not have a good fit.

Because fit is often a problem in applying theories to social work practice, the social worker must become familiar with several theories of practice. Pincus and Minahan (1973) comment that "any one theory cannot be expected to be adequate for all situations." Most social work educators agree that practitioners need to select the theory and interventions that have the best fit with the client situation. Furthermore, the theories used should be valid, that is, empirically demonstrated to be effective. A common term for this understanding is systematic eclecticism. This means knowing a number of different theories and interventions and being able to use them systematically, depending on the needed fit. For example, according to the latest literature, the most valid theory and intervention for treating depression is cognitive therapy. The social worker practicing systematic eclecticism would be familiar with cognitive therapy and recognize the fit between depression and cognitive distortions.

In this chapter you will be reading about four different theories and their application to a case example. The first case study presents an application of ecological theory. Ecological theory is important for social work because it is considered to be a unifying framework (Germain, 1981; Germain & Gitterman, 1980). It is a unifying framework because it provides a theory to answer the question, What do social workers do? Although this theory is broad without much specification about practice guidelines, Maluccio and others have translated the theory into practice principles.

The case studies by Thyer and Siegel represent two major theoretical perspectives in clinical social work: behavior modification and ego psychology. Although these two perspectives are major theories for many social workers, they rely on very different assumptions about human behavior. Behavior modification examines such variables as antecedents and consequences to discover their contribution in maintaining dysfunctional behavior. Ego psychology examines mastery of ego functions within the context of developmental stages and life tasks. Both theories offer useful guidelines in working with clients.

The last case study, by LeCroy and Rank, demonstrates the utility of integrating and combining different theories. Theories may not necessarily be incompatible with one another. By integrating different theories, you have a variety of vantage points from which to understand your client's behavior, and this can offer you different perspectives on how to help this person.

The challenge of learning social work is before you. You must grapple with a number of different choices and assimilate a large body of knowledge. Use this challenge to make social work exciting. Don't oversimplify what it takes to provide good social work services. Accept that this is a complex profession and that you must continue to learn everything you can in order to serve it well.

## References

Germain, C., & Gitterman, A. (1980). *The life model of social work practice.* New York: Columbia University Press.

Germain, C. (1981). The ecological approach to people-environmental transactions. *Social Casework, 62,* 323–333.

Pincus, A., & Minahan, A. (1973). *Social work practice: Model and method.* Itasca, IL: F. E. Peacock.

# CASE STUDY 1.1

*An overview of ecological theory is presented and applied to a case requiring intensive casework services. A theme throughout the case is client empowerment.*

## Questions

1. How did the social worker mobilize the client's assets?
2. How was the client prepared to confront new situations and stressors that she will encounter later in life?
3. How can client strengths be used in the therapeutic process?
4. How did the interventions used in this case represent an ecological approach to practice?

## ECOLOGICALLY ORIENTED, COMPETENCE-CENTERED SOCIAL WORK PRACTICE

*Anthony N. Maluccio, Shelley Washitz, and Mary Frances Libassi*

Social work has long focused its practice on the person in her/his environment. Ecological theory helps implement this historic commitment. In conjunction with ideas about promotion of competence in human beings, ecological theory undergirds an approach to social work practice that focuses on understanding and enhancing the dynamic transaction between people and their environments. Following a summary of this theoretical perspective, this chapter presents a case study illustrating the major principles and guidelines of ecologically oriented, competence-centered social work practice.

## THEORETICAL PERSPECTIVE

The ecological paradigm draws from such fields as ecology, systems theory, anthropology, and organizational theory. In particular, it builds on ecology as a metaphor and thus on the study of the interactions between living organisms and their environments. As noted by Germain (1979, p. 7):

> Ecology rests on an evolutionary, adaptive view of human beings (and all organisms) in continuous transactions with the environment. As a metaphor for practice, the ecological perspective provides insight into the nature and consequence of such transactions both for human beings and for the physical and social environments in which they function.

As reflected in the above quote, a central feature of the ecological perspective is its view of people and environments as parts of a unitary system in which each continually shapes the other (Germain, 1979). The person and the environment are understood to be complementary, independent parts of a whole. By thus offering a broad conceptual lens for viewing human functioning and needs, the ecological approach underscores that social work intervention should be addressed to the interface between human beings and their impinging environment. In short, social workers seek to influence change in both the person and the environment.

The ecological perspective is complemented by a competence orientation that contrasts with the more typical pathology or deficit model of social work. Competence refers to the repertoire of skills and abilities that enable the person to function effectively. When viewed within an ecological framework, competence can be defined as the outcome of the interplay among:

- A person's capacities, skills, potentialities, limitations, and other qualities
- A person's motivation—that is, his or her interests, hopes, beliefs, and aspirations
- The qualities of the person's impinging environment, such as social networks, environmental demands, and opportunities

While the metaphor of ecology provides a way of perceiving and understanding human beings and their functioning within the context of their environment, theories about competence and its development lead to *competence-centered social work practice*, a perspective that holds that the promotion of competence in human beings is a central function of social work intervention (Maluccio, 1981). Competence-centered social work practice embodies a set of attitudes, principles, and strategies designed to promote effective functioning in clients by focusing on their unique coping and adaptive patterns, mobilizing their actual or potential strengths, emphasizing the role of natural helping networks, and using environmental resources as major instruments of help.

## PRACTICE PRINCIPLES AND GUIDELINES

Ecologically oriented, competence-centered social work practice is characterized by a number of key principles and guidelines, which are summarized below. These are adapted from more extensive discussions of the life model of social work by Germain and Gitterman (1980); the eco-systems perspective by Meyer (1983, 1988); and the competence orientation by Maluccio (1981).

### View of Human Beings and Problems

Human beings are viewed as striving, active organisms with strengths and potential for growth and development throughout their lives, as long as the proper environmental supports are available to them. Moreover, human beings are motivated to achieve competence in their coping with environmental challenges (White, 1963).

Human difficulties are defined as "problems in living" resulting from the lack of fit between people and their environments. Problems are located within the transaction between people and their environments rather than within the person. The concern with pathology is balanced by an explicit focus on the person's strengths and potentialities. Major categories of problems in living are:

- Life transitional problems and needs, including developmental crises, status and role changes such as marriage or divorce, and crisis events
- Interpersonal processes including relationship and communication problems
- Environmental problems resulting from discrepancies between people's needs and available resources

### View of Clients

Clients are regarded as partners in the change process and defined as resources, as having assets and potentialities that can be mobilized on their behalf. Pathology is recognized, but emphasis is placed on engaging and mobilizing the strengths and potentialities of clients. There is also emphasis on client autonomy, initiative, and action.

Workers are viewed primarily as enabling

or change agents who play diverse roles and use varying approaches so as to provide the conditions necessary for clients to achieve their purposes, meet life challenges, and carry out their developmental tasks. The helping process is characterized by mutuality and sharing.

## Unit of Attention

The unit of attention or focus of helping efforts is expanded in both assessment and intervention: attention is paid to the person and environment and the transactions between them. Assessment includes evaluation of the quality of the environment as well as the person's functioning, and it underscores these questions:

- What is there in the client's physical or social environment that is supportive, nutritive, enriching, or suited to the person's needs, styles, and qualities?
- What is there in the environment that is unsupportive, stressful, destructive, or inconsistent with the person's needs and qualities?
- What needs to be changed, removed, or added so as to render the environment richer and more supportive for the person?

## Intervention

The worker's intervention is addressed to the transaction between people and their environments. It can focus on improving the coping of the individual, changing the environment, or both.

Practice activities are varied and determined by clients' needs and qualities more than one's preferred modalities. Helping efforts are located as close as possible to the client's natural life space. Such location enables the worker to understand and assess a person's life situation, take full advantage of the therapeutic potential of the client's life processes, and use strategies such as life space interviewing. Location of help at these "crossroads of life" has the potential for being preventive as well as rehabilitative.

Practitioners work with or on behalf of clients to restructure or enrich their environment, as a means of facilitating coping and adaptation. There is emphasis on mobilizing resources in the client's social networks; creating new networks when necessary; and in general using strategies of environmental modification.

In addition, the client's own life experiences and actions are regarded as valuable means to strengthen adaptive capacities and promote self-esteem and competence. The worker aids the client in seeking out activities that promote personal growth, the learning of social skills, and the development of competence. Especially crucial in this regard are social skills training, self-help groups, and other approaches focused on educating rather than treating the person.

The following case example illustrates the use of the key principles and guidelines outlined above. In particular, the case exemplifies the importance of evaluating and appreciating the impact of the environment on human functioning and development; the view of clients as autonomous organisms motivated to achieve competence in dealing with life challenges; the role of clients as partners in the helping process; the use of life experiences and events as instruments of help; and the emphasis on restructuring and enriching the client's environment by identifying and mobilizing resources in the clients and their social networks.

## CASE EXAMPLE

### Referral

Carrie Brown* contacted my agency, an outpatient substance abuse counseling program,

* This is not the client's real name. To maintain confidentiality, all clients' names have been changed.

by mail and requested "someone to talk to on the outside" or "she'd go crazy." Carrie was well known to the agency, as she had been a resident of our inpatient program and had maintained infrequent and informal contact since her discharge. I was asked to contact Carrie and offer our agency services to her.

I prepared for my initial call by looking through agency records regarding Carrie's life and situation. It was a discouraging picture. Carrie was 19 years old. Her history and development were characterized by numerous family crises, including physical and mental illness, substance abuse, sexual abuse, and foster care placements. For example, Carrie's mother had been diagnosed as bipolar/schizophrenic and hospitalized for an extended period. Despite this treatment, she eventually died of a drug overdose. Carrie had been sexually abused over an extended period, first by her father at age 7 and then by a member of one of her foster families. She and her family had received numerous services throughout the tumultuous years. Carrie had been hospitalized on several occasions as a result of substance abuse and suicide attempts. In one instance, she had been discharged from the hospital because it was thought that the program could not affect her destructive relationships and behaviors. The records reported that Carrie was noncompliant and hostile and denied any need for treatment.

I was aware of the number of diagnoses she had been given by previous practitioners, including depression; adjustment disorder of adolescence with depressed mood; poly-substance abuse; schizo-affective disorder; and borderline personality disorder. Her psycho-social stressors (Axis IV of DSM-III) were consistently rated as severe. Her highest level of adaptive functioning (Axis V) was rated as poor. I.Q. testing revealed functioning within the borderline range, and recommendations did not highlight strengths or hope for increased capacities. As one psychological eval-uation stated: "She is limited intellectually, has poor reality testing skills and limited ability for insightfulness, and is symptomatically resistant to the usual modes of intervention."

Most recently, Carrie had been living with a boyfriend, a 35-year-old Vietnam veteran with problems of substance abuse. Amazingly, this boyfriend had been trying to curb her substance abuse but in a threatening and violent manner. During this time, Carrie began working as a nurse's aide in a rehabilitation hospital. Somehow, she was managing employment in the midst of this turbulent life.

With this factual information, I tried to prepare myself for entering Carrie's world, so as to appreciate her struggles and strivings to achieve competence as she faced many life difficulties. I tried to imagine what she must be feeling: the desperation, the hopelessness, the anxiety. I reflected on the developmental tasks she was coping with, that is, searching for an identity, struggling with issues of sexuality and intimacy, desiring a sense of competency and self-esteem.

I wondered what had caused her to reach out for services, when her experience with so many services had been negative. I realized that even though she was seeking services, much of the success of the initial engagement would result from the way in which I offered her my services. It would be crucial to do so in a way that respected her past experiences but proposed new ways in which we *could* work together on *her* agenda.

### Initial Phase

And so, Carrie and I met. I found that her goals were general—she could no longer tolerate her situation. She thought and even talked of suicide. She wanted her life to change but did not know how or where to start to bring about any change. She was quite clear that she would not accept a referral to a mental health center for therapy. "All they ever wanted to talk about was my father." She was clear she wanted to work on her "reality" problems. I felt comfortable in accepting her "real world" as our unit of attention. It fit with social work purpose and with my agency's function.

I was conscious of the dismal prognosis other practitioners had formulated for Carrie, but I tried to put that aside and view her problems as manifestations of a lack of fit between her needs and the resources in her environment, that is, as outcomes of the transactional processes in her life. For this reason, I proceeded to carry out an expanded assessment, including an evaluation of both the person system (biopsychosocial) and the impinging environment.

Our initial task was to explore Carrie's life situation, to look at her personal and environmental resources in order to mobilize her strengths, both environmental and personal. I used as guidelines the techniques of competence clarification, that is, "the process of identifying and understanding the person's capacity to deal with environmental challenges" (Maluccio & Libassi, 1984, p. 51). This technique involves clarifying (1) the competence of the client system; (2) the characteristics of the impinging environment; and (3) the goodness of fit between person and environment.

*Clarifying the Competence of the Client System.* I realized that biologically and developmentally Carrie was at the stage of late adolescence. She was searching for an identity. Further, she had needs for achievement, for recognition of accomplishment of some kind in order to achieve such an identity. Her past experiences had not prepared her for the challenges of this life task. She had been physically, sexually, and emotionally abused. Parenting had not been consistent and responsive to her needs. Carrie had not experienced the "normal" socialization process in her family or the school and had not emerged with a sense of competence and worth. Rather, I found that she had great difficulty trusting

others, and she felt shame, guilt, and inferiority.

Carrie also struggled with feelings of stigma as a psychiatric patient and a drug abuser. Although her identification with the drug culture was stigmatizing, it did give her an identity, a role, a language, a function. Her use of drugs helped her cope with the other stressors in her life. In sum, Carrie was struggling to fulfill her "normal" status and role tasks while coping with the stress generated by the exceptional demands of her stigmatized or devalued status (Germain & Gitterman, 1980).

But, the more I came to know Carrie the more I realized that there were latent personal strengths and potentialities. She was a giving, nurturing, kind person. She enjoyed being with people and helping people. Although her current depression was causing lethargy and lack of motivation, case records describing prior experiences with Carrie revealed an underlying energy and motivation. She had survived multiple destructive experiences and was still reaching out for help, guidance, and nurturance. In many ways, she was still the young child whose needs had never been met. It was that childlike quality that charmed and engaged people. The potential did exist for the development of corrective relationships to nurture growth and competence for Carrie.

*Clarifying the Characteristics of the Impinging Environment.* Several relevant and salient features of Carrie's environment emerged. First, she had not received appropriate services from the treatment programs in which she had participated. Rather than seeing her behavior as an indication of the need for continued treatment, various practitioners had branded Carrie a rule breaker and a noncompliant and unmotivated client. The policies and procedures of the agencies where she had received services, including my own, were a major environmental barrier to treatment.

In addition, Carrie's environment was far from nutritive or supportive. She had numerous concrete needs, particularly financial and medical. She and her boyfriend owed back rent and utility and phone bills. There were several medical concerns, some of which related to the abuse of drugs and alcohol. Also, she was underweight and malnourished, complained of constant headaches, and had occasional blackouts. She had earlier been diagnosed as having a seizure disorder, but it was difficult to determine whether this was due to the alcohol abuse or to a neurological disorder. And yet she was not receiving any medical services.

Carrie's social networks were minimal and, in most ways, destructive. Her family network of sister and brother reinforced her drug problems by their own drug use; at the same time, however, it provided important support and love. On the other hand, the "druggie" network to which she belonged was maladaptive and impeded her strivings for growth and health. Acceptance and membership were based on continued drug use. But, for Carrie, the pressure to be accepted was extremely powerful. She also had a powerful relationship with her boyfriend. The boundaries of this relationship were rigid and isolated and undermined Carrie's growth and identity. She described her experience of this relationship as feeling trapped, held prisoner. And yet, there appeared to be some sort of love that was manifest in the boyfriend's concern about Carrie's addiction.

*Clarifying the Goodness of Fit Between Person and Environment.* Carrie had a number of strengths, notably a giving nature and a motivation for change. At the moment, she was overwhelmed by a number of negative environmental factors, previously identified, and was using maladaptive methods as coping techniques. A positive environmental experience that supported and promoted her adaptive functioning and even competence was her job. Although Carrie initially stated that she hated it, further clarification revealed that she indeed found great fulfillment through working with the elderly, talking to them, and caring for them. This positive experience was one of the prominent features in her transaction with the environment: it seemed to release her adaptive potential and promote her self-esteem.

**Ongoing Phase**

As Carrie and I planned for intervention together, on the basis of the above clarification, I was convinced that much of our efforts should focus on Carrie's natural life experiences and processes. The overall goals for our work together were to improve her biopsychosocial functioning, release her adaptive capacities, promote her competence, and strengthen her ability to exercise autonomy and control over her life situation. In working with her toward these goals, I deliberately regarded her as someone who was striving toward growth, who was a resource on her own behalf, and who could learn through more positive life experiences. I saw my primary role as supporting her in these efforts and providing growth-producing opportunities.

We began our work with the traditional format, that is, 1-hour sessions in my office. I soon realized that Carrie was uncomfortable in this situation. Accordingly, I changed the treatment environment to suit her comfort, and we met in her apartment and had coffee together. The length of the sessions varied according to her need. In short, I adapted the helping format to meet her needs and desires rather than my own or my agency's.

The early work with Carrie was painstakingly slow, frustrating, *and* scary. It seemed as though we took one step forward and 10 steps back. Although we had set as a goal the reduction/elimination of drug abuse, it became clear that Carrie was not ready to give this up.

Her identity and social relationships were very tied up with the drug culture. She refused my suggestion that we attend Alcoholics Anonymous (AA) or Narcotics Anonymous (NA) together. Carrie did not believe that these groups could provide her with a social network.

Of particular concern were her chronic suicidal ideation and feelings of apathy, which were most acute when she was drinking heavily. I was never really sure whether I would see her again or read about her in the local obituaries. These drinking bouts also affected her ability to work, which had been a major step toward competence and self-esteem. My therapeutic support did not seem to be influencing her behaviors or feelings at all, even though she appreciated and respected our time and work together.

I questioned whether there was a biological base to Carrie's drinking and depression. I was aware that her mother had suffered from mental illness. I suggested that she and I should explore the possibility of somatic therapy/medication. At first she resisted, fearing yet another label and the stigma attached to any form of mental illness. Playing the role of educator, I helped Carrie understand the nature of mental illness as a brain dysfunction and the ways in which psychotropic medication could be useful in alleviating some of the troublesome symptoms of the illness. We discussed her prior experience with the side effects of medication and the importance of finding the right medication for her, on the basis of her knowledge of her feelings and responses.

With her increased knowledge and altered perceptions, Carrie was agreeable to a psychiatric consultation. My task now was to obtain such a consultation without the procedural hassles so often encountered. For example, the mental health center required that anyone seen for a psychiatric consultation be willing to participate in therapy with a staff member

of the center. Carrie was unwilling to enter into yet another therapeutic relationship. Fortunately, I was able to convince the center's staff that my therapeutic work with Carrie was an adequate substitute. Getting the system to alter its policies was difficult, and yet my working relationship with key people in other agencies paid off. The consultation resulted in a prescription for medication, but Carrie was given considerable opportunity for control, input, and autonomy in its use.

At this point, life events intervened and had a powerful impact on Carrie's motivation and the direction of our work. She became pregnant and made a conscious decision to keep the baby and raise it on her own. Our goals and tasks for our work were reformulated to meet this new life challenge and take advantage of the new life experiences. Together we began to identify what supports she needed to promote her competence as a mother and what changes were necessary in her behavior and life-style. It was amazing to watch her give up old patterns of thought and activity. For example, she immediately stopped using drugs and alcohol. The awareness of the life inside of her and its preciousness to her was the motivation that was not present before. She wanted to give her child every possible chance to come into the world whole and healthy. It was for her child and his life that her life now had value and meaning. My goal was to build on this strength and this value and to extend these positive feelings and values to Carrie's concern for herself. As described by Golan (1981), a new, altered life space impels the person to set up a cycle of internal and external changes aimed at improving the "fit" between herself and her environment.

Carrie's response demonstrated how life changes can create new potentialities for actions when the client receives support and encouragement from the worker and other significant persons in her social networks.

During this period, Carrie, in fact, began to take independent action to secure prenatal care and followed through with appointments and self-care. My role became one of validator, providing feedback to her that highlighted the effectiveness of her actions and her growing competence as a responsible future mother *and* as a person.

Another role I played was that of broker, as Carrie began to need services from the public welfare system. I helped cut through the chaos, the red tape, and the humiliation by helping Carrie obtain necessary verifications, file forms, and so on. I also provided transportation to appointments and companionship and coaching for the numerous interviews necessary to obtain entitlements and services. Carrie continued to follow through and take action on her own behalf, therefore not decreasing her level and feelings of competency drastically. Indeed, the frustration of dealing with the public service system may have helped promote new and healthy coping mechanisms.

In addition, I identified sources of needed services for Carrie, such as income and health insurance through Aid for Dependent Children; nutrition and health information through the Women, Infants and Children's Program (WIC); and pregnancy and parenting information through the Visiting Nurse Association. Carrie and I worked as a team on arranging these services, with my serving as enabler, resource, and coach and with Carrie following through to obtain the services. In varied ways, I thus helped her to modify and restructure her environment, to make it more nutritive, and to render it more suited to her changing needs.

Another focus of intervention was explicit use of life experiences to promote growth through teaching and modeling new skills and behavior in a way that enhanced self-esteem and promoted competence and autonomy in Carrie. One experience was particularly memorable. In keeping with the ecological orientation, I accompanied Carrie on some of her errands, thus participating in her real-life experiences. In the course of using the WIC vouchers, Carrie felt particularly humiliated. When she reached the check-out counter, the vouchers had to be approved by the manager. The clerk waved the vouchers in the air as she called for the manager's attention. These actions, and the delay in the check-out line, brought the attention of all and considerable embarrassment and humiliation to the consumer.

After one such experience, Carrie refused to use the vouchers and spent what little income she had on groceries. I tried to depersonalize the situation and help her see this as a problem with the system. As a social worker, I considered trying to change the system through bureaucratic means but decided that was not feasible. Accordingly, I attempted to influence the system on a more individual level by educating the cashier and surrounding customers as to the nature and purpose of the WIC program, as I proceeded through the check-out line purchasing groceries *for* Carrie.

Carrie and I also worked to strengthen her natural support systems by strengthening her ties to her brother and sister and by improving her relationship with her boyfriend. All of them became invested in Carrie's pregnancy and offered considerable support and attention—at times, too much attention. She and I discussed and role played ways to communicate her feelings and needs to her family so that she could benefit from their support but not be overwhelmed and smothered by it. Through this process, she strengthened her social skills and self-image.

### Ending Phase

Carrie gave birth to a healthy baby boy. She obtained her High School Graduate Equivalency Diploma and her driver's license. She found a job working part-time as a home-maker for the elderly. She began to feel that she no longer had to live with her boyfriend but could make it on her own. In our work together we explored options for new living arrangements for her and the baby. It was evident that her feelings of self-worth had increased tremendously: Carrie's strength as a survivor had indeed developed into competence as a mother and as a person.

As we ended our work together, we reviewed the accomplishments of the past few months. I used these accomplishments to reinforce her developing feelings of competence and her sense that she was facing the future with a new measure of confidence in her own abilities. We highlighted her strengths and the major skills she had learned and discussed how these could be useful to her in facing problems and challenges she would encounter in the future. Carrie continued to resist all efforts to link her with organized groups such as AA/NA or parenting groups. However, she was aware that she needed support, and so we worked together to improve relations with her family as well as a young mother close in age whom she had recently met and identified as a friend and confidante.

Finally, we evaluated our work together. It had been fulfilling for us both. I suggested that this kind of helping relationship characterized by authenticity and sharing would be useful to her whenever she felt overwhelmed by life's problems and needs. And so, our work together ended, as we considered future crises she might face and identified her personal strengths and environmental resources available to her, including the agency's services, that could be mobilized to support and nurture her in meeting whatever problems and challenges came her way.

## References

Germain, C. B. (1979). Ecology and social work. In C. B. Germain (Ed.), *Social work practice: People and environments* (pp. 1–22). New York: Columbia University Press.

Germain, C. B., & Gitterman, A. (1980). *The life model of social work practice.* New York: Columbia University Press.

Golan, N. (1981). Building competence in transitional and crisis situations. In A. N. Maluccio (Ed.), *Promoting competence in clients—A new/old approach to social work practice* (pp. 74–100). New York: The Free Press.

Maluccio, A. N. (1981). *Promoting competence in clients—A new/old approach to social work practice.* New York: The Free Press.

Maluccio, A. N., & Libassi, M. F. (1984). Competence clarification in social work practice. *Social Thought, 10,* 51–58.

Meyer, C. H. (1983). *Clinical social work and the eco-systems perspective.* New York: Columbia University Press.

Meyer, C. H. (1988). The eco-systems perspective. In R. A. Dorfman (Ed.), *Paradigms of clinical social work* (pp. 275–285). New York: Brunner/Mazel.

White, R. (1963). *Ego and reality in psychoanalytic theory.* New York: International Universities Press.

*The case study uses various components of social learning theory in successfully intervening with a phobic disorder. The client left treatment with a sense of accomplishment and a set of new strategies and behaviors that could be used in future situations with similar circumstances.*

## Questions

1. How does social learning theory explain the development of phobic disorders?
2. What treatment strategies are used to help the client change his phobic behaviors?
3. What factors do you believe led to the successful outcome in this case?
4. How was the client involved in the treatment planning?

## SOCIAL LEARNING THEORY IN THE TREATMENT OF PHOBIC DISORDERS

*Bruce A. Thyer*

I closed the file and sat back in my chair, reflecting on the materials I had just finished reviewing: client's name, Mr. Donald Scott, age 54, married for 30 years to his present wife and employed for over 25 years at an automobile manufacturing plant outside of Detroit. All potential clients of our busy Anxiety Disorders Program completed and mailed in an extensive questionnaire packet for review prior to their first appointment. In these materials Mr. Scott indicated that his presenting problem was being "terrified of people," and my eyeballing of his Fear Survey Schedule and Symptom Checklist 90-R responses certainly supported that view.

The phone buzzed, and my secretary told me Mr. Scott was in the waiting room. As I entered the room, Mr. Scott and his wife looked up. They were sitting close together listlessly flipping through the tattered magazines on the table in front of them. I introduced myself, asked Mr. Scott to accompany

me to my office, and suggested to his wife that she might find it more comfortable to wait in the hospital cafeteria down the hall. She agreed and went to have a cup of coffee, promising Mr. Scott to be back after an hour went by, the time I estimated that he and I would be together.

Mr. Scott sat in the indicated chair alongside my desk, and I went into my routine spiel about who I was, my background, and the operation of the Anxiety Disorders Program, an interdisciplinary outpatient treatment clinic affiliated with the Department of Psychiatry at the University of Michigan Hospitals in Ann Arbor. I asked him to tell me why he had come to our clinic, and his story went as follows.

He had always been a somewhat nervous fellow, and for almost his whole life he had felt extremely uncomfortable around other people. His fears were so extreme that in the presence of others, unless he had some secure object to sit on or lean against, he would develop very obvious tremors in his arms and legs. This of course made people stare at him, leading to a vicious cycle of anxiety feeding back upon itself. He had adapted to these fears by restricting his social life to a very great extent. He never went out to parties, had discontinued receiving communion at church (since this involved standing in line), and would not go to fast-food restaurants or to bank tellers or attend popular movies. His wife was distressed, not only for him but because her own social life was correspondingly curtailed. He was viewed by his co-workers and acquaintances as somewhat of a curmudgeon.

His story took over 20 minutes to tell. He was articulate, earnest, and clearly at his wit's end. He knew he wasn't crazy, he said, but he felt like he acted that way sometimes. I asked him if he had anything else to add to his description of his difficulty. He did not, so I proceeded to inquire about some other possibly important features. If no one else was nearby—for example, if Mr. Scott was in the woods—he could walk alone or with his wife without discomfort or support. If approached at work by his supervisor, Mr. Scott could lean against his workbench and remain free from distress, but if the same person approached him in the middle of the room, after a few moments of conversation Mr. Scott could feel "the shakes" coming on and would invent some excuse to sit down or would scuttle over to the wall and lean against it.

Apparently this problem had been present for years, with no sign of its lessening. He was moderately depressed over these circumstances but was unequivocal that the social fears came first. He was convinced that if he could overcome them he would no longer be depressed.

By this time I was reasonably sure that Mr. Scott met the DSM-III criteria for social phobia. I took down the worn green book from the shelf over my desk and read the relevant passage aloud to him: "A persistent, irrational fear of, and compelling desire to avoid, a situation in which the individual is exposed to possible scrutiny by others and fears that he or she may act in a way that will be humiliating or embarrassing" (American Psychiatric Association, 1980, p. 228). "Does any of that sound familiar?" I asked. Mr. Scott's face lit up. "Do you mean that there are other people like me?" I assured him that such was indeed the case and proceeded with further inquiries.

"As best as you can recollect, when or how did this problem with shaking develop?" Well, he knew all right; it was 35 years ago when he was in the army. During a morning roll call all the troops in his unit were assembled at attention when, suddenly, Mr. Scott's commanding officer stomped up and planted himself in front of Mr. Scott, verbally abusing him in a stentorian voice for all to hear, ostensibly because of some infraction Mr. Scott had committed. The abuse was both obscene and prolonged and was listened to avidly by the other soldiers. Dictates of military discipline prevented Mr. Scott from replying, even though, as it subsequently emerged, the commanding officer had picked the wrong man! It was not Mr. Scott who had committed the infraction but some other G.I. Finally the officer stormed off, leaving a quivering Private Scott feeling horribly humiliated and enraged at the unjustness of it all.

Ever since then, according to my client, face-to-face contact with others made him feel extremely upset and tremorous. Further questions revealed that the shaking was not evoked by small children, only by adults, but apart from that it reliably occurred every time he stood face to face and unsupported with someone (except for his wife and children). Apart from these social circumstances the shaking never appeared. "What do you think would happen, Mr. Scott, if you found yourself forced to stand in front of someone without the opportunity to escape? Have you ever tried that?" "NO!" he replied. "I think that would drive me out of my mind!"

Our time was about up, so I informed Mr. Scott that he had been most helpful and that I thought it was likely we could assist him to overcome his problem of shaking. We arranged a second appointment the following week. I also gave him a copy of *Living with Fear* to read, a self-help book by Marks (1978), which describes in easy-to-understand language the various kinds of phobias and their behavioral treatments based on social learning theory.

In writing up my notes, it seemed to me unlikely that Mr. Scott's tremorousness could be attributable to an organic problem such as vestibular dysfunction or to some form of movement disorder such as Parkinson's disease. The specificity of the controlling stimuli argued against that possibility. Although there were some symptomatic features superficially similar to agoraphobia, the absence of spontaneous panic attacks excluded both panic disorder or agoraphobia as differential diagnoses. He was not taking any medications with tremorous side effects, and he was in good physical health.

I had not conducted a formal so-called "mental status" examination with Mr. Scott, since it was obvious from his written materials and our interview that he was well oriented and was not psychotic or cognitively impaired. I knew from the literature on the etiology of phobic disorders that his case was fairly typical: most individuals who meet the criteria for simple or social phobia report that the onset of their fears was associated with a traumatic experience with the objects or situations they had come to fear (Ost & Hugdahl, 1981). This seemed likely in his case. He could recall the precipitating event clearly, and the problem had never occurred prior to the episode in the army. He was a high-functioning person in virtually all areas of his life, excluding those related to his fears. There was no evidence of

marital or family distress, apart from that engendered by his phobia.

## CONCEPTUAL FRAMEWORK

I believed that it was reasonable to hypothesize that Mr. Scott's social fears were generated through respondent (that is, Pavlovian) conditioning processes. An initially neutral stimulus (having someone stand in front of him) was paired with an extremely aversive event (humiliation, embarrassment, lack of opportunity to respond). This association resulted in the formerly neutral stimulus coming to elicit reactions similar to those he experienced during the initial aversive event. In more technical terminology, the event of face-to-face confrontation changed from an unconditioned stimulus to a conditioned one and came to elicit a conditioned response (anxiousness, tremors, and so on) similar to his unconditioned response following his being verbally attacked.

Such powerful and enduring effects following "one-trial learning" have been well demonstrated in laboratory conditioning research with human beings (Malloy & Levis, 1988) and are extensively supported by both formal studies on the etiologies of clinical phobics and at the level of anecdotal reports (Marks, 1987; Ost & Hugdahl, 1981; Thyer, 1981; Thyer & Curtis, 1983). Once a conditioned fear reaction of this nature is set up, then operant conditioning processes come into play. Every time Mr. Scott successfully *avoided or escaped* from a face-to-face interaction during which he felt anxious, it is possible that the relief he felt accompanying such escape or avoidance served to *negatively reinforce* such behaviors. Negative reinforcement (which is not the same thing as punishment) is the process whereby behaviors are strengthened by the removal of aversive states or events. Everyday examples include turning down the volume of excessively loud or obnoxious music, putting on sunglasses in bright light, removing a chafing shoe, and so forth. Such acts are likely to be strengthened by their effectiveness in providing some form of relief. Similarly, Mr. Scott's escape and avoidance behavior, including holding onto secure objects or leaning on tables, chairs, or walls, provided him with relief from the noxious state of severe anxiety/agitation. Such behaviors would be correspondingly perpetuated, perhaps for very long periods of time.

The practice-research literature has clearly shown that the treatment of choice for phobic disorders is a clinical procedure known as real-life exposure therapy (Marks, 1987; Thyer, 1983, 1987). Exposure therapy is effective in producing substantial therapeutic gains for between 80 and 90% of clinical phobics, improving not only behavioral avoidance but subjective fears and physiological arousal as well. Such gains are well maintained, with controlled follow-up studies often lasting for years. Relapse following exposure therapy is low, and there is no evidence of the development of symptom substitution (Marks, 1987). I also knew that exposure therapy is usually quite well tolerated, poses few side effects, and is highly acceptable to most clients if properly explained and conducted.

It seemed to me that exposure therapy was the first treatment option I should explore with Mr. Scott. In the event it would prove unacceptable to him I was prepared to offer a program of exposure conducted in fantasy or of more traditional (and labor intensive) systematic desensitization. The patient self-help book I had asked Mr. Scott to read, *Living with Fear*, describes the theory and conduct of real-life exposure therapy, so I knew he would have some background in what I was proposing when he returned for his next visit.

## THE TREATMENT PROCESS

Mr. Scott did arrive on time for his next appointment; he had read the book and was full of questions. I first dealt with his questions and then described in easy-to-understand language how I viewed the nature of his problem. I outlined my rationale for beginning with a course of exposure therapy, if he was agreeable. I also explained treatment alternatives but noted that they were liable to take much longer and be somewhat less effective. I assured him that there would be no tricks or surprises, that everything would be explained to him in advance, and that his permission would be obtained prior to introduction of new levels of exposure. Furthermore, he could terminate a session any time he felt it necessary.

With these reassurances he was ready to proceed. After explaining the following procedures, we began as follows. I pushed all the office furniture against the walls, leaving an open area about 8 by 8 feet square. I described to Mr. Scott the use of the subjective anxiety scale, whereby he could roughly quantify his feelings on a zero (feeling completely relaxed) to 100 (absolutely panic-stricken, as frightened as he had ever been in his life) scale. Such scales are commonly used in social work practice (Hudson & Thyer, 1987), and this particular one has reasonably good convergent validity, correlating well with physiological measures of arousal (Thyer, Papsdorf, Davis, & Vallecorsa, 1984).

As I sat in my chair I had Mr. Scott stand in the center of the room, unsupported. He was comfortable. I then obtained his permission to stand directly in front of him about 1 foot away. Mr. Scott was about 5'8", whereas I am a little over 6 feet tall, so I more or less loomed over him. Within a few moments a remarkable transformation came over my client. He developed obvious tremors in his hands, arms, and knees and became quite agitated. "See," he said, "It's always like this; I have to sit down!" I was appropriately supportive and encouraged him to remain standing there, which he did with a great deal of difficulty. Profuse perspiration broke out on his forehead, and he made several abortive movements toward the wall.

I kept up a running chatter about how well he was doing, that soon the reaction would subside if he would only give it time. I asked him to reflect on and tell me about his internal sensations, and every two minutes I had him rate his level of anxiety using the zero to 100 scale described above.

As social learning theory predicted, soon Mr. Scott's anxiety reaction began to subside. After about 12 minutes the tremors began to diminish, the sweating stopped, and he began to feel better. I encouraged him to note these reactions, and he was quite astounded when after 20 minutes he found himself relatively calm and relaxed yet had not had to resort to any external means of support to lean on or to sit down. "I can't believe it! I haven't done this in over 30 years, to stand in front of someone and not shake!"

I terminated the exposure procedure after some 20 minutes had passed, and we sat down over a cup of tea to process what had happened. I once again explained to him how respondent (that is, Pavlovian) theory would predict how a conditioned response (his shaking and other upsetting reactions) would slowly undergo extinction if the conditioned stimulus (someone standing in front of him) were constantly repeated or continued. The difference, I noted, between the experience he had just undergone with me and the routine episodes of exposure he encountered in everyday life was that the exposure was prolonged until he was calm and that operant avoidance behaviors (leaning on a wall, fleeing the situation, sitting on a chair, and so on) were not permitted to occur. By repeating such experiences over and over in progressively more difficult and realistic life situations, I thought he would be able to overcome his social fears, irrespective of their severity or duration.

His skepticism had vanished, since he could see that substantial therapeutic changes had

literally occurred before his very eyes. He was almost euphoric as we made our third appointment (second treatment session) for the following week. In this second treatment session I basically repeated the procedure employed the previous week and did so again during our third session. I recorded Mr. Scott's subjective anxiety rating during each of these therapeutic trials, and the data are depicted in Figure 1. As can be seen, the severity of Mr. Scott's peak anxiety reactions declined over the course of the sessions until this exposure technique elicited very little response by the third trial.

Over the next few weeks I moved Mr. Scott from the confines of the consulting room to more real-world contexts. I reserved the private use of a large instructional auditorium and repeated the exposure process of me standing in front of him, this time with Mr. Scott being dozens of feet from any means of support. I went with him to nearby movies on dollar night, when the lines stretched around the block. I had us take our place at the end of the slowly moving line and engaged my client in conversation. "Could you tell me what your worst fears would be in this situation?" "Sure, I am afraid I would start to shake and that people would notice and laugh at me." "OK, let's see what would actually happen. I will begin to shake like you used to as we stand here, and you carefully watch the reactions of others. Will you do that?" With his consent I began to display a palsylike reaction in my crooked right arm as we shuffled up the line. After we got to the ticket window several minutes later I pulled Mr. Scott out of line and we rejoined it at its end, repeating the exposure cycle. "Well," I asked, "what did they do?" "Most people ignored you, or if they noticed they looked away." "Yes, that was my impression also. Now let's try something else. I would like you to deliberately shake like you used to, to try and bring attention to yourself, so you can gain a more realistic idea of how

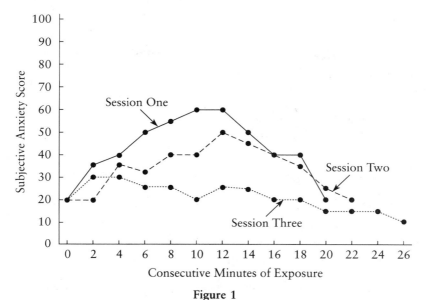

**Figure 1**

Client's subjective responses to three consecutive sessions of exposure therapy for a social phobia. (From B. A. Thyer [1987]. *Treating anxiety disorders: A guide for human service professionals.* Newbury Park: Sage.)

people would respond." With a little coaxing he complied, and of course nothing untoward happened.

After our success at the movies I asked Mr. Scott to undertake some carefully structured homework assignments relating to his self-exposure to situations he formerly avoided. For example, I asked him to go to church and to sit in the back and join the communion line just before the communion service was over when the line was at its shortest, then to begin joining the line each time it was a little longer at subsequent services.

He came back for a few more scheduled sessions with me. For example, we went to McDonald's during the lunch rush and stood in the lines. After one trial with me, I had Mr. Scott go through the line alone and buy a drink, fries, or a burger. All progressed relatively smoothly. At his own initiative he attended a wedding and stood in the receiving line. He sought out co-workers and engaged them in conversation while carefully refraining from any avoidance behaviors. I gradually faded my involvement in Mr. Scott's treatment: he came to see me a few more times, wherein I basically served as a consultant to his own self-exposure homework tasks; then we had a few appointments by telephone; and finally I was simply available as necessary.

Three years later I tried to call Mr. Scott at home one evening but he was not there. I spoke with his wife instead, who informed me, after I identified myself, that he was out with his bowling league! She remarked that he seemed like a changed man, for the better; that they now had an active social life; and that he was no longer troubled by "the shakes."

## CONCLUDING REMARKS

I believe that as a case example Mr. Scott's story reasonably illustrates the integration of social learning theory into social work practice. The etiology and maintenance of the client's problem was conceptualized in terms of the principles of both respondent and operant learning processes. Similarly, the treatment program was developed with these processes in view, and the success of social work intervention corroborated (but of course could not confirm) the validity of these etiological hypotheses. Treatment involved elements of respondent conditioning (prolonged exposure of a conditioned stimulus resulted in the extinction of the conditioned response) and operant conditioning (refraining from negatively reinforced avoidance behaviors such as seeking support or sitting down resulted in the operant extinction of these actions as well). Throughout treatment I modeled reactions I wished Mr. Scott to develop and used his realistic observations of how people reacted to his and my deliberate shaking in a therapeutic manner.

The client was thoroughly involved in treatment. He was given appropriate reading materials describing the nature and treatment of problems similar to his. These were discussed in our sessions, and I was open and aboveboard in all respects with regard to how I thought we should proceed. I obtained his consent for all the procedures used prior to their employment and facilitated the generalization and maintenance of treatment gains by taking the therapeutic process out of the confines of the consulting room and into the real-world contexts of Mr. Scott's own life. I gradually faded my own involvement in the active management of the case as Mr. Scott undertook more and more of the therapeutic tasks on his own.

In keeping with the tenets of contemporary clinical social work practice, I based my treatment program on the empirically based practice-research literature and employed rudimentary single-case evaluation procedures to help ascertain that Mr. Scott had benefited from treatment. Although the case seems relatively straightforward, it is a mistake to conclude that behavioral social work practice requires any lesser degree of clinical skill and acumen or complexity of conceptualization than other approaches to practice. Conventional therapeutic relationship variables are cultivated, but their role is seen more as adjunctive to treatment than as a central therapeutic mechanism.

## References

American Psychiatric Association. (1980). *Diagnostic and statistical manual of mental disorders* (3rd ed.). Washington, DC: American Psychiatric Press.

Hudson, W. W., & Thyer, B. A. (1987). Research measures and indices in direct practice. In A. Minahan (Ed.), *Encyclopedia of social work* (pp. 487–498). Washington, DC: National Association of Social Workers.

Malloy, P., & Levis, D. J. (1988). A laboratory demonstration of persistent human avoidance. *Behavior Therapy, 19,* 229–241.

Marks, I. M. (1978). *Living with fear.* New York: McGraw-Hill.

Marks, I. M. (1987). *Fears, phobias and rituals.* New York: Oxford University Press.

Ost, L., & Hugdahl, K. (1981). Acquisition of phobias and anxiety response patterns in clinical patients. *Behaviour Research and Therapy, 19,* 439–447.

Thyer, B. A. (1981). Prolonged *in vivo* exposure therapy with a 70-year-old woman. *Journal of Behavior Therapy and Experimental Psychiatry, 12,* 69–71.

Thyer, B. A. (1983). Treating anxiety disorders with exposure therapy. *Social Casework, 64,* 77–82.

Thyer, B. A. (1987). *Treating anxiety disorders: A guide for human service professionals.* Newbury Park, CA: Sage.

Thyer, B. A., & Curtis, G. C. (1983). The repeated pretest-posttest single-subject experiment: A new design for empirical clinical practice. *Journal of Behavior Therapy and Experimental Psychiatry, 14,* 311–315.

Thyer, B. A., Papsdorf, J. D., Davis, R., & Vallecorsa, S. (1984). Autonomic correlates of the subjective anxiety scale. *Journal of Behavior Therapy and Experimental Psychiatry, 15,* 3–7.

*The case presents the application of object relations theory in conducting marital therapy. Clinical techniques based on this approach are described with an emphasis on the personal growth of the clients.*

## Questions

1. How can the marital difficulties of the clients be explained using object relations theory?
2. What clinical techniques are used to deal with the marital difficulties of the couple?
3. How is interpretation used in helping the clients resolve their difficulties?
4. What are the major differences between this approach and the previous case study based on social learning theory?

## OBJECT RELATIONS MARITAL THERAPY: ENGAGING THE COUPLE

### Judith Siegel

Pete and Carla had interviewed three other marital therapists before they met with me. They were bright, articulate, and highly motivated—surely the kind of clients most social workers would be pleased to work with. In fact, they were a difficult treatment case, one that exemplifies the challenges of engaging a couple in treatment.

### THE CLIENTS

Pete, age 35, was a tall, well-groomed man with a soft, pensive manner of speaking. He seemed polite and well-intentioned but was sufficiently vague and rhetorical to keep me guessing about his real feelings. Carla, an attractive woman in her early thirties, was sociable but at the same time guarded and controlling. She was the more outgoing of the two and was engaging but slightly theatrical.

As I probed into their current situation, the stress in this relationship was readily apparent. Pete had recently moved home after a month-long separation. The couple had been together four years and had been distant and unhappy for most of that time. Pete's perspective of the marriage was resigned and very pessimistic. Carla's temper flared quickly, and she scorned Pete's moods, rigidity, and pessimism. Each blamed the other for not listening, not caring, and not giving enough. Not surprisingly, each felt attacked, misunderstood, and unloved.

### FAMILY BACKGROUND

Pete had little recollection of his childhood but initially described his family as "normal." The eldest in a sibship of three, he grew up in a middle-class Irish-American family. He later revealed that his father had a painful, deteriorating arthritic condition that caused him to lose his job at a young age. Although Pete did not remember open conflict between his parents, there was a cold war that led to their separation while Pete was in college. His father committed suicide 5 years later.

Carla was born in Austria and has one younger sister. Both were physically abused by an alcoholic father and emotionally abandoned by a depressed, self-absorbed mother. Carla's grandmother, who was the only loving adult available to her, died just after Carla immigrated to the United States. Carla married at a young age and divorced after her only child was born. She married again for "mutual convenience" and divorced 4 years later.

Carla and Pete were enrolled in the same university for graduate studies and met shortly before Pete's graduation. Pete was attracted to Carla's looks, confidence, and outgoing personality. Carla found Pete to be attentive, attractive, and very accepting of both herself and her daughter. They were married within the year.

The couple had gradually found fault with each other's friends and soon were socially isolated. Lack of money created additional stress. Pete had changed careers twice, and Carla would work only in commission-based jobs. Although each superficially supported the other's career decisions, they also blamed each other for not being more successful. The couple rarely made love, and they avoided meaningful conversation, as it invariably led to conflict. When they fought, Carla would become intensely angry and threaten divorce. Pete would become cold and withdraw for days.

## ENGAGING THE COUPLE

Both Carla and Pete tended to see each other and their marriage as "all" or "nothing." They were extremely vulnerable to criticism and were easily wounded by their partner's disapproval. Each blamed the other for causing their profound unhappiness, but at the same time, each was invested in saving the relationship. The splitting, blaming, and intense unresolved conflict led me to speculate that this was a narcissistically vulnerable couple (Feldman, 1982; Lansky, 1981; Slipp, 1988). Narcissistically vulnerable adults are especially difficult to engage in treatment. They are uncomfortable about needing help, worried about losing control to a therapist, and afraid of being exposed or humiliated by their partner. The therapist must create a safe environment wherein each spouse can feel responded to and yet protected. In order to accomplish that, I interrupted the couple's direct communication whenever they became too critical or devaluing of each other. Conversation would be redirected through me, until control was reestablished. The first time fighting started I immediately interrupted and defined their anger as being useful but, at this particular moment, destructive. I asked Pete and Carla to slow down so that I could get to know them well enough to provide the special treatment that was best suited to their needs.

From the beginning my questions were intended to create an observing "team ego." Narcissistically vulnerable couples need help in differentiating in ways that encourage individuality but do not rupture the couple identity. The therapist's validation and equal interest in each person's separate perspective helps establish the therapist's genuine interest and impartiality.

I also normalized the stigma each felt about failing in their marriage and needing professional assistance. I applauded them for seeking help and thought it was revealing that they cared enough about their marriage to go through three consultations. These interventions were formulated to help this couple feel accepted and safe in a new and threatening environment. Each could feel that I was not going to take their partner's side and that I would not allow the sessions to become destructive.

## TREATMENT TOOLS

### Countertransference

An object relations marital therapist must pay special attention to countertransference reactions throughout the treatment process (Kernberg, 1965; Scharff & Scharff, 1987). This couple's style of interviewing me immediately sparked my awareness of severe esteem and control issues. The way this couple flirted with intense eruptions of anger also gave me early awareness of their attempt to triangle responsibility onto me. My ability to acknowledge and accept my reactions to this couple freed me from acting out and also gave me an intimate understanding of the effect Carla and Pete had on each other. Assessment would involve pursuing each of these areas in more depth.

### Defining the Projective Identifications

The therapist's main task after creating a safe therapeutic environment is to engage the couple in exploring the ways they overreact to each other. Object relations therapists assume that partners involve each other in reenacting earlier relationship trauma and in reexperiencing old wounds. Framo described this process as "irrational role assignment," but it is more commonly referred to as projective identification (Framo, 1970; Grotstein, 1981; Sandler, 1987; Zinner & Shapiro, 1972).

An object relations marital therapist defines and interprets irrational interactions in ways that link perception, feelings, and behavior to the family of origin dynamics. I often use the analogy of a "bruise on a broken bone." An emotionally injured spouse is confirmed in his/her perception of being hurt or bruised by a mate, but the intensity of the pain and the subsequent reaction is ascribed to a broken bone lying beneath the more recent injury. The bone was broken before the partners met,

and yet each spouse perceives the partner as being completely responsible for his/her pain.

Pete and Carla had each been deprived of emotional confirmation and desperately needed to be noticed, validated, and responded to. Each had difficulty asking to be cared for but would be hurt and disappointed if his/her unarticulated need was not responded to. The cycle of hope, neglect, and disappointment that had been established in their youth was repeated, but this time, Carla and Pete each became more assertive and angry at their unresponsive object. Through this interaction each was able to reexperience feelings of being unloved or, in the reverse position, being unfairly criticized and rejected.

Analysis of projective identifications gives the social worker access to unconscious intrapsychic conflicts and unresolved issues. Once the irrational dynamic has been observed and delineated, the worker must establish its childhood origin. Narcissistic adults block, split off, or deny their most painful childhood disappointments, and uncovering the past may provide to be a challenging task (Miller, 1981). Pete, for example, had very few memories of his early family life but assumed that everything was "fine." I observed that as he talked with me about unpleasant experiences, he seemed detached and intellectual. As I probed his own awareness and comfort with his feelings, we both realized how shut off he was from his emotional self. I asked him why he thought his parents needed him to be emotionally self-sufficient, and he was able to remember his father's constant pain and his mother's exhaustion at having to hold a full-time job and raise three boys with little help from her self-absorbed husband.

At this point I was able to reframe his complaint that Carla never noticed his moods or seemed to care how he was doing. I suggested that this was a statement of his growth in wanting to finally be acknowledged. I also pointed out how Carla's self-centeredness must revive repressed anger and frustration at having to minimize his own needs in order to take stress off the family. Pete could intellectually agree and could understand how Carla's lack of attentiveness was a bruise that pressed on the broken bone of being forced into early self-sufficiency in childhood. He could then better understand the intensity of his emotional reaction and begin to process the experience of being hurt and disappointed.

Carla was able to acknowledge how frustrating it was for her to be expected to read Pete's mind and be criticized and punished by his withdrawal. When this happened, Carla would reexperience her own childhood pain of being criticized by an unreasonable alcoholic father and her reaction of deep shame, fear, and resentment of being unfairly punished. Pete's withdrawal reminded her of her mother's abandonment, and this would strengthen her resolve to never trust or depend on anyone again.

The projective identification pattern described above occurred frequently and caused this couple considerable pain. I interpreted that both Carla and Pete had survived childhood by learning not to trust too easily. As children, they both had compromised too much of themselves and had become overly self-sufficient and distrustful of intimacy. Their arguments enabled them to avoid getting too close and allowed them to protest their past in an active way. The couple could see how they each had some responsibility for perpetuating this pattern and how, ultimately, it caused each of them pain that they could choose not to repeat any more.

## Empathic Listening

Object relations therapists respect the importance of the "holding environment" in all relationships (Scharff & Scharff, 1987). Adults who have impaired object relations tend to blame others for their pain and to be very defensive when others blame or criticize them. As a result, narcissistically vulnerable couples have great difficulty discussing problems and resolving fights. Rarely is an attempt made to understand each other's point of view, and complaints quickly flare into intense battles.

Pete and Carla were aware of their problem with conflict. As a result of not being responded to, each had clung to specific memories of being disappointed and hurt. It is impossible to rekindle intimacy in a relationship where there is no trust or opportunity to demonstrate caring.

In order to let go of past hurts, Carla and Pete needed their partner to listen and acknowledge their feelings. Empathic listening can be achieved by channeling communication through the therapist. In the early phase of this couple's treatment, I would have Carla tell me why she was upset and have Pete tell me what he understood when she had finished. I would interrupt his immediate reaction to dismiss her complaints or defend his own viewpoint and instead keep him focused on Carla's feelings. I would then ask Carla if Pete had understood her correctly, and if she didn't think so, urge her to repeat or add more information in order to make it more clear. Spouses that are too entwined frequently expect their partner to "know" how they feel without conversing. After some initial discomfort, Carla and Pete began to value being listened to and understood. Each could see how much easier it was to respond to his or her partner's hurt when it was not presented as criticism or blame.

## Joining Forces to Restore "Middle Ground"

Object relations theory places heavy emphasis on the defense mechanism of splitting and its role in distorting perception and creating unstable relationships (Akhtar & Byrne, 1983; Zinner & Shapiro, 1975). Adults who split tend to evaluate themselves and others in "all or nothing" ways and are often angry and abrupt in their intolerance of imperfection. This is an important dynamic to tackle as early in the treatment process as possible. Narcissistically vulnerable couples immediately overvalue the therapist who helps them mend or who stabilizes their relationship, but they will likely react to their first setback in an intense way.

In the first session, I had identified Pete and Carla's shared tendency to react to disappointment in an extreme manner. Both were able to see how quickly their good feeling toward each other could crumble and how unpredictable the roller-coaster pattern of their emotional life was. When Pete came to our third session acting despondent and withdrawn, I could relate his mood to a minor fight that the couple had had during the week. Whereas Carla was delighted that they had been able to stop the fight before it became destructive, Pete felt completely discouraged and pessimistic. He felt hopeless about their relationship and skeptical of my skills as a marital therapist. My ability to hold Pete's disappointment and engage him in better understanding this experience as splitting helped him recover his good feelings toward his marriage and the therapy.

## SUMMARY

The narcissistically vulnerable couple's success in engaging in marital therapy is enhanced by the therapist's awareness of both intrapsychic and interpersonal dynamics. The social worker's ability to predict the couple's sensitivity to criticism and their difficulty in relinquishing control to a stranger will prevent power struggles and alienation of the client from the worker. Once a safe environment has been created, the worker can assess the countertransference and projective identifications to better understand the couple's fundamental problem areas. The past is drawn on to make sense of each spouse's view of self and the relationship patterns. The couple's tendency to overvalue/devalue must be addressed early in the therapy in order to bring stability to the couple and to the treatment. As the worker helps the couple look at their interaction from a new perspective, an "observing ego" is developed. This and the guided empathic listening help the couple resolve old hurts and begin the process of renewing intimacy. The stage has been set, and the couple can knowingly commit to the work that lies ahead.

## References

Akhtar, S., & Byrne, J. (1983). The concept of splitting and its clinical relevance. *American Journal of Psychiatry, 140*, 1013–1015.

Feldman, L. B. (1982). Dysfunctional marital conflict: An integrative interpersonal-intrapsychic model. *Journal of Marital and Family Therapy, 8*, 417–428.

Framo, J. (1970). Symptoms from a family transactional viewpoint. In N. Ackerman & K. Pearce (Eds.), *Family therapy in transition*. Boston: Little, Brown.

Grotstein, J. S. (1981). *Splitting and projective identification*. New Jersey: Jason Aronson.

Kernberg, O. (1965). Notes on countertransference. *Journal American Psychoanalytic Association, 13*, 38–56.

Lansky, M. (1981). Treatment of the narcissistically vulnerable marriage. In M. Lansky (Ed.), *Family therapy and major psychopathology* (pp. 163–182). New York: Grune & Stratton.

Miller, A. (1981). *Prisoners of childhood*. New York: Basic Books.

Sandler, J. (Ed.). (1987). *Projection, identification, projective identification*. Madison, CT: International Universities Press.

Scharff, D. E., & Scharff, J. S. (1987). *Object relations family therapy*. New Jersey: Jason Aronson.

Slipp, S. (1988). *The technique and practice of object relations family therapy*. New Jersey: Jason Aronson.

Zinner, J., & Shapiro, R. (1972). Projective identification as a mode of perception and behavior in families of adolescents. *International Journal of Psychoanalysis, 53*, 523–530.

Zinner, J., & Shapiro, R. (1975). Splitting in families of borderline adolescents. In J. Mack (Ed.), *The borderline states in psychiatry* (pp. 103–122). New York: Grune & Stratton.

# CASE STUDY 1.4

*This case study presents a multiple perspective—the combination of three different but related theories. Each theoretical approach suggests a different perspective from which to view the problem and suggests different but related ways to intervene.*

## Questions

1. How does each theoretical perspective explain the difficulties presented in the case study?
2. In what way is the combination of theoretical perspectives helpful in working with the couple?
3. What clinical interventions resulted from the three different theoretical perspectives?
4. How does this case study demonstrate the role of theory in social work practice?

---

## TOWARD A MULTIPLE PERSPECTIVE IN FAMILY THEORY AND PRACTICE: SOCIAL EXCHANGE, SYMBOLIC INTERACTIONISM, AND CONFLICT THEORY

*Craig Winston LeCroy and Mark R. Rank\**

I greeted Bill and Judy and asked them to come into my office. They both looked agitated as I explained to them my role and goals for this first visit. As I got to know them I discovered that they had been married in their early twenties, and like many couples, after 6 years of marriage, they were experiencing serious problems that had been getting progressively worse.

Bill and Judy were a well-educated professional couple. Judy told me about her career in business and her recent job promotion. Bill spoke about the difficulties of pursuing an advanced degree in administration. As I listened to their stories I could see how they had drifted from one another, each pursuing new life tasks and directions.

For Judy this meant becoming less interested in their relationship and for the first time

* Reprinted from *Family Relations*, 1983, vol. 32, no. 3, pp. 441–448. Copyright 1983 National Council on Family Relations. Reprinted by permission of the NCFR.

noticing an attraction toward other men. Prior to Judy's having begun her career, Bill was her best friend and only source of companionship. Now she has made many friends at work and has been going out after work with her friends. Bill, who has remained isolated in his attempt to study and get through school, has become more demanding in terms of Judy's commitment to their relationship. When I asked about recent conflicts, they described frequent fights over how much time should be devoted to being together as opposed to going out and being with other people.

I listened to them discuss this problem, and the following is an account of what I heard:

*Bill:* I don't understand why you have to come home so late.

*Judy:* I don't have to come home so late; I want to spend more time by myself.

*Bill:* What do you mean by yourself—you're going out with other people.

*Judy:* That's not the point, Bill, I need time by myself and with other people.

*Bill:* Why do you need time with other people?

*Judy:* Because I enjoy being with the people from my office.

*Bill:* I wouldn't mind, but you never want to spend any time with me.

*Judy:* Bill, we do spend time with one another. We're with each other every day.

*Bill:* You're not committed to this relationship anymore.

*Judy:* I don't know how I feel about this relationship. I need time to be myself.

## THEORETICAL PERSPECTIVES

There are three complementary theories—symbolic interactionism, social exchange, and conflict—that can help us obtain a better understanding of Bill and Judy's situation. Symbolic interactionism stresses that individuals gain meaning about the world by interacting with their social and physical environments. This environment includes family, peers, social groups, media, and so on. Through interaction, interpretation of symbols, and the filtering process of the mind, meaning about the world and the self is acquired—the "looking glass" phenomenon. Individuals also conceptualize of themselves and others in terms of roles.

Social exchange theory focuses on human interaction occurring in terms of exchange. The theory suggests that individuals attempt to maximize rewards and minimize costs in their exchanges so as to obtain the most profitable outcomes. Thus, rewards − costs = profit, and the maximization of profit is assumed to be the goal of the individual. Profit is sought through the use of bargaining with one's exchange partner(s). Thibaut and Kelley (1959) argued that individuals evaluate the rewards and costs of a given relationship in terms of a standard (comparison level) that

represents what they feel they deserve. When outcomes fall below the comparison level, one seeks out alternatives that are perceived to offer better outcomes than the current relationship. In this situation, if one's "levels of alternatives" are greater than the existing outcomes, the individual or group will leave the relationship for the alternative relationship. A serious gap in this theory concerns how one comes to define what is a reward or cost. It is at this point that symbolic interactionism serves to complement social exchange theory.

Conflict theory emphasizes that conflict is natural and inevitable in all human interaction. Conflict is viewed as an assumed and expected part of all systems and interactions, including family systems and marital interactions. Thus, if husband-wife or parent-child goals are in frequent conflict, the issue is not avoidance but rather how to manage and resolve conflicts. As Eshieman (1981, p. 54) has noted, "Conflict, rather than being disruptive or negative, may strengthen relationships and make them more meaningful and rewarding than they were prior to the conflict." From this perspective, marital harmony is maintained only through negotiation. One particular source of conflict among dyadic relationships is a perceived unequal exchange between partners. This idea ties into the earlier discussion of social exchange theory. When, for example, one partner of a marital dyad perceives that a relationship is no longer equitable (or that the outcomes fall below their comparison level), conflict is a likely result. Whatever the outcome, conflict is likely to lead to reorganization of the exchange relationship.

To summarize, social exchange theory, symbolic interactionism, and conflict theory may be viewed as possessing complementary aspects that, when taken together, may present a fuller understanding of social behavior. Although social exchange theory answered some questions, it left others unanswered. Thus, while individuals enter into exchanges

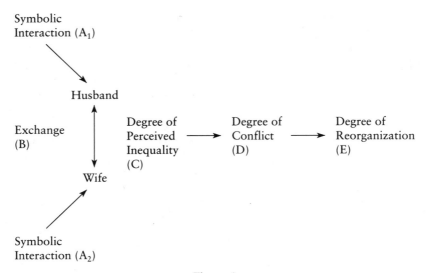

**Figure 1**

A model for integrating multiple theoretical perspectives

with others and are motivated to maximize rewards and minimize costs, social exchange fails to emphasize the process whereby individuals define what is a reward and what is a cost. Symbolic interactionism addresses this issue. Moreover, it implies that definitions of rewards and costs are rarely static, which in turn creates changing exchange relationships. As exchange relationships change, the potential for conflict arises. Subsequently, conflict theory offers an additional complementary viewpoint to social exchange theory. This leads to either reorganization within the exchange or reorganization by leaving the exchange, and thus the process begins again as illustrated in Figure 1.

Using these theories to examine more closely Bill and Judy's relationship suggests a better understanding. How might what has happened to this couple be explained? First it is clear that Judy is learning new things about herself through her interactions with others (refer to point A2 in Figure 1). Her values and

perceptions of rewards and costs have been changing. She is beginning to value experiences and contacts outside the domains of her relationship with Bill. On the other hand, Bill's values and perceptions have remained fairly consistent over time (point A1). As a result of this, what was once a satisfying (and equitable) relationship has now changed (point B). For Judy, her interactions with her co-workers have caused her to reassess her relationship with Bill. Her concepts of rewards and costs have shifted. Consequently, both Judy and Bill feel that their relationship with each other is no longer equitable (point C). Judy feels that Bill is making unnecessary demands on her, and Bill feels that Judy is no longer committed to working on the relationship. Neither partner is experiencing the level of profit that he/she was at the beginning of the marriage. This in turn has created a substantial amount of conflict between Judy and Bill (point D). The presence of such conflict will inevitably lead to some form of reorganization (point E). This reorganization may involve negotiation to reestablish equal reciprocity, trial separation, or perhaps divorce.

## CLINICAL INTERVENTION

Symbolic interactionism provides a means for Bill to understand how and why Judy's values and behaviors are changing (point A2 in Figure 1). Likewise, Judy needs to understand how things from her point of view have suddenly changed. The therapist may want to engage both Bill and Judy in a process of mutual role taking so that each can begin to understand a little more about the other person's position in the relationship as well as his/her own position. This helps each partner in the relationship make sense out of his/her experience. Steinfield (1978) discussed this method of decentering in relation to family process to bring about change in marital relationships.

The next point of intervention could then be focused on how expectations regarding one another have changed. Expectations are developed by the way in which behavior is perceived and understood. This would be a starting point for initiating some action on their behalf. The couple needs to move beyond "first-order labels" and learn to use "second-order labels" (Watzlawick, Weakland, & Fisch, 1974). In this manner Bill would more accurately perceive Judy's role and interpret her actions not as rejection of him (first-order label) but as a need for her to spend more time developing her own potential as a person (second-order label). Similarly, Judy would not react to Bill as if he was fighting this need of hers (first-order label) but would react out of a desire to make their relationship work (second-order label). As the couple learn to change their expectations of one another they can begin to reestablish their relationship. Marital therapists like Martin (1976) and Sager (1976) have stressed the importance of clarifying expectations for facilitating marital harmony.

A second point of intervention rests on the foundation of each person having a better understanding of the other such that a process of changing behavior can be activated. Social exchange theory revolves around trust (Blau, 1964), trust resulting through reciprocal investments made in the relationship by each party. Bill and Judy do not have a compatible "comparison level" such that there is equal interest in and reinforcement derived from their relationship (points B and C). This would suggest the need to help the couple develop a means to increase positive exchanges with each other. Stuart (1980) discussed the technique of "caring days" which would be applicable here. This is seen as one way of helping the couple build trust in the relationship. The technique is based on the idea of exchanges, investments, and credit balances. Stuart described how "the caring-days procedure prompts nonreciprocated investments in the present, with the recording chart serving as a 'receipt' for the investment, and with the very real possibility that reciprocal positives will be experienced in the future" (p. 203). In this way Bill and Judy can begin the process of building trust so that investments made will be reciprocated. Their behavior toward one another can become more positive, changing the nature of their current interactions with the goal of increasing the mutual enjoyment each can experience from the other.

Last, conflict theory directs the therapist to consider strategies oriented toward maintenance of the relationship (points D and E). Conflict is presented as a natural and inevitable part of marital relationships. Because it is inevitable, the couple is taught ways of resolving unforeseen conflicts that are bound to arise in the future. In addition to using procedures that have been the focus up to now—decentering, use of second-order labels, positive exchanges—the couple is taught how to resolve conflicts through problem solving and/or contracting. Bateson (1972) suggested that in order for a couple to deal effectively with conflict they need to be able to identify conflictual issues, get beyond defensive and emotionally toned responses, use problem solving, and have sufficient commitment such that exchanges will be reciprocated in the future. Specific procedures such as problem solving (Jacobson & Margolin, 1979) and contracting (Murstein, Cerreto, & MacDonald, 1977; Stuart, 1980) can be useful at this stage of therapy.

In summary, it is clear that there are several points and styles of intervention available to the therapist. By bringing to bear more than one theoretical perspective to the problem, a more effective treatment may be obtained. The difficulties facing Judy and Bill occur at points A, B, C, and D in Figure 1. Each theory builds on the other in order to provide a more complete understanding of the various marital processes facing this couple. Through such understanding, the clinician is in a better position to deal effectively with conjugal problems.

## CONCLUSION

A multiple theoretical approach offers the practitioner various lenses through which to view families. By using both a telephoto and a microscopic lens, one may gain insight into differing though complementary phenomena. So too with the family. Multiple perspectives from which to view marital relationships can provide insights and direction in clinical practice. In the case example, the various theories were applied in such a sequence that each theory could be adopted to provide a point of intervention to maximize treatment goals. All three theories proved to be complementary in a way that each built on the other. This ap-

proach allows a level of understanding for various marital processes that are necessary to deal effectively with the complex dynamics of dyadic relationships. The theories can and should be applied at different points in time, as each is better suited for addressing certain problems depending on the circumstances. In the case example a focus on understanding, decentering, and/or role taking was believed to be a critical initial step (guided by symbolic interaction). Behavior change was activated by calling on an exchange model whereby the couple could increase mutual enjoyment and rebuild trust. Last, it was recognized that the couple would continue to face critical problems throughout the marital life cycle. Therefore, conflict resolution through problem solving and contracting was seen as a step toward inoculating the couple against future crises they will inevitably confront. It is hoped that family practitioners will begin to investigate the untapped potential of a multiple perspective in their practice.

## References

Bateson, G. (1972). *Steps to an ecology of mind*. New York: Ballantine Books.

Blau, P. M. (1964). *Exchange and power in social life*. New York: Wiley.

Eshieman, J. R. (1981). *The family: An introduction* (3rd ed.). Boston: Allyn and Bacon.

Jacobson, N., & Margolin, G. (1979). *Marital therapy: Strategies based on social learning and behavior exchange principles*. New York: Brunner/Mazel.

Martin, P. A. (1976). *A marital therapy manual*. New York: Brunner/Mazel.

Murstein, B. I., Cerreto, M., & MacDonald, M. G. (1977). A theory and investigation of the effect of exchange-orientation on marriage and friendship. *Journal of Marriage and the Family*, 39, 543–548.

Sager, C. J. (1976). *Marriage contracts and couple therapy*. New York: Brunner/Mazel.

Steinfield, G. J. (1978). Decentering and family process: A marriage of cognitive therapies. *Journal of Marriage and Family Counseling, 4,* 61–69.

Stuart, R. B. (1980). *Helping couples change: A social learning approach to marital therapy.* New York: The Guilford Press.

Thibaut, J. W., & Kelley, G. H. (1959). *The social psychology of groups.* New York: Wiley.

Watzlawick, P., Weakland, J. H., & Fisch, R. (1974). *Change: Principles of problem formulation and problem resolution.* New York: W. W. Norton.

# 2

CASE STUDIES

# IN CHILD AND FAMILY WELFARE

CHILD AND FAMILY WELFARE REPRESENTS social work's concern with the well-being and protection of children and the support and rights of families. Child and family services are typically needed when parents are unable to care properly for their children, when children have special needs, or when certain resources are needed. Current estimates indicate that over 15% of social workers are employed in this field (National Association of Social Workers, 1983). Although historically child and family welfare has been considered the heart of social work, in recent years interest in this field has declined. This is unfortunate because there are great opportunities to use a range of social work skills in this setting.

There are many roles for social workers to play in the field of child and family welfare. Social workers are child protective service workers, adoption workers, foster-care specialists, residential care workers, and sex abuse therapists. The settings for child and family welfare are equally broad: residential care centers, state departments of welfare, state departments of health (pregnancy prevention), and family counseling centers. The case studies in this chapter represent some of these settings. In each of the cases the social worker uses two fundamental skills: relationship building and contracting.

Since the beginning of the profession the social work relationship has been seen as a principle of effective practice. The skill of developing effective social work relationships is capitalized in one essential skill: empathy. The development of empathy, which is the ability to perceive and communicate the feelings and experiences of the client, is widely recognized as a necessary, although not always sufficient, condition of effective practice. Almost every approach to treatment recognizes the importance of building a good worker–client relationship in creating change for the client. A good rapport enhances the client's interest in being open and honest with the worker, encourages the client to explore his or her issues completely, and motivates the client toward change. An effective worker–client relationship builds the relationship components of liking, respect, and trust that result in the relationship consequences of communication, openness, and persuasiveness (Goldstein, 1980).

Each of these case studies represents an example of the contracting process. Contracting is considered one of the essential components of effective social work practice. A contract is an agreement between a social worker and a client about the work they agree to do together to accomplish their goals. It involves three essential aspects: (1) clarifying the purpose, (2) clarifying the roles and responsibilities of each person, and (3) reaching an agreement about the work to be done together (Schwartz, 1971).

Clarifying clients' expectations will enhance your ability to work effectively. Clients, as you might imagine, have many expectations regarding how a social worker can help them. They might question, for example, How is this person going to help me? Have I made the right decision to seek help? What is the likelihood that I will be helped? What are the fees? How long is this likely to take? and so on. Therefore, a critical part of the helping process is clarifying the client's expectations and determining how they match with your ability and the available resources.

This chapter presents several different cases that all revolve around child abuse. Child abuse is a complex problem in our society, and each case study approaches the problem from a different context, agency position, and treatment perspective.

DeMaria in her case study works intensively with parents who have abused their children. It is a good example of the importance of relationship building. She is clear and structured in her approach to reparent her clients. The case study by Krugman is similar because of the exemplary relationship he establishes with his clients. Engaging the violent couple into a long-term relationship of therapy is a respectable accomplishment. His work demonstrates the skill of "starting where the client is at." Krugman also establishes a clear contract with his clients, which is necessary in case situations where you are responsible for the protection of your client. The case by Sammons describes a completely different context, the inpatient hospital. She describes a multidisciplinary team approach to dealing with a complex case of childhood schizophrenia and sexual abuse. Here the social worker is involved in many aspects of the treatment and planning for her client. The case by Barrett and Trepper deals with the complex issue of denial in families where there is child sex abuse. The authors demonstrate a carefully constructed sequence of actions that emphasize empathy and encouragement for giving up the denial.

In all of these case studies there was an abusive relationship going on. The social worker had to clearly establish that he or she would not allow such an abusive relationship to exist. In each case are examples of how the social worker went about protecting the best interests of his or her client. As you read the case studies think about the contracts that were developed between the social workers and others involved in each case. Also, think about how the worker–client relationship was critical in the success of these cases.

## References

Goldstein, A. P. (1980). Relationship enhancement methods. In F. H. Kanfer & A. P. Goldstein (Eds.), *Helping people change* (2nd ed.) (pp. 18–57). New York: Pergamon Press.

National Association of Social Workers. (1983). Membership survey shows practice shifts, *NASW News, 28,* 6–7.

Schwartz, W. (1971). On the use of groups in social work practice. In R. R. Roberts & H. Northern (Eds.), *The practice of group work.* New York: Columbia University Press.

# CASE STUDY 2.1

*This case demonstrates how family therapy can be applied to cases typically found in the child welfare system. A model of reparenting with the goal of reunification is presented.*

## Questions

1. What do you think might be some of the special difficulties of working with child abuse and neglect cases?

2. How is reparenting used in this case to help the mother change her abusive behavior?

3. How does the social worker use her relationship with the clients in encouraging them toward change?

4. Working with child abuse and neglect cases can be challenging because of the complexity and intensity of the problems. What kinds of things can be done to provide the support needed for social workers working under these types of circumstances?

---

## FAMILY THERAPY AND CHILD WELFARE*

*Rita DeMaria*

Jean, the 25-year-old mother of three children—each of whom had a different father—worked as a Go Go dancer to supplement her public assistance checks. Her working hours were constantly changing, and frequently her children, the eldest of whom was 8 years old, were left alone for long periods of time. Jean had no explicit rules for her children, but they were expected to "behave" and not cause her problems. When they did, like the time her 6-year-old shoplifted a water pistol, she saw no alternative but to beat them. They frequently showed up in school with welt marks. As harsh as Jean was when she thought her children were out of control, she was a pushover at other times, indulging her children with presents and ignoring misbehavior when she did not feel like being a disciplinarian. Over-

all, her treatment of her children bordered on the verge of neglect and abuse. Although Jean was opposed to the idea of her children being taken away from her, she faced this prospect. Such a separation was not foreign to her experience. As a child, Jean herself had lived in a child-care institution.

Jean is typical of the single mothers involved with the child welfare system. To a family therapist it is obvious that Jean and her children would benefit from family therapy. However, family therapy is not typically the treatment of choice in child welfare agencies dominated by a child advocate service philosophy. Many child welfare workers share the attitude of a caseworker who once came up to me after a workshop I had given on working with the natural families of foster children to voice her skepticism about the likelihood of reuniting foster children with their natural parents. She related a gruesome incident of a

* Reprinted from the *Family Therapy Networker*, January–February, 1986. Reprinted by permission of the author.

parent's abuse that forced amputation of a child's limbs. Her position was that it was too dangerous to take chances with children's lives and that family work could prolong a child's involvement with abusive and destructive parents.

I have seen that family therapy can work with child welfare cases. At the Institute for Comprehensive Family Therapy, we have developed a treatment and training approach that has worked well with these families.

In 1976 I was the project director for a special community-based family therapy program. Our goal was to work with families of acting out and delinquent youth. Everyone in the community was excited and cooperative—the police, the schools, the probation department, and the child welfare department. But one year and 100 cases later, only two cases had been referred to us by the child welfare department.

In 1979, Sam Kirshner and I founded the Institute for Comprehensive Family Therapy (ICFT). Part of our goal was to implement family-centered services in the child welfare field. Since then, ICFT has provided training to over 35 child welfare agencies, public and private, and consulted on hundreds of cases.

We aimed to reach the families most in need and most resistant to treatment. These families have been described as "fragmented, disenfranchised and formed by persons who have practically no semblance of the meaning of parenthood—they themselves have not had parents" (Polansky, Chalmer, Buttenwieser, & Williams, 1981). These are the kinds of parents whose children languish in foster care year after year: people like Jean but usually with even fewer resources.

Clinically, these families present unusual challenges. For one thing, they often lack many of the creature comforts middle-class mental health professionals take for granted. They may have no telephones, no transportation, no money, and no homes. Their lives are dominated by the stresses of poor health, moderate to severe psychopathology, educational deficiencies, poor job records, and lack of social supports. "Mapping" these families usually reveals convoluted relationships. There can be numerous paramours, stepparents, half-siblings, and other difficult to classify relationships.

Most often child welfare cases involve young mothers who may be promiscuous, psychotic, and drug and/or alcohol addicted. Two important studies can help us understand the problems that lead to these young women having their children taken away. In a study of neglecting families, Polansky et al. (1981) found clear evidence of profound developmental lags and maturational deficiencies in the neglectful parents. Greenspan and Porges's study (1984) with "at-risk" children through the Clinical Infant Developmental Program at the Mental Health Study Center, National Institute of Mental Health (NIMH), sheds further light on how families end up at child welfare agencies:

> In spite of definitional differences, there has been general consensus on the clinical characteristics of these families. They tend, for example, to be need-oriented, and to have difficulty in anticipating and conceptualizing the consequences of their actions. The parents operate on a survival basis, often competing with their children for concrete, as well as psychological and social supports.

## REPARENTING

Comprehensive family therapy (CFT) focuses on therapy as a reparenting process. This is an especially effective way of approaching the families one encounters in the child welfare system. CFT aims to provide corrective emotional and behavioral experiences for the parents themselves so that they can more effectively parent their own children.

The first step in CFT involves developing a

parental attachment between therapist and client. The therapist's initial task is to assess a client's experience in his or her family of origin and determine what kind of parenting style is needed—nurturing, disciplining, or programming. Bonding between therapist and client is facilitated by the development of a relationship that contains elements of familiarity. For example, in the early stages of treatment, a person who has been abused and demeaned would be uncomfortable with, but hungry for, a nurturing reparental relationship. Therefore, a CFT therapist would be likely to develop a demanding, tough stance toward this kind of client, later softening to provide the nurturance and validation so desperately needed.

Of course, establishing this kind of initial therapeutic bond is difficult—especially with the kind of disadvantaged people involved in the child welfare system. Jean, to whom you have already been introduced, was quietly resistant to treatment from the outset. After attending the first two family therapy sessions she simply did not show up for the third appointment. The therapist, sensitive to the reparenting issues in the case, called her and asked why she did not come for the appointment. "I forgot" was the response. The therapist scheduled another appointment. Jean came for the appointment and was curious about why the therapist had called. The therapist replied, "Because we have a relationship, and I wanted you to know that I take this seriously. I cannot help you if you do not come for the appointments."

Jean needed someone who would be demanding of her and who could also command her attention and respect as her own parents never had. In this situation the therapist confronted Jean's ambivalence about making her life better and said she would help only if Jean demonstrated her willingness to work—by coming to sessions on a regular basis.

Jean kept the next several appointments and then, predictably, stopped coming. Again, the therapist called her. This time Jean was told that she was being charged for the missed appointment, and a new appointment was set up for the next day. This kind of testing of the therapist is a recurring theme in child welfare cases, and the therapist must develop an appropriate, therapeutic reparenting posture. In many of these cases perseverance and commitment are essential ingredients.

Soon after therapy resumed, Jean revealed for the first time that she had been abandoned and abused (physically, sexually, and emotionally) by both parents and that she taught herself to live life by the rules of the street. Jean has now been in treatment for a little less than 4 years. Her treatment has included many sessions with her children as well as her paramours, but for the most part, the treatment has involved primarily Jean. The therapist's role has been to become the "good enough" mother that Jean never had.

One of my favorite anecdotes is about the day Jean came and told her therapist that the school was going to place her son in a special school for learning disabled children. At age 6 he could not read and was very disruptive in class. During that session the therapist vividly depicted the possibility that the boy's school failure might lead to delinquency, to lifetime criminality, or psychosis.

The next week the therapist went with Jean to the school for the "placement" conference. The school psychologist began the meeting by apologizing. It seemed that in the last week Daniel was a changed boy, and the teacher had written a special note on his behalf to keep him in the regular classroom.

"What happened?" everyone asked Jean.

"I had a talk with him," she said calmly.

Later when the therapist questioned Jean about the change in events, Jean said, in her usual naive way, "Why I talked to him the way you talked to me. What else was I supposed to do?"

The relationship between Jean and the therapist allowed her to take a proper parental relationship with her son. Over time, variations on this theme occurred with each child, and Jean has acquired much more competency in her ability to parent. Current treatment is focused on developing skills in effectively disciplining her children.

The bonding that took place between the therapist and Jean allowed the development of a relationship in which Jean could experience discipline in a positive way, not as abuse or emotional rape. This is a critical step in her development as a parent. Previously the "discipline" that she employed was abusive and, consequently, her tendency was to back off from disciplining her children on a regular basis.

The 4 years Jean has been in treatment is a long time for family therapy. However, Jean and her family had previously been on public assistance for over 13 years. As a child, she had been placed in a child-care institution for 5 years (where she was also physically abused). Altogether, she and her children have had more than 30 years of involvement with the public welfare system. Her siblings (seven of them) are still on public assistance. Including her siblings and immediate extended families, the number of years of treatment is over 200! These kinds of statistics are all too typical of child welfare cases.

## THE CASE OF MARY

The child welfare system has classically been a reflection of parens patras doctrine—the state becomes parent in order to protect or rehabilitate the child. Mary is an example of a child who needed the state's protection and also needed big changes in her family. She was 16 years old and been picked up for drunk driving. She refused to go home and instead stayed with a friend. When a probation officer came to talk with Mary, she told her that her brothers—older and younger—were "messing with her" and that she also had an outbreak of venereal herpes. The probation officer, then in a CFT training group, scheduled a family therapy session to discuss Mary's return home.

Although both Mary's parents had agreed to come to the session, only her mother showed up. Under the guidance of a consulting CFT therapist, the first session was spent convincing the mother of the validity of Mary's claim and enlisting her support to bring in the husband. We learned, too, that both mother and father had previously undergone psychiatric hospitalization. The mother had attempted suicide. The oldest daughter was married to an abusive husband. Four boys remained at home—one had dropped out of school and all of them were drinking. The father was a truck driver with an erratic schedule and an alcohol problem.

The male consulting therapist and trainer took a nurturing but demanding posture toward the mother. These were classic systems maneuvers to put the mother into the executive position. The therapist ensured that the mother felt not only the strength of the therapist but his understanding as well. The father did in fact come to the second session in which he was told why his daughter did not want to come home. The therapist (also a male) pressed the father to be specific and concrete about what he was going to do with the boys to ensure that the "messing around" stopped.

The father had come from a family in which he was one of 17 siblings. He called himself "a loner who had to scratch for everything he had." He also acknowledged that he knew nothing about fathering. He had never felt "at home" in his family of origin, and it wasn't any different now. The therapist took a "fathering" stance toward this man, which created a relationship in which the father could seek advice and admit to his shortcomings and weaknesses. The progress in this family over time has been significant. The marital relationship has improved dramatically, and Mary has recently entered college—the first person in her family ever to do so.

## REFLECTIONS ON WORKING IN CHILD WELFARE

There are currently more than a half million cases in the child welfare system. It is important to keep in mind that child welfare is called on to serve children when all other institutions, including the family, have failed. Consequently, these families are notoriously difficult to engage. In training caseworkers, our programs focus not only on developing family assessment and intervention skills but also on creative ways to develop relationships with the more fragmented and disengaged families.

In one case, a caseworker obtained agency permission to install and pay for telephone service for a mother who had not had contact with her 6-year-old son since he was less than a year old. The mother lived in another state, and there was no other realistic way to maintain weekly contact. The caseworker had to work through numerous channels and red tape to receive the necessary approval. As a result, the mother did in fact establish a relationship with her child. Reunification became a possibility and then a reality.

The high staff burnout rate in child welfare programs is a crucial problem. The case examples discussed so far clearly show that the families that are referred to child welfare have a tremendous need for security and relatedness, which are difficult to achieve when staff are coming and going at a more rapid pace than the treatment process itself. The average length of time a caseworker stays with a public agency is 2 years. Supervisory personnel tend to stay a little longer—5 years on the average. Combine this with the fact that caseworkers are generally underpaid and unprepared for the overload of complex, dysfunc-

tional client families and you have a situation in which the least experienced people are expected to "do something" with the most difficult families.

Even though the child welfare system consistently maintains a child advocate position, each agency has its own organizational style and preferences. Advocacy can mean prevention as well as intervention. The style is most evident in the role that the agency expects the caseworker to take with his or her clients. Is the worker's role administrative, managerial, or direct service oriented? If the agency is service oriented, with a belief in the value of casework, it is more likely the staff will accept training and integrate new skills into their practice.

But is casework really therapy? Who should provide family treatment? This was definitely one of the more complex and distracting issues that we had to address in forming our training programs at ICFT. One way we learned to prevent unnecessary conflict was to define training or service as "intensive family casework." Such terminology is congruent with almost every agency's philosophy. Each agency can then develop their unique brand of family-centered services. For example, some agencies will develop specialized family therapy units. Other agencies will take a more generic approach and apply family therapy principles and techniques on a "unit" or program basis.

Many caseworkers and casework supervisors have participated enthusiastically in Institute training programs. These staff have tended to stay with the agency longer and move into supervisory and middle-management positions. But ultimately, they, too, move on to the programs that afford them greater clinical variety and professional satisfaction.

The clinical demands of this work can deplete even the most optimistic and successful staff members, clinicians, and trainers. There seems to be a limit to the number of severely dysfunctional families any one therapist can work with successfully on a daily basis. That is what makes the child welfare system such a humbling experience. Even though family therapy is a powerful tool, the mess, the demands, and the commitment required by the system as well as the family are great. However, the use of our reparenting model has resulted in unusual success in reaching many of the families.

With perseverance, realistic goals, and clinical skills, progress is inevitable. Indeed, the county agency that once had only those two families to refer to our family therapy project was able to reduce the actual number of children in institutions by over 65% between 1979 and 1982. With an emphasis on family work they have also established an impressive network of family-centered services throughout their county and have moved to providing generic family-centered services themselves.

## References

Greenspan, S. I., & Porges, S. W. (1984). Psychopathology in infancy and early childhood: Clinical perspectives on the organization of sensory and affective-thematic experience. *Child Development, 55*, 49–70.

Polansky, N. A., Chalmers, M. A., Buttenwieser, E., & Williams, D. P. (1981). *Damaged parents: An anatomy of child neglect.* Chicago, IL: University of Chicago Press.

# CASE STUDY 2.2

*The couple in this case developed a relationship that incorporated significant incidences of violence. Breaking this pattern of violence became the goal for successful resolution of the problem.*

## Questions

1. How does the social worker challenge the family's values in this case?
2. What factors could be attributed to maintaining the violence in this family?
3. How was the couple kept involved in the treatment?
4. What personal attributes or family experiences do you have that could affect your ability to work with similar cases?

## CHALLENGING THE TRADITION: IN SOME FAMILIES, VIOLENCE IS A WAY OF LIFE

*Steven Krugman**

A dog barked at me while I waited on the porch of the ramshackle house for someone to open the door. A young woman in her mid-20s wordlessly let me into the kitchen. There, five or six adults were sitting around the table, smoking cigarettes, and drinking coffee. A baby slept in a port-a-crib, while two older boys played with used auto parts in the living room.

The baby and the two boys were the ostensible reason I was there. A social worker at the hospital where the baby had just been born had learned that the infant's mother, "Kathy"—the young woman who had let me in—had a long history of drug abuse and that both she and her two young sons had been beaten by her first husband. The worker, concerned about Kathy's ability to take care of her new baby, had filed a child abuse and neglect report. I was there following up on that

report as the representative of a family intervention team of the State Department of Mental Health. I had already gotten some background information on Kathy. She was a tough Boston Irish tomgirl grown older and a little wiser over the years. At 17 she'd married a man who worked sporadically, sold drugs, and regularly abused her and their two boys. After one especially vicious beating, Kathy's brothers helped her escape and return to her parents' home. That ended the marriage. Back home she quickly resumed her long-standing job of taking care of everyone else and keeping the lid on the ever-stewing pot of family conflict. She was the fourth of 10 children. She'd kept out of trouble by staying close to her volatile, sometimes alcoholic, mother; running errands; and hauling in stray family members. Then she met 40-year-old "Tony," whose maturity seemed to offer the possibility of a more stable, less violent family life. They had been married for 2 years.

The relationship with Kathy was Tony's

* Reprinted from the *Family Therapy Networker*, May–June, 1986. Reprinted by permission of the author.

third try at a family. His first marriage had broken up because his wife wouldn't take his abuse and left with their daughter. According to him, the second marriage "just ended," that's all. Tony carried himself like a coiled spring and let everyone know he was not someone to mess with. But evidently someone had ignored those signals along the way— Tony had once done 10 months for assault.

Tony offered me a seat and went on talking with his buddies. I just sat there wondering if either Tony or Kathy would acknowledge that we had set up a meeting a few days before. Neither did. Finally I said we needed to get started. With drudging ceremony Tony ushered his friends from the kitchen, shrugging his shoulders and asking one of them to wait in the living room.

I explained about the report I had received from the hospital's protective worker. Tony immediately let me know that he wanted to be no part of whatever I was selling. Everything was fine except for the "goddamned Department of Social Services." Neither he nor Kathy needed any help and I should better leave. I felt like an intruder and was more than a little intimidated by Tony and his friends. Kathy hardly said a word. There was no room for discussion. As I left, I told Kathy and Tony to call if they felt I could be of use.

## A SURPRISE CALL

The following Sunday night I answered a crisis call. It was Tony. Kathy was in the hospital. She'd "hurt herself" while high on valium and alcohol. Could I see the two of them? The next morning I learned that Kathy had been stuporous and badly bruised when she was admitted to the hospital. The emergency room sent her to a shelter for battered women. The kids seemed to be all right.

Later that day Kathy came to the session with an advocate from the shelter. She and Tony cried together while the shelter worker and I sat by uncomfortably. They were both

tremendously apologetic and remorseful. Kathy was angry at herself for breaking a promise she had made to Tony about using pills. She was, however, confused about how she had gotten so bruised. Tony swore he'd only "slapped her around a little" to revive her. He said that he'd been scared to death when he saw her looking all doped up.

I asked Kathy if she knew what Tony wanted her to do. She said, "Sure. Stop using pills. Be home when the boys get home from school. Stay in at night because it's too dangerous. Not see anyone, just wait for him." As she spoke she got angrier and more sarcastic. "Yeah, I know what he wants. He wants to control me."

Still smarting from my first encounter and puzzled by Tony's call to me, I wanted to shift the responsibility for choosing therapy to the clients. "It seems to me that you've both apologized and forgiven each other. The last time I spoke with you Tony told me that everything was okay. I wonder if there's any need for us to meet? Maybe Kathy should go for counseling at the shelter." This time they both said that they wanted to go to therapy—they didn't want this relationship to go down the tubes like the others had.

## CHALLENGING THE FAMILY'S VALUES

Once I began meeting with Tony and Kathy it was clear that they were much more experienced than I with violence of all kinds. Both had grown up witnessing violence at home and in the street. They jokingly called their neighborhood "Dodge City." During the two years they'd been married, Tony had threatened Kathy numerous times; shoved her on two occasions (prior to the current incident); pushed around Kathy's 9-year-old son, Kevin, several times; and had a fight with her ex-husband. Yet these acts had barely registered on their scale of life events.

With Kathy and Tony, as with other violent

couples I see, the first phase of treatment was governed by three principles:

1. *Safety First.* I help the victim and the family establish as much safety as they can. To do this I negotiate an explicit contingency plan in which both partners agree on how they will deal with a violent crisis. The plan then becomes a technique for creating alternative choices like "time out" periods and physical separation, to counter abuse and victimization. My emphasis on the plan challenges the family's belief that now that treatment has begun the danger is over. I insist that it lies ahead.

2. *Responsibility and Control.* With violent couples it is essential to give a clear message that the hitter is responsible for his hitting and that rationalizations like "she provoked me" or "I couldn't help it" are not acceptable. Tony insisted that when he hurt Kathy he was "out of control." I told him that I had a hard time believing that an experienced street fighter like him had so little control over his hands. He repeated my observation, enjoying the irony. There was something about this way of looking at his relationship with Kathy that struck home with him. Invoking the image of the battle-scarred street fighter unable to control himself with his wife provided tremendous leverage throughout the course of therapy.

3. *The Rights of the Victim.* Along with the emphasis on the responsibility of the abuser comes a concern with the rights of the victim—namely the right not to be hit. In many families this challenges the accepted value system regarding the use of physical force. While emphasizing that Tony was also hurting and needed help, I strongly supported Kathy's right not to be hit or coerced. "I've never had a safe place," she told me. "I want my home to be safe."

After 4 months of weekly meetings with Tony and Kathy there had been no further physical battles, and I confronted a familiar problem in working with violent couples. If you succeed in putting a check on the violence, the family's motivation to change is likely to diminish dramatically. Going from the crisis and initial engagement to a longer-term working alliance is difficult. Many cases get lost at this point. Making the transition to ongoing treatment requires either a high degree of motivation within the family (often the wife says "Unless you change I'm leaving") or consistent external pressure coming from the courts or the Department of Social Services (DSS). At times, family and church networks can provide it as well.

Violent families rely heavily on denial and minimization as a way of warding off feelings of being out of control and being vulnerable. Dropping out of therapy at the first sign that things are better is a predictable response. After all, going on in treatment means dealing with upsetting memories and experiences.

So, when Christmas arrived, Tony and Kathy decided to break for the holidays and call me if they wished to see me again.

## PHASE TWO

What happened next makes the case of Tony and Kathy unusual in my experience. Typically, either one or both of the partners in a violent relationship are reluctant to be in treatment. The investment of the mental health system with such couples is more in the way of crisis intervention than ongoing treatment. If therapy is to continue past the initial crisis, the therapist must ally with both partners while, at the same time, insisting that the violence must stop. This can be a difficult balancing act to pull off. Somehow, in this case, both Kathy and Tony had come to see me as someone who had something to offer, and 4 months later I heard from them again.

Tony, working long hours and under a lot of financial pressure, "lost his cool" one night, pushed Kathy around, and slapped her. In a similar incident some days before, Tony slapped Kevin after the boy told him "not to yell at his mother." Kathy was furious. She told Tony, "I did what you asked. I haven't used valium. But I married you to spend time with you and you're never home. I need my own life. You can't control me. I won't put up with your hitting and shoving me and the boys. I don't want those kids hit by anyone ever again."

Tony seemed to get the message and reaffirmed his commitment to no more hittings. I agreed with Kathy that Tony was trying to control her life, but I reframed it as "too much caring." Tony agreed to see me individually to find some better way of handling Kathy's wish for more autonomy.

Meanwhile, Kathy's son Kevin told his guidance counselor about the violence at home. Another DSS worker got involved and raised the question of whether Kathy's three boys should be removed from the home. Though no specific action resulted, Kathy became very anxious at the possibility of losing custody. She even talked about leaving Tony if staying with him jeopardized her custody of her sons. For the first time Kathy and Tony were faced squarely with the possibility of losing either their children or their marriage.

## OTHER SYSTEMS

A basic ground rule in working with violent family situations is to make use of all available community resources. Yet anyone who has ever dealt with the courts and DSS knows that their interventions are often ineffective and poorly coordinated. In this case, though I had worked closely with the protective agency, the threat to remove Kathy's children was never discussed with me. I suggested a meeting to develop a plan including the school and DSS, but before the meeting could be held, the caseworker left the agency. The case, evaluated now as "low risk," went unassigned for

months. A relieved Kathy and Tony left therapy once again.

About 6 months later Tony and one of Kathy's brothers had a terrible fight over some money that had disappeared from the house. The police, arresting no one, filed a child abuse report. A new worker was assigned, and the family was once again encouraged to resume treatment.

By this time the pattern of ebb and flow of tension was becoming clear, and together we focused on understanding how the episodes of violence fit into Tony and Kathy's life with each other. Tony had long ago cut himself off from all familial ties. As is true for many men, abusive and nonabusive, his wife had become his sole source of emotional attachment. Yet her wish that he be home more left him feeling "hemmed in" and anxious about making enough money.

The later and harder Tony worked, the more entitled he felt and the more alone and vulnerable to her family Kathy found herself to be. Furious at Tony for not fulfilling the role of protecting her from her family, which he had assumed earlier in their relationship, she distanced herself by using drugs and going out with friends. Tony experienced this withdrawal as deeply threatening. His fear and anxiety would generate a crisis of violence that, like a violent summer storm, would clear the air and reestablish their connection.

As they came to recognize that violence was their way of regulating closeness when no other means seemed available, Kathy and Tony began to feel more connected. He began to come home for dinner several nights a week. They agreed to set limits with Kathy's intrusive family and become more involved with the boys.

By this time, the pattern in Tony and Kathy's relationship with me was also becoming clearer. Some crisis or external push (for example, from a new DSS worker) would trigger a new round of therapy. We'd meet regularly for several months and then the demands of daily life would override our scheduled meetings. I framed the waning energy as Tony and Kathy's taking control of the therapy. We ended this phase with me saying, "Call me when you'd like to meet again. Remember, you don't have to wait for a crisis."

## TRANSGENERATIONAL ISSUES

Tony called 6 months later to report another crisis: Kathy had moved out with the boys. They had had a fight, but—he emphasized—he hadn't hit her. When I saw Tony and Kathy together, I learned that her mother had died, her father had moved in, and in his wake the brothers and sisters followed through the open door. "I've lost control of my house," she said.

Tony said, "This is how it started. I thought that when her mother died, we should take care of her dad. Kathy blew up. She said, 'If you like my family so much you can have them.' I was hurt. But when she said she was leaving I saw red."

The death of Kathy's mother brought all the transgenerational themes underlying their conflicts into focus. Kathy had been ambivalent about her mother all along. Her covert function as surrogate mother became overt when "mom" died, as did her life-long resentment over being put in that role. For Tony, having Kathy's father around was a little like having his own deceased father around again.

Creating boundaries around the nuclear family with Kathy's father living there was next to impossible. Finally, pursuing the issue of how Kathy and Tony could be available to each other in the midst of all this generated the idea of a vacation. "Pops" could either go with them to Florida or go stay with one of her older sisters. With great difficulty Kathy allowed her father to live elsewhere.

A year later he was still living with her older brother, and Kathy and Tony were together and doing well.

## CONCLUSION

Physically violent families tend to be closed systems. They are organized around secrets and a fearful view of the world. Obtaining the trust of such families is a trick in itself. Engaging the abusive members, along with others in the family, means going from being seen as a nosy intruder to a valued resource who can help the family to change what hurts.

Engaging any closed or rigid family system is a challenge, but with violent families the challenge goes deeper. The therapist takes a clear moral position on the unacceptability of violence in the family, a position that typically challenges the family's subcultural values. By supporting the vulnerable members—both those being hit and victimized and those who feel emotionally one-down and disempowered—the therapy begins to help the individuals and the family reorganize around their needs for physical and emotional safety.

Although they hardly matched the stereotype of the ideal therapy consumers, Kathy and Tony went much further in exploring the roots of the violence in their relationship than most couples I have treated. In each installment of their treatment, we were able to focus more on the larger familial context maintaining their problem. Recently, I spoke with Kathy to sound out how things were going for her and Tony. "Good and bad," she told me. "Things between Tony and me are fine. He hasn't been violent in years. When things get 'tight' we talk it out—like you taught us. I'm not afraid any more that he's going to hurt me. That's the good news. The bad news is that my dad's back with us, and he's driving me nuts!"

# CASE STUDY 2.3

*Multidisciplinary team work in a hospital setting calls for a variety of social work functions. This multifaceted case study illustrates the detailed tasks of this type of social work.*

## Questions

1. What is the role of the social worker on the multidisciplinary team?
2. What are the social work tasks once sexual abuse has been identified?
3. How does the social worker provide case coordination for the multidisciplinary team?
4. How does the social worker's role shift in response to the changing needs of this case?

## CLINICAL SOCIAL WORK IN A MULTIDISCIPLINARY TEAM: AN ADOLESCENT INPATIENT PSYCHIATRY CASE

*Catherine Sammons*

In a number of practice settings, the social worker is at the hub of a network of professional disciplines and social agencies. Although social work training is oriented toward direct clinical interventions with the client, the practitioner must also master the role of coordinator of the various "players" who interact to affect the client.

This case is presented to highlight the complexities and special issues in clinical social work as practiced in a multidisciplinary team. The setting is a locked inpatient hospital unit for adolescents with severe psychiatric disorders, including schizophrenia, autism, mental retardation, and affective and conduct disorders. Patients typically stay for 2 to 3 months and receive a comprehensive evaluation, initial treatment, and recommendations for ongoing treatment. Frequently, the postdischarge disposition plan involves placement in a residential treatment center.

### THE CRISIS OF DISCLOSURE

About 20 team members and clinical trainees from the adolescent service were assembled in a large meeting room for their weekly case conference. The trainee for this day's case presentation, a child psychiatry fellow, provided a brief history of the patient. She was beginning her fourth week of hospitalization and was thus well known to the team.*

The senior child psychiatry professor, a jovial and kind-spirited older man, smiled as the patient, Debby, a black 14-year-old, was escorted into the room and seated next to him at the front of the group. Debby appeared calm and cooperative as the professor asked her a few general questions about the events leading up to hospitalization. At one point, he asked, "Have you ever had any unusual experi-

---

* To preserve anonymity, this case is a composite description, with features of several patients.

50

ences?" This question is a typical probe for unusual thoughts, perceptual illusions, or hallucinations.

However, Debby's calm answer was like a quiet bomb in the room: "Yes, my father's been screwing me." "What do you mean by that?" said the professor; like everyone else in the room, he had been caught off-guard, but unlike them, he had to mobilize himself and continue the interview. Debby went on to define in clear, calm terms her sexual molestation for the past 2 years by her adoptive father.

Aware and experienced in this all-too-common problem among children and adolescents, the team was not surprised by the content of the disclosure so much as its timing. This was not the presenting complaint at admission, and no clues had been detected during the first month of treatment. Yet another problem had to be added to an already lengthy list for this adolescent, necessitating a marked change in her treatment and in the role of the social worker.

## THE BACKGROUND

Debby was brought to the hospital by her adoptive father, Mr. Smith, a white 58-year-old small-business owner whose wife of 24 years, a black woman, had died 6 months before, after a short bout with cancer. He described himself as a recovering alcoholic. He appeared depressed, still grieving the loss of his wife, and yet he portrayed himself as devoted to the care of his two adoptive children, Debby and her adoptive brother, Billy, a white 14-year-old.

Mr. Smith had brought Debby to the hospital because she had exhibited a sudden change in personality, from an easygoing, happy young teen with mild mental retardation to a depressed, tormented individual. She had been troubled by auditory hallucinations (voices telling her to jump off a building "to die and

be with my mother"), somatic and religious delusions, and thought broadcasting and insertion. The family noted Debby becoming withdrawn, confused, and illogical in her speech. She was also wakeful at night, paced frequently, and had a greatly reduced appetite.

The family configuration was fairly complex and perhaps best conveyed by a diagram. (See Figure 1.)

Debby's household at the time of hospitalization included herself; her adoptive brother, Billy; her adoptive father; and longtime family friend and housekeeper, Helen. Debby's sisters all resided in the same city.

## TEAM TREATMENT GOALS AND INTERVENTIONS

The adolescent unit team generated the following treatment goals for Debby:

1. Recovering basic mental health (decreasing delusions, hallucinations, and depression)
2. Being and feeling safe and protected from further emotional and sexual exploitation
3. Resuming age-appropriate (chronologically and developmentally) daily activities
4. Strengthening emotional bonds with supportive family members
5. Working through the grief of losing her mother
6. Securing an appropriate discharge disposition arrangement in which the first five goals could continue to be addressed

In order to make progress toward these goals, Debby needed the assessment and intervention of several team members of various professional disciplines who could accurately evaluate and treat this adolescent and her family.

The case coordinator, a medical doctor in advanced psychiatric training (postresidency fellowship), was the primary therapist for

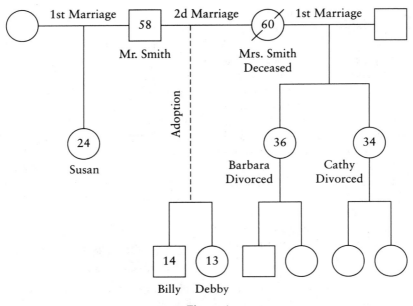

**Figure 1**

A family tree diagram

Debby, seeing her at least three times per week. He also prescribed and monitored medications. However, his key role in the inpatient team was to integrate the team's assessments into a comprehensive diagnostic picture and coordinated treatment effort. The case coordinator also conducted family meetings in collaboration with the unit's clinical social worker. In those meetings, the cotherapists obtained the clinical history (medical, developmental, and psychosocial), oriented family members to the inpatient unit program, and provided family updates regarding Debby's clinical status and response to treatment. They also assessed family functioning to determine adaptive and maladaptive aspects of family interaction (that is, ways in which family relationships inhibited or enhanced Debby's functioning).

The psychologist evaluated Debby's intellectual and emotional status by administering standardized tests. Even when nonpsychotic,

Debby appeared emotionally immature, with a poor vocabulary and academic underachievement. A complex diagnostic task was to differentiate between temporary impairment in cognitive skills secondary to psychotic symptoms and mild mental retardation as an underlying, preexisting developmental disability.

The occupational and recreational therapists assessed Debby's leisure time skills, her ability to interact appropriately with peers in both task and social groups, and her fine- and gross-motor functioning. The inpatient educators performed a complete educational assessment and provided a daily special education classroom program during the hospitalization.

A psychiatric nurse designated as Debby's "primary nurse" formulated a nursing care plan that addressed all areas of daily living: eating, sleeping, personal hygiene, general health, and relationships with peers and staff in the adolescent unit milieu. The nurse helped

Debby adjust to the unit's behavioral system, she developed individualized behavioral contracts, and she provided emotional support to Debby on a daily basis.

The speech and language therapist clarified and described language deviances versus delays and also provided guidelines for team members to enhance Debby's verbal skills.

Following the sexual abuse disclosure, an extensive physical examination was performed by a pediatrician with specialized training and experience in evaluating sexually abused youths. She noted key physical signs of abuse, described these in a formal report (with diagrams), and later testified in court, with her examination as evidence for the prosecution. Because of her expertise, she was able to accomplish these interventions with sensitivity, so that Debby did not feel further "invaded" but rather supported.

## THE ROLE OF THE SOCIAL WORKER

In addition to the basic social work functions of family assessment, support, and therapy, in the case of Debby (as with most inpatients), the social worker performed a number of other interventions. Debby's disclosure of sexual abuse necessitated (in accordance with state law) immediate telephone and written reports to the local department of children's services and the police department in the city in which the abuse occurred. The social worker typically either makes these reports herself or assists the case coordinator, a trainee, in doing so. Furthermore, the social worker maintained telephone contact with these agencies to keep informed of the progress of their work. This was relevant for both clinical treatment (for example, learning that the father had been arrested and conveying this information to the patient) and disposition planning (for example, Debby was designated a dependent of the

court, and the children's services worker was responsible for appropriate placement).

As treatment progressed, it became clear that Debby could benefit from longer-term psychiatric care at an adolescent residential treatment center. The social worker investigated various programs and, in conjunction with children's services, facilitated Debby's smooth transition from the intensive hospital evaluation unit to an appropriate placement.

Another community agency relevant to Debby's case was the local center for developmentally disabled persons. The social worker initiated and monitored the application process so that Debby would become eligible for future services such as vocational and independent-living training. Also, since the course of schizophrenia is unpredictable, one possible future scenario was that the psychosis would resolve (or stabilize), and Debby would benefit from other developmental disabilities settings and services.

The social worker's direct clinical work with Debby and her family occurred within a context of intensive, daily contact; information exchange; and coordination with the case coordinator and the rest of the team. From the perspective of the team social worker, the various role relationships formed a pattern like that exhibited in Figure 2.

## FAMILY INTERVENTIONS

Following the disclosure of sexual abuse, Debby adamantly refused to see or talk with her father. This was an adaptive response in several ways: it protected her from further abuse, intimidation, guilt (which might increase if she had to witness her father's sadness and complaints about the arrest), and shame (he was then blaming her).

The disclosure created a crisis situation for every family member, and alliances shifted. Figure 3 illustrates how the therapists' initial

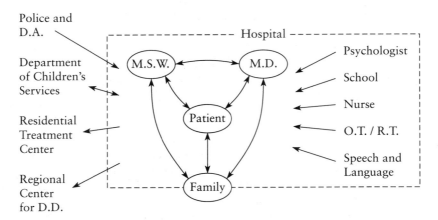

Police and
D.A.

Department
of Children's
Services

Residential
Treatment
Center

Regional
Center
for D.D.

Hospital

M.S.W.        M.D.

Patient

Family

Psychologist

School

Nurse

O.T. / R.T.

Speech and
Language

**Figure 2**

Role relationships and communication

perception of family members' relationships changed after disclosure.

Clearly, a major breach in the father–daughter relationship occurred. Also, Debby's contacts with her brother became brief, superficial in content, and limited to phone conversations because Mr. Smith refused to bring Billy to the hospital for visits or family therapy.

Two of Debby's three adult sisters became very involved and intensified their contacts with Debby. One sister, Barbara, coped well with her understandably "mixed-up" feelings of surprise, anger at Mr. Smith, sadness for Debby, guilt over not detecting the problem herself, uncertainty about Debby's psychiatric problems, and intense desire to protect Debby and participate in disposition planning. The second sister, Cathy, could not accept Debby's report as truthful; she insisted that Debby's psychiatric problems had distorted her sense of reality and past events so that Debby was mistakenly blaming their father instead of the "real" perpetrator. Although Cathy was overwhelmed with sorrow and pity when visiting Debby, she appeared to feel more sympathy toward Mr. Smith and to perceive him as the victim. (Note: one hypothesis that might explain Cathy's reactions was that perhaps she

also had been molested by Mr. Smith during her childhood or adolescence and that acknowledging Debby's victimization would threaten her long-standing denial and refusal to disclose such early events in her own life. She might also experience particularly acute guilt if she had been victimized first and had failed to warn or protect her younger sister. Although we could never confirm or refute this theory, we did learn that both Barbara and Cathy had fended off a number of inappropriate sexual advances from Mr. Smith as older teens and adults.) The third sister, Susan, did not contact the hospital and had little contact with Barbara and Cathy.

The social worker and the case coordinator, in weekly sessions with Mr. Smith, assessed his reactions to the disclosure as partial willingness to accept that the abusive events had occurred but complete denial that he was the perpetrator. He attributed Debby's "false" report to her "confused mental state." The therapists attempted to educate him about the nature of schizophrenia and specific ways in which it had distorted Debby's thinking, feeling, and perceiving. However, the details of the disclosure, her later interviews with police and district attorney, her daily behavior, and the medical evidence were all consistent with a

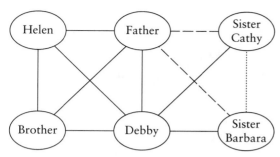

Initial Assessment of Family Relationships

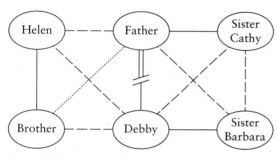

Revised Assessment of Family Relationships

```
┌──────────────── Key ────────────────┐
│ ——— = strong, positive   —\\— = broken   │
│ — — = disrupted, conflict  ········· = unknown │
└─────────────────────────────────────┘
```

**Figure 3**

Initial and revised diagram of family relationships

truthful report. The therapists told Mr. Smith that there were many reasons to believe Debby and no reasons to disbelieve her. Understandably, the therapists' position vis-a-vis Debby's report served to distance Mr. Smith from the therapeutic process. An already guarded client withdrew even further. Meetings focused primarily on treatment updates and disposition planning, although the therapists attempted to offer support by acknowledging how painful and difficult this period was for Mr. Smith and to encourage him to seek support from his brother and to obtain counseling outside of the hospital.

The social worker was inundated by phone calls from sisters Barbara and Cathy, so frequent visits with Debby were arranged. At the social worker's suggestion, all of Debby's visits with family members were monitored by staff. At most visits, the social worker herself served as monitor. She facilitated Debby's communication with the sisters, protected Debby from grilling or accusations, monitored Debby's reactions, and afterward interpreted Debby's behavior to the sisters (sorting out various influences such as developmental delay, psychotic themes, medication planned effects and side effects, and temporary mood state).

As Mr. Smith's legal rights as a parent decreased because of Debby's becoming a dependent of the court, parenting functions were dispersed across a group of adults. First, Debby experienced acute feelings of loss and abandonment due to the death of her adoptive mother, who had been very nurturing and supportive to Debby. Second, the housekeeper, Helen, had served as a second mother to Debby for many years, but in the course of disclosure, Debby stated that she had previously told Helen of the abuse and that Helen had even observed inappropriately intimate behavior between father and daughter. However, Helen now denied any prior knowledge. Debby thus felt ambivalent about Helen: this adult would not openly support or defend Debby, but she continued to be warm, caring, and supportive of efforts to restrict Mr. Smith's contact with Debby.

Third, Debby was confused by Cathy's questioning the truthfulness of her disclosure and by this sister's emotional intensity. On the other hand, Debby felt validated and strengthened by her contacts with her sister Barbara. Finally, coloring all of Debby's feelings was the sense of betrayal and anger she felt toward her father and now had permission to express.

In addition to this complex pattern of emotional parenting that evolved within the family, other adults assumed other parenting role functions as well. The children's services social worker became the action planner and decision maker (with court authority) regarding where Debby would live on discharge and how family contacts would be managed. The hospital continued to provide for all aspects of Debby's daily needs.

The hospital social worker's primary function vis-a-vis these parenting figures was to coordinate and facilitate. Not all parties would accept support or allow a therapeutic alliance to develop with the social worker. Frequent communications with all parties (including a primary relationship with Debby) were necessary to understand the various points of view, levels of understanding, and emotional reactions, especially as these pertained to the selection of a long-term residential treatment program. The hospital and children's services social workers collaborated in researching placements, mailing admissions packets (reports describing Debby's diagnoses, treatment, and recommendations), and arranging for preplacement visits by Debby and her sister Barbara. Although the children's services worker was the primary source of guidance regarding the policies and procedures of dependency hearings and court-ordered placements, the hospital worker's close relationships with Debby and her sisters meant that she was the primary provider of the therapeutic rationale for a particular placement, and she offered encouragement, reassurance, and assistance in reducing anxiety during the difficult transition from hospital to placement.

## SUMMARY

The rich detail and depth of a case such as Debby's is difficult to convey in any written depiction and especially one this brief. However, the case overview offered here is meant to illustrate three points about social work practice in an inpatient psychiatric setting:

1. The clinical complexity and multiproblem nature of hospitalized clients
2. The social worker as a team member, encompassing both the multidisciplinary hospital team and outside community agencies
3. The various other roles and functions of the psychiatric hospital social worker apart from narrowly defined therapeutic interventions during formal therapy meetings.

# CASE STUDY 2.4

*Child sex abuse is a growing problem that concerns social work. In order to intervene effectively in such cases, the worker must be prepared to address denial on the part of family members.*

## Questions

1. What function does denial play for the individuals or families that feel compelled to engage in this action?
2. What are the various types of denial and how can the social worker respond to each type?
3. What are different strategies that can be used to confront denial?
4. What factors led to the successful disclosure of child sexual abuse in this case?

## TREATMENT OF DENIAL IN FAMILIES WHERE THERE IS CHILD SEX ABUSE

*Mary Jo Barrett and Terry S. Trepper*

One of the most frustrating elements of treating incestuous families is the tendency of their members to engage in active denial. Therapists are only human; they find incestuous abuse as abhorrent as most people. Many therapists, who expect at least a modicum of remorse by the offending father* and sympathy for the child from the nonoffending mother, are incredulous when confronted with denial from both. The denial of abuse then may become the focus of a power struggle between the clinician and the family, with the result being that the therapy becomes stalemated.

This chapter will discuss the function of de-

nial, outline the various types of denial that may operate within a family, and present a case example that illustrates how denial can be effectively reduced. These interventions for denial are part of a larger program for treating child sexual abuse that we will first briefly describe.

The program has been in operation for over 10 years and has treated hundreds of families, offenders, and victims. It is an intensive program, based on the Multiple Systems Model (Barrett, Sykes, & Byrnes, 1986; Trepper & Barrett, 1989), which assesses and intervenes in the many "systems" that contribute to the expression of incest. Families are seen for an average of 18 months in family, marital, individual, and group therapy. Other important systems, such as the parents' families of origin or the victims' social network, are also incorporated into the treatment.

Therapy occurs in three distinct stages: Stage 1 is called "Creating a Context for Change," and its purpose is for the therapist

---

* In this chapter, the term *father* will be used to refer to the offending parent; *mother* will be used to refer to the nonoffending parent; and *daughter, son,* and *child* will be used to refer to the child-victim. This convention makes for easier reading and should in no way be construed to suggest that only fathers abuse children, nor that only girls are victims. Also *father* and *mother* are used to refer to *stepfather* and *stepmother*, again for consistency and ease of reading.

to join with the family, network with involved legal and social agencies, create the reality that change is possible, provide a common language that will be used throughout treatment, and reduce the family's resistance to change. During Stage 1, the most vigorous effort to understand, work with, and potentially ameliorate the denial occurs. Stage 2, "Challenging Behaviors and Expanding Alternatives," is characterized by intensive therapeutic challenges to the style and structure of the individual and the family that has contributed to its vulnerability to incest. In this stage, intense individual therapy takes place. If the family or individuals are still engaging in the more subtle forms of denial, it is challenged during this stage. Stage 3, "Consolidation," is when the family is expected to incorporate the changes made during Stages 1 and 2 of therapy into their daily life with a minimum of therapist involvement. Here denial is discussed in the past tense, with the client being asked to examine what purpose his or her previous denial served and how to prevent denial from being used as a coping mechanism in the future.

## PURPOSE OF DENIAL

We have found it most helpful to consider denial as a special case of a family's natural resistance to change, to therapy, and to the intrusion into their lives by outsiders. Denial, like all resistance, is not necessarily pathological but can be an important and understandable protective device. Whether it is psychological denial, where it is unconscious and unavailable to the client even when confronted with reality, or social denial, where the decision to deny is conscious, the underlying purpose is protection of the individual and/or family from the overwhelming psychological and social consequences of incest. This may be considered analogous to the body's production of endorphins to mask overwhelming physical pain. Offenders deny in order to save themselves from legal repercussions and/or to de-

fend against the psychological and emotional pain of their childhood trauma that contributes to their abusive behavior. Nonoffending parents, mostly women, are often forced by society to deny because of their economic and emotional dependence on men, the offenders, and because they wish to protect themselves from emotional and physical pain.

The benefits to the therapist in viewing denial as a strength rather than a deficit are numerous. Instead of seeing the client's denial as hostility against the therapist, which can only lead to a defensive posture, the therapist who views denial as self-protection and a coping mechanism is free to treat it as any other clinical interaction. A positive view of denial allows for a more positive and respectful view of the client; this opens up the possibilities for a functional relationship. Demanding the extinction of denial as a coping mechanism is an irresponsible position for any therapist to take. When understanding denial, the therapist can expect its occurrence, build a more effective therapeutic relationship, and plan strategies to intervene.

Most therapeutic programs expect the offender to accept responsibility for the sexual abuse as part of the treatment goals. This goal must be kept in mind throughout the program. Even when accepting the protective component of denial, the therapist should be cautioned never to appear to accept the denial of the abuse itself. The therapist who appears to accept the denial may be tacitly excusing the abuse and may contribute to the befuddling of reality that may lead to long-term psychopathology for the abused child. The challenge for the therapist is to accept the underlying reason for denial but not the denial of the abuse itself.

## TYPES OF DENIAL

In the course of our work, we have identified four types of denial commonly present in the family. Of course not every family member denies, and any family member may manifest more than one type of denial. These types are (1) denial of facts; (2) denial of awareness; (3) denial of responsibility; and (4) denial of impact.

## Denial of Facts

Denial of facts refers to the direct and open challenge of the reality of the incestuous abuse. A family member can deny that the abuse ever occurred at all or deny certain facts associated with the abuse. Denial of facts is the most difficult with which to intervene and, if it persists, can have the most serious long-term consequences for the child because it assaults the very core of his or her reality. Younger children may grow up never really knowing whether what they think they experienced really occurred. When there is denial of the facts by the perpetrator and/or by the non-offending parent, it is as if the child is being victimized twice: first by the abusive act and next by the act of denial. We consider the denial of facts so potentially detrimental that we do not choose to have a child in session with a parent who is denying facts.

Not surprisingly, the abusing fathers deny facts more often than other members of the family; about 30% of fathers in our program denied facts on entering therapy. Most often this denial is seen as a way to protect them from prison terms, and in fact attorneys advise fathers in our program to admit to as little as possible in therapy, since it could be used against them in court. We know our experience is not uncommon from other sexual abuse programs. Therapy becomes little more than a continual reiteration of, "I didn't do it; I don't know why she said it."

About 15% of our nonabusing mothers deny facts at the beginning of the program. Most often the mother's denial occurs in tandem with the father's denial, but denial can occur when a mother denies the facts, even when both the father and the daughter admit to them. "She is lying, and maybe some of what he says is true, but she is making it worse, and he is going along with it to help his case."

Only about 4% of the victims in our program deny the facts. When they do so, it is usually to protect the father from being removed from the home or to keep him from going to jail. It is a reality, that in order to protect the child from further abuse, families often are separated and, unfortunately, this is not always done in a consistent or therapeutic fashion. The child is told, "Tell me about the abuse and nothing bad will happen to you," and when she/he does, the family is split up, he/she may be in a foster home, and the father may go to jail. Consequently it is not uncommon for an abused child to recant his/her story in an attempt to save the family. The child has been put in that position before, the position of sacrifice.

It is always an unsettling possibility that the members of the family are denying because the abuse actually did not occur. In the past we have been able to say with certainty that in most cases when a child reports that he/she was sexually abused it likely did occur. It is now becoming somewhat less certain, especially in some savage custody cases where children are coerced by one parent into saying that the other sexually abused them. We recommend a complete social, psychological, and medical investigation to take place in these cases. However, it is still our experience that most cases, where the child has accused the parent of abusing him or her, are true.

## Denial of Awareness

Denial of awareness is where a family member admits to the possibility of abuse but denies being cognizant of it when it happened. This form of denial is usually psychological and more conducive to therapeutic intervention. Offenders deny awareness approximately 20% of the time and usually say that they either were drunk, suffering from posttraumatic stress disorder, had a blackout, or perhaps thought they were with someone else because it was night and dark.

When mothers deny awareness they will say things like "I knew something was wrong in my house but I never knew it was this" or "I can't believe it was happening right in my own household." Less common but of more concern is the situation where the daughter told the mother about the abuse, but the mother now states that she does not remember her daughter doing so. This form of denial is a reflection of the emotional, economical, and social disabilities the mother suffers as a result of having a spouse's or significant other's abuse. She must maintain that it did not happen in order to maintain stability in her life.

Child victims also deny awareness. This is often a very protective and functional dissociative device. Victims claim that they were asleep when the abuse occurred, or they turned it into a dream or fantasy, or they don't remember much because they pretended it happened to someone else and they were just watching. This type of denial of awareness is often coupled with a mother or father who is denying the facts.

## Denial of Responsibility

Denial of responsibility occurs when a family member admits to the facts about the abuse, remembers many of its occurrences, if not all of them, but suggests that someone other than the abusing father was responsible. Fathers and mothers may blame the daughter for being seductive and do not acknowledge that the daughter learned this behavior through them. Men often blame their wives for being sexually unavailable to them, again not recognizing their role in the abusive act.

Women often deny the responsibility of their husbands or boyfriends. They may ascribe responsibility to the daughter, to alcohol, or to themselves. To acknowledge that the responsibility is the offender's once again puts a woman into the bind of "Am I better

off with or without him?" and the choice of denial is understandably based on an emotional, physical, and economic set of circumstances.

For the children, it is most common for them to believe that they caused their own abuse. Blaming oneself stems from a combination of several possible origins. First, being a victim and living with parents who are being victims to one another and to society, the child supports what he/she already believes and that is "bad things happen to bad people"—in other words, learned victimization. Or self-blame may be an attempt to protect the family and themselves. Children can protect the family by creating the reality that it was their fault and no one else should be punished. If they blame themselves, then they do not have to acknowledge the psychological or emotional problems of either or both of their parents or caretakers. Finally, children of all ages feel responsible for and in the center of the world around them. Part of the normal developmental process is children's understanding, over time, of what they are responsible for and what they have control over in the world. During this crucial developmental phase is often when children are abused sexually, physically, and emotionally. When victims become developmentally thwarted through the trauma, so does their belief system that they are basically bad, and the adults whom they are taught to trust have hurt them because they deserve it. If they deserve this cruel treatment then they must be responsible for it.

## Denial of Impact

With denial of impact, the family member admits to the facts of the incestuous abuse, was consciously aware that it happened, and accepts that the abusing father is ultimately responsible for its occurrence. However, the family member does not accept the seriousness of the abuse, how the abuse may have negatively affected the victim and the entire family's functioning, or the potential for long-term psychological damage.

Abusing fathers in our program deny impact in some manner almost all of the time. Statements like "It was only fondling" or "She didn't seem to mind" are quite common. Mothers will often feel that what happened to the child is not as bad as what is happening now to the family after the crisis of discovery. And the children, who deny impact 46% of the time, feel that the abuse had little impact on their life.

The denial of impact is a way for members to protect themselves and each other from acknowledging the potential for the long-term emotional and psychological effects of sexual abuse. It's the mind's way of saying, "If what happened is no big deal, then what will happen to me as a result will be no big deal either."

## TREATMENT OF DENIAL

The ultimate goal in the treatment of denial is to have it end. However, there are no certain techniques that will end an individual or family's denial, particularly because the denial serves very protective functions. Because we see denial as a necessary attempt by the family and its individual members to protect themselves, we do not take its appearance as a personal affront. We approach denial with a strategic focus rather than directly challenging the symptom. In other words, we have found that the most therapeutic approach that we can take with denial is to not allow ourselves to become overly organized by the outcome. We do not have the eradication of denial as our only outcome goal. Instead our primary goal is to eradicate abusive, oppressive, and violent interactions between family members, and work toward this goal can begin while members are in denial. Paradoxically, the less we are organized by the denial and thus do not have a medical approach, the easier it is to

establish a therapeutic relationship with clients and help them face the pain and destruction that often accompanies their admittance.

In this chapter, we will illustrate, through case dialogue, three interventions that we most frequently use when confronted with denial: (1) normalization; (2) negative consequences of change (Fisch, Weakland, & Segal, 1982); and (3) pretend techniques (Madanes, 1981).

### Normalization

There are two premises we maintain when normalizing denial. The first is that denial is a normal defense that humans use as a means of reestablishing power and control in their lives and a method of self-protection. The second premise is that we believe that people are basically good and that they aspire to attain that goodness and inner peace. In the face of denial, therapists sometimes find it difficult to maintain these beliefs, but if one does, there is much more freedom therapeutically.

The operation of normalization is a long and tedious process where the therapeutic rhythm is crucial. The therapist is understanding and empathic with clients' need to deny and simultaneously is helping them see that it is in their own best interest to take responsibility for their feelings and behaviors in order to obtain inner peace. The dance between these two realities, protection of self and true goodness of self, continues throughout therapy.

### Negative Consequences of Change

The therapist helps clients to take a close look at the negative consequences they will encounter if they give up their denial. One of the functions of the abusive behavior is an attempt on the part of the offender to gain power and control in his life. The acknowledgment of sexually abusive behavior can represent the ultimate loss of power—going to jail. By examining the negative consequences of an admittance, the therapist can help reframe this loss of control (Fisch et al., 1982; Haley, 1984). This intervention is used repeatedly in every stage of the program and with every type of denial. We want clients to recapture control over their lives in a nonabusive form. The therapist explores the problems that accompany change and potential solutions to these new problems. This exploration helps prevent future abusive situations not only in the family but often in society, that is, courts or jail. For example, an offender can explore all the ways he will be hurt if he admits the abuse, and he can plan with his therapist and attorney a more rehabilitative consequence. Mothers can take a painful look at their economic situation, if they choose to believe the child, and prepare to function independently if that becomes necessary.

## Pretending

The therapist creates an "as if" scenario with clients that allows them to talk about the sexual abuse, their own victimization, and their views on family, self, and the world without admitting to anything. For example, the offender would be asked to pretend that he was a victim of sexual abuse: how does he think it would have happened to him, or how does he think it would have felt to have no one believe him? Or "if" their daughter/son had been abused by their spouse, what would a mother do in that situation? This gives persons permission to explore the possibilities and still maintain their necessary control and protection.

These are only three examples of how denial is managed in a case; however, they are the primary interventions used when helping family members master their denial. The interventions are not separated in the treatment but are interwoven with each other in many of the sessions. The case example that follows contains excerpts of actual sessions when the therapist, through individual, family, marital, and group treatment, is helping a family

weave their way through the complicated tapestry of denial.

## CASE EXAMPLE: THE QUES CASE

We first met the Ques family in much the same manner that we meet the majority of our families: through the state social service department. In cases of child abuse, the systems involved are much larger than that of just the family; consequently, the treatment must take all these systems into consideration. In the first call from the state worker, the therapist discovered that both the family and the worker were very angry. The worker was angry about the family's denial and resistance, and the family was angry about what they considered false and unfair allegations. Prior to the first meeting with the family, we attempt to determine the viewpoints of all the parties involved in the case, as well as their expectations of therapy. It is crucial to understand the legal status of the case, that is, is there criminal court or family court involvement. The worker's perspective of the Ques family provided us with facts and some interesting opinions. First some facts: the family consists of father, Mark, a 38-year-old male; mother, Doris, a 36-year-old female; Sandra, one of the alleged victims, a 14-year-old female freshman in high school; Sally, another alleged victim, a 12-year-old seventh grader; Donny, an 8-year-old male second grader, and, finally, Dotty, a 4-year-old female. The family was living together at the time of the report, and the two oldest daughters were placed in foster care because of the father's and Sally's denial of the sexual abuse. At the time of the referral, there was no criminal court involvement; all legal actions were taking place in the juvenile court proceedings.

Sandra was at a friend's house one day looking very depressed and preoccupied. After much coaxing, it seems, she finally was convinced to tell her friend what was bothering her. This is when she revealed that her father had been fondling her. The friend, although sworn to secrecy, was extremely upset and confused and decided to tell her own mother, who then reported the abuse to the authorities. The Department of Social Services investigated the report, and although the father and Sally, the second oldest daughter, denied the allegations, the report was considered to be substantiated, and the two oldest daughters were removed from the home for protective custody.

The opinions of the state workers provided a bit more information. The investigative worker was convinced that the girls had been abused and was extremely punitive with both Mark and Sally for denying. He swore to the father that his time had come and he would make sure that he would be punished for his crime. The follow-up worker, on the other hand, was not so convinced that the allegations were very severe, and she was much more concerned about some of her more serious cases. These two opinions were confusing for the family members, and all parties involved were angry about the manner in which they were treated.

We began treatment with a series of individual sessions for the father, the mother, and the two victims. The two younger children were also seen after the mother, father, and two victims had been seen. In the sessions with the youngest we would attempt to find out what the kids thought was going on and their reasons for their sisters' absence. After some initial assessment we would also explore with them any problems they saw in the family. Excerpts from their sessions are not in the chapter because of this chapter's emphasis on denial. With the rest of the family, our only goal for the first few meetings was to establish trust and attempt to gain some foundation for mutual respect in order to assure their return to therapy.

In this session, the therapist has already spent some time visiting with the client and getting to know him and is now beginning to work with him on normalizing the situation.

*Therapist:* (to father) I know you have been through a lot lately.

*Mark:* Damn right, and I am plenty mad that I have to be here.

*Therapist:* I don't blame you. But we both have to be here. You can say we both have a mandate from the state. Can you think of any way I can help?

*Mark:* The only way anybody can help is to get me out of this mess. Sandra is a spoiled brat. She was mad at me for punishing her, and this is how she decided to get me back. These kids get these ideas from TV, and now I am paying for it. Do you have any idea how I am being ruined because of this?

*Therapist:* You must feel completely out of control of your life.

*Mark:* I am completely out of control, but in this family I am never in control anyway.

*Therapist:* Can you tell me other ways that you are out of control at work, at home, or anywhere else?

In this session, the therapist only explores and empathizes with the father's feelings of being out of control and discusses his attempted solutions on regaining control. There is no discussion for the first few meetings with him about whether he did anything sexually abusive or not.

In the sessions with the daughters and the mother, the themes that are being created are very similar. Primarily, the therapist is helping them see that their ambivalence is normal— the ambivalence between wanting the abuse to stop and at the same time not wanting their father/husband to be punished severely or the family broken apart.

*Therapist:* (to Sally, the daughter denying any abuse) You must be very confused by all of this. I imagine that you want to believe your sister, and of course, if your father is touching you in ways that he should not be touching his 12-year-old daughter, you must want him to stop, and yet you don't want anyone to be hurt because of this.

*Sally:* Sandra only cares about herself. She doesn't care that she is ruining the family. She likes it in the foster home because she can always have her way. I want to go home. If she doesn't change her story that will never happen.

Later during the session, the therapist summarizes for Sally what she has heard.

*Therapist:* Sally, what you have shared with me today is very similar to what many boys and girls who have been sexually abused by their fathers tell me. I know that you have not told me that anything has happened, and right now I don't want you to tell me. (The therapist is pacing the client, in an attempt to help Sally maintain control over the situation.) But you have told me that life is terrible now and would only get worse if your father did do anything to you or your sister and that you just want this to all go away. If your father sexually abused you, and I believe that he did abuse your sister (the therapist is supporting her denial but not maintaining it), I can assure you that a part of him wants help to stop hurting the two of you. It is possible for him to be a good father and a good person and for you to love him and for him to have done a terrible thing to you and your sister. My job is to help him change that part of himself that is hurtful.

Working with a mother who is in denial about the sexual abuse of her children is one of the most difficult jobs of a therapist. Our society holds mothers almost solely responsible for the well-being of children and forgets how nearly impossible that is for a woman to do on her own. In the following session, the therapist is once again normalizing the ambivalence that the mother must be experiencing in this situation.

*Therapist:* As a mother, you are in a terrible position, probably the most difficult position that any mother could ever be placed in. It must feel like you must choose between your husband and your daughter.

*Doris/Mother:* It is impossible. I cannot win no matter what I do. That is why I am doing nothing, and everyone is telling me I am such a bad mother.

*Therapist:* Is Mark telling you that too?

*Doris:* Sure. He says if I had not been so easy on the kids that Sandra would have never thought that she could have gotten away with this. I am no good no matter which way you look at it.

*Therapist:* Do you believe that too?

*Doris:* Yes, I know Mark is not lying. He would never do that, but what would make Sandra tell such a lie? I don't know what she is up to.

*Therapist:* Maybe neither of them is up to anything. Maybe they are both just trying to protect themselves from some pretty terrible things. Unfortunately, everyone is turning to you to be the judge, jury, and therapist.

*Doris:* What do you mean?

*Therapist:* Everyone is depending on you to figure out if it happened or not and to make everyone work together to work it out. I don't think you can or should do that Doris. I think you have to let me work with them, and maybe you just have to believe them both right now.

*Doris:* How can I do that?

*Therapist:* I am not sure how you can do that, but I can tell you how I do it. I believe that Sandra was hurt by Mark in some sexually abusive way, and I believe that Mark must deny right now in order to take care of himself, and that is normal. I also believe that good people do some pretty terrible things. They don't want to, and they can change, but they do them. And I believe if you came out on one side or the other right now you would be in a lot of pain and overwhelmed, and you don't have to do anything until you are ready.

The therapist helps the victim make some sense of her family's denial through normalizing the denial and her own denial of impact.

*Therapist:* What are you thinking about what has happened since you told your friend about your father's abuse of you?

*Sandra:* It is not as big a deal as everyone is making it out to be. He is a jerk, but he has done a lot worse things to me than anything with sex. I don't know why everyone is making such a big deal out of this. That is what I think.

*Therapist:* That makes sense to me. You want your dad to stop the "bad" stuff, but you did not want all this to happen. That is the worst part of this whole thing—no matter what you do you keep getting hurt. (Sandra begins to cry and the therapist continues.) Right now you don't have to do anything. The rest of the people in your family have to decide what they are going to do.

*Sandra:* They have decided not to believe me and to turn against me.

*Therapist:* I am not sure they have decided not to believe you. I think they have decided to protect themselves. How could pretending that the sexual abuse didn't happen be protecting, let's say, your father for instance?

*Sandra:* Well, if he never admits it, things can just stay the way they are, and he won't have to suffer at all.

*Therapist:* It must feel like he is still abusing you.

*Sandra:* Yeah, it does.

*Therapist:* What about your mom? How could she be protecting herself and your sister?

*Sandra:* My sister, that's easy. I didn't want to believe it was happening to me for the longest time. I would have said it wasn't true too until I had just had it and wanted it all to stop. I sometimes now wish I hadn't said anything either. It is terrible now. My mom, I don't know. I could never not believe my kid. And I'd never let my husband do anything like that to my kids.

*Therapist:* You have every right to be mad and feel hurt. I just want you to know I am not so sure that your mother doesn't believe you and believes him. I think it is more that if she says anything out loud she is not sure what will happen to her and the rest of the kids. She is working on getting strong enough to have her voice. It just may take longer than you or I, or she for that matter, would like.

The therapist takes as neutral position as possible in regard to the denial but not in regard to the abuse. In the following sessions the

therapist incorporates both negative consequences of change and pretending to help the family creatively find alternative solutions to the dilemma of maintaining denial.

*Therapist:* Mark, pretend with me for a second. Let's just say that portions of what Sandra is alleging are true. Remember I am just pretending. What do you think would happen if you admitted or agreed with what she was saying?

*Mark:* I know what you are getting at.

*Therapist:* But it is something we have to think about. There are a lot of negative consequences to finally taking control of the situation in a real way. You have always talked to me about being the man of the house. Your family needs you to be the man now and have power like you have never had it before, and that is the power to not hurt others in order to help yourself. You have told me numerous ways that you have done that. So let's just pretend now that you took control. What would happen to you?

*Mark:* My life would be over. I'd go to jail, and I'd kill myself before I would go to jail. There is no way I did anything or will admit to doing anything.

*Therapist:* Do you think more suffering is going on now or if you took responsibility for your mistake?

*Mark:* There would be more suffering if I said something. It would be much worse.

*Therapist:* Worse for you or for the family?

*Mark:* For me and for everyone if I said something.

*Therapist:* I am not so sure it would be worse for your family if you admitted to the abuse. Now they are confused, accused of lying, and separated. The kids are not with their siblings or their parents. Their mother is being ripped in two. Much could be helped if you were strong enough to talk about what happened and the problems that led up to it. And now you are choosing to have your family suffer more.

*Mark:* I guess for now I am. But you act as if you know everything. You don't know.

*Therapist:* I know what Sandra says, and I know you would have a lot of problems if you admitted anything and that you are not strong enough yet. I guess for now you have made your choice who is to suffer.

As the therapist builds on these small changes, the client begins to explore potential ways that both he and the family can have protection. For example, jail certainly is not the only alternative to admission, and the offender can discuss with his attorney other options like treatment, probation, or even work release. When jail and subsequent suicide appears to be the only alternative, denial seems to be a much more attractive option.

When the mother pretends to believe her daughter and imagine the consequences, she becomes overwhelmed with the prospects.

*Doris:* I could never survive. (Notice how all the family members are trying to figure out how to survive, in their own individual set of circumstances.) I really would be a terrible mother then. The kids and I would be on the street. Even if I could find a job that made as much money as Mark's did, how would I watch the kids or be there when they needed me? I could never protect them. My family would probably turn against me, and my friends would be disgusted.

*Therapist:* Is the image worse than what you are experiencing now?

*Doris:* I am not sure. I just wish it could be different.

*Therapist:* And if you had control over it being different, how would that look?

*Doris:* Of course I would believe my daughter and help Mark get help, even if he was out of the home for a while. If he could still work and not abandon us, then maybe it could be better.

*Therapist:* Could you ever talk to Mark like you are telling me?

The therapist, after a few more sessions similar to this, helps Doris confront Mark during a couple session. They begin to explore alternative solutions that might still protect themselves but be far less hurtful to the children.

*Therapist:* Mark, tell Doris some of the things that you believe she would do if her husband ever abused her kids. She is used to the same pretend stuff that you and I do in sessions.

*Mark:* I think you would try to kill anyone that would do that to our kids. I sure would. I know you'd divorce them, and you'd try to get everything they got and leave them ruined. I wouldn't blame you because I'd do the same thing.

*Doris:* I used to think that, Mark, but after therapy and the group I am not so sure anymore. I think I would want to understand more how someone I love and lived with all these years could be both good and bad, strong and weak. I would want my family to heal. We can never heal this way. The longer it goes on, the less respect I have for you. Now I would respect you for helping to save the family before we are completely destroyed. I see things a little differently now.

After 5 months of treatment, Mark admitted to fondling both girls. Both Sandra and Sally confirmed his reports. Mark moved out of the house and was sentenced to 4 years probation and mandatory treatment. He is still working and supporting the family, and Doris got a part-time job during school hours. The girls moved back into the house. Mark stopped denying the facts, but that was only the beginning of therapy; there were still many layers of work to do.

*Mark:* I realized that it could be better for the girls and me if I said what really happened. Doris really convinced me when she said that she would try to stay with me and that she believed a good man could do something terrible. I still think things could have been figured out on our own without all these people involved. But what's over is over, and we have to get on with our lives.

## SUMMARY

In this chapter, we have discussed that all child sexual abuse cases have some level of denial: denial of facts, denial of awareness, denial of impact, and/or denial of responsibility. Therapists, because of the social-political climate in which we work, become overly invested in eradicating denial before they begin treatment. We view denial as a normal and functional coping skill used by family members. In Stage 1 of our three-stage model, the three primary interventions used to focus the treatment are normalization, negative consequences of change, and pretending. The therapy takes on the pace of the client and helps each individual and the family explore alternative solutions to their emotional and social welfare problems. As they see more alternative solutions to life's problems, they can slowly put their lives back together, piece by piece.

## References

Barrett, M. J., Sykes, C., & Byrnes, W. (1986). Systemic model for the treatment of intrafamily child sexual abuse. In T. S. Trepper & M. J. Barrett (Eds.), *Treating incest: A multiple systems perspective*. New York: Haworth.

Fisch, R., Weakland, J. H., & Segal, L. (1982). *The tactics of change: Doing therapy briefly*. San Francisco: Jossey-Bass.

Haley, J. (1984). *Ordeal therapy*. San Francisco: Jossey-Bass.

Madanes, C. (1981). *Strategic family therapy*. San Francisco: Jossey-Bass.

Trepper, T., & Barrett, M. J. (1989). *Systemic treatment of incest: A therapeutic handbook*. New York: Brunner/Mazel.

# 3

# IN FAMILY THERAPY

THE EARLY FOUNDATIONS OF SOCIAL WORK practice were firmly rooted within a family perspective. Mary Richmond, one of the great leaders in social work, wrote in 1930 about the importance of the family. Richmond believed that the family was a pivotal institution about which human lives evolved. Although the history between social work and the family has not always been strong, today much, if not most, of social work is practiced from a family perspective.

The strong family emphasis is due largely to the family therapy movement, which began in the 1950s. That movement continues as social workers and other professionals specialize in family treatment. Social workers work with families in numerous capacities, such as offering assistance to families who are grieving over loved ones, providing divorce mediation, performing family therapy, working with families who have abused their children, doing case management with families confronting developmental disabilities and chronic mental illness, and working with foster families that provide a family substitute. Clearly families are an important part of social work practice.

The family therapy, or family systems perspective, perceives individual dysfunction as largely related to the dynamics of the family. Family practitioners typically see symptoms of family members as a systemic function in the family. The treatment focuses not on a client with symptoms but on a family with certain dynamics influencing the symptoms. The assessment of a family examines the functional relationship between the individual problem and the dynamics of the family. A classic example would be a family with a child behavior problem that is functionally related to the couple's marital difficulties. In this example, the child's behavior problem becomes the central concern for the couple, and it serves the purpose of reducing their marital discord. Although a family perspective is a powerful way to understand families, it is equally important to understand the relationship between individual and family dynamics and environmental factors. A family perspective has often led practitioners to neglect the importance of individual and environmental factors.

All family therapy approaches address some aspect of the family, but there are important differences in the way different models conceptualize, operationalize, and intervene to help families. Walsh (1983) classifies the family therapies into two major categories: (1) growth-oriented approaches, which include psychodynamic, Bowen family systems and experiential models, and (2) problem-solving approaches, which include structural, strategic, and behavioral models of practice.

These family therapy approaches attempt to understand how families function and use a variety of different concepts to understand families. Some of the more familiar concepts include family structure and power; family boundaries; communication and interactional patterns; family rules, myths, and rituals; family decision-making processes; and family roles. In general, the family therapy practitioner gathers information about the sequences and patterns of behavior, the emotional and cognitive reactions of family members, and the specific actions of family members.

Whatever the approach in working with family members, it is critical to successfully engage them in the treatment. This requires good clinical skills such as providing reassurance and normalizing problems (helping clients understand that when in stressful circumstances it is understandable that problems exist), communicating empathy to family members, establishing positive expectations for change, and encouraging positive motivation.

The case studies in this chapter demonstrate many of these clinical skills and present some different models of family treatment. The chapter begins with a case study by Eddy, who helps family members resolve their grief over the suicidal death of a family member. It demonstrates the use of a particular family therapy procedure: ritual. Gladow and Pecora present a detailed account of how the Homebuilders program works toward family preservation. This case study presents a clearly specified treatment model with lots of concrete examples. de Shazer's case study focuses on domestic violence, and he guides you through a "solution-oriented" approach to treatment. Curry's case study centers around a family's adjustment to the sobriety of a family member. The study points to the complexity of understanding family functioning.

## Reference

Walsh, F. (1983). Family therapy: A systemic orientation to treatment. In A. Rosenblatt and D. Waldfogel (Eds.), *Handbook of clinical social work* (pp. 466–489). San Francisco: Jossey-Bass.

# CASE STUDY 3.1

*Suicide can dramatically crystallize a family into a pattern of sadness and grief. Social workers can use strategic therapy techniques to mobilize a family into positive action.*

## Questions

1. What responses might be expected from family members as they grieve the suicidal death of a member?
2. How can anniversaries and rituals used to mark sad occasions be helpful to families?
3. What are some ways a social worker "joins" with a family?
4. What are some of the family therapy techniques used to help mobilize this family into problem-solving action?

---

## COMPLETING BRAD'S DREAMS

*David Eddy\**

A few months ago a former trainee living in Iowa phoned for an emergency consultation with the warning, "I think I've got a challenging one for you this time." While working at a psychiatric hospital, she had been assigned the case of a 15-year-old boy, "Adam," who was hospitalized after telling an outreach worker that he planned to kill himself on the anniversary of his brother's death. Two years earlier his only sibling, Brad, age 15, had committed suicide.

The therapist reported that the entire family—mother, father, and most of all Adam—was depressed. The previous year they had all had a very difficult time passing the anniversary of Brad's death. A shroud of guilt enveloped them. Contacts with friends or relatives who might have helped them through the loss were limited. Holidays were not celebrated, special occasions were avoided, and visitors

* Reprinted from the *Family Therapy Networker,* September–October, 1986. Reprinted by permission of the author.

were not welcome. Since Brad's suicide, time had stood still.

For Adam, Brad's death meant the loss of a best friend as well as a brother. They had played, shared secrets, and even planned future exploits together. The day that Brad shot himself, he had asked his brother to come to the basement with him. Adam, suspecting some sort of joke, had not gone. A short while later Brad was dead and Adam's guilt and doubts began. Had Brad intended to take Adam with him on his journey?

The therapist said on the telephone, "I've never seen such a hopeless family. Where should I begin?" I realized that it was essential to talk about Brad, but in what context?

I remember an idea being developed by Cloe Madanes about reducing a client's feelings of depression, worthlessness, or guilt by motivating him or her to perform anonymous good deeds. I suggested that the therapist ask the family if they would prefer to discuss Brad immediately or at some agreed on time in the future. After discussion of Brad began she was able to say that she had noticed a valuable ability in this family to look to the future and that that's what she wanted to talk about. She should say that Brad obviously had been a young man with dreams and a desire to make contributions. What accomplishments would he have made in life? She was to prompt the family's responses, if necessary, by asking about Brad's interests, likes, special projects, friends, and so on. Throughout, the emphasis was to be on the positive, and the family was to be given as much time as they needed to discuss Brad and his potential contributions. Then the therapist was to make a summary speech along the following lines:

> You are all very fortunate to have known Brad so well that you can clearly imagine all he would have accomplished. Knowing you, I have little doubt he would have done all you've mentioned and probably more. You've been left with much to be done on Brad's behalf, so I suggest we begin. Your love for Brad is great, and yet your thoughts of him are troubled. You have an opportunity to complete Brad's dreams and bring peace to your thoughts of him.
>
> To begin, you must each make a contribution on his behalf. At a time of your choosing and in a way known only to you, you are to do a special good deed for someone on Brad's behalf. You each knew Brad in a unique way, so your good deed should reflect all that he meant to you. This should be done on a date of your choosing. The date is to become a celebration of Brad and his life. It is very important, however, that it be done anonymously so that you've done it on Brad's behalf and receive no personal credit. Each year this date is to be celebrated through a special effort. Each of your efforts, however, is to be known only to you.
>
> In addition, you are to have a family meeting and together plan a special good deed project. Again, as with your personal effort, the project is to be an anonymous contribution on Brad's behalf. The project should express your combined efforts. It should be on a date that be-

comes an annual occasion to celebrate Brad as a member of the family.

The therapist was delighted. A call to action was just her forte, hopefulness was her strength, and subtle persuasion was a special talent. She would begin immediately.

Two weeks later the therapist reported that the family agreed immediately to discuss Brad. Each contributed to the discussion of what Brad would have accomplished. While at first there was a sense of hopelessness about all that was lost with his death, a marked change resulted when the therapist outlined the plan of action for each family member and the family as a unit.

Several sessions followed, each more positive than the last. A sense of purpose and well-being began to appear in the family, along with a reduction of guilt. Adam was released from the hospital, and, at an informal ceremony before discharge, he presented the staff with a baseball cap that was a special trademark of his. Only the therapist knew that the cap had originally belonged to Brad. Mother got a job that she enjoyed—her first employment in 20 years. The father became active in teaching a seminar on self-esteem.

The presenting drama in this family revolved around self-inflicted violence. Brad had killed himself, and Adam said he planned on doing the same. It might have been tempting to inquire into the circumstances of Brad's death, but I thought such an approach was unlikely to raise the family from the grimness of their loss and their feelings of hopelessness.

It seemed to me that the therapist needed to project the family into the future, beyond their quiet depression. I wanted her to prepare the family for a discussion that would lead to action. Families filled with regret and guilt frequently engage in "if only . . ." conversations about things they wish they had done. This plan addressed what each person and the family "could do."

As with most therapy, the question of how to begin was essential. In a directive therapy, there is a careful balance between joining people and telling them what to do. Courtesy is a powerful joining approach and was emphasized in asking permission to discuss Brad and in listening respectfully to each person. Milton Erickson was noted for a carefully planned balance between telling people what to do and remaining courteous. In this case, the balance was achieved by offering a choice—"Would you prefer to discuss Brad now or a while later?"—while giving the implicit message that Brad would be discussed.

The major challenge of this therapy was to rally the family to action. Before that could be done, the therapist needed to create a context that would overcome the finality of Brad's death. By inquiring about what Brad would have accomplished, the therapist enabled the family to project him into the present and future.

The speech the therapist presented was intended to inspire, motivate, and persuade the family. Word selection, order, and pacing usually require a thoughtful delivery. Practicing such speeches may be helpful, though risk of losing spontaneity is always a concern.

Persuading families is one aspect of a directive therapy. If, however, a useful plan of action is not developed to change the sequence within the family, the therapy is likely to fail. Performing anonymous good deeds that could be attributed to Brad offered this family the opportunity to forget their "if only . . ." wishes and engage in activities that were hopeful and helpful.

The therapist had said that no one would be asked or was to discuss what was done on Brad's behalf, and, therefore, she had no way of knowing what each person, or the family, did as their good deed. The community was small, however, and over time she was able to detect the contributions of each member of the family. In particular, it was impossible for her to miss a television program done by a family about the loss of a son and brother through suicide. The program was filled with hope and fond memories as Adam and his parents talked about Brad.

# CASE STUDY 3.2

*Intensive in-home services are a powerful social work tool for helping families. This case study illustrates the use of goal setting and relationship building, which are critical in the Homebuilders model of home-based treatment.*

## Questions

1.  What are some examples of relationship building used in this case?
2.  How did the social worker intervene to reduce conflicts between the father and son?
3.  What is a "teachable moment," and how was this incorporated into the treatment?
4.  What are some of the advantages and disadvantages of a home-based treatment model?

---

## HOMEBUILDERS: HELPING FAMILIES STAY TOGETHER

*Nancy Wells Gladow and Peter J. Pecora*

The following case involves conflict between a single-parent father and his 13-year-old son. The treatment agency is the Homebuilders Program of the Behavioral Sciences Institute (BSI), headquartered in Federal Way, Washington. Homebuilders is an intensive, home-based family preservation services program. BSI contracts with the state of Washington and city of New York to provide Homebuilders services to families who are in imminent danger of having one or more children placed outside the home in foster, group or institutional care. Home-based family preservation programs currently exist in many states, and 28 states have at least one program attempting to replicate Homebuilders. Although theoretical approaches, clinical techniques, caseloads, and length of treatment vary from program to program, the basic goal of most programs is the same. This goal is to prevent unnecessary foster or group-home placements of children outside the home and to help multiproblem families cope with their situations more effectively.

Of these programs, Homebuilders is the most intensive in terms of its short time frame of 4 to 6 weeks per family and low caseload of two families per therapist or counselor. (Therapists provide an average of 36 hours of face-to-face and phone contact to each family.) The program is a skills-oriented model that is grounded in Rogerian, ecological, social learning, and cognitive behavioral theories. The intervention involves defusing the immediate crisis that led to the referral, building a relationship with the family, assessing the situation and developing treatment goals in partnership with the family, and teaching specific skills to help family members function more effectively and achieve these goals. Evaluations of Homebuilders indicate that the program is highly effective in reducing out-of-home placements and increasing the coping abilities of family members (Fraser, Pecora, & Haapala, 1988; Haapala & Kinney, 1988; Kinney, Madsen, Fleming, & Haapala, 1977).

Referrals are made to the Washington Homebuilders program through Child Protective Services (CPS) and Family Reconciliation Services (FRS), which are two subunits of the public child welfare agency. In CPS cases the caseworker determines that placement of one or more of the children outside the home will occur if the family does not make certain changes to ensure the safety or well-being of the children. In FRS cases either parents or children have themselves requested out-of-home placement for the child due to family conflict or child behavior problems. In FRS cases, caseworkers may refer the family to Homebuilders as a way to work out the problems that are making placement a serious consideration.

## CASE OVERVIEW

The following case study highlights some of the Homebuilders treatment philosophy and techniques with an atypical, but increasing, type of case situation: a single-parent father and his son. However, this case was similar to most cases in that the family had a history of family problems and conflict. In this case, the child had no previous out-of-home placements: 21% of Homebuilders clients have already experienced previous placement. Selected client sessions are described for each of the 4 weeks of service. All the names and identifying information have been changed to protect the family's privacy.

Because of space considerations, the three contacts and work with the boy's mother are omitted along with the contacts made with the school psychologist and other school personnel. In addition, a considerable amount of time was spent working with the father regarding his use of marijuana, which was not interfering with his job performance but was a concern to his son.

Interventions such as working with a local church and Narcotics Anonymous (NA) were attempted (with some success) but will not be discussed in order to focus on the therapist

interventions regarding client relationship building, chore completion, school behavior, and anger management.

## INTERVENTION

### Week One: Gathering Information, Relationship Building, and Setting Treatment Goals

It was 7:30 P.M. as I drove up for the first time to the Barretts' small three-bedroom house located in a working-class neighborhood. The referral sheet from the FRS caseworker said Dick Barrett had been a technician for a large manufacturer in Seattle for 10 years and that his 13-year-old son, Mike, was in seventh grade. FRS became involved after Mike had told his school counselor that his father had been smoking marijuana for 15 years. (This was the first time that the state had come into contact with his family.) Mike said he hated drugs, was tired of his father's constant yelling, and wanted to be placed outside the home. He also said he was afraid of his uncle, who had been living with the family for 2 months. The school counselor had already been concerned about Mike, a seventh grader for the second year, who frequently neglected to turn in his homework and disrupted class by swearing at both students and teachers. Mike had already been suspended twice that semester. The referral sheet said that Dick voluntarily agreed to have the uncle move out and to quit using drugs, although he was unwilling to begin a drug treatment program. It also said the family had tried counseling several months ago through a local agency, but Mike had disliked the counselor and refused to continue.

Dick, a tall man of around 50, opened the door soon after I rang the bell. Dick invited me to sit at the kitchen table and called for Mike to join us. The family cat jumped on my lap. Dick and I began chatting about cats as

Mike slowly walked into the kitchen, looking at the ground and making grumbling sounds. Mike smiled when he saw Tiger sitting on my lap and being scratched under the chin. Mike began to tell me stories about Tiger, and I responded with interest and a funny story about my own cat. I felt no pressure to hurry the counseling session along, as taking time for small talk and showing interest in what was important to family members was a key element of relationship building that would be the foundation of any later success in confronting clients and teaching new behaviors.

Dick began to discuss the difficulties his family had been experiencing. He said he was upset about Mike's behavior problems and lack of motivation in school. Dick said he had tried everything he knew to get Mike to improve but with no success. As Dick talked, I listened reflectively—paraphrasing parts of the content and feelings that Dick was expressing. For example, when Dick said, "Mike does not even try to improve his behavior in school," I responded with, "It is frustrating for you that Mike does not seem to want to improve." After Dick spoke about Mike's abilities being much higher than his actual achievement, I said, "So it seems pretty clear that Mike has a lot more potential than he is using."

Reflective or active listening serves several purposes. First, it helps family members deescalate their emotions. As they tell their stories and begin to feel that someone understands, they calm down and are more likely to be able to take constructive steps to improve their situation. Second, by conveying understanding, active listening helps build up a positive client–therapist relationship. Third, active listening helps the therapist gain more information about the family without having to ask a lot of questions. People frequently expand on their stories when the therapist is listening reflectively. Asking many questions seems to limit what people say, and it creates the impression that the counselor is the expert who will "do something to" the family. With Homebuilders clients, it works better to recognize and treat clients as partners in the counseling process. Clients have more information about their lives than does the therapist, and their active participation in the change process is crucial. However, sometimes asking a few key questions at the right time is the most efficient way to gain behaviorally specific information. For example, in this situation. I wanted to know just what Mike's grades were. (He was in three special education classes and was earning one B and two Cs in those. In his other classes he was earning two Fs and a D.)

As Dick talked, Mike remained silent, although his facial expressions and body movements frequently suggested anger toward his father. "You do not look too pleased, Mike," I said. "What do you think about all this?" Again I listened reflectively as Mike began to talk about how he hated school and his father's frequent yelling. Mike told stories about a number of arguments he and his father had that resulted in both of them swearing and saying things calculated to hurt each other. Dick agreed that this was true. I summarized, "So learning how to fight less and deal with your anger constructively is something both of you might like?" They both nodded. Dick went on to say, "Mike makes me so angry. If he would not say some of the things he does, I would not get so mad." (I thought to myself that Dick could benefit from learning a basic principle about anger: no one can *make* you angry—you are responsible for your own anger. I did not mention my thought at this point, however, because pointing out errors in thinking and teaching too soon before there has been time for sufficient information gathering and relationship building is often ineffective.)

"You have mentioned that you argue a lot more than either of you would like. Tell me what kinds of things you argue about," I requested. Dick described frustration about trying to get Mike to do chores around the house, saying if Mike was not willing to help he would prefer Mike find somewhere else to live. Mike complained that his Dad was always ordering him around. Dick had been working especially hard lately to fix up the house so that it could be sold in a few months and finances between him and Mike's mother could be resolved. Dick and his ex-wife had gone through a difficult divorce 3 years ago after 28 years of marriage and four children, the older three being over 18 years of age and currently living on their own. Through mutual agreement, Dick had received custody of Mike.

"I get the picture from the caseworker that drugs have been a big issue in your family," I commented. Dick described how he had been smoking marijuana for about 15 years. He said he had also gotten into "some other things" during the time his brother-in-law, Mike's uncle, had been living there. Dick said once the school and the caseworker became involved, he realized it was important to have his brother-in-law move out, which he had done. Dick said he had stopped using other drugs and had also voluntarily stopped using marijuana a few days ago. Dick stated that he respected Mike's right to live in a drug-free home and that he thought it would benefit himself as well to stop his drug use. "I can't afford to get fired if my work finds out about this," Dick commented.

"What do you think about this, Mike?" I asked. Mike remained silent. "If I were you, I might be a little worried that my Dad was not really going to quit using drugs," I said. "Is that anything like you are feeling, or am I way off base?" Mike opened up a little to say that his Dad had said he would quit before and had never stuck with it. Mike talked about how his siblings all use drugs and how he had been scared when, 3 years ago, some "bikers" had

come to the house to get his oldest sister to "pay up" on some drugs. Mike said he also worried about having his father's health go downhill from drug use. I could tell from Dick's expression that this was probably the first time he had heard Mike express these concerns openly.

Soon it appeared that Mike was getting tired, and it was time to end this 2½ hour initial session (about the average amount of time for a first-session Homebuilders program). I explained more of the specifics of the Homebuilders program and gave them my home phone number as well as the backup phone numbers of my supervisor and our beeper. All of this is an effort to be available to clients 24 hours a day, 7 days a week. I then summarized the session in terms of treatment goals. "It sounds like what you two most want help on is (1) working out a way to build in more cooperation on household chores; (2) learning how to fight less and to deal with anger more constructively; (3) Dick, your receiving support in your efforts to be drug-free; and (4) improving your school performance, Mike. Is that how you see it?" They both nodded. Summarizing in this way checks my perception of the family's priorities for change and also gives direction for future counseling sessions. In this intake session with the Barretts it was easier to establish goals than it is with many families. There is really no rush to determine all five treatment goals (a typical number for a 4-week intervention) at the intake session, although Homebuilders therapists generally try to have one or two goals established by the end of the first week.

The last thing I did during the first visit was to set up individual appointments with Dick and Mike. Unless family members are opposed to them, individual meetings can be helpful initially to gather additional information and continue building relationships. Later, one-to-one sessions can facilitate work on each person's goals. I gave Mike a sentence-completion sheet to fill out for our next session and checked to make sure he understood how to do it.

When I came back 2 days later to pick up Mike for our individual session, he was listening to his stereo. I listened to a few songs with him. As we drove to McDonalds, we talked about various musical groups and our favorite TV shows. He seemed to be feeling much more comfortable with me by the time we sat down with our Cokes and french fries. I looked over the sentence completion sheet, which included sentences such as "My favorite subject in school is _____," "In my spare time I like to _____," and "I feel angry when _____." Instead of asking Mike a lot of questions, which teenagers frequently dislike, I read some of his answers in a tone of voice that encouraged him to expand on the topic. When he did, I listened reflectively to his responses, and he frequently elaborated even further. I learned that he was especially upset about his father yelling at him on a daily basis. When his father yelled, Mike found himself quickly feeling angry and sometimes yelling back. I reflected Mike's feelings of worry, embarrassment, fear, and anger about his father's use of drugs. I also checked out with him what kind of system they used at home regarding who did what household chores and if Mike earned an allowance. (I was thinking that coming up with a mutually agreed on chore system might be the first goal we would tackle because it was so important to Dick and was a goal with which we were likely to make concrete progress.) Mike said there was no system—his dad just gave orders and Mike either complied or didn't. I suggested a system whereby he earn an allowance for doing certain agreed on chores, and I asked what he thought a fair allowance would be, assuming his father would approve of this plan. He said the plan sounded agreeable and suggested $8 per week. I gave Mike an assignment to complete before the next meeting. He

was to write down (1) two things he'd like to be different in his family; (2) two things he could do to help get along better with his dad; and (3) two things his dad could do to help them get along together better.

My appointment with Dick alone began with his showing me the work he had done around the house to get it ready to sell. This led him to talk about his past marriage with Rita, his feelings about the marriage ending, and how Mike had gone back and forth between their homes for almost 2 years up until about a year ago. Dick thought some of Mike's troubles were due to his going from home to home, plus the pressure of Dick and Rita's continual fighting. After an hour of active listening to these subjects, I felt pleased that Dick was opening up, warming up to me, and appearing relieved to get some of these things off his chest. When he brought up his older children's drug involvement, I saw it as an opportunity to gently begin talking about his own drug use. (This is an example of a "teachable moment." A teachable moment is a time when clients may be particularly receptive to learning because they can see the relevancy of it in their lives.) We then spent some time discussing this issue and developing a plan of action.

Before ending the session, I introduced the idea of having Mike's chores be based on allowance. Dick's reaction was positive, saying he thought more structure would be helpful. I noted two benefits to such a system: (1) Mike would experience the consequences of his actions, and (2) it would reduce the number of times Dick would need to tell Mike what to do. Mike had developed a tendency to blame much of his behavior on others rather than taking responsibility for his actions. In addition, like most teenagers, Mike hated to be told what to do, yet their previous system was based completely on Dick giving daily instructions. We briefly discussed what he thought a reasonable allowance would be. We agreed to negotiate this new system with Mike at the next session. I also gave Dick the same homework assignment I had given Mike.

## Week Two: Active Work on Goals

As Mike, Dick, and I sat down together in the living room, I asked how things were going. Meetings often start in this way, as events may have recently occurred that need to be discussed or worked out before clients will be able to concentrate on the current agenda.

When I asked if they had done their homework, Dick had and Mike hadn't. Dick agreed to do something else for a few minutes while I helped Mike complete the questions. Then both told what they would like to be different in their family. Dick said he would like anger to play less of a role and for the home to be drug free. Mike said he would like less arguing and to go places together more. In discussing what each person thought he could do differently, Dick said he could try not to get angry when frustrated, and he could also be more consistent with Mike. Mike said he could help more around the house and try not to get angry so much.

On the subject of what the other person could do, Dick said Mike could be more responsible with housework and schoolwork. Mike said his dad could stay off drugs and yell less. I took this opportunity to talk about how problems in a family are almost never one person's fault and how each family member can do things that can help the other family members. I also noted the similarities in the changes they wanted and stated that I had some ideas that might help them with some of these changes.

Next we began work on the new chore system. I explained that we would be deciding together what chores Mike would be responsible for, when they were to be done, how much allowance he would earn, and what he did and did not have to pay for with his allowance. We began by writing a list of all the chores possible and gave Mike a chance to pick some he would be willing to do. Dick added a few he would like Mike to be responsible for. After a little more negotiation, we came up with a list both felt they could live with. Mike said he really did not like doing chores. Rather than letting Dick jump in with a lecture, or responding with one myself, I opted for humor. I chuckled and told Mike I certainly could understand that, as Ajax and vacuum cleaners had never thrilled me either. I gave a couple of examples of how my husband and I split up chores so that neither one of us would have to do all of the work. Then Dick and Mike decided how often each chore needed to be done, to what standards, and by what time of the day. We discussed which chores involved the most and the least amount of work and determined point values for each.

In deciding on allowance, Mike thought $8 per week was fair, and Dick thought $6 per week was more appropriate. After discussing it further, we agreed on a system whereby Mike's basic allowance would be $6, and all he would have to pay for was his own entertainment. On the weeks when he earned 97% of the points or above he would get a $2 bonus and earn $8. We put this all onto a chart and filled it out as though Mike had done a perfect job (see Figure 1). The crossed-out squares on the chart indicate days the chore need not be done.

On a blank chart we wrote the possible points next to each chore and agreed on the time when Dick would check the jobs and fill in the points. We specified which day would be "payday" and where the chart would be placed. When Mike got a phone call, I took the opportunity to share with Dick some hints on making the chore system work most successfully. I suggested he use the chore checking as a chance to develop good will with Mike by praising him for work he does well. I gave Dick a handout on "97 Ways to Say 'Very Good.'" I also suggested that when Mike did

| Behavior | Mon | Tues | Wed | Thur | Fri | Sat | Sun | Total |
|----------|-----|------|-----|------|-----|-----|-----|-------|
| Straighten bedroom (by 5 pm) | 2 | 2 | 2 | 2 | 2 | 2 | ✕ | 12 |
| Bring in wood (by 5 pm) | 2 | 2 | 2 | 2 | 2 | 2 | 2 | 14 |
| Do dinner dishes (by 9 pm) | 3 | ✕ | 3 | ✕ | 3 | ✕ | ✕ | 9 |
| Take out garbage (by 9 pm) | 2 | 2 | 2 | 2 | 2 | 2 | 2 | 14 |
| Vacuum house (by 6 pm) | ✕ | ✕ | ✕ | ✕ | ✕ | 9 | ✕ | 9 |
| Change cat litter (by 6 pm) | ✕ | ✕ | ✕ | ✕ | ✕ | 2 | ✕ | 2 |

Every 10 pts. = $1.00                                      Weekly Total     60
58–60 pts. = $6.00 + $2.00 bonus
Sunday evening payday
X = Chore not required on that day

**Figure 1**
Weekly chore chart

not do a chore or when he did it poorly, Dick handle it matter-of-factly rather than with anger. Past experience indicated that Mike became less cooperative when Dick was angry.

The last session in week two was with Mike and Dick together. Mike was upset because his father had not filled in the chore chart the past 2 days. We got the chart off the cupboard and filled it in together. Dick agreed with Mike that Mike had done all his chores so far that week. I encouraged Dick to appreciate Mike's efforts and success, and we practiced this. Mike enjoyed the encouragement.

Because anger management was one of our main goals, I introduced the topic by showing a picture of an "anger thermometer" (see Figure 2). I talked about "0" as the point where a person was calm, relaxed, and feeling no anger at all. At "2" or "3" a person often felt irritated or frustrated. At "5" a person was

definitely angry, at "6" or "7" quite angry, and by "9" or "10" so enraged that he or she was out of control. At these top points people often say and do things that they would not otherwise say or do and that they often regret later. I had both Mike and Dick identify times they had been at various points on the thermometer. They both acknowledged that some of their most hurtful and useless fights had occurred when they were at a "9" or "10" on the scale. I asked them to identify physical symptoms they experienced at various points on the scale, especially at "7" or "8" before they were out of control (for example, having a fast heart beat, feeling hot, or having sweaty palms). I requested that they identify how they could tell that the other person was at these points. We then discussed the concept of removing oneself from the situation before losing self-control in an effort to avoid destruc-

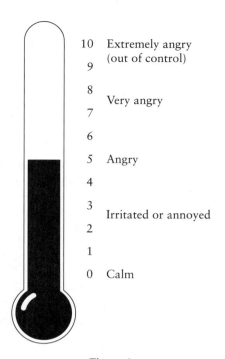

10  Extremely angry
       (out of control)
9

8
    Very angry
7

6

5  Angry

4

3
    Irritated or annoyed
2

1

0  Calm

**Figure 2**
Anger thermometer

tive fighting. I said that their symptoms at "7" or "8" should be seen as cues to temporarily leave the situation. We discussed where each person could go to calm down (for example, Mike to his bedroom, Dick to the basement to work on a project). Mike and Dick agreed they would try to remove themselves from the situation to avoid fights.

At some point when we were alone Dick commented, "If Mike would just do what he is supposed to do and not talk back to me, I wouldn't have this problem of anger." I gently challenged him. "I see things a little differently. I agree that Mike doing his chores and schoolwork would help. And certainly the way Mike talks to you has an influence on how you respond. But I see your response back as your responsibility and not Mike's. Each one of us is responsible for our own behavior—Mike for his and you for yours. In

fact, the only behavior any of us can truly control is our own." Dick thought a minute and agreed.

We got back together with Mike and I talked with the two of them about using "self-talk" to decrease and control anger. To illustrate this point, I gave several examples. Then we read a short children's story together called *Maxwell's Magnificent Monster* (Waters, 1980b). This story illustrates the point that our self-talk causes us to become angry. Mike put the two concepts together and said that the monster was when a person was at a "9" or "10" on the anger thermometer. Dick was quiet and seemed reflective. He said he liked the story and asked to keep it for awhile.

## Week Three: Teaching, Learning, and Some Application

The first session of the week was spent initially with Dick alone. Dick talked about the meeting he had gone to at school that morning with Mike and the school psychologist. It was the first day back after vacation, and Dick had been required to go because Mike had been suspended the 2 days before the break. I listened reflectively as Dick told of "Mike's rude behavior" toward him and the psychologist. Dick expressed his frustration at not being able to "make" Mike improve in school. I reiterated that a person has the greatest control over his own behavior and that Dick could only do so much to influence Mike. I suggested that concentrating on staying drug free, decreasing his own angry responses, and being consistent with checking and praising Mike on chores are all areas he could control that could indirectly have an impact on Mike's functioning at school. We reexamined the ineffectiveness of yelling as a means to improve Mike's school performance. I suggested he not spend too much energy on this issue now and let Mike have more responsibility or ownership for the school problems.

Mike then joined us, and we talked about the morning school appointment. When I brought up the issue of Mike's behavior with the school psychologist, Mike quickly mentioned some things his Dad had said to the psychologist that had embarrassed him. I said I could understand his embarrassment. However, his actions and words toward the school counselor were still his responsibility and could not be blamed on his father. I reinforced the idea that what he says and does is his responsibility, just as what his father says and does is his father's responsibility. Because I knew this was a message Mike would not like hearing, I said it in a concise and friendly way and then moved on to the next topic. Dick said Mike had been doing extremely well on chores and had earned the full $8 the past week. It was obvious from Mike's expression that he liked hearing his dad's praise.

The next day I picked Mike up at school, and we went to McDonald's again for our session. Mike had a long list of complaints about his father especially, that his dad got upset and yelled about such small things. Mike said he also worried about his dad drinking more beer. I simply listened, focusing largely on reflecting the feelings Mike was expressing. At one point I used a sheet with 20 feelings and accompanying faces showing those feelings. I had Mike pick out the feelings he felt frequently and explain when he felt them. My hope was that simply having the opportunity to vent his emotions would be helpful to Mike. However, I purposely avoided any statements blaming his father. I wanted to encourage Mike to take responsibility for his own actions rather than blaming someone else for everything. I talked with Mike about what he could and could not control. I mentioned that he could not control his father's substance abuse, that this was largely his father's choice. I suggested a number of phrases that he could use to share his feelings about it with his father, if he would like. (Example: "When

I see you drinking beer, I feel scared and worried.") We discussed the support group his school counselor had told me about—a group for teens whose parents have problems with substance abuse. Mike made an agreement with me that he would go once and evaluate it. I talked about how Mike does have control over his own behavior, both at home and at school. I said I thought it was great he was doing his chores so regularly and how this had already improved things. I listened to Mike's feelings about school and then talked concretely about all the positive things his dad, counselor, and I saw in him. I encouraged him to try a little harder in school and talked about the potential of increased self-esteem and future employability. We also discussed a few career possibilities, and I told stories of some people I knew who had dropped out of school early and ended up in very low-paying jobs.

During the next session with Dick, I asked if he had read the article I had given him at our last meeting—"The Anger Trap and How to Spring It" (Waters, 1980a). Dick said yes, that it made an excellent point. He was able to summarize the main idea: anger is a choice, and there are other choices available. I emphasized that by opting to interpret a situation in a different way (changing one's self-talk), anger can be reduced and more helpful responses can be chosen. I explained again the basic concept of rational-emotive therapy (RET). This time I drew the RET triangle as I illustrated that it is not situations or events (A) that cause feelings (C) but rather our self-talk or interpretation (B) about the situation (Ellis & Harper, 1975). (See Figure 3.) I gave some examples from my own life, and Dick was able to identify some situations in which using this technique could have helped him.

We discussed a handout on "The Six Steps to Anger" (Hauck, 1974) that identifies common self-talk leading to problematic anger, and then I provided him with a list of calming self-talk and challenges to angry self-talk. We

Belief or
Self-Talk / Interpretation

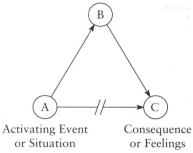

Activating Event          Consequence
or Situation              or Feelings

**Figure 3**

The rational-emotive therapy triangle

discussed the need to catch oneself using anger-producing self-talk and to substitute that with calming self-statements. When a friend of Dick's dropped by, we had covered so much material—Dick had been very eager for help with anger—that I saw it as a good time to end. I quickly gave Dick a book I had bought for him, one of the Hazelden Daily Meditation Series based on the 12 steps of AA (Hazelden Foundation Staff, 1988). I knew that the book fit well with the concepts Dick admired in his church group, and it could be helpful to him in his struggle with substance abuse. Dick was surprisingly touched that I would buy him this. He read the meditation for that day out loud. (Dick's readiness to accept and use written materials is definitely greater than most Homebuilders cases. A large percentage of clients will not read materials, so therapists spend considerable time discussing and role playing concepts with families.)

The third session of the week, held with both Mike and Dick, was very encouraging. They were in good moods when I arrived, having spent a fun afternoon riding dirt bikes together. They said they had forgotten how much fun each other could be. When Dick said he planned to do more things with Mike in the future, Mike was visibly pleased. When

I saw that the chore chart was filled out and that Mike had done all his work for the second week in a row, I smiled and complimented Dick and Mike.

Dick said he had been working on the anger management techniques we had discussed and that they were helping. He gave an example of an incident that had occurred that morning in which Mike had approached him angrily. Rather than responding with anger as he previously would have done, Dick had been able to remain calm. Dick said it kept Mike from escalating and resolved the situation sooner. Mike confirmed that his dad was calming down and that this made it more relaxing to be at home.

The remaining time was spent learning the skill of "I-messages." I explained the basic concept of I-messages as a way of communicating how another person's actions are affecting you in a manner that is most likely to be received well. The point of an I-message is to say how you feel without attacking the listener's self-esteem or saying things that are going to make the other person more defensive (Gordon, 1970). To illustrate, I told of a situation and then stated my feelings in an unhelpful, critical, and blaming way (a "You-message"). For example, "You were a thoughtless idiot to have left the gas tank empty when you came home last night. You never think of anyone but yourself." We discussed how they felt hearing that statement, how likely they were to want to cooperate with me, and what they felt like saying in return. Then I expressed my feelings in "I-message" form. "When you left the gas tank on empty, I felt irritated because I had to go to the gas station first thing and ended up being late for work." We discussed the difference. I pulled out the anger thermometer and pointed out how I-messages can be used when a person is at a low point on the scale. This increases the chances of resolution of the problem at an early stage and avoids the "gunnysacking" effect that can occur when a person lets a lot of irritations go unaddressed. Dick said he had a tendency to hold back his irritation and shared a few examples of this.

I diagrammed the parts of an I-message on a large pad I had brought along. "When you __(behavior)__ , I feel __(emotion)__ because __(effect on you)__ . I gave Mike and Dick an assignment to write four I-messages for one another: two using positive emotions (proud, happy, relieved, and so on) and two using uncomfortable emotions (angry, hurt, discouraged, and so on). While Dick worked on these on his own, Mike and I moved to another room where I helped him write his. We then shared what they had written and discussed the experience.

## Week Four: Progress Continues but Setbacks Occur

Dick said he was hungry and wanted to go to a nearby coffee shop when I arrived for our appointment alone. I drank coffee while he ate dinner. He said Mike had continued to do well on his chores. Dick said he thought the system was helping, and he had even noticed Mike looking for ways to improve the decorating in his bedroom. Dick said he was calming down quite a bit after realizing that he could choose responses other than anger. He said Mike also seemed calmer and that they were warming up to one another.

Mike and I had our last individual session at the same coffee shop to which Dick and I had been. Mike said he had seen his father using marijuana the previous evening. Mike expressed concerns that Dick would stop doing the chore chart, become more irritable, and use drugs more often after I was gone. We talked about some ways the likelihood of this could be minimized. I said I would have a follow-up session or two with them. I encouraged Mike to look at the behavior he could

control and stressed that rather than giving up, he could put his main efforts into continuing to do his chores and his homework and working on the anger-management skills we had learned. Briefly, I went over the RET triangle with him, as I had with Dick, and gave him a list of possible calming self-statements. I suggested he consider using an I-message to tell his dad how he felt about seeing him use marijuana again. We wrote out a couple of possible I-messages together.

The next evening I received a phone call from Mike. I asked if he had shared the I-messages. He said no, that he had gone right to bed. He went on to say that he had been suspended from one day of school for saying "Jesus Christ" to the teacher that day. I listened reflectively to his story and feelings. Knowing that saying "Jesus Christ" at his house was part of the norm, I was not surprised that he felt puzzled about how it led to suspension. I talked about why that might have been offensive to the teacher and how different types of talk were appropriate for different settings. We went on to discuss different teachers' expectations for quiet versus talking when students are finished with work. Mike said he was shocked that his dad had not yelled at him when he learned of the suspension. Dick had simply said, "School is your responsibility." Mike said the two of them had agreed Mike would be restricted to the house on the day of suspension. I was very pleased to see that Dick had been able to apply the concept of letting Mike take greater responsibility for school and avoid making it another area of major friction between them. It was clear from Mike's response that Mike was more able to look at his own behavior when the problem was not complicated by an enormous argument with his father.

The termination session was with Mike and Dick together. First we discussed school issues. Dick said he had talked to the school counselor, who said Mike had indeed improved on getting his homework in, although his classroom behavior was still a problem. We discussed some ideas Mike could try: saying his angry words to himself rather than out loud, keeping an index card with the calming self-statements on it in his notebook to read over when getting angry, and picking a student whom he likes (but who also gets along with teachers) to model after. We also discussed the possibility of Mike being placed in a classroom for behaviorally disordered students, an idea the school counselor had suggested. Dick said he had consciously chosen not to get mad about Mike's school suspension, saying he had realized it would not help either of them. I praised Dick for this and asked Mike if he had noticed his father getting angry less often. Mike said, "No kidding. My dad's attitude has really changed." Dick and I could not help but chuckle at Mike's comment, but it was obvious it meant a lot to both Mike and Dick.

We looked at the chore chart. Dick said Mike had earned the full allowance for that week, too. I raised Mike's concerns that the chore chart would not be continued after I left. We agreed that Mike could remind his dad to check chores if he forgot. We role played how Mike could phrase his request to maximize the chances of Dick responding favorably.

We discussed the progress they had made over the past 4 weeks: Mike was doing chores, and there were fewer arguments over this subject; the frequency and intensity of fights had decreased as they were able to express feelings; Mike was making small improvements in school; and there had been progress in getting Mike into a more appropriate classroom setting. Mike and Dick both said they were getting along together better, despite Dick's less frequent but continued use of drugs. Dick said he no longer wanted Mike to live elsewhere,

and Mike agreed. We set up a follow-up appointment for 2½ weeks later.

## CONCLUSION

This case illustrates some of the treatment techniques used by Homebuilders' staff to help families change their behaviors. In the Barretts' case, these included using a mutual goal-setting process, chore charts, the anger thermometer, rational-emotive therapy, I-messages, and other anger-management techniques. It demonstrates how intensive home-based services can help families improve their functioning in a variety of areas. Part of the reason for the effectiveness of these interventions is due to a flexible treatment model that can address a wide variety of family problems, the therapist relationship with the family, and the emphasis placed on teaching clients techniques to resolve real-life problems.

## References

Ellis, A., & Harper, R. A. (1975). *A guide to rational living*. North Hollywood, CA: Wilshire.

Fraser, M. W., Pecora, P. J., & Haapala, D. A. (1988). *Families in crisis: Findings from the family-based intensive treatment project* (final technical report). Salt Lake City, UT, University of Utah, Graduate School of Social Work, Social Research Institute, and Federal Way, Washington, Behavioral Sciences Institute.

Gordon, T. (1970). *Parent effectiveness training*. New York: Peter H. Wyden.

Haapala, D. A., & Kinney, J. M. (1988). Avoiding out-of-home placement among high-risk status offenders through the use of home-based family preservation services. *Criminal Justice and Behavior, 15,* 334–348.

Hauck, P. A. (1974). *Overcoming frustration and anger*. Philadelphia: Westminster Press.

Hazelden Foundation Staff. (1988). *Touchstones*. New York: Harper/Hazelden.

Kinney, J. M., Madsen, B., Fleming, T., & Haapala, D. A. (1977). Homebuilders: Keeping families together. *Journal of Consulting and Clinical Psychology, 45,* 667–678.

Waters, V. (1980a). *The anger trap and how to spring it.* New York: Institute for Rational Living. (Mimeograph)

Waters, V. (1980b). *Maxwell's magnificent monster.* New York: Institute for Rational Living. (Mimeograph)

# CASE STUDY 3.3

*This case illustrates the importance of specificity and early introduction of goals in brief treatment. The case presentation includes a sequence of self-questions that the social worker can use to obtain specificity and establish goals in treatment.*

## Questions

1. How does the social worker establish treatment goals in this case?
2. Why is it important to talk about change and solutions as early as possible in treatment?
3. What are some of the principles of brief treatment illustrated in this case?
4. What is the value of "simplicity" in this case example?

## SOLUTION-FOCUSED THERAPY

*Steve de Shazer**

Most case studies focus on the presenting complaint and/or some diagnostic category. The following case study takes a radically different approach, focusing instead on what it is that the client and therapist do together to solve the problem they are discussing. This approach may appear excessively limited and minimalist; however, this conversation is what happens when client and therapist are doing therapy, and, in a very real sense, it is the only hard data therapists have.

This case study should not be misread as "how to treat 'domestic violence'" or "how to treat two adult children of alcoholics" or "how to treat two (former) alcohol abusers," or even "how to treat people who hit each other." And it should not be misread as "how to treat couples." That is not the point. Each case is seen to bear a family resemblance to every other case.

* The author wishes to thank the other members of the team for their contributions to the model described in this chapter: Insoo Kim Berg, Wallace J. Gingerich, Eve Lipchik, and Elam Nunnally.

## SESSIONS ONE AND TWO

### Constructing a Complaint

The district attorney ordered a young couple to therapy after the police had been called to intervene in the couple's fight, one that included enough physical violence that they both had to go to the hospital. At the very start of therapy, Mr. S declared that he came to therapy only to stay out of jail, and Mrs. S said she came because "down deep" she knew he "wants to change." He disagreed: it was his wife that needed to change because, after all, it was her nagging and her failure to understand him that led to the fights.

Periodically during their 5 years together, they had had arguments that led to physical fights, and the most recent episode was not the first that had required medical treatment for one or the other. Following the most recent episode, Mrs. S had moved out for a short time, and, prior to returning home, she had seen a lawyer. But she did not want a divorce, even though she thought they had less than a 50/50 chance of living together without more violence. He too wanted the marriage to work out, and he thought they had an 85 to 90% chance of living together without violence. As we continued to talk about things, it became clear that both wanted to make their marriage successful, and each of them was willing to change if the other one did.

## Searching for Exceptions

Once we have confirmed the complaint, we look for exceptions to the rule. As we talked, it became clear, for the first time to all of us, that violence erupted in less than 10% of their arguments (they might have 10 to 12 per week). Of course that is 10 too often, but—nonetheless—they knew how to argue without getting violent, and whatever they did was 90% effective. But they were not able to describe what either of them did that worked.

## Setting Goals

"Suppose that one night, while you both were sleeping, there was a miracle, and this problem was completely solved. What will each of you be doing that's different the day after the miracle?" They both described more frequent touching, more frequent laughing, more feeling like they were "one, together" rather than "two, apart." They also saw themselves arguing without the fear of violence.

In 20 years of doing brief therapy, this "miracle sequence" is one of the most effective ways I have found to help clients specify (relatively) concrete and specific goals. Too often, when people are directly asked about goals, they will respond with global statements, that is, "communicating better," or "not getting violent," which are very hard to measure.

The first question I ask myself when I take a break to think things over (or to consult with the team behind the one-way window) in any first session is:

1. Is there a complaint?
   *Yes   No*

A "yes" answer means that therapy has begun. At this point, a solution has been described in such a way that it confirms that they have a complaint to work on together. Ending the violence was important to them, and they both knew they both would have to change, even though they both thought that the other one needed to change more. Indeed, this couple wanted to make changes so that they could remain together.

These questions are phrased in this simple "yes-no" format as a result of our current work on developing an "expert system" for case consultation (Goodman, Gingerich, & de Shazer, 1989; Kim, de Shazer, Gingerich, & Kim, 1987). Situations in which the answer is "no" are beyond the scope of this case study presentation (see de Shazer, 1988).

Clearly, physical fights did not occur every time they had a disagreement or argument. They perceived the fights as the rule, and arguments that did not lead to fights as an exception to that rule. Unfortunately, whatever is going on when fights do not happen is poorly described.

The second question I ask myself is related to the first:

2. Are there exceptions?
   *Yes   No*

Most of the time, in fact, the rule "the complaint always happens" is not in effect. Therefore it is likely that a solution can be built on what they are already doing. The behaviors that are useful in having arguments without violence are already in their repertoire.

The third and fourth questions are:

3. Is there a goal?
   *Yes   No*

4. Is the goal related to the exception?
   *Yes   No*

As a consequence of reaching their goal, they will feel confident that any arguments they have will not lead to violence. Clearly, the goal is related to the exceptions, and therefore promoting the exceptions will probably help them reach a satisfactory solution. This follows the first rule of brief therapy: if it works, don't fix it.

Repeating the exception or forcing the non-violent argument pattern will probably be easier when they know what behaviors to look for. Thus, I gave them the following task:

"I want you to secretly notice what she does that prevents any argument you might have from becoming violent, and I want you to secretly notice what he does that prevents any argument you might have from becoming violent."

## Eliciting Solution Talk

Ten days later, I opened the session with this question: "So what is better?" They reported that there had been no violence and that things were better in general.

It is important to start talking about change and solution as early in therapy as possible (Gingerich, de Shazer, & Weiner-Davis, 1988), and, in particular, we have found that opening the second and later sessions with a question about how things are better is a good, simple way to convey to the client that improvement is expected as part of the normal course of therapy.

I take a general report of improvement like this to mean that the clients and I were on track in the first session and, further, to mean that whatever they were doing right needs to be explored and identified.

## Marking Differences

There had been some arguments, one of which was a "near miss." There were four elements in their description of that episode that were not part of the violence pattern:

1. The argument took place in the kitchen (the violence tended to happen in the living room);
2. He initiated the handholding (which he had never done during an argument);
3. They were arguing across the table (there was no table in the living room);
4. She responded with a squeeze and a smile.

Thinking things over, the first question I ask myself during the break in the second and subsequent sessions is:

1. Are things better?
   *Yes   No*

The second question is:

2. Is the client closer to the goal?
   *Yes   No*

And a related third question is:

3. Has the goal been reached?
   *Yes   No*

The "yes," "yes," "no" sequence of answers to these three questions in this case suggests that we follow the second rule of brief therapy in designing any intervention: once you know what works, do more of it. Their descriptions of how they handled the near miss are obviously related to the goal, but neither of them is confident that the goal has been reached.

If the answer to the first question had been "no," things are not better; then the third rule of brief therapy would have applied: if it doesn't work, don't do it again—do something different.

4. Have differences or changes been reported in behavioral terms?
   *Yes   No*

5. Are these differences members of the same class as the exceptions?
   *Yes   No*

The two "yes" answers to these questions give further indication that therapy is "on track."

After listing the four steps they have invented during the near miss, I suggested that, since they had never argued in the kitchen before, "whenever you find an argument starting outside the kitchen, you should get up and move to the kitchen." This they agreed was possible and might prove good enough.

## SESSIONS THREE, FOUR, AND FIVE

Over the course of these sessions, on a 10-point "confidence scale," her confidence rose from 2 to 7, and his remained stable at 8. During this entire period, the task was the same: "Continue to pay attention to what you do that increases your confidence and the other's confidence that you have solved the problem."

## SESSION SIX

A "checkup" 6 months after the fifth session revealed that there had been two incidents where he had slapped her, either of which they thought would have gotten out of hand the year before. They were quite pleased with their progress and were very confident that they had "all but" solved the problem. On the confidence scale, she was at 8, whereas he had slipped to 7, and both of them agreed that they only needed more time to become completely confident.

It is important for neither the clients nor the therapist to mistakenly think that slaps in this situation were a relapse. Indeed the violence still is part of their life, but—and this is a big "but"—they did not allow the episodes to escalate.

I suggested to them the following rules, which make explicit some of the elements in their new (nonviolent) argument pattern.

"Obviously, you need to continue doing what works. I have some ideas for you that might prove helpful in preventing troubles."

*Rule 1:* When you two are discussing anything, and she says "I don't know" to you, believe it. Then the topic or subject of discussion must be dropped for 24 hours at least, unless she brings it up again.

*Rule 2:* When in doubt about what is going on between you, you must walk away and give her time.

*Rule 3:* You are to reward him whenever he follows rules 1 and 2.

*Rule 4:* If you feel that you are "drifting apart," then, paradoxically, you need to spend the next weekend apart.

We scheduled another "checkup" for 6 months later.

The scheduling of a weekend apart (which they had done every so often in previous years) was designed to help them not "try" to fix things when they thought they were drifting apart. Previous attempts to "fix" things had helped to increase intensity in the relationship and to put them under stress, which still provokes occasional violence.

They reported a complete lack of violence during this 6-month period, and both felt extremely confident that the solution was complete. This time, she rated her confidence at 9.5, and he rated his at between 9 and 9.5. I ended the session early, wishing them the best of luck.

## CONCLUSION

Approaching cases in this way helps therapists figure out what to do and what to focus on. Although it may seem to ignore many of the issues therapists sometimes think germane, this way of thinking about doing therapy focuses on successfully developing solutions to the clients' complaints, whatever these complaints may involve. The pattern of therapy from session to session, as described by the questions and their "yes" and "no" responses, focuses on success and on figuring out what went wrong when things do not go according to plan.

This case study was not meant to fully describe the approach but only to show the efficacy of the model in dealing with a case that many therapists might label as "difficult." Just because the clients describe a complicated, complex, or even confused problem with lots of issues does not mean that the therapy needs to be equally complicated, complex, or confusing. In fact, this situation, perhaps more than many other ones, calls for the therapy to be as simple as possible. Of course, the simplicity of the model does not necessarily make it easy to use. The model is only meant to clarify "what to do" and leaves the question of "how to do it" in the hands of the individual using the model. For a broader and fuller description of this approach and the research and theory behind it, see de Shazer, 1988.

## References

de Shazer, S. (1988). *Clues: Investigating solutions in brief therapy.* New York: Norton.

Gingerich, J., de Shazer, S., & Weiner-Davis, M. (1988). Constructing change: A research view of interviewing. In E. Lipchik (Ed.), *Interviewing.* Rockville: Aspen.

Goodman, H., Gingerich, W. J., & de Shazer, S. (1989). Briefer: An expert system for clinical practice. *Computers in Human Services, 5,* 53–68.

Kim, J., de Shazer, S., Gingerich, W. J., & Kim, P. (1987). Briefer II: An expert system for brief therapy, IEEE stems man and cybernetics Annual Conference.

# CASE STUDY 3.4

*Codependency is being increasingly recognized as an important issue when working with alcoholic families. This case study illustrates a developmental approach to family problems and presents interventions designed to minimize codependent behaviors.*

## Questions

1. What behaviors suggest codependency in a family system?
2. What function does alcoholism serve in this family?
3. What developmental changes were confronting the family in this case?
4. How did the interventions promote change in this family?

## A FAMILY SYSTEMS APPROACH TO THE TREATMENT OF CODEPENDENCY

*Christine Curry*

The term *codependency* refers to a pattern of behavior in which the individual's assessment of self-worth is based on external referents. Because the focus is outside of oneself, the codependent's need for personal validation is often met by excessive caretaking of others to the neglect of himself/herself. The codependent underreacts to internal cues regarding feelings and situations and finds it difficult to make decisions and choices based on personal needs. The codependent demonstrates a preoccupation with the behaviors and feelings of others, inappropriate levels of guilt when attempts are made to be assertive, fears of abandonment, and tremendous resistance and anxiety when feelings begin to emerge in therapy.

Within dysfunctional family systems, this overfunctioning becomes acute as the codependent strives to compensate for another's perceived, or actual, loss of role functioning. Because this caretaking function is reinforced by the family system, it is unlikely that the codependent will experience enough con-

scious discomfort to initiate changes. The impetus for intervention will be more likely to occur around a life stage transition or the cessation of problematic behavior in a family member. At these times, the carefully nurtured balance of the family system experiences disruption, and unfamiliar, unpredictable demands create high levels of stress. It is at these times that the codependent faces the loss of familiar relationship patterns and may seek treatment on behalf of another family member. Because the family is so integrally bound in maintaining codependent behavior, family therapy is essential in its treatment.

Jean was such a client. Her marriage of 25 years was under extreme stress because of events surrounding her husband's decision to discontinue drinking after 20 years of active alcoholism. Despite the realization of her wish that he stop drinking, Jean reported in our first telephone contact that the family was "even worse," referring to an increase in conflict between her husband and their 18-year-old son. She stated that at different times, both her son and her husband had threatened to move out. Jean noted that her physician husband had recently completed a 28-day inpatient program for alcoholism following an intervention by his colleagues. He had been sober for 6 months and was attending two Alcoholics Anonymous (AA) meetings per week. She suggested that counseling would assist her in "calming down" her son and husband. I requested that the entire family participate in therapy despite her misgivings over including her 21-year-old daughter and her husband. Jean agreed to ask everyone to come the next week.

Jean arrived at the first session accompanied by her husband, Bill, age 49; her son, Charlie, 18; and daughter, Amy, 21. Jean was a thin, intense, rather dowdy 48-year-old homemaker, who looked older than her years. As she described her assessment of the problems at home, she tightly smiled at Charlie as if to check out her statements with him. She used the pronoun *we* to describe his persistent problems with authority figures. Jean noted that she frequently intervened in Bill and Charlie's arguments in order to keep them from "getting totally out of control." Often, she would spend hours speaking individually to husband and son, in order to "help them understand each other." She was distressed by Charlie's increasing reluctance to talk over his problems with her and his occasional flashes of temper where previously they had enjoyed a very close relationship. Jean stated sadly that "before, I could tell when he wasn't happy because I knew what he was feeling even before he did." She described how helpful and supportive Charlie had been in the past when her husband had "his problem." Throughout her discourse, Jean referred only obliquely to her husband's long, stormy relationship with alcohol and vigorously discounted my suggestion that she had also been affected to a great degree.

Throughout the first several sessions, Bill continued to take a rather passive role, glancing noncommittally in Jean's direction when she was asked to comment on the marital relationship. He appeared to defer to her assessment of the difficulties between he and Charlie, except to note that they got along fine when they were alone together. When asked, Bill stated that his relationship with Jean had waned for many years and that he was unsure of what he felt now that he was no longer drinking. Observing the pained look on his mother's face, Charlie interrupted his father and reminded him about the sacrifices Jean had made on behalf of the family. Bill responded by challenging Charlie to describe how his "delinquent behavior" had helped things. Jean immediately rushed to limit this first direct exchange between the two by reminding her husband that she had already spoken to Charlie about "how we are going to deal with our DWI (driving while intoxicated) charge." Amy remained very quiet throughout the first sessions, except to support her father's comments about Charlie. She became tearful as he commented on the deterioration of the marital relationship, yet she was unable to verbalize any thoughts or feelings except to state "It just seems like everyone is so upset all the time now."

In this beginning stage of therapy my goal was to hypothesize what function Bill's alcoholic behavior had served for this family and what dilemmas and challenges were precipitated by its subsequent absence. During my exploration of the family's behavior before, during, and after one of Bill's drinking episodes, it became clear that alcohol abrogated Bill's discomfort with intimacy and closeness. He felt, and was perceived by the family as, "more approachable" after several drinks. As his disease progressed, he frequently became enraged by his son's oppositional behavior. Jean, terrified by glimpses of her own unacknowledged anger at her husband, became an expert in diminishing the intense feelings between father and son by rerouting communication through her. Bill's periods of sobriety were accompanied by intense remorse and guilt, and he relinquished his role as husband and father to Jean's attempts to create the perception that everything was perfect. She appeared fearful of abdicating her role as family caretaker and increased her efforts to help by reinforcing the dependency of Bill and Charlie on her capable shoulders. As the stress increased at home it was no longer punctuated by the tension-relieving cycle of Bill's binge drinking and subsequent remorse and withdrawal. In addition, several factors increased the stress—among them, Charlie's age-appropriate desire to emancipate himself from his family of origin and Bill's growing self-esteem and his demands for intimacy and closeness in the marital relationship.

These changes had severely compromised Jean's coping mechanisms and ushered in a dawning awareness of her own feelings, which had been suppressed in the service of her role as caretaker. This role was being challenged by Amy's impending departure to medical school and Charlie's threat to move out. She felt as though these events were a sign that she was losing control through her personal inadequacies in making everyone happy. I discussed with the family some of the common dynamics for the newly recovering family and recommended they consider participating in family therapy for the next 6 months. My goals for Jean were to assist her to recognize her feelings, to support her efforts to decrease her controlling behavior, and to help her meet her needs for closeness within the marital relationship. These goals were complementary to our agreement that the overall goal of therapy would be to assist the family to meet the challenges of sobriety.

During the next three months, the family attended sessions on a weekly basis. Jean's role as the primary spokesperson became more limited through my support of other family members' contributions through circular questioning. The focus continued to be on creating boundaries between family members and encouraging direct communication. Jean was helped to relinquish some of her responsibility by reassigning it to other family members. The family was given several tasks for the purpose of intervening in triangulated relationships and cross-generational coalitions.

During one session, Jean was able to verbalize her fears that if she let go of her acknowledged control, the family "would explode." She described her wish to be taken care of yet how difficult it was to trust Bill's request that she share her feelings as he had been urged to do in treatment. I supported Jean to verbalize some of her emerging feelings about past and present events in the safe environment of the family session. She became tearful and stated that she was terrified that Bill would lose his temper and get drunk. She was reluctant to share parenting responsibilities with him, stating that "the kids are all I have to make me feel like I'm worth anything . . . that's why it's so hard when they act like they don't care about me." Bill reiterated his desire to share more of the parenting, yet also acknowledged his ambivalence about seeing Jean more vulnerable and indecisive. Despite his wish to have her "share feelings openly" it was clear that everyone in the family was quite uncomfortable when Jean discussed her feelings of anger and sadness. Amy, seeing this as Jean abandoning her father, attempted to protect him by suggesting that her mother was "selfish." Because this occurred in a family session, I was able to help the family recognize and talk about the anxiety that new behaviors had created for everyone. In order to assist the couple to move through this transition, I assigned them tasks where they "courted" each other in establishing a "new" relationship.

At the end of the third month, an anxious

Jean reported that Charlie had been arrested for another DWI. As he moved beyond the guilty bravado in his description of this latest episode in an escalating series of misadventures, it became apparent that he was reacting in part to Jean's growing autonomy. He had encountered her diminished attention as well as a greater degree of accountability, from both parents, for his behavior. Jean was able to resist her first impulse to rescue Charlie, and with Bill's support they confronted him about his irresponsible behavior and drinking problem. It was becoming clear that the shift in the family's organization had revealed years of denial regarding Charlie's out-of-control drinking. Early on, I had made participation in Alanon a prerequisite for Jean's therapy, and it was at this juncture that her growing involvement with other mothers in this self-help community really paid off. Several months later, on follow-up, Jean revealed that she and Bill asked Charlie either to leave home or to get treatment for his alcoholism, and he had chosen the latter.

During the last month of therapy, the sessions revolved around Bill and Jean. Amy had left for medical school with expressed relief that her participation in family sessions had ended. Charlie had angrily refused to participate, as he viewed the sessions as "being just for my mom and dad, anyway." I spent most of the sessions working with the couple on their families of origin and helping them understand how their respective early experiences impinged on their marital relationship. As we worked on Jean's genogram, she discovered that her father's chronic absence was due to his alcoholism, which had never been acknowledged by her mother. In her role as her mother's confidante, Jean's earliest memories were of guilt and responsibility for failing to ameliorate her mother's sadness and anxiety. In the absence of a viable marital relationship and her father's advancing alcoholism, her parents had colluded to keep her at home to "take care of mom." As the only child, Jean felt responsible for maintaining the tenuous equilibrium of her family. She was able to write a letter to her deceased father and in this way release some of her feelings of anger, sadness, and loss that she recognized she had displaced on Bill since her father's death shortly after her elopement with Bill.

At the end of the contracted 24 sessions, Bill and Jean agreed to return for marital therapy to continue their exploration into the "silent years" as Jean termed the last 15 years of their marriage. She realized that her fragile sense of self was still vulnerable to Bill's disapproval and that she still encountered difficulty in avoiding "catching everybody's feelings like the flu." Jean wanted to work on her relationship with Amy, however she recognized that this would require patience and understanding, since her daughter might not be ready to address their rather estranged relationship. She continued to struggle with control issues yet was able to recognize that the impulse to "make everything perfect" for everyone else coincided with her need to be perfect, lest she be abandoned. With the support of her Alanon group and marital therapy, Jean reported on follow-up, one year later, that "things were going well, not perfect." She had recently been hired for a part-time position and was using her prodigious helping skills as a hot-line volunteer one night a week. She was able to recount several instances where she recognized control returning to her relationships and discovered that she was able to address the feelings beneath. Jean closed our phone conversation by relating her discovery that in her anxiety to avoid the "scary" feelings, she had also closed out the wonderful ones that she was now able to experience in her life.

# 4

# IN TREATING ADULT DYSFUNCTIONS

It is estimated that 2 out of every 10 adults in the United States suffers from one or more mental disorders. Mental disorders include such problems as anxiety disorders, substance abuse, affective disorders (such as depression), and schizophrenia. The care and treatment of people who suffer from these disorders is provided by social workers, psychiatrists, psychologists, and mental health nurses. However, the social work profession provides the bulk of mental health services. These services are provided in a variety of settings including community mental health centers, private psychiatric hospitals, child guidance clinics, psychiatric clubhouses, group homes, and state and county hospitals.

Much of social work concerns the management and treatment of adults who suffer from such mental disorders. Such problems present special challenges to social workers. The social worker may be involved in clinical treatment; case management—especially through aftercare treatment planning; development and coordination of community services, for example, establishing clubhouses for persistently mentally ill clients; life skill training to help clients function in the community; court proceedings that involve commitment and guardianship; and family counseling.

The case studies in this chapter present examples of practice with adults who suffer from various mental disorders. In each case the difficulty the person faces produces disability in his or her personal, social, or occupational life; the difficulties therefore qualify as mental disorders

Social workers need to learn about different mental disorders, but it is important to point out that mental disorders, not individuals, are classified. Thus clients diagnosed using the DSM-III as having a particular disorder are different in many ways. The only similarities are the symptoms that represent the disorder. As Maxmen (1987) points out,

"Some schizophrenics (and diabetics) are delightful, some obnoxious, some brilliant, and some stupid. When, for brevity's sake, a patient with schizophrenia is called a 'schizophrenic,' it should be done with the understanding that the disorder is an attribute of the person, and never his totality" (p. 5).

Because each of the mental disorders is quite different, social workers must obtain and master specialized knowledge in order to provide effective services and treatment. This knowledge includes what treatments are effective with different disorders, the effects of various medications on the disorders, how to best manage each case, and how to use community and social supports. The case studies presented in this chapter show the diversity of social work practice in treating adult dysfunction and demonstrate the need for this specialized knowledge. Geary presents a case study that focuses on depression, one of the more frequent adult disorders, showing how to use cognitive therapy with a depressed man. The study is a good example of treatment effectiveness because cognitive therapy is recognized as the treatment of choice for depression.

Liebman's case study is about a person who suffers from crippling anxiety, and he describes what is referred to as an Ericksonian approach to working with this disorder. Milton Erickson has had a profound impact on the field of psychotherapy with his emphasis on both hypnosis and family therapy. In Liebman's case study, the elements of Ericksonian therapy are present: ritual, reframing, hypnosis, and a solution-oriented focus. This case study also describes a team approach to treatment.

Richard Whiteside addresses a disorder that has increased dramatically in the last 10 years: bulimia—an eating disorder. He offers an example of an adult disorder that must be understood and addressed in the context of the family. Although he worked individually with the client, he hypothesized that her symptom must be understood in relation to her family. He describes a brief therapy approach to help the client give up her binging episodes.

José Ashford and Larry Whirl present a case study that exemplifies forensic social work. In this setting, assessment and attention to details are critical as one attempts to make conclusions about an individual's mental competence at the time of a crime.

## Reference

Maxmen, J. S. (1987). *Essential psychopathology.* New York: W. W. Norton.

# CASE STUDY 4.1

*Depression is one of the most common problems among adults. This case presents the most widely used treatment for depression: cognitive therapy.*

## Questions

1. Why is cognitive therapy considered the treatment of choice for depression?
2. What are the central concepts of a cognitive approach to treating depression?
3. What is the function of task assignments in this approach to treatment?
4. What cognitive therapy techniques were most helpful in reducing the client's depression?

## INDIVIDUAL TREATMENT OF DEPRESSION USING COGNITIVE THERAPY

*Brent B. Geary*

Jim was a 42-year-old, divorced, unemployed man who sought psychotherapy for depression, complaining that "every area of my life is a mess." His 14-year marriage had ended 8 years earlier, and he stated, "I just never have recovered from that." Jim made several attempts to change from an unsatisfactory career in computer programming but had not found a vocational niche. When he entered therapy, Jim was living with his sister and her husband. Although they were well-to-do and supportive, it was apparent from Jim's description that their patience with his situation was wearing thin.

The client grew up in a secure but emotionally unexpressive home. He and his sister, who was 2 years younger, both did well in school. Jim progressed through college with a B average and married during his junior year. He obtained a job with a growing data-processing firm on graduation. Well-liked by his fellow employees, Jim was recognized several times for profit-generating innovations he devised. After he turned 30, however, he experienced increasing disenchantment with his work and

distance from his wife and two sons. He discovered that his wife was having an affair with another man. Several sessions of marital therapy proved ineffective. Jim's wife filed for divorce and moved with the children to a neighboring state to live with her new lover. Jim had tremendous difficulty coping with the transition, and his job performance deteriorated significantly. Approximately 6 months after the divorce, Jim terminated employment with the company.

Jim attempted to establish several consultation and free-lance business ventures, but all failed within a year. These entrepreneurial forays were generally impulsive and not well thought out. He eventually landed a job as a counselor at a residential facility for delinquent boys. He remained in this position for 3 years and found particular enjoyment and satisfaction in teaching the youths computer skills. Jim developed novel treatment programs incorporating computers, which proved to be quite successful. The lack of an advanced degree hampered his advancement, however, and Jim found himself "topped out" in the organization. His savings depleted from the failed business endeavors, Jim was unable to meet financial obligations (including child support) on his meager salary. This situation forced him to leave the treatment facility, to everyone's regret, and accept his sister's offer to live temporarily with her family. Here he had remained for 15 months, without employment, when he entered therapy.

Information gained from Jim during the intake interview signaled that cognitive treatment was appropriate. The client had undertaken psychotherapy intermittently over the past 6 years. He described these ventures as "focusing on my feelings" and as being highly expressive (that is, cathartic) in nature. Though he was helped to feel better, he stated "I still don't think very well of myself." Several other indications of cognitive dysfunction were present in his self-report: Jim said that he frequently found himself "brooding" and that, even when his mood lightened, "I'll talk myself back down into depression." When asked what he meant in describing himself as his worst enemy, Jim said that he believed the root of his problems lay in "these thoughts I carry around inside of me." The client denied suicidal ideation or intent but added "I don't want to live like this the rest of my life, and I'm beginning to wonder if things will ever change." Jim reported that his sleeping and eating patterns were only sporadically disrupted; social activities ("I rarely go out") and cognitive functions ("I can't seem to think clearly") evinced general and lasting disturbance. Cognitive therapy was indicated as the treatment that would best address the modalities (behavioral and cognitive) showing the most dysfunction.

## OVERVIEW OF THE INTERVENTION

Succinctly, the aim of cognitive therapy is "to help depressed individuals to identify, evaluate, and modify their dysfunctional personal paradigm" (Covi, Roth, & Lipman, 1982, pp. 459–460). Beck (1976) hypothesized that the "personal paradigm" is a unique assumptive framework that underlies psychogenic depression, containing an individual's negative beliefs regarding himself or herself, the world, and the future. Cognitive therapy defines three essential concepts as central in specifying and altering a depressogenic personal paradigm. *Cognitions* are ideas and images brought to consciousness in a given situation. Cognitions exert direct influence on affect and behavior, comprising what an individual thinks *in* (not about) a particular occasion (Rush, 1983). *Schemata* are assumptions or beliefs that are formed by early experience and that guide the content of cognitions. The manner in which experience is evaluated and distorted is determined by a person's schemata (Beck, Rush, Shaw, & Emery, 1979). *Cognitive distortions* are logical errors that result from negative cognitions. These inaccurate inferences and conclusions regarding events serve to intensify depressive symptoms (Hollon & Beck, 1979).

Cognitive therapy is an active and directive approach that employs didactics extensively to supplement the ongoing supportive therapeutic relationship. A "collaborative empiricism" is fostered in which therapist and client together formulate treatment strategies (Beck et al., 1979). Cognitive therapy is designed to be delivered in a negotiated, time-limited procedure, generally 15 to 25 sessions.

Jim was seen on 21 occasions over a period of 6 months. The framework of his sessions was tapered so that he received therapy twice per week for 4 weeks, once weekly for 8 weeks, four times biweekly, and in a follow-up session one month after the previous visit. Sessions were typically structured in the following format:

1. Reactions to the previous session
2. Events since the last session
3. Homework review
4. In-session agenda

5. Formulate homework
6. Feedback and process commentary

Jim completed the Beck Depression Inventory (BDI) (Beck, 1978) before each session to provide a marker of progress. The Automatic Thoughts Questionnaire (ATQ) (Hollon & Kendall, 1980) was filled out monthly to determine the nature and frequency of Jim's self-statements. The client purchased, read, and completed exercises in *Feeling Good* (Burns, 1980), a self-help book about cognitive therapy that serves as a valuable adjunct to treatment.

## THE COURSE OF THERAPY

The first four sessions with Jim, completed over a 2-week period, were devoted to establishing rapport and gaining a history, providing a rationale for treatment, and educating the client regarding the nature of depression and the cognitive model. Jim's BDI scores ranged from 28 to 32, indicating moderate to severe depression. Although the client indicated that he experienced nothing more than passing ideation regarding suicide, this was closely monitored. Jim stated that he was less likely to perform self-injurious acts "now that I'm finally doing something constructive for myself" (that is, engaging in therapy).

Jim read the first two chapters of *Feeling Good*, remarking "This book was written about me!" This provided an opportunity to "normalize" his depression, pointing to the frequency of dysphoria and depression in the general population and helping to alleviate the client's self-imposed onus of thinking himself different (that is, inferior), isolated, and unique. Jim reported that a typical day consisted of "sleeping a lot, watching some tube, and talking to my sister's family until they get sick of me." He left the house very little and communicated only sporadically with friends and acquaintances ("Who wants to hear a depressive's tale of woe?"). When he did go out into public, Jim said that he felt like he was wearing a neon sign that read "I'M DEPRESSED" and that people were uninterested in him.

Behavioral measures were begun in this initial phase of therapy to counteract Jim's low activity level and social withdrawal. He started a Daily Activity Schedule (Burns, 1980, p. 88) with mastery and pleasure ratings. Jim also collaborated in devising graduated task assignments, keyed to ventures he had been meaning to undertake but had not achieved. These activities ranged from taking walks to going to the public library to shopping for cards and small gifts to send to his children. In addition to reactivating the client, these strategies served as tangible indications of Jim's motivation and compliance. They also opened the door to both in-session and experiential challenging of Jim's self-negating set. When Jim reviewed accomplishments in his task assignments during sessions, it was commonplace for him to punctuate his reports with statements such as "But that's no big deal," "I feel stupid telling you these silly things," and "Anybody can do this stuff." The therapist acknowledged that the activities were small, perhaps even silly, but that the accumulation of small steps formed the pathway to change. Jim's alterations in volition were also highlighted; he was continually reinforced for choosing to help himself. To strike these points home, Jim was asked to twice daily (for example, at noon and at bedtime) review his Daily Activity Schedule and then, on a separate paper, write what he would have done in that given time (for example, a morning or afternoon/evening) before he entered therapy.

The client was highly cooperative in completing his homework assignments. Though he continued to disparage the activities, he increasingly anticipated and vocalized the therapist's counter ("I know, I know. . . . It's a small thing but it shows progress"). His activity level increased; it seemed appropriate to move into examination of Jim's cognition process.

The next six sessions were primarily devoted to illustrating the thought-affect-behavior sequence, identifying patterns of cognitive distortion, and specifying cognitions that gave rise to Jim's negative moods. The client's reading of Chapters 3 through 9 in *Feeling Good* supplemented the therapy. Jim's BDI values ranged from 22 to 29, and he reported for the first time seeing some hope in his situation, though he quickly tempered his proclamation with skepticism that results could be lasting.

Jim quickly became adept at isolating thoughts and images that contributed to his feelings of sadness, anger, frustration, anxiety, and the like. He began to recognize cognitive errors at every turn in his thinking. When asked which distortions seemed to be most frequent, he replied "All of them." Questioned further, he listed "all-or-nothing thinking," "minimization," "should statements," and "labeling" (terms from *Feeling Good*, pp. 40–41) as most prominent. Jim completed the Automatic Thoughts Questionnaire; his most frequent self-statements clustered in the negative self-concepts and negative expectations dimension (Hollon & Kendall, 1980). He remained relatively active, with periodic lapses. However, Jim remarked that he had become "trapped" because, during periods of inactivity, "all I think about now is my distorted thinking, and I'd rather be doing things."

A method for combating Jim's negative automatic thoughts was instituted in session. The client began to counter his harsh self-statements by use of the "triple column technique" (Burns, 1980, p. 60). In the first column, Jim entered automatic thoughts he noticed; in the second column, he identified the cognitive distortion(s) contained in the self-statements; and in the third column, he generated rational and reasonable responses to the automatic thoughts. For instance, Jim found that he frequently said to himself "I should be doing better than this" (first column), which involved a should statement, minimization, and all-or-nothing thinking as cognitive distortions (column two). He was able to counter with "Although at times progress seems slow, I am doing better and better" and "What I'm doing now is better than before, and I can reasonably expect to continue improving" in the third column. Jim likened this process of offsetting negative automatic thoughts to "reprogramming the old computer."

The next several weeks (around sessions 12 to 15) contained events that proved to be vital in Jim's therapy. A relapse occurred, evinced in the client's BDI scores (which rose to 32 and 30 at sessions 12 and 13, respectively) and his report that his mood plunged despite his attempts to counter depressogenic self-statements. While exploring and working to identify what was different during this time (when his mood dived), the following interchange took place:

*Client:* Well, I was beginning to feel better and I was more active, so I began to think about getting back to work. But I got this wave of panic and despair.

*Therapist:* Panic and despair. Any particular thoughts or images as you felt that?

*Client:* Yeah, like "I can't cope," "I can't handle work." All of a sudden I felt as though life was sweeping me aside. I had this picture of myself swimming out into the ocean toward something but being pushed back to shore by the waves. It was like I was powerless, like I was at the mercy of the waves and the tide.

*Therapist:* So, it was like you were trying to "get back into the swim" vocationally, but there were these powerful forces working against you.

*Client:* Right . . . and I had a lot of other thoughts whenever I considered working.

*Therapist:* What thoughts?

*Client:* Like, "I'll never hold a good job," "They'll [employers] reject me," "I guess I'm unemployable."

*Therapist:* And that would indicate what about you?

*Client:* Well, that I'm powerless to earn my own way . . . that if I can't even handle a job . . .

*Therapist:* Then that would mean what about you as a person?

*Client:* That would mean I was pretty worthless. I mean, if I can't even hold a job, what good am I to anybody?

*Therapist:* If I can't demonstrate that I'm competent then I'm worthless.

*Client:* Yep.

Jim's rich imagery and his developed ability to recognize automatic thoughts yielded valuable clinical material. This exchange and further probing evoked memories for the client. In particular, Jim remembered numerous instances as a child when he felt powerless to elicit affection and emotional expression from his parents. His achievements at school, though, reliably drew their praise and attention. He remembered his father, a successful business man, rewarding these accomplishments with money. But he was then sent out on his own to buy things for himself with the money. And he remembered continuously buying and paying for things with his childhood and adolescent friends. "I worked a lot as a kid—paper routes, lawn-mowing jobs, stuff like that—so that I'd have money to spend and be able to keep my friends," Jim reminisced. His descent into depression began when he couldn't "keep" his wife, even while he was succeeding at work. And the failed attempts to revive his career made him feel even more hopeless about proving his value as an individual.

This turning point in Jim's therapy marked a shift in the level of analysis of Jim's automatic thoughts. Specifically, it represented a transition from *horizontal exploration* to *vertical exploration* of the client's thoughts (Safran, Vallis, Segal, & Shaw, 1986). Horizontal exploration surveys automatic thoughts across a variety of contexts. This process serves to demonstrate to the client the relationship between thinking and mood and provides a general indication of the client's thinking style. Vertical exploration pursues deeper meanings behind automatic thoughts, particularly those that reflect on the client's sense of self. This latter procedure uncovers core cognitive processes—central assumptions and beliefs that make up the schemata. In the present case, the event of considering work evoked numerous negative automatic thoughts for Jim. The collaborative investigation of these thoughts by the therapist and the client revealed that his sense of personal value was highly dependent on performance and material gain.

The focus of treatment turned to devising behavioral assignments that would disconfirm Jim's depressogenic assumptions. He talked to his sister and reestablished contact with friends and acquaintances. He discussed therapeutic insights with people and received valuable feedback that they cared about him, not his material products. Jim arranged an extended visit with his children, during which he concentrated on his relationship with them rather than activities and gifts. He began volunteer work 5 hours per week at a convalescent center. And, he obtained a dog at a local animal shelter, remarking "She doesn't care what I have or what I make—she just loves me."

Jim's BDI scores progressively decreased, reading 14 (mild mood disturbance) by the 18th session. His visits with the therapist were spaced to once every 2 weeks. Jim reported that, although he at first had difficulty believing his worthiness independent from his performance, "It's hard to ignore the evidence" he accumulated in his experiences. In-session work concentrated on defining realistic expectations of himself and future planning. His gains were reinforced and consolidated.

When Jim presented for the follow-up session 1 month after his previous visit (BDI = 8; much less frequent negative self-statements on the ATQ), he listed several notable changes in his life. He had secured a part-time job and a small apartment for himself and his dog. He was still performing the volunteer work and was initiating a social life. Though he still had his "ups and downs," he had become adept at stopping himself and using cognitive strategies to reappraise situations. Jim reported greater confidence, enjoyment, and fulfillment and an enhanced sense of security. He promised to check in periodically with the therapist and to return promptly if he encountered difficulty.

In closing, Jim returned to symbolism of an earlier session. He stated that he had replaced his former neon sign with a new one that read "I'M WORTHWHILE." "You know," he said, "people respond to this one a lot better. So do I."

## DISCUSSION AND SUMMARY

The foregoing account illustrates a straightforward use of cognitive therapy in the treatment of depression. This particular client was highly motivated and quite compliant. It is common for depressed individuals to require more protracted therapeutic efforts at various treatment junctures than did Jim. But the sequence of therapy remains essentially the same: stabilization of the client's mood, instillation of hope, behavioral activation, application of cognitive strategies, and establishment of an orientation to the future.

Cognitive therapy is primarily indicated when clients' thought patterns constitute the modality of most dysfunction. Other treatment approaches may be more appropriate when affective reactions, interpersonal dynamics, or physiological functioning dominate presenting concerns. Careful initial assessment is essential to match intervention strategies to the client modality producing the most distress (Rachman, 1980).

When cognitive therapy is employed, *Feeling Good* frequently serves as a valuable adjunct to ongoing therapy. The book is written in a very readable style and helps to bridge in-session work to clients' everyday life. Extensive clinical material is generated from client reactions to the reading, the completion of (or failure to complete) activities recommended in the book, and pertinent issues contained in the topical chapters (for example, anger or self-esteem).

Other adjunctive strategies are easily incorporated into treatment with cognitive therapy. Social skills training, marital or family therapy, clinical hypnosis, group psychotherapy, and other treatment approaches can effectively supplement cognitive therapy. A strength of cognitive therapy lies in its structure, which encourages a comprehensive treatment package; practitioners can remain mindful of potentially beneficial points of departure and supplementary work.

Cases such as Jim's, in which long-standing depression patterns are counteracted, provide therapists with some of the most tangible and heartening products of their efforts. Cognitive therapy has significantly enhanced the therapeutic repertoire available to combat depression. It is nice to remember that this translates into enhanced lives for thousands.

### References

Beck, A. T. (1976). *Cognitive therapy and the emotional disorders.* New York: International University Press.

Beck, A. T. (1978). *Depression inventory.* Philadelphia: Center for Cognitive Therapy.

Beck, A. T., Rush, A. J., Shaw, B. F., & Emery, G. (1979). *Cognitive therapy of depression.* New York: Guilford Press.

Burns, D. (1980). *Feeling good: The new mood therapy.* New York: Morrow.

Covi, L., Roth, D., & Lipman, R. S. (1982). Cognitive group therapy of depression: The close-ended group. *American Journal of Psychotherapy, 36,* 459–469.

Hollon, S. D., & Beck, A. T. (1979). Cognitive therapy of depression. In P. C. Kendall & S. D. Hollon (Eds.), *Cognitive-behavioral interventions: Theory, research, and procedures.* New York: Academic Press.

Hollon, S. D., & Kendall, P. C. (1980). Cognitive self-statements in depression: Development of an Automatic Thoughts Questionnaire. *Cognitive Therapy and Research, 4,* 383–395.

Rachman, S. (1980). Emotional processing. *Behavior Research and Therapy, 18,* 51–60.

Rush, A. J. (1983). Cognitive therapy for depression. In M. R. Zales (Ed.), *Affective and schizophrenic disorders: New approaches to diagnosis and treatment.* New York: Brunner/ Mazel.

Safran, J. D., Vallis, T. M., Segal, Z. V., & Shaw, B. F. (1986). Assessment of core cognitive processes in cognitive therapy. *Cognitive Therapy and Research, 10,* 509–526.

*Brief treatment combining strategic techniques with hypnosis is illustrated in this case. It is presented within the framework of an Ericksonian approach to treatment.*

## Questions

1. What are the primary goals of the Ericksonian approach to treatment?
2. How does this approach to treatment view the client's symptoms?
3. What was the function of using hypnosis in this case?
4. How did the future projection exercise help this client?

## BRIEF TREATMENT OF ANXIETY

### Michael Liebman

This case study is based on an experiment in team-oriented brief psychotherapy. Our four-person team was given a client who had a severe anxiety problem. We had a maximum of six sessions to produce a "cure." The team had never worked together before. Each session was to be videotaped. The client was to complete a short anxiety scale prior to each session and at 3 months following the completion of the therapy. The results and the supporting videos and documentation would be presented at a conference in 4 months regardless of the outcome.

Therapy took place at the Milton H. Erickson Center for Hypnosis and Psychotherapy in Phoenix, Arizona. The center had recently opened, and the staff was just beginning to work together for the first time. The center philosophy is based on brief, strategic psychotherapy using an Ericksonian perspective. There were two primary goals to the exercise. First, the clinical director wanted to force the concept of brief work. Many of the staff had not worked in a brief context prior to their association with the center. Second, the exer-

cise was to serve as a team-building experience. The staff members were divided into therapy teams, and each team was given a client referred for treatment of severe anxiety. The following is an account of one team's experience.

Jay is a 43-year-old man who recently moved to Phoenix from the Midwest with his wife of 8 years and his stepson. Jay has two children by his first marriage. He previously owned his own business but was never able to make a success of it. In recent years, he earned a marginal living as a salesman. He tried several sales jobs since moving to Phoenix, but he is unhappy with his work and uncomfortable in a large city. Jay makes a very pleasant presentation: he is tall with a slim build, is well-groomed, and has good social skills. He is above average in intelligence.

Jay's presenting problem is severe bouts of social anxiety, primarily in situations where he is "in the spotlight." These anxiety episodes are most acute in his work setting, primarily when he calls on new clients. He stated that he becomes obsessed with thoughts about bad things that people might think about him. He blames this anxiety for his limited success as a salesman. He is concerned that his wife is losing patience with his continued inability to earn an acceptable income. He received therapy before but found little relief.

Jay had developed quite a repertoire of strategies over the years in his attempt to cope with his anxiety. Self-medication with alcohol was his most frequently employed coping mechanism. He often stopped at bars before sales calls and imbibed until the anxiety was quelled. Unfortunately, many times Jay found himself still at a bar when he was supposed to be at a client's office. A second strategy he tried was pulling his car over to take a nap. Short naps turned into long ones. He also tried meditation but often fell asleep. At times, the anxiety developed into a heightened and persistent pattern. At these times, Jay crossdressed. Sometimes his wife would find him relaxing comfortably at home in her attire. She would complain that this was disgusting and threaten to leave.

Jay believed that his problems were caused by hypercritical parents. They were socially conscious and often publicly condemned Jay's behavior and dress. His father was a "self-made man" and a major executive with a large corporation in a "factory town." Jay remembers his father as tough and demanding, kind of a "bully." He remembers his mother as passive and critical.

Treatment began with a primary therapist working with Jay; the remainder of the team observed behind the mirror. During the first session the therapist made many references to the team treatment approach, attributing power and mystery to the team. The team called in on a phone that connected the team behind the mirror with the primary therapist. Each team member had the opportunity to ask questions and direct treatment. This served to reinforce the team's presence in the therapy.

Our approach was based on Ericksonian therapy, which led us to focus on three primary goals: interrupting the pattern of behavior, changing the perception of the problem, and eliciting the resources, strengths, and solutions from within the client. These primary goals form what many people refer to as solution-oriented therapy. Indeed, Milton Erickson was never very fond of a pathological approach to treatment. His orientation to therapy is known to be *solution* oriented as opposed to problem oriented.

Traditional psychotherapy has as its focus the elimination of difficulties, whether they are behaviors, thoughts, or past difficulties. There is an underlying pathology that needs to be addressed in therapy. Erickson's approach views symptoms as patterns that are difficult to change because they serve a function for the person, albeit at an unfortunate cost. This constructional approach focuses on constructing new patterns that produce more desirable outcomes for the person. Symptoms are accepted at face value and, rather than eliminated, are worked into part of the solution. Erickson did not focus on eliminating people's patterns; instead he helped people develop the resources to change those patterns. He was a master at observing and using the strengths within people and constructing new, more functional patterns of behavior.

The focus on outcomes begins with the therapist's attempt to get the client to describe how things would be different if therapy were successful. In the case of Jay, he was asked, "How will you know when therapy is over and successful?" His response was, "When the thought of presenting myself to a potential client I don't know doesn't provoke a thought in me about what he'll think of me." Once the goal of therapy is clarified, the focus shifts to constructing solutions.

At the end of the initial session, Jay was given a homework assignment. It was employed to assess compliance and gain more exacting information regarding the nature of his anxiety. The homework assignment asked Jay to focus on aspects of his client during his anxious periods. He was to observe, in careful detail, behaviors of the client, interpret his observations, record his experience, and bring the notes to the center a day before his next appointment. This directive required Jay, who was concerned about his inward anxiety, to focus outwardly. It was designed to change his experience in the interview and to interrupt his familiar pattern. Such an experience could give Jay a feeling of control; he could begin to do things differently. We also thought that this was something Jay could accomplish, and we wanted to gain his compliance early on in the therapy. The design was to get him involved in the therapy, bind him to the treatment, and increase his expectation that change could happen. We sent him on his way, and the team sat down to discuss what our next steps might be.

When Jay returned, he reported that he had complied with the homework assignment. He complained that he was not sure what the homework was about or whether or not it was helpful. As work with Jay continued, it became evident that he resisted positive interpretations by the team. The team maintained an indirect approach to the therapy. Indirect strategies such as suggestions, reframing, metaphors, and task assignments were used throughout the six sessions with Jay. For example, the nonspecific interpretation "The team is very impressed with the small but significant changes *you* have begun to make" was offered at one point. Jay appeared confused and offered a vague statement consistent with the feedback. His statement, as vague as it was, served as a springboard. The team supported and amplified his comment that change was occurring. There was a constant reminder to Jay that he was effecting the change. The team wanted Jay to internalize his own changes and sense of control.

During the second session, the primary therapist introduced the idea of hypnosis to Jay. He immediately became anxious. He talked about not wanting to do hypnosis, at least not now. He was not sure he could be hypnotized. He felt he was doing fine with the therapy as it was. Two team members from behind the one-way mirror entered the therapy room and introduced themselves. We talked to Jay about the nature of his anxiety. We explained to him that trance was a common experience and that his anxiety was framed as a "negative trance state" with emotionally debilitating consequences. Jay was told that he could learn more about hypnosis and learn to exercise more control over his trance states. Jay agreed to try, and the therapist initiated an induction using direct suggestions with increasingly indirect and metaphorical content. The focus of the hypnosis was on the process of change: feeling more comfortable with himself, developing his own resources, learning to let go of things, making changes, and allowing things to happen.

The use of hypnosis at this juncture was designed to help Jay mobilize his inner resources. A hypnotic trance is a unique state—one of heightened awareness in which feeling states are intensified and past events are more vivid. Often people are able to gain new perspectives on problems and new understandings about potential solutions. Jay responded favorably to the hypnosis. He asked many questions after he reoriented from the trance. Jay was told to pay more attention to his trance states during the week.

When Jay came for the third session, it was apparent that something was different. He appeared enthusiastic and reported that he had experienced a good week. The team decided to strategically restrain his progress. Jay was told that although the team was pleased with his changes and improved mood, there was concern that he might be moving too quickly. He responded with confusion and indignation. He assured us that he was doing just fine and that he could handle doing well. The team agreed but suggested that the pace of his progress would remain a concern.

During hypnosis in session three, themes from the previous trance work were reinforced. In addition, age regression was elicited to address childhood issues. Jay responded very well. He recalled an event at "Greezy Creek" when he was a young boy learning to ride a bicycle. Jay's father was very critical of him. In spite of his father's abuse, Jay was able to stand up to him by learning to ride that bike. This event seemed to hold a deep meaning for Jay. He became excited and wanted to talk about it at great length. At the close of the session, we gave Jay an "ambiguous function assignment." We told him to climb Squaw Peak, a local mountain and popular hiking attraction in Phoenix. This was one of Dr. Erickson's favorite homework assignments. The team suggested that Jay would notice certain things about himself and about other people. He was instructed to go slowly but steadily up the peak and to make a mental record of things he noticed. He could tell the team about his experience in the next session. He asked for more information, but the team declined while encouraging his compliance with the task.

This homework allowed Jay to consider, in great detail, the extent to which he really wanted to solve his anxiety problem. By allowing him time to reflect in a prescribed directive, Jay was encouraged to delve into his own resources and develop greater determination than had ever existed before in working on his own goals in treatment.

Of course, all of our strategic interventions involved ritual, that is, action—doing things outside the context of the therapy. The nature of the ritual, especially the Squaw Peak experience, helped change the nature of Jay's anxiety. Consider his symptoms—nervousness, tension, fear, negative self-evaluations—and the experience of the Squaw Peak ritual—a calm, relaxed, and self-reflective hike. This experience helped him capitalize on his own resources, recognizing that he can be calm, relaxed, and positive in self-evaluation—he can change. In this respect it can also be considered to have some metaphorical qualities. Follow a different path; do some things differently in your life. We believe the homework was meaningful to him because it included a lot of ambiguity or confusion. This meant he had to find the meaning behind the experience, but when he did, it had an important influence on him.

Furthermore, these experiences interrupted his pattern. It was a different experience, and it served to "break up" his previous problem-solving efforts. It allowed him to initiate a new behavior and to choose his own direction in life. At the same time, he was being encouraged to change within the context of the therapy. It was a good intervention in that it allowed him to follow the general course of therapy and also to achieve some autonomy in making his own decisions. It allowed Jay to solve the problems he brought to the therapy.

Jay reported to the fourth session again in a positive mood. He told us that he had quit his current sales job. He decided to sell products with which he was more familiar. He and his wife went out several times during the week, something they had not done in some time. They had several conflicts, and Jay stood up for himself. His wife, Marsha, said that he reminded her of the man with whom she fell in love and married.

The team congratulated Jay, telling him that he had done even more than expected, but the team again strategically restrained the change process. Jay was told that several of the team members were now persuaded that he could handle these new changes. One team member, however, was concerned that he was moving too quickly and that a relapse might occur. This was a delicate intervention. Given Jay's propensity for attributing power to others' opinions of him, the team had wanted to be careful. Dividing therapeutic sentiment allowed the team to simultaneously reinforce Jay's progress while paradoxically urging ratification of his gains. In order to reject the equivocal evaluation of him, Jay was forced to solidify the more functional behaviors he developed. The team fostered a context in which Jay could prove its opinion wrong only by taking more positive steps.

The team concluded that we had achieved the brief therapy goals at this juncture in the treatment. The goal now was to "nail in" the changes. Jay was asked to keep a daily journal of his new thoughts, feelings, and behaviors and to drop the journal off 2 days before his next session. In this way, the team would be able to review what he did prior to meeting with him. He complied.

In session five, the initial interactions were more relaxed and conversational. This was encouraged to allow Jay to change his position in therapy from a "one-down" position to a more equal position. Jay seemed to enjoy more personal and supportive contact with the therapist. In the second half of the session, the team called in on the phone to suggest a future projection exercise. Jay was asked to leave the therapy suite and reenter as if it were 6 months later. An interview was conducted, looking back over the elapsed time. Discussion centered on the changes he had made and how they persisted. Other life goals he wanted to achieve were enumerated. This strategy was designed to make the changes cognitively concrete and suggestible. The focus was now on future attainment—how to make the future different.

At the conclusion of the session, we told Jay that the team had devised a homework assignment for him. He became excited. Ap-

parently, he had come to value the tasks the team had assigned him. Unexpectedly, the team asked Jay to develop his own homework assignment, something personally meaningful. He was requested to complete the assignment and was told that the team looked forward to discovering what he did.

In the sixth and last session, Jay reported a good week. He was interviewing for several jobs with kitchen cabinet companies, the business he had owned in the Midwest. He and his wife were continuing to do well. The team entered the therapy suite and told Jay that we had enjoyed working with him. We concluded the therapy.

The experiment was a success. The team was able to develop an effective context for brief, solution-oriented psychotherapy. Part of our experiment was to assess the effectiveness of the treatment, so we conducted a single-subject evaluation. These designs are suited to an integration of research and practice. They allow for evaluation of a client's progress over time through the use of repeated measures by using the client as his/her own control. We chose The Clinical Anxiety Scale (Thyer, 1987) as our primary measure. As a secondary measure we administered a self-esteem scale, the Index of Self Esteem (Hudson, 1982).

Figure 1 presents the data for Jay, showing the results of the Clinical Anxiety Scale and the Generalized Contentment Scale. The Clinical Anxiety Scale shows that Jay's anxiety was significantly reduced over the course of the therapy. He began therapy with an initial anxiety score of 72. The value obtained at his last session was a score of 31. This would appear to be a significant therapeutic gain. The Generalized Contentment Scale also shows improvement over the course of the six sessions. Reducing anxiety probably led to a concomitant improvement in self-esteem (a lower score indicated improvement in esteem). A 3-month follow-up measure indicated that the gains Jay

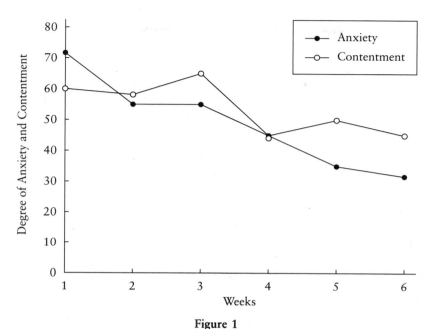

**Figure 1**

Degree of anxiety and contentment during 6 weeks of treatment

had accomplished in the six-session program were holding. In summary, the outcome data suggest that therapy was effective in significantly reducing the degree of anxiety Jay experienced.

The team was able to apply Ericksonian principles in both the hypnotic and the non-hypnotic aspects of the therapy. The brief focus forced the team and the client to attend to the change process and to use resources efficiently. The team believed that its focus on the therapy process rather than the support and rapport function was instrumental in the success of the work.

### References

Hudson, W. W. (1982). *The clinical measurement package.* Homewood, IL: The Dorsey Press.

Thyer, B. (1987). *Treating anxiety disorders: A guide for human service professionals.* Beverly Hills, CA: Sage.

# CASE STUDY 4.3

*Although treatment with this client is conducted individually, many aspects of the treatment reflect a family systems approach. In this case the powerful symptoms of binging and purging are redefined as behaviors that the client can control and eliminate as a method of responding to familial problems.*

## Questions

1. What is the purpose of ritualistic task assignment in this case?

2. What is the value of redefining a symptom as a voluntary behavior that the client can choose to control rather than accepting the client's perception that the problem behavior is an involuntary behavior?

3. Why is it so important for the client to keep the task a secret between the client and the practitioner?

4. How did the individual treatment in this case affect the marital and family systems?

## THE WIN-WIN BIND

### Richard G. Whiteside*

"Janice," a stylishly dressed 28-year-old, made a good living as a clothing designer at a trendy shop in Washington, D.C. Although she presented herself as vivacious and outgoing, inwardly she felt helplessly enslaved to her 7-year-old pattern of compulsive eating of junk food, followed by ritualistic vomiting. These bulimic episodes took place an average of 10 times a week.

Janice was married to "Jim," a construction worker with an erratic income who drank heavily and abused drugs, particularly cocaine. Ever since their marriage a year earlier, Janice and her husband had lived in a wing of Jim's parents' house. Janice was eager to move out, but even though Jim promised that they would soon begin to look for a place of their

own, he never took any steps to make that possible. Instead, he grew more and more involved in the difficult relationship between his ailing father and unhappy mother.

Janice had previously been in family therapy along with her husband and her family. The therapy succeeded in enabling her to give up her bulimia, but she relapsed 3 months after termination. At the time I became involved with the case, her husband, Jim, refused to continue in therapy, maintaining that Janice's bulimia was now her problem to solve.

I agreed to see Janice alone. In my initial assessment, I was struck by her strong sense of responsibility for her divorced mother and three younger sisters, who all complained constantly to her about their problems. Janice's efforts to offer suggestions and help, however, were invariably unsuccessful, and she usually wound up being criticized for her efforts and

* Reprinted from the *Family Therapy Networker,* September–October, 1986. Reprinted by permission of the author.

feeling like a failure. For example, once after a shopping trip with one of her sisters, Janice was devastated when her sister took back the dress she had bought and blamed Janice for persuading her to make a bad selection. Similarly, Janice would be distraught after long-distance phone calls with her mother that left her feeling that she hadn't been helpful enough.

Janice's position in her family would change dramatically, however, when the focus shifted to her binging and vomiting. Instead of expecting something from Janice, everyone would offer support and forget their own problems and come to her aid. Thus her bulimia became a powerful tool enabling Janice to elicit support from her family and at the same time helping her family put aside their own difficulties. As might be expected, when she stopped being bulimic, Janice once again felt the burden of listening to her family's complaints and trying to offer assistance. I hypothesized that Janice's bulimia helped her family, whereas her not being bulimic immobilized them. So why not switch the pattern?

I began by explaining to Janice that she needed to take a week to decide whether or not she really wanted to solve her problem. Her determination would be important as she would need to carry out a very precise and demanding plan. The next week she agreed, and the following directions were given:

1. The plan was something only she and I would know about. It had to remain secret from her family.
2. Each time Janice binged, she had to call each family member and offer to help them. If they declined, she must insist. She had to do whatever they demanded, with no demand being too great.
3. She was to wear the same ritualistic clothes in calling her family as she did while vomiting.
4. She had to keep a record of the amount of time it took to shop, binge, and vomit. She was then to spend double that amount of time helping her family members.

This series of directives had a number of goals. The directives were to mirror Janice's symptom as much as possible, down to having her wear the same clothes when she called her family as when she vomited. The directives were also designed to redefine the problem behaviors Janice regarded as involuntary—her bulimia and her need to help her family—and turn them into things she could consciously choose to do. Further, by instructing her to keep elaborate records, the directives required her to focus more and more of her attention to her behavior. As Milton Erickson demonstrated in many cases, the more you are directed to pay attention to a preoccupation, the more difficult it becomes to maintain it.

Of course, the directives also made it more difficult for Janice to binge and vomit. But even if she did, the consequences would force her to intensify her relationship with her family in a way that was likely to lead to spontaneous change. Either Janice would eventually get fed up with her continuing servitude to her relatives, or they would begin to feel odd about accepting her unsolicited offers of help. And even if they didn't, Janice would be offering useful service to her family under her own direction rather than theirs. Essentially Janice was placed in a win-win bind. Either she would just give up her presenting symptom or she would act in ways that would make it more and more difficult for her to continue in a pattern of family relationships that she said she wanted to change.

In the first week, Janice spent 6 hours shopping, binging, and vomiting and thereby committed herself to 12 hours of service to her family. Nevertheless, she only gave them half that time, saying that she couldn't think of other ways to help. I challenged her by asking if she was serious about giving up her bulimia and presented her with a list of things that she could do. I told her she could call her mother and get her to air all of her complaints, or she could take her lonely sister to a dance and introduce her to a man, or she could even brighten her most irritating sister's disposition by volunteering to clean her apartment. Janice said she got the idea.

She binged and vomited for 2 hours the following week and therefore owed her family 4 hours of service. Janice took her lonely sister for a walk and also started her most irritating sister's stalled car all by herself, refusing to let her sister call for automotive assistance. I remarked that surely her family needed more than 4 hours of her help and maybe they felt deprived. Janice laughed. She has not vomited now for 18 months.

In her relationship with her husband, Janice's bulimia served to protect him from having to face any of his problems. As long as she was preoccupied with her own difficulties, she was unable to demand anything from him. Once she was able to give up her bulimia, however, Janice was able to become much clearer about what she wanted for herself and firmer in dealing with Jim.

For some time Janice had wanted to move out of Jim's parents' home and into a place of their own, but Jim had always balked. Supporting Janice in her attempt to create a boundary between her husband's ties with his parents and her own relationship with him, I recommended that she set a date to move out and do it, with or without Jim. At the eleventh hour, Jim decided to leave with his wife.

Jim continued to refuse to attend any therapy sessions, although he expressed a willingness on the phone to stop using drugs. The focus at this point became working with Janice, helping her to help her husband beat his drug habit. I instructed her to take charge of the family finances and the credit and money cards, cutting off her husband's access to funds to support his habit until he became drug free. Once Jim saw that Janice was serious and that unless he shaped up she would leave him, his drug abuse and drinking stopped. Eventually, Janice was even able to persuade Jim, who had taken sole responsibility for helping his parents during his father's illness, to get his brother involved. This was something Jim had stubbornly refused to do up until that point.

A follow-up 18 months later revealed that Janice was pregnant and had had no recurrence of bulimia. Jim was working full-time as a construction worker. I also learned that, without professional assistance, Janice and Jim had been able to handle a crisis a year earlier. Following the death of his father, Jim had begun to drink heavily and together with Janice had moved back home to be with his mother. After some months of watching Jim's functioning decline, Janice realized that they were returning to an old, destructive pattern. As she had earlier, she decided to move out and set a date to move again to a place of their own. They did. Janice indicated that she and Jim still struggle at times, but she believes their marriage is now on a much firmer foundation.

# CASE STUDY 4.4

*The challenge of forensic evaluation presents the social worker with tasks uniquely different from other social work practice areas. In this case study a step-by-step process and rationale for social work forensic evaluation is presented.*

## Questions

1. What is the role of the social worker on the forensic evaluation team, and how does this differ from other social work roles?
2. What is the social worker's goal in forensic evaluations?
3. Why is a mental status evaluation conducted, and how does this evaluation provide useful information for the forensic evaluator?
4. How does the social worker use the information obtained in the forensic evaluation to reach conclusions and form recommendations about the defendant?

## FORENSIC SOCIAL WORK: A CASE OF INFIDELITY, INTOXICATION, AND HOMICIDE

*José B. Ashford and Larry Whirl*

Mr. Jonathan Armstrong was referred to a community-based Forensic Psychiatric Center in Toledo, Ohio, by Judge William Potts from the Lucas County Court of Common Pleas under the provisions of the Ohio Revised Code Section 2945.40 (Not Guilty by Reason of Insanity). Mr. Armstrong was in pretrial status on two counts of aggravated murder. Judge Potts indicated on the center's referral form that Mr. Armstrong did not have a history of assaultive behavior and that the court was ordering the forensic center to address the following questions: (1) Was Mr. Armstrong in full possession of his mental capacity at the time of the offense? (2) Did he understand what he was doing at the time of the offense and the seriousness of his actions? (3) To what extent did alcohol contribute to Mr. Armstrong's commission of these offenses?

The judge's clerk made additional comments on the agency's referral form. She pointed out in the section on the referral form that asked for additional comments that the police indicated in their report that Mr. Armstrong had been drinking heavily prior to the instant offenses. Besides these additional comments, the judge's clerk enclosed copies of the police report, the indictment, and an official report of the defendant's arrest history.

Because this court-ordered evaluation involves one of the most difficult questions for a forensic evaluator to assess, I knew that I would have to gather as much information as possible about the circumstances surrounding the defendant's alleged offenses before beginning my initial interview with him. In particular, I needed to review the police report and any official statements made by the defendant in order to question him about factors that might have a bearing on his mental state at the time of the offense. As a member of the forensic psychiatric team, my task as the social worker is to perform the initial interview with the client, do collateral interviews with relevant witnesses or family members, obtain pertinent releases of information, and render an opinion regarding the defendant's mental state at the time of the offense.

In order to accomplish the prior tasks, I had to read the police report carefully in order to follow up on any discrepancies in reported facts between the perceptions of the defendant and those of the police officers. This is not to say that the defendant is always the incorrect party, but in many instances gross discrepancies in the facts can give a clue as to whether the defendant is malingering. It also can provide useful information in assessing the defendant's present mental state. That is, information from the police report can be very helpful in assessing whether a defendant is confabulating because of a mental disorder or a mental deficiency such as Wernicke's Korsakoff's psychosis.

After preparing for the evaluation, I interviewed Mr. Armstrong at the Lucas County jail on November 27, 1989. The evaluation commenced at 9:00 A.M. and terminated at 10:50 A.M. Mr. Armstrong was cooperative throughout the evaluation. He entered the interview room willingly but appeared anxious throughout the interview process. In fact, he remarked at the beginning of the interview that he was feeling "extremely nervous" and that this was something that he had always had problems with. Before I began his formal evaluation, I discussed the issue of confidentiality or the lack thereof. I also explained to him the nature and the purpose of the evaluation. After I completed these tasks, he informed me that he understood this and agreed to participate in the evaluation given these constraints. He also told me that he understood that he was being evaluated to determine his mental condition at the time that he is alleged to have killed his wife and her lover. After verbally discussing these issues with him, he signed a written statement that warned him of the lack of confidentiality during the evaluation and of his right to refrain from making any statements that he thought might hurt his chances in court. In essence, I did not begin the interview until the client had signed an admonition against the lack of confidentiality and the defendant conveyed in his own words its significance.

Mr. Armstrong is a 50-year-old, widowed, white man who is of average build, has a relatively pale complexion, and appears approximately his stated age. At the time of the interview, he was unshaven but neatly dressed in green jailhouse coveralls that had long underwear protruding through his sleeves. Because he appeared nervous, I realized that I might need to take longer than usual in trying to build rapport with him before I would begin to test the credibility of his statements surrounding his involvement in the two murders. With this end in mind, I decided to approach more neutral issues before discussing the specifics of his crimes. I have learned over the years that gathering neutral information on a person's background is helpful in getting a baseline on the defendant's functioning before approaching the more sensitive topics surrounding the issue of criminal responsibility. That is, I use a review of the defendant's social history to establish rapport to obtain data relevant to the legal concerns in the evaluation and assess the potential for alternative motives or explanations. In performing these tasks, I have found that I always have to remind myself that my role as a forensic social worker is more that of an investigator than that of a traditional clinical social worker.

As you will see in this review of the defendant's history, I am trying to obtain from Mr. Armstrong any information that may have a bearing on our opinions regarding his mental state at the time of the offense. I recorded the following social history:

Mr. Armstrong was born in Bay St. Louis, Mississippi, to Thomas Armstrong and Ann McDonald. He was raised in an intact family with one brother and one sister. He was the youngest member of his family. His family moved to Toledo when the defendant was 11 years of age. He described his mother as a nice woman who is often aloof. When asked to clarify this description, he stated that "if I would tell her I loved her, she would say okay. If I would try to show her affection by trying to hug her, she would generally pull back." He went on to say that he found this behavior quite troubling.

Mr. Armstrong described his father as basically being a nice guy but went on to say that his father was prone to having emotional outbursts. These outbursts involved the father yelling and screaming at members of the family. Mr. Armstrong's mother died 4 years ago from a heart condition. His father, who is 85 years of age, still resides in Toledo. The defendant informed me that he currently has a very good relationship with his father.

Mr. Armstrong attended school up until the 10th grade. He said that he quit school to take a job and help out with the family's finances. He reported that while in school he did not have any significant problems. He denied temper tantrums, cruelty to animals, fire setting, and school fighting. He also denied the use of a transitional object, thumb sucking, and nail biting. He reported having infrequent nightmares and being enuretic up until the age of 6 or 7.

At 15 years of age, Mr. Armstrong began working for a house painter and doing other odd jobs. However, he maintains that he was unable to land a good paying job that had any degree of permanency. When the Korean Conflict broke out, he enlisted in the United States Army. He was in the army for only one year because he was discharged for a medical condition. He received a medical discharge for "trench foot" and has a medical disability of 30% from the service because of this condition. After being dis-

charged from the military, Mr. Armstrong returned to Toledo and moved from factory job to factory job. In 1963, he hurt his back while he was employed at Jeep and eventually had to leave and go on permanent disability. The defendant has not worked since 1965 and has been on disability since 1966.

The client married in 1956, and three children were born as a result of that union. He had two daughters and one son in this marriage. He and his first wife divorced in January of 1969. He said that she divorced him primarily because he began drinking heavily following his back injury. He reported that before marrying his second wife, he lived with one other woman for a little over a year but left her because of her infidelity. He also stopped dating another woman that he had a real interest in when he found out that she was seeing other men. The worker questioned him about how he felt about what happened in both of these relationships. His answer was precisely the same as he gives in relation to his recent wife's behavior: "It hurt me."

As far as his alcohol and drug history are concerned, he stated that he believes that he began to drink around the time that he was discharged from the army. He stated that he drank quite a bit at times but generally limited his drinking to weekends when he was off from work. He also pointed out that his alcohol usage never interfered with his employment record. Furthermore, he insisted that he never drank to excess and has always been a very moderate drinker. He claimed that the most he drank was probably a case of beer in slightly less than 2 weeks. He also added that there were times when he would drink six or seven beers a day on each day of the weekend but would then not have any beer for a week. He claimed that he quit drinking about 5 or 6 months before he met his second wife. This was because drinking interfered with the control of his diabetes. In 1988, he was found to have late-onset diabetes.

As far as drugs are concerned, he denied the use of street drugs but said that he has taken a good deal of Valium. He was taking Valium before and after his hospitalization in early 1989. In September 1989, he went to the hospital because he was having dizzy spells, as well as to get treatment for his high blood sugar. When the doctors evaluated him, they discovered that he had severe coronary artery disease and that it was probably providing some interference with his circulation to his brain. He was operated on in late September, during which grafts on both the anterior and posterior coronary arteries were done. Before and after this operation, he maintained that he was taking Valium. He maintained that after being discharged from the hospital, he was taking 5 mg of Valium (a minor tranquilizer) and 100 mg of Darvon (a pain killer) three or four times a day. From Mr. Armstrong's description, it is very difficult to know exactly how much of this medication he was taking on the day of the alleged offenses. This is because at one point he said that his medicine was in his wife's possession, either in her purse or on top of the refrigerator. As you will see in later discussions about the circumstances surrounding the offenses, he stated that he couldn't remember the last time he had any pills on the date of the alleged offenses but thought it was 2 or 3 hours before he had the drink at his cousin's house. Because he had not been at his home since about 9:30 in the morning, this did not appear to be a reasonable assessment; that is, it was not reasonable, since it was estimated that he had the drink at 6:30 in the evening at his cousin's house. When this discrepancy was pointed out to him, he then remembered that he was carrying an old prescription bottle around with him with some of his pills. However, this bottle was not among the contents found in his possession when he was booked at the county jail.

After feeling that I had a fair picture of his history, I thought that it was time to perform a formal mental status examination (MSE). As a forensic social worker, I always perform a MSE on any offender that I am evaluating for the courts. I use the data from this evaluation of the defendant's mental functioning to assess the reliability and validity of his or her statements. The data also provide me with information that could be suggestive of the defen-

dant's mental state at the time of the offense. That is, it is suggestive of the defendant's past mental state, but it cannot be assumed that the defendant's mental state remained constant (Melton, Petrila, Poythress, & Slobogin, 1987). Whenever I find in the evaluation that a defendant is suffering from a mental disorder, I generally assess whether this disorder is interfering with his or her ability to be truthful. For example, a paranoid or suspicious individual is likely to deny many forms of inquiry simply out of fear. If such a situation presented itself in this evaluation, then the issue of Mr. Armstrong's competency to stand trial would supersede the issue of his sanity at the time of the offense. In essence, the mental status examination serves a number of key functions in a forensic evaluation.

I always perform a formal mental status evaluation on every client that I see in a forensic evaluation. In a formal mental status evaluation, my goal is to systematically test a wide range of the defendant's mental functions. In my review of Mr. Armstrong's history, I did not detect any major deficits in affect, thought content, thought process, or memory suggesting the presence of a mental disorder. My observations from this examination were as follows:

Mr. Armstrong appeared to be of average intelligence, and his answers to questions were logical, coherent, and relevant. His verbalizations were soft and generally at a slow rate. Emotionally he appeared to be mildly depressed. When he was asked how he felt, he stated that it is still very painful for him. The worker then asked him to be more specific, and he stated that it is something emotional—"he feels bad deep down inside to think that he could have done what he is accused of doing." However, he reported no physical signs of depression.

His recent and remote memory appeared intact. He was oriented to time, place, and person. His verbalizations and speech were at an average rate, and the client would present moderate amounts of data spontaneously. Mr. Armstrong denied hallucinations and delusions, and no evidence of either hallucinations or delusions were elicited during the evaluation process.

After completing the MSE, I thought that I had an appropriate baseline of the defendant's functioning and that I was ready to focus on the circumstances surrounding the offense. Although voluntary intoxication with alcohol or drugs may not ordinarily serve as a basis for an insanity defense, there are specific instances where forms of intoxication can be deemed a legitimate basis for an insanity defense. These instances are (1) involuntary intoxication, (2) delirium tremens, (3) pathological intoxication, and (4) permanent psychosis due to alcohol. Because pathological intoxication was a reasonable hypothesis in this case, I realized that I needed to obtain data that would either confirm or dispute whether or not he experienced an unusually severe reaction to a small quantity of alcohol. In addition, I needed to know whether he had prior knowledge of alcohol bringing out this type of reaction. Last, I needed to rule out whether he voluntarily took alcohol with his medications on the date of the alleged offenses. These questions addressed several preliminary hypotheses that I would have to rule out in my efforts to test the defendant's credibility. Mr. Armstrong's description of the events leading up to the current offenses were as follows:

After Mr. Armstrong's children left home, he sold his home and moved in with one of his favorite cousins who lived in Toledo. Shortly after he had moved in with his cousin, his wife (the victim) began coming over to visit his cousin on one pretext or another but apparently to see Mr. Armstrong. She lived across the street from his cousin. He believes that she began making these visits sometime in late July. After a couple of visits, she started bringing over meals that she cooked for him. She also would bring him "special treats" that she had purchased for

him at the store. Much to his surprise, she came over one day with a document that was her will. In this will, she left him all of her possessions. He stated that his initial reaction was that he wanted no part of this. He was troubled primarily because she had other relatives, and he was confused as to why she would leave her possessions to him. Mr. Armstrong maintains that she told him that she had made her will out to him because she had frequent difficulties with members of her family and did not want them to get anything that was hers.

He was also troubled by her will because she was living with a man whom he presumed was her husband. However, he later learned that he was her common-law husband (Bill) and that she was in the process of getting a divorce from him. After making her will out to Mr. Armstrong, she constantly tried to convince him to move in with her. The defendant states, however, that he took the position that he did not want to move in with her as long as her husband was still living with her. Approximately 2 weeks after the victim proposed to Mr. Armstrong, she got her husband (Bill, the other victim) to move out. Within 3 weeks, the defendant moved in with Ms. Johnson. After they moved in together, they decided to remodel her home since she had the house put in both of their names. In order to accomplish this task, they borrowed $6,500 to fix up the house. The defendant states that after they borrowed the money he would work long hours each day making repairs around the home. While this was going on, Ms. Johnson (the victim) would receive daily visits from her former husband, Bill. When Mr. Armstrong confronted her about his frequent visits, she responded by saying that he was only coming over to check on whether he had received any mail.

In late August, Mr. Armstrong claims that he began experiencing dizzy spells and blackouts and attributed these difficulties to his diabetic condition. At this point he decided to go to the hospital for a checkup. After some tests, his doctor decided to admit him to the hospital because he had a major problem in the circulation of his blood to his heart. In addition, they informed him that he needed immediate surgery but did allow him to go home on furlough while they scheduled a room to do his surgery. While on furlough, Ms. Johnson insisted that they go and get a marriage license. When they went to get the license he learned that she had been divorced three times. However, she had told him that she had only married Bill, her common-law husband. When he confronted her about this, her reply was that it was just a minor error. About this time, Ms. Johnson started disappearing for most of the day and sometimes at night. On one particular day, she said that she was going to the dentist, and when she didn't return after a considerable length of time, Mr. Armstrong said that he was concerned about what might have happened to her and called the dentist's office. However, they informed him that she had not been in for a visit. After learning this, he went out looking for her and found her at Bill's apartment. He said that this made him think twice about marrying her, but when he confronted her about being with her ex-husband, she said that she was there because they were debating whether her ex-husband should be able to count her as a dependent for the previous year. Mr. Armstrong returned to the hospital on September 27. On September 28, Ms. Johnson came to the hospital with a marriage license, and they were married in the hospital chapel.

When he got out of the hospital on October 9th, he learned that his new wife had spent all of their money, and she changed completely toward him. In fact, on the way home she informed him that she did not want to have sex with him any longer. After returning home from the hospital, Ms. Armstrong refused to cook breakfast and dinner for him. She also demanded that he begin cooking for himself and doing more work around the house. In the defendant's own words, he stated that "she changed completely toward me, and this made me become extremely nervous." In fact, he stated that he ran out of his prescription for pain pills about a week early because he began taking more and more medication to feel better. In addition, he reported that he began taking Valium (5 mg) three or four times a day that had been prescribed for his wife. He stated that his wife

had just about any type of medication around the house. He also reported that he felt miserable the day before the instant offenses and that he took several types of medication to feel better. In particular, he recalled taking Valium and some of his own prescription for Darvon. On the day before the instant offenses, Ms. Armstrong received a call from her ex-husband. She talked to him and then got dressed, got their lunch ready, and left. She said that she was going to the doctor's and Mr. Armstrong asked to ride along with her. She began yelling at him and told him that she could not bring him along with her because she had to run several other errands after the visit.

Mr. Armstrong reported that his wife once again did not return home at what seemed to be a realistic time, and he once again checked up and found out that she had never made her appointment and was again at Bill's apartment. He said that "both times that I found her there it felt like my heart would burst right out of my chest." When he went to Bill's apartment and knocked on the door, Bill came to the door and let him inside. He said that he confronted his wife with the fact that she had told him she would never go back to Bill's place without him. He said that he told her at that point that he was going to get a divorce. Mr. Armstrong maintains that he then left Bill's apartment and went home and slept in another bedroom that night and called to make an appointment to discuss this matter with his minister.

The next morning the defendant went to see his minister. When he returned from his meeting with his minister, he took some of his belongings out to his car. At that point, his wife indicated that she wanted him out of the house. He told her that he would move out and informed her that he would spend the night at his cousin's place across the street. After he left the house at about 9:30 A.M., he went to visit his father to discuss his circumstance. He says that he left his father's place at about 1:30 in the afternoon and then stopped in to see his attorney. He then returned to his home to get some of his things and ran into his wife. They got into an argument, and she said that she was going to get her step-brother to come and change the locks on the house. He was asked if he took any medication when he returned, but he stated that he did not get a chance to get anything because his wife was so angry. He was asked where he kept his medication, and he replied that it was either on top of the refrigerator or in her purse. When he left the house, he said that he got in his car and drove around for a while and then went to see his cousin around 6:30 P.M. When he got to his cousin's home, his cousin was "pretty much loaded." He pointed out that his cousin was a relatively heavy drinker. When he arrived there were two or three bottles of scotch on the table. He told his cousin about his problems with his wife and said that she had threatened to have him beat up if he ever tried to return to her home. At that point, he said his cousin went into his bedroom and brought out a gun, put it down on the table, and said "No one will beat you up if you try to get into your own home with this." Mr. Armstrong reports that he initially did not take a drink with his cousin, but his cousin kept pushing him to have a drink with him. He also pointed out that the last thing that he had had in his stomach was a cup of coffee that he had with his minister. Finally he gave in and drank a splash of scotch with water. He said when he drank the scotch, all of a sudden he felt completely different. He felt as though he were floating; he felt very happy; he felt as though he were free. He remembered laughing; then he got so that he couldn't feel his body; he remembers pinching himself and laughing because he couldn't feel it. He took another drink diluted with water and then took another shot straight. When asked the last time he had taken any medication, he stated that he had taken Valium and Darvon approximately 2 hours before he had the drink. When he was confronted, however, he stated that he really couldn't remember. He said that he thought his cousin left and went to sleep sometime around when Mr. Armstrong took the shot of straight scotch. The next thing he remembered was falling through the door of the home in which he and his wife had been living. He thought maybe he pushed the door down with his shoulder but had no clear recollection of doing so. He also remembered seeing a light in the living room and starting toward it and then seeing a light going on very quickly in the bedroom. He then started for the bedroom. Then he recalled Bill getting out of the bed naked and shouting at him. He also remembered Bill making threatening gestures at him, and the next thing he knew there was a loud explosion. He said he did not see a flash; he just heard a noise, but he didn't know where it came from. He only remembered one such explosion and then remembered being in his car, but he is not quite sure where this was. He then reported that he recalled standing in front of the police station looking at it, knowing that something was wrong and that he had to tell the police about something. He doesn't remember going into the police station, but he remembers talking to the police about something. Things then went blank. The next thing he said that he remembered was going from the jail to the court house. He said, however, that his memory was blurred from here on and was not very clear. He also stated that he remembered having Dr. Stevens, a doctor, come in to see him at the jail. He cannot remember, however, the date that this took place. At this point, the client was very emotional and constantly was fighting back his tears. He said that he was not clear about when he went into the medical unit at the jail and remained confused for several days on that unit. He also pointed out that he really did not become oriented until sometime around the third day that he was on the unit. When challenged about what he meant by the term *oriented,* he responded by saying that he really did not realize where he was until the third day.

Because Mr. Armstrong was suggesting that he experienced some selective amnesia for events surrounding the commission of these offenses, I realized that I had to be careful in rendering a clinical opinion. In particular, I did not want to overstep my expertise, since the issue of amnesia presented in this case involved intoxication, medication, and other health concerns. That is, I realized that I lacked the necessary expertise for making a valid distinction between "registration" amnesia due to drugs or alcohol and "recall" amnesia due to repression or blocking mechanisms (Melton et al., 1987). Because of these concerns, I requested Mr. Armstrong's permission to obtain the records from the medical staff at the jail.

On leaving the interview, I went immediately to the medical staff and waited until they released his records. From this material, I learned that the admitting notes on the medical unit made no mention of any confusion and indeed talked about his being quite pleasant and cooperative. The notes summarizing the mental status examination that the psychiatrist performed on Mr. Armstrong at the time of the admission indicated that he was oriented to person and place but was confused about the date. Notes in his medical record from nursing and medical staff suggested nothing that would indicate that he was confused during his stay on the unit. Besides obtaining releases from the jail, I obtained all the other necessary medical and military releases of information relevant to the case and requested that I have his permission to interview his cousin. Because I did not have relevant third-party information available when I formulated my report and conclusions, I had to make a tentative assessment regarding the issue of the defendant's criminal responsibility. My impressions were:

1. From what I can reconstruct in this evaluation from Mr. Armstrong's recall of the circumstances surrounding the offense, medical records at the jail, and other third-party accounts, Mr. Armstrong was, according to his own statement, emotionally overwrought 24 hours prior to the alleged offenses. However, there is nothing in what he told me to suggest that this amounted to a mental illness. In addition, he has not had a history of serious mental disorders and was rational throughout the evaluation process. He also did not present with any evidence of residual forms of schizophrenia or any other major form of mental disorder.

2. Mr. Armstrong's medical records indicated that he had a mild degree of impairment in the circulation to and through his head. Because I am not qualified to determine whether he had enough insufficiency in circulation of blood to his brain to account for his disturbed behavior, I must defer this issue to the psychiatrist and await the results of the psychological testing. However, there was nothing in his present mental status examination that indicated any gross cognitive impairment or memory deficits.

3. From what I can reconstruct, it would appear as though the combination of alcohol and the lack of food for some 24 hours or more led to a lessening of inhibitions, which permitted this sort of behavior to emerge in an individual who prior to this had been a completely nonaggressive sort of person. I am unable to determine whether or not the medication he was taking contributed to this, since I do not know whether he was actually taking it. This is something that the other evaluators should devote some attention to trying to clarify. They also need to address whether or not Mr. Armstrong's reaction was an abnormal reaction or one that might be expected because of the combination of alcohol and minimal food. In other words, the results from my evaluation suggest that the other evaluators need to rule out whether Mr. Armstrong had a pathological or simple intoxication.

4. The reports from the prosecutor's office refer to the presence of videotapes. I do not know when these tapes were taken. If they were taken within several hours of the alleged offenses, they would be of great help in assisting the other evaluators on the team in determining exactly what Mr. Armstrong's mental status was at that moment. I would be particularly interested in knowing if his memory for the events was clear at that time. Certainly, if

it was, one can only conclude that the lack of memory at this time is probably not due to an alcohol-induced amnesia and not to a Valium-induced amnesia but to the repression of what must be very painful memories.

In sum, I thought that it would be premature for me to render an opinion as to whether or not the client had a condition that impaired his mental capacity to such an extent that he either did not know what he was doing was wrong or was incapable of refraining from the commission of these offenses. That is, I did not think that I had sufficient information to conclude with any degree of scientific certainty that the client did not experience a substance-induced amnesia or pathological intoxication. Furthermore, I thought that the relationship between these diagnoses and the legally relevant behavior of concern in this evaluation exceeded my own area of expertise as a forensic social worker, unlike other DSM-III-R diagnoses.

### Reference

Melton, G. B., Petrila, J., Poythress, N. G., & Slobogin, C. (1987). *Psychological evaluations for the courts: A handbook for mental health professionals and lawyers.* New York: Guilford Press.

# 5

# IN PREVENTING PROBLEMS AND DEVELOPING RESOURCEFULNESS

TRADITIONALLY, SOCIAL WORKERS HAVE waited until clients presented themselves for help, usually after their difficulties became quite serious. However, another option is for social workers to intervene at an earlier point in time and help clients learn the skills needed to cope with future difficulties. Indeed, preventive approaches to social work are needed in order to reach out to clients before problems become serious. This is what is meant by "primary prevention"—reducing the likelihood of new clients needing help in a population.

Because there are so many social problems and so many people needing help, it is important to have services that reach people quickly. Methods for preventing problems and developing resources can respond to this need. Krumboltz and Thoresen (1976) discuss several characteristics of such programs.

First, preventing problems and developing resourcefulness programs are designed to benefit people who have not specifically asked for help. Many people could benefit from social work services who have not specifically asked for help or cannot ask for help. For example, teaching parents positive parenting skills is likely to have long-range benefits for children although they have not asked for help. Other people may not be aware that they are "at risk" for developing mental health problems or becoming too stressed or that they are in need of some social service.

Second, such programs are designed to reach large numbers of people. Much of direct practice is directed toward individual casework, counseling, or case management. Programs for preventing problems and developing resourcefulness are designed to benefit groups of individuals such as families, classes, schools, and communities.

Third, such programs many have indirect effects. Because of the broad focus in these programs, their effects are often indirect and influence individuals other than those specifically targeted. For example, a program designed to provide support to caregivers would be expected to benefit both the caregivers and the individuals being cared for. Likewise, a stress management program should reduce stress for the participants but also have a positive impact on all those who come in contact with the less-stressed participants.

Fourth, many of these programs become self-perpetuating. Numerous preventive interventions are designed in such a way that once established they can continue. For example, in some prevention programs each new set of leaders will train the next set of leaders. The result is that the preventive intervention can have continued impact.

Social workers play a critical role in the development of preventive interventions. A focus on prevention is consistent with social work's purpose of alleviating distress and helping people realize their aspirations. Often it is up to the social worker to design a program that encompasses both treatment and prevention goals. As you read the case studies in this chapter, consider how the social workers intervened to prevent clients from needing additional help.

This section begins with Black's engrossing description of her work in a homeless shelter. Although this is not typically what would be considered a prevention program, it is nonetheless a program designed to develop resourcefulness among people who are often depleted and demoralized. Magen and Rose present a detailed description of how a stress management group is conducted. Stress management is a logical preventive intervention for addressing the complexities of postmodern life. Peak and Toseland's case study addresses the needs of caregivers of frail older persons. Caregivers are "at risk" because they often feel unprepared for their role, isolated in caregiving situations, and abandoned by friends and family members. This case study is an excellent example of group work that provides social support and improved coping skills in addressing stressful caregiving situations. Milne discusses the use of divorce mediation as a means to prevent further disruption among family members who are in the process of separating. Divorce mediation is a unique combination of law, social work, and counseling. The chapter by Mondros and McGuffin is an attempt to address a community-level problem—a city that was falling apart at the seams. It is an important contribution because the social work function is a clear example of community organizing.

## Reference

Krumboltz, J. D., & Thoresen, C. (1976). *Counseling methods.* New York: Holt, Rinehart and Winston.

*Emergency shelters for the homeless present a glaring example of the serious social problems that confront social workers. This poignant account of one worker's encounters during a typical week at one such shelter documents the multiple problems and challenging demands made on social work.*

## Questions

1. What unique difficulties confront homeless people in their day-to-day lives?
2. What were the primary tasks of the social worker at the shelter?
3. How can social workers design shelters to better meet the needs of homeless people?
4. What social policies can be developed to prevent homelessness or reduce the need for shelters?

## THE SHELTER: EVERY DAY IS A STRUGGLE TO KEEP THE FAITH

*Lascelles W. Black\**

### MONDAY

The morning light is gray and the wind blowing down the hill is cold, damp, and seems like the breath of the large brick building that dominates the skyline. It is not really the tallest structure in the neighborhood, but it is the most imposing, appearing in the winter half light like a cross between Castle Mordor and Darth Vader's winter home. It was built as an Armory, a war-like building, designed to be formidable, constructed to keep people out, not to welcome them like the large church diagonally across from it. Now it is a shelter, a place where more than 600 homeless men seek refuge.

New York City's Human Resources Administration runs the shelter; their staff provide case management and medical and job referrals. The shelter's client-staff turnover is

\* Reprinted from the *Family Therapy Networker,* November–December, 1987. Reprinted by permission of the author.

high, mainly because of burnout. Few people can face the anger and depression of the men for long.

I work for a Community Support Systems Program placed within the shelter and administered by a nearby hospital. We provide mental health counseling, family therapy, job counseling, referrals to alcohol and drug abuse programs, and occasionally assistance with carfare. But one of our most important services is the free phone we provide. It is a major help to people in the shelter who don't have the money for a phone call and has made the difference in many men getting and keeping a job, renewing severed family ties, and getting themselves placed in needed programs.

Inside, I climb to the third floor where I am greeted by five or six clients waiting for our program to open so that they can get a cup of coffee; the shelter does not provide coffee for the residents. I make a phone call to the clinic on the first floor (operated by another nearby hospital) to inform our program's female staff members who prudently wait there, that I, a male, have arrived. After making coffee, the staff—one psychiatrist, one administrator, two social workers, two case managers, and a secretary—begin seeing clients. I am a case manager here, and I work primarily with the "first timers," recent arrivals to the shelter. My job is to help them get out of the shelter before they are "shelterized," absorbed and lost within the shelter system.

Part of my caseload consists of clients who are "established" in the shelter system and have learned to survive here. One client is an artist, Hispanic, in his mid-30s. He speaks as little as possible to the staff or other clients. This man approached me on the main floor about 2 months ago and asked if we provide art materials in our program. I told him about our art class. Now he comes here daily and does his paintings of bowls of fruit and landscapes in the Impressionist style. His pictures radiate light and color and tell of memories far from this city.

Then there is the "caretaker," a client who believes he looks after us. He is a 30-year-old white man who has spent, by his estimation, more than 20 years in mental institutions. His experience has made him very good at assessing when other clients are suicidal or losing touch with reality. He likes to make coffee, clean the office, and do errands for staff, but he does not like to be thanked or told he is doing a good job. Another client I call the "sleeper," a black man in his early 20s, who spends most of the morning or the afternoon sleeping on the couch. He has politely declined offers of assistance but has promised to talk with us soon.

Although we were set up primarily as a mental health program, we are open to all clients with no appointment necessary. Because the circumstances that lead to homelessness and shelter life itself are very depressing, we see anyone who is depressed; the client does not have to be in crisis. Although the majority of the men in the shelter are from the neigh-

borhood, the shelter does not bring a family perspective to bear on their problems. But our program does when possible assist clients to maintain or reestablish family contact.

Today I have a new client. He was a sergeant in the Vietnam War and is still having trouble adjusting to peacetime and finding a place in our society. Well-groomed, well-dressed, well-spoken, and apparently well-fed, he does not fit the stereotypical image of a homeless man. But for his age, I think, he could reenlist. Then he tells me his problem. He has recently been released from prison, after serving 8 years, and he is hooked on heroin again. He wants a methadone program. We discuss the ramifications of this; there are some professionals who think that replacing one addiction with another is not really helping the client and that the side effects of methadone can be quite severe. It might be better to get into a drug-free program. The choice is the client's, however, and he has been in a methadone program before and sees it as his only answer.

I make phone calls to several programs and find two that will see him tomorrow. One said it will take 10 days for him to be accepted, and the other said 5 days. He chose the quicker acceptance, although I told him the other is a better program. He wants to get out of the shelter as soon as possible. He tells me about his wife and children whom he has not seen in more than 6 years, although he has kept in touch by mail and phone. "She wouldn't divorce me even though I begged her to, because she still loves me." Why hasn't he seen them for so long? He didn't want them to see him in prison, and now he doesn't want them to see him hooked. He firmly believes a methadone program will help him take control of his life. I think to myself that methadone didn't work before—why should it work now? Before we conclude, I ask him about combat flashbacks. He says, "I have dreams about the war," but he doesn't consider these flashbacks. We make an appointment for him to attend a Vietnam Veterans group.

During the lunch hour I meet with John English and his parents. John is a 36-year-old man who came to the shelter after a quarrel with his stepfather. He believes that the police have implanted a radar device in his brain so that they can keep track of him. "They did this," he said, "because they think I attacked a woman." But he explained that when he broke the bottle against the wall he meant her no harm; he was only trying to stop the voices swearing in his head. She was a bystander who was frightened by his behavior and screamed for the police. He spent a month on Rikers Island for this. Now he believes the police can read his thoughts from six blocks away, and he can hear them doing this. The voices, which he calls projections, still swear at him.

John decided to prove his independence and sanity by leaving his stepfather's home and finding a place of his own, and to do this he chose the shelter as his base. It is fairly typical for younger men to come directly from home to the shelter, as lack of available housing leaves them no other choice. But John is not typical because of his age and his mental problems.

In the family meeting, Mr. English tries to reason with John and, when John feels cornered by his stepfather's reasoning, he complains that the smell of the old man's breath is overpowering him. Mrs. English, who has had multiple sclerosis since a year after her marriage, criticizes them both for not listening to what she is saying. During a pause in the argument I ask Mr. English if he really expects John to be logical. He says no. John then tells him, "Just because I can't be logical doesn't mean I can't make sense." Mr. English thinks this over and agrees that John can make sense. They start listening to each other. Mr. English now tries to understand what John is saying instead of trying to convince him to follow instructions. John eventually agrees to let his

stepfather help him find a safe place to live, and Mr. English agrees to let John stay at the shelter until the new home is found. Mrs. English says, "That's what I was trying to say."

## TUESDAY

I receive a letter from a postmaster in a small town in Florida. It is about a former client, Mr. Duncan, and the news is good. I recall the case. The old man was traveling from Massachusetts to Florida, and he changed trains in Penn Station. He fell asleep in the station and woke up to find all his belongings and identification gone. Only his bus ticket receipts remained in his pocket. After the police brought him to the shelter, I made phone calls to various agencies who assist travelers, but to no avail. One social worker yelled over the phone at me, "You must be new. Don't you know all the old bums in the city want to go to Florida for the winter?" Shelter staff and people from other agencies just did not believe his story. I chose to persist.

Getting information from Mr. Duncan was a slow process. He had had a stroke, and his memory was impaired. He said he had daughters living in the city, but he hadn't seen them since their early teens, and he was not sure how long ago that was. I tried the telephone directory without success. Then I asked how he supported himself in Florida. By fishing, he said, and trading some of the catch for the things he needed. How does he pay his rent? "Oh," he said, "I'm on social security." A call to the social security office verified this (he remembered his social security number). His next month's check was mailed to the shelter.

This process of seeking aid for him took 1 month. Prior to his leaving for Florida, I gave him two self-addressed envelopes and asked him to write me so that I would know he had arrived safely. Another month went by and I did not hear from him, so I wrote the postmaster in his town. He had told me he picked up his mail at the local post office and was known there. The postmaster's letter said Mr. Duncan arrived safely; he was doing fine and remembered me. The postmaster also advised that I not expect a letter, since while Mr. Duncan said he would write, he would likely forget again in a few minutes.

Just before lunch the veteran returns from the methadone program. He is feeling very happy because he is positive he will be accepted there. He says he is determined to stop using heroin, and in fact he has not used it in more than a week. This proves his high motivation, he says. How can I tell him this does not help his chances of being accepted into the methadone program?

After lunch I accompany another case manager who is escorting her client to the hospital. The Emergency Medical Service had to be called because he was decompensating rapidly and having dangerous hallucinations. He is another veteran, a marksman in the army, who has suffered brain damage, most probably from drug use.

Talking with his worker, the client, Carlton, alternately becomes the four or five different people who "live inside" him, including a very seductive woman and a dangerous man who could hurt people. In the ambulance he keeps repeating, "I see Carlton over there. He says, 'I'm the real Carlton.' I say, 'Shit, that's why I'm crazy.'" Then he starts mumbling what sounds like gibberish to me, and I marvel at his worker's ability to understand his speech. Carlton cooperates with the process of hospitalization to the best of his ability, but his admission takes the whole afternoon. The hospital keeps him for observation.

Shelter residents like Carlton seldom have friends, as the mentally ill do not usually interact with the rest of the population and the healthy residents tend to ignore them. Often if they have money, a welfare check or cigarette money from the family, they are robbed and exploited. In fact, robbery and exploitation

are quite common in the shelter, and that is why the men form groups, not formal organized gangs but a buddy system where friends back each other. The population is too transient to form gangs, and sometimes the man who is a buddy in the morning will steal your bus fare for a fix or a drink at night. There are few close friendships here.

But there are good deeds done here also. Last night an old man came in, lost and confused, with $279 in his pocket. He would not trust staff to put the money in the safe. A young man, a drug addict, stood by the old man's bed all night to make sure that no one robbed him while he slept. Staff found the old man's family today. The young man said he did it because "He looks like my grandfather."

## WEDNESDAY

This morning William Hartley is waiting for me when I arrive. There is always that one client who gets to you, the one who can get behind your screen of objectivity and occupy your mind even in your leisure hours. That is how William affects me. He is a 27-year-old man who looks like he is 20 or 21. The hardships of his life do not show on his face. He has served 5 years in prison for armed robbery, but his manner is gentle and polite. His acts of violence have mostly been directed at himself.

On my second day on the job our entire staff was called down to the main floor to deal with a crisis. There was a man up in the rafters threatening to jump. That man was William Hartley. The fall, at least 50 feet to the concrete floor, would certainly have killed him. The workers and some clients quickly piled mattresses below him. People were shouting, "Don't do it." One young man yelled, "Jump! It'll bring the TV cameras, and then people will know what it's like in here." Security guards dragged the troublemaker from the building. Meanwhile, the man in the rafters pulled out a rope made from knotted bed sheets, tied one end to the steel beams, and slipped a noose over his head. When his girlfriend and his 2-year-old son were brought to help talk him down, he screamed in agony, "Get my son outta here! Whose crazy idea was that?" Finally, another shelter resident succeeded in talking him down, and police and emergency medical services took him away.

The next morning William became my first client. He was raised by foster parents and was about 12 years old when he met his biological mother. He was visiting the younger sister of his foster mother, and she casually introduced him to another woman in the apartment saying, "This is your real mother." William kept in touch with his mother, and after the death of his foster parents, he moved in with her and his half-brothers. He was about 19 at the time.

William could not believe his mother loved him, and she could never do enough to convince him that he meant as much to her as her other children. She explained the circumstances of his birth, how she was a young girl unable to care for herself and a baby. They were deserted by his father, so she left him with the older, childless couple. I got this information from both William and his mother with whom I spoke on the phone because she would not meet with me. Ms. Hartley spoke with both of us often on the phone, and William visited her home, but she would not let him move in with her again because she was convinced that would cause trouble for the whole family. I supported her in this decision, and William came to understand her point of view. It took weeks of counseling and phone calls to his mother, but he eventually got a job and moved away from the shelter. The last I heard from him he was doing well working as a security guard. Now he is back.

William sits at my desk with his chin on his chest and his hands between his knees. When I ask him what brings him back to the shelter, he whispers one word, "Crack." He was living with his cousin's family, but they kicked him out because he stole from them. Could I help him get his things from them? Could I help him get his job back? He says his use of crack has not affected his work because he only used it on his days off and he did not miss a day of work until his cousin threw him out. I tell him that he is deceiving himself if he thinks crack has not affected his job performance; I ask him if he has been late other times also. Sometimes he did use the drug when he had to be at work the next day. We talk about the dangers of addiction, the physical, mental, and emotional damage crack inflicts on users and their families, but he has heard it all before.

I have seen other clients like this who made it out of the shelter but return when trouble strikes and there is no one else to turn to. This is especially true when the trouble involves drugs and the man's family refuses to take him back because they have already been burned so many times in the past. In those cases the man either returns to the shelter or sleeps in abandoned buildings. Returning to the shelter can be an indication that someone is sincerely trying to change. I believe this is true of William.

With William's agreement, I set up an appointment for him with a physician I know who works with crack users. Then I call his cousin to discuss the possibility of William returning to remove his belongings from the apartment. The cousin is adamant; he will not allow William to reenter the apartment and will put the things out on the street. Valuable things could get stolen that way, I remind him. The cousin does not want that to happen so he suggests that I come for the things while William waits in the street. I agree.

I call William's job, and his boss says he has been a good and reliable worker. He is only angry that William has been absent without calling. I let William speak to him, and William explains that family troubles have kept him from work. I wonder to myself if I am doing the right thing by passively supporting this half-truth. I decide that my role as advocate dictates I should not intervene because that would destroy his second chance with the company. William is told to report to work the next morning.

William waits in the car while I go up to his cousin's apartment. His cousin turns out to be not a blood relative but a life-long friend who really cares for him. He is deeply hurt by William's theft and does not want to hear the promise of compensation that I bring. He is touched when I tell him that William wants his little girl to keep the portable TV; nevertheless, he wants William to stay away from him and get his act together. He is sorry William had to return to the shelter (he lived there himself briefly), but he also thinks this is light punishment for what William did. If another man had stolen his stereo he would have pressed charges. I collect the garbage bags of clothes and tapes and bring them down to the car. I wonder if the things his cousin said are true, that William is just a people user and doesn't give a damn about anyone. If so, why did he give his TV to the child? A portable TV is a precious item in a shelter. We return to the shelter.

I have just finished my lunch when Arthur Brown comes into the office. He is speaking to himself in angry tones. Since there is already a client at my desk, I tell Arthur I will see him next. He makes a nasty comment about drug addicts, meaning my client, then leaves the office. Later Arthur comes looking for me. He walks past me and goes directly to the center of the room and challenges me to come fight him. I offer to talk over the problem right away, but he doesn't want to talk. He says he wants to "beat the shit" out of me. I ask what he thinks I have done to anger him. He says I

prevented him from getting a job. I quickly think back to last week. Arthur, who is mentally handicapped and unable to read, applied for a job well beyond his ability and asked me for a reference. I told him that I could not do that because I would only be setting him up for a failure. I suggested another job instead where he would have more supervision. He refused my offer, and I had not seen him since then. Now he is standing in the middle of the room yelling at me.

Again I try to get him to talk to me, but his anger escalates, and he rips off his shirt. I warn him that I cannot permit this behavior to continue and advise him that I will have to call security if he does not get control of himself. The threats and verbal abuse continue. I look around the room. There are several clients sitting around, but most of them are ignoring us. One staff member tries to calm her clients during this outburst; another remains busy at his desk; only one comes to my aid. He tries to reason with Arthur and places himself between us. Now Arthur has to look over my co-worker's shoulder to swear at me.

These incidents have happened before. When staff get in trouble there is a dangerous lack of support, and this is affecting the morale of the program. Finally my director tells me to go call security. I descend three long flights of stairs knowing that if Arthur breaks away and comes after me I don't stand a chance on these stairs. I report the incident to security, and five guards remove Arthur from the office.

The threat of client-on-client violence is ever present, but client violence toward staff seldom occurs. Clients' resentments toward staff are more likely to be expressed through a slashed tire or a broken car antenna, which are hard to trace, than with a direct assault. Staff members are concerned that there isn't an effective policy for dealing with these incidents, and there is not enough security to offer adequate protection.

## THURSDAY

This morning I do outreach. I go down to the ground floor of the shelter and try to engage new clients. I look out onto a sea of beds, more than 300 of them, spaced about 3 feet apart. The old men and the physically handicapped are placed in a separate corner, away from the other men, to minimize their chances of being exploited. Men can be robbed at night when the lights are dimmed and they are sleeping, but the old are easy prey anytime.

The bed linens are all that familiar shade of institutional white, except for the occasional colored or patterned pillow case someone has brought from wherever used to be home. A few men are lying in bed; some are still getting dressed to go out to whatever their day's activity will be—job search, apartment search, family connection, drug connection. They get dressed standing in full view of everyone. They are depersonalized and accustomed to the lack of privacy and make little or no attempt to cover themselves even when female staff pass by.

I see a young man carrying a large garbage bag. I approach and greet him. He says he is doing fine. I tell him about our program and invite him to come visit us. He says he is not interested. I ask what's in the bag. "Empty soda cans," he replies. He collects them for the deposits. I tell him he could get four or five Coke bottles a day from our office. He replies, "I don't do bottles, only aluminum cans." As he walks away I make a note to speak with him again next week.

Another young man I speak to says that the CSS program I work for only has crazy people. That preconception is the biggest obstacle to getting people involved in our program. I tell him that I know the staff is a bit off the wall, but most of the clients are quite sane. He says his name is Ivan and he may come to talk to me tomorrow. What's wrong with right now, I ask? He says maybe he'll see me later. We pick up about 20% of our clients through outreach; the rest are referred to us by shelter staff and other clients. I wander around talking to more residents before going back to the office.

Ivan has come to see me. I ask him what made him decide to come up and he says, "I don't really have my shit together like I pretend down there; I need help." He is 21 years old. His mother caught him with a couple of friends using cocaine in her home, and she kicked him out. She told him not to return until he has a job, an apartment, and a bank account and is drug free. That was 2 months ago. He had not seen or heard from her since. He is worried because they both have no other family; his father is recently deceased. His mother has a heart condition, and he is concerned that something may happen to her and that he won't be around to help.

I ask if he is drug free now, and he says he is. He broke off with those friends a month ago and came to the shelter. I ask him, "Why not call your mother now and let her know where you are? She might think you are in jail or worse." It had not occurred to him that she might be worried also. He is afraid to call her and asks me to do it for him.

I call Ivan's mother at work, and she is grateful for news that he is all right. If she hadn't heard from him by the weekend, she was going to report him to the police as a missing person. She says, "Yes, I told him to get out and get a job, but I didn't say he couldn't phone or come visit." I give the phone to Ivan.

I have found that reestablishing family contact is easier if I make two things clear at the start. I am not trying to convince the family members to take the client back into the home, and I am not holding the family responsible for the client's homelessness. Once this is understood, people are more open to discussion and helping their homeless relative.

## FRIDAY

William is waiting for me this morning, dressed in his security guard uniform. He is smiling and standing straight, and he tells me he is going to work at noon. His job means a lot to him because he gets to work with a dog and he guards an apartment building where families with children live. He loves the attention he gets from the children. He hopes to have a family of his own one day. "No," he tells me, there is no chance of his getting back with his son's mother. She won't even let him see the boy. William is angered by her actions, but he stays away because he is afraid she will call the police on him again. He has not kept the appointment I made for him with the physician because he is feeling fine and he wants to work. I remind him that the large quantity of crack he told me he used can cause physical damage and he should have an examination. He takes the physician's number and uses my phone to make an appointment for next week. I ask when he plans to get help with his drug addiction, and he replies that he is not addicted. He insists he has no desire to use drugs and he is going to work, save his money, and get out of the shelter again. "What will happen," I ask him, "when you cash your next pay check and you have all that money in your hand?" "I won't spend it," he tells me, "I will put it in the shelter safe and only take out enough each day to go to work."

William thanks me again for helping him get his clothes from his cousin's place. He admits again that he is partially right. He has proved he can save money and get out of the shelter; his problem is that when he is living on his own he gets involved with the wrong

kind of friends. He makes an appointment to see me next week, and he leaves for work.

I haven't seen the artist since Monday, so I ask the clients where he is. They tell me that he left for California on Wednesday. He did not say much about leaving, just that his family agreed to have him live with them again and sent him a ticket, so he left. Now I think I understand the quality of the light in his Impressionist paintings. The shimmering light, the wide open spaces were his memories of the home he had left.

Ivan has come to see me. Again he thanks me for making the phone call to his mother. He had dinner with her last night, and he is spending the weekend with her. I listen while he reviews the events that preceded his departure from his home. He lived with his mother and his father all his life. He is their only child. Last summer he lost his job, and since his father was ill he did not try to find another job; instead he stayed home to look after his dad. When his father died in the fall, Ivan and his mother did not talk much about their loss. They grieved silently and separately. With his father gone, Ivan found himself with time on his hands. He had used drugs occasionally before, and he started hanging out with unemployed friends. Soon they were using Ivan's home as a safe-house in which to get high, and it was during one of these parties that his mother came home early and caught him with cocaine.

Ivan tells me that he always was able to talk things over with his mother, but that day she went into a blind rage and would not listen to anything he said. Ivan understands the feeling of betrayal piled on loss that his mother experienced. He does not expect her to tell him he can move back home after this weekend. He knows he will have to make his own home now, but he also knows he has not lost his mother.

After lunch the veteran comes to see me. He asks me to phone the methadone program to find out if he has been accepted. I make the call, and the news is not good. I am told that the client's sample tested negative, no trace of illegal drugs, and I should advise him to return to the methadone program Monday morning and give another sample. I am told he will understand the message. I relay the information to him and tears stream down his face. "Do you know what they are telling me to do, sir?" he asks. "I have no money! Do you know what I will have to do to get $10? I don't want to do that any more!"

John English and his stepfather have come to see me. Mr. English has found a basement apartment that is acceptable to John, and John is moving there today. It is quite far from his parents' home, but it is near his aunts and cousins, so he will have family contact and Mr. English won't have to respond to every minor crisis personally. The person renting John the apartment has known him for many years and understands his condition. I ask him about getting back on his medication, but he refuses to do that. He reasons that since the medication can't cure him there is no point taking it. I tell him that I understand what he means, but I disagree with him, and I ask if he knows the difference. He replies, "Yes! I disagree with Donald Trump building big apartment buildings for the rich when poor people can't find anywhere to live; but I understand that cities like to compete for who has the tallest buildings." He is right; just because he is not logical does not mean he can't make sense. John tells me that if the voices become too much for him he will go to the hospital. The Englishes thank me for my help, and I thank them for coming to say good-bye.

It is snowing when I leave work today. I look out at the empty lot directly across from the building. It is strewn with garbage and weeds. I wonder if in the spring the men would like to clean it up and use it as a recreation area. I wonder if in the spring I will still be working here. The burnout rate is very high among the staff. I am aware that my own sense of burnout comes more from the constraints of the larger systems than from the problems of the men. I ask myself why I do this work. I think I do it because I like being with people and helping when I am able to. I am disturbed and distressed every day as I pass the empty apartment buildings that stand decaying near the shelter. These empty buildings could be rehabilitated were it not that the city responds to plans for more shelters more readily than plans for affordable housing. I know that almost anyone can become homeless; I have met PhDs, teachers, and businessmen living here alongside the untrained, the unskilled, and the mentally ill.

The cold wind hits me, and I button my coat against the chill. It is hard to think of spring at this time, but this must be what it is like for the men in the shelter. It is the faith that conditions will change that keeps them going every day, and I share that faith. Of course I am speaking of the ones that haven't given up. Many have. And what of their families? What conflict rages within Ivan's mother tonight while she wonders if she did the right thing? Is Mr. English wondering, as I am, if John's voices will drive him from the apartment back to a mental hospital? Where is Arthur tonight? I had heard that he was suspended from the shelter Wednesday night for fighting with another client. I have no idea what will happen with any of these men. I only know that I am never bored working at the shelter and being invited each day to enter the lives of so many people. And at those moments when a client and I develop trust in each other, I am at once honored and humbled.

# CASE STUDY 5.2

*Multiple methods are used in a group format to reduce stress. This case study presents a highly structured model of group treatment that emphasizes systematic collection of data, use of empirically based techniques, and a group format for teaching stress management.*

## Questions

1. What group leader skills were demonstrated in the case study?
2. How were group members involved in the treatment process?
3. How did the group leader gather feedback from the group members and incorporate it into the group process?
4. What were some of the key techniques used to reduce stress among the group members?

---

## THE MULTIMETHOD APPROACH TO STRESS MANAGEMENT

### Randy Magen and Sheldon D. Rose*

To provide an overview of the multimethod approach, we present a case study of a typical group, a stress management group, in this chapter. We focus on the tasks of the group leader, the group interventions, the data-collection procedures, and the generalization strategies used over the 10 sessions. We include brief excerpts from all 10 sessions and the pregroup and postgroup interviews. The strategies and principles covered in this book are noted parenthetically where appropriate.

An agency that served its clients primarily through group programs decided to include as clients those suffering from stress disorders. Trained and interested leaders were available, and the need in the community was made apparent by the number of people who had already referred themselves. Other clients were recruited by means of public service advertisements in the local newspaper.

Those who called the agency received a brief description of the program and how it would be carried out. The telephone interviewer explained that the groups would meet for 2 hours once per week for 10 weeks. Costs and other conditions of membership were also clarified. The applicant was informed that the group had four major components: relaxation training, social skill training, cognitive restructuring, and group exercises. Members would be provided selected readings and would have the opportunity to examine and work on specific stress problems of concern to them. If the caller was interested, an appointment was made for an individual pregroup interview that would last about an hour. Further information was provided in this interview. The client was tested with the measures described later and interviewed to determine the specific parameters of the stress. The interviewer also explored situations the client wanted to work on in the group. The following interviewees agreed to come to the stress

* Reprinted from Sheldon D. Rose (1989), *Working with adults in groups*, San Francisco: Jossey-Bass. Reprinted by permission of Jossey-Bass Inc.

management group being offered at that time. (The specific information was gathered at the pregroup interview.)

On the bulletin board in her physician's waiting room, Ellen M. noticed a poster recruiting members for a stress management group. Ellen reported in the group that she has been managing a clothing store for the past 12 years. Until recently, she had lived alone, a situation with which she was content. Last month, Ellen's 15-year-old grandchild came to live with her. Ellen's peaceful rural life has been shattered by loud music, phone calls, and the responsibilities of caring for a teenage girl. Ellen told the interviewer that she feels a great deal of stress from having to deal with her grandchild.

Susan B.'s friend, noting her inability to handle the transition from high school to the working world, told her about the stress management group. Susan had graduated from high school 2 years earlier. Since graduation, she had been working as a secretary for an insurance company. Many of Susan's friends moved away or went off to college. Susan feels alone in the world and wonders if she will ever fall in love. She doesn't like her job and doesn't know what to do about it.

Jim W.'s social worker at Catholic Social Services referred him to the stress management group. Jim works on the line at a factory. His wife of 14 years recently moved out and is divorcing him. Jim feels depressed and nervous. The effect of the divorce seems to have resulted in constant stomachaches and feelings of uneasiness. He has little idea of what to do with his life.

Rosemary M., who also read about the group in the newspaper, is a homemaker. She has a husband and two daughters. Now that her children are older and need her less, she feels bored with life. The stress of this period in her life has left Rosemary without purpose and with a sense of hopelessness. She also complains of increasing insomnia.

Janet A. noticed a poster in her dormitory advertising a stress management group. Janet is an undergraduate student at the university. Every semester she feels so much anxiety that she fails to complete most of her assignments. She has dropped more classes than she has completed. Janet has been told by her advisor that if she does not complete her work, she will not be permitted to finish college. This threat adds to her inability to function.

## ASSESSMENT

Since all the assessment interviews were structured similarly, we focus on Jerry's pregroup interview. On arrival, Jerry asked more about the group. After his questions were answered, he was given three paper-and-pencil assessment instruments—the Profile of Mood States (POMS) (McNair, Lorr, & Croppleman, 1971); the Symptom Check-List-Revised (SCL-90-R) (Derogatis, 1983); and the Hassles Scale (Kanner, Coyne, Schaefer, & Lazarus, 1981)—to estimate level of stress and coping skills. Jerry took about 25 minutes to complete the three tests.

After Jerry completed the Hassles Scale, the group leader, Lydia, discussed those items that were scored "3" (that is, occurred often). Some of Jerry's "often occurring" hassles included having too many responsibilities, having trouble relaxing, having problems getting along with fellow workers, not liking fellow workers, being dissatisfied with his job, worrying about the decision to change jobs, and being concerned about getting ahead. The discussion of these hassles revealed that Jerry was feeling pressured by work and by his partner. Jerry readily identified these as two issues he would like to deal with in the group. (The reader should note that the tests were used not only to obtain a score, which was later used to evaluate outcome for Jerry and the group, but as a point of departure for determining specific situations on which to focus interventions in the ensuing weeks.)

To assess Jerry's ability to use the group effectively, Lydia asked him about his previous experiences as a member of groups. Lydia inquired how Jerry felt about talking and sharing his problems with six to eight strangers. In addition, Lydia asked about Jerry's specific social skills and skill deficits and the situations in which these skills were manifested. Jerry stated that he had participated in several discussion groups at his church. He added that he had been in a weekend encounter group that he did not like, although he did feel it opened him up a little. He remarked that he might be hesitant at first in talking with strangers, but once others began to talk, he thought that he would have little trouble participating. (On the basis of Jerry's successes in past groups and his avowed willingness to participate, the leader concluded that Jerry could effectively use the group but would have to be eased in slowly at the beginning.)

Finally, Lydia reviewed with Jerry the treatment contract, which covered extragroup tasks, types of interventions, attendance, promptness, and other issues. Jerry asked how much time the extragroup tasks would take. Lydia responded that because they were negotiated, it would be up to him. Both Jerry and Lydia signed the contract.

Prior to the first session, the group leader examined the assessment on all clients. She redesigned the format of the 10-session group based on the common need for the modeling sequence to enhance social skills and the expressed need for relaxation training to help cope with minor stressors. Although these two elements were to be given proportionately greater emphasis, no interventions from the general format were dropped.

## GROUP SESSIONS

The 10 group sessions could be roughly divided into three phases. The early phase con-

tinued the orientation and assessment begun in the pregroup interview. In addition, group cohesion was built up, and basic training in dealing with stress was initiated. Provision of information and skill training were continued in the second or middle phase. Clients began to identify and work on their own unique problems. In the final phase, clients focused on more complex stress situations and began to prepare to transfer what they had learned in the group to the real world.

### The Initial Phase: Sessions One Through Three

In the first session, the leader's goals were for group members to learn about each other, to increase their attraction to one another (group cohesion), and to continue to identify and further clarify their target problems. For the first exercise, members broke into pairs and took turns interviewing each other for 2 minutes each. Suggested interview questions were put on the chalkboard as a means of reducing anxiety. When members returned to the large group, they introduced their partners. Their partners reminded them when they forgot anything. These introductions were accompanied by some joking and laughter. (Introducing one's partner rather than oneself is likely to reduce initial anxiety. Moreover, this exercise elicited the active participation of all members within a few minutes in the first session. Broad participation, as well as a snack in the midgroup break, is likely to increase group cohesion.)

After a minilecture on the nature of stress and stressors, the members completed an individual checklist to identify their specific physical cues of stress. First Lydia, as a model, and then the members, one at a time, summarized their unique physical stress responses before the group. After the break in which decaffeinated (!) coffee and soft drinks were served, each member described a stressful situation recently encountered and their response to it.

(During both exercises, Lydia noted that Rosemary and Ellen chatted with each other but did not participate in the general group discussion, except when called on.)

To prepare for the next week, Lydia suggested two extragroup tasks. In the first, members would monitor their daily stress levels on a 10-point scale. The second task was to record their physical cues when feeling high levels of stress. When the members agreed to these suggestions, Lydia asked them to report on their monitoring at the beginning of the next session. Lydia mentioned that because self-monitoring was probably not a common experience for them, they might require a system to remind them. Jerry, who stated that he never forgot anything, was the only one who did not develop such a system. (It should be noted that to increase the likelihood of compliance, extragroup tasks were negotiated rather than assigned, and use of a self-monitoring system was encouraged.)

At the end of the first session, Lydia distributed and explained the postsession questionnaire, which is used to collect the members' perceptions of the session. Three of the questions asked were (1) How useful was this session? (2) How supportive were the other members? and (3) How close do you feel to other members? Although these questions were open-ended, Lydia noted how hard the members had worked and looked forward to the next session. (The leader in the early sessions attempts to find every opportunity to reinforce the real achievements of individuals and the group.) Ellen said she would bring cookies next week to enliven the break. Lydia chatted informally with the members as they slowly departed.

As members arrived for the second session, Lydia purposely sat between Rosemary and Ellen to encourage them to talk to others in the group. She chatted with both while the others arrived. Lydia praised those who were present for their punctuality and started the session on time to establish promptness as a norm, even though Jerry and Janet had not yet arrived. As they trickled in, Lydia smiled and indicated the free seats to them, and said "We've just started." (Apparently, by reinforcing those who were on time and not commenting on the tardiness of the latecomers, the norm was established. For the remaining sessions all but one person arrived on time.)

In session two, after Rosemary read the agenda, Lydia briefly summarized the postsession evaluations from the first group meeting. Lydia remarked that group members had given the group a 3.8 on a 6-point scale for usefulness. A few of the members' written responses to the open-ended questions were read aloud. Lydia stated that one member remarked that he had found learning about other people in the group helpful. Another member wrote that Lydia had used some technical words that she did not understand. In response, Lydia asked the group if there were any specific terms she had used the previous week that could be clarified. No one responded. Lydia stated that she would attempt to use clearer language in the future. She also encouraged members to stop her when something was unclear. (Several principles should be noted here. First, if evaluations are to be used, they must be commented and acted on. Second, by using feedback, the leader provides opportunities for the members to assume increasing responsibility for structuring the group. Third, by having the members read the agenda and encouraging them to ask questions, the leader decreases her activity and increases participation by the members.)

The next agenda item, as in all sessions, was review of the tasks performed between sessions. Lydia asked members to state what parts of the extragroup tasks they had completed. Three members responded that they had written down physical stress cues in their diary, and five members remarked that they had monitored their stress levels, though not every day. Jerry said he was too busy to do any of it. As each person mentioned an achievement, Lydia offered praise, giving little attention to those who did not complete tasks.

Next, Lydia noted that most people did some part of the task. She then remarked that homework is not something one does on a regular basis when no longer in school. Members expressed a variety of other reasons for not doing the homework completely: "having a busy week," "not remembering," and "not understanding what I was supposed to do." Jerry, in particular, noted that he should have developed a reminder system for himself, as he was more forgetful than he thought. Once the obstacles were identified, Lydia asked for suggestions as to what members could do to overcome them. Many ideas were generated. One was that each member could call another group member between sessions to remind him or her to do the homework. In line with another idea, Lydia would spend the last 10 minutes of every session explaining the task and responding to questions. All the suggestions were evaluated, and the two mentioned here were selected by the group to be implemented. (Note that as in most groups, homework completion rates were low at the second session and required attention; in this case, the leader made use of group problem solving rather than attempting to solve the problem herself.)

One additional theme of session two was introduction to relaxation training. After a brief review of the use of relaxation to cope with stress, Lydia cautioned members about muscle spasms, medications, and other factors that in combination with relaxation might result in negative side effects. Lydia then led the group through progressive muscle relaxation in which she had them alternately tense and relax muscle groups. The group members were asked to rate their tension before and after the exercise. After the relaxation practice, members discussed their response to the exercise, and several agreed to try relaxation at home. At the end of the session other homework assignments were negotiated in pairs and then read to the group. Finally, the members completed the postsession questionnaire. As they drifted out of the room, they talked informally with each other.

The third session was similar in many respects to the second. As Lydia reviewed the experience with the extragroup tasks, she noted enthusiastically that almost everyone had completed the tasks. Lydia also informed the members that their evaluations of the group had gone up dramatically this week. Several members noted that they could better understand what happens in this kind of group and how it might help them. Two people expressed their enthusiasm for relaxation in particular. Lydia concluded the evaluation by saying that she was pleased that each person was finding his or her own way of making the group useful.

Lydia then introduced a new group exercise designed to help members identify and change those thoughts that seemed to increase stress, such as putting oneself down or making a catastrophe of an insignificant event (self-defeating thoughts). As this exercise involved assimilation of a great deal of information, Lydia supplemented the instructions with a handout explaining the exercise and wrote down the important points on a chalkboard. Lydia began the exercise by providing a rationale to show the link between self-defeating thoughts and stress. This rationale also demonstrated how a person can replace self-defeating with self-enhancing thoughts. (In the dissemination of information, the leader made use of a number of didactic strategies, audiovisual aids and demonstrations, brief lectures with ample opportunity for questions, and handouts to supplement the lecture. This, like all lectures, was held to a maximum of 5 minutes to maintain members' attention.)

Lydia modeled a number of different types

of self-defeating thoughts, which were identified and discussed by the members. For example, one type of self-defeating thought is "absolutizing." Lydia said "One of the things I have often said to myself just before a meeting is, 'I'll never be able to explain that concept understandably.'" After the group discussed why this statement might be self-defeating, Lydia demonstrated how she would stop it. She would yell "Stop!" to herself. She then immediately replaced her earlier statement with "Clear explanations are sometimes difficult for me, but if I take my time and check to see whether people understand, I can do a better job of explaining concepts." Next, the members discussed how the latter statement was more effective and honest than the first. (To increase self-disclosure the leader modeled self-disclosure. In addition, she involved the members by having them discuss her self-statements, which was less threatening than discussing their own.)

The members were asked to read a list of 10 different self-statements, after which they took turns identifying the self-defeating or self-enhancing and changing the self-defeating to self-enhancing statements. After the 10 statements had been reviewed and modified, each member was asked to contribute a personal self-defeating statement.

*Rosemary:* When I start to worry at night, I say to myself, "I'll never be able to sleep—there's nothing I can do about it."

*Janet:* Sometimes when I'm studying, I think I'm just too dumb to do this kind of work. I should drop out of college.

*Jim:* I keep thinking, "I failed with my wife; I'll probably fail with every other woman I come into contact with." Sometimes I add, "My life is finished."

*Susan:* Today I just met a new guy at the office, and I said, as usual, "No sense talking to him. He won't like me, anyway."

*Jerry:* I can't think of one at all. While the others were talking I kept worrying about it. I don't know why it is, but when anyone asks me to do something, I always freeze.

*Group Leader:* Can anyone find a self-defeating statement in what Jerry just said? [Occasionally, members are not able to come up with a self-disclosing response during an exercise. Usually, the leader acknowledges the difficulty and goes on. In this case, the self-defeating statement was obviously implied, so the leader involved the group in helping Jerry find it.]

After each of these statements, the other members pointed out why the given statement was self-defeating and brainstormed about how to replace it. For example, Rosemary replaced her "I'll never be able to sleep" with "It may be difficult for me to sleep, but if I relax it sometimes helps a lot." (Throughout this and most exercises, the leader praised members on their work, for example, for successfully identifying and changing self-statements, for giving feedback to each other.)

Session three ended as did the earlier sessions with additional relaxation practice, group task planning, and a postsession questionnaire. To prepare for session four, Lydia carefully explained the principles of problem solving. For the extragroup task, all the members agreed to record specific stressful situations in which they were dissatisfied with the way they coped. Lydia handed out the criteria for selecting a stressful situation and provided the members with examples of situations that met these criteria.

At this meeting, Lydia noticed that Rosemary and Ellen were addressing most of their comments to the group at large even though they sat together. During the session, Jerry was somewhat reluctant to talk about himself, although he had comments for the others. (Unless the lack of self-disclosure is persistent by one person or characterized by several group members, the leader would not act on such observations; however, should it persist or include more than one person, the leader might deal with it as a group problem.)

## The Intermediate Phase: Sessions Four Through Seven

In the fourth session, after review of the previous week's data, the monitoring of extragroup tasks, and the rate of completion (which continued to be high), Lydia provided a feedback exercise. After breaking into pairs, each member wrote down one specific thing that his or her partner had done well in the group and one specific thing the partner might do differently. Using general feedback criteria as a guide, they provided their partners first with positive feedback, then with constructive negative feedback. Each member was evaluated with respect to how well the criteria had been met.

After this exercise, Lydia talked briefly about the relationship between stress and unsatisfactory performance in interpersonal situations. She provided the group with some examples, and some members came up with some of their own examples. Then Lydia described how one can learn concrete skills in handling difficult situations by getting ideas from others, by demonstration, by practice, and by feedback. She noted that we would be doing a lot of role-playing demonstrations and practice in the group from now on. Lydia then suggested that they look at the stressful situations they had observed during the week.

Each member had the opportunity to present and to deal systematically with his or her own problematic situations. Jerry brought up a situation even though he had not agreed to the previous week. (Some clients function better if they feel free to do what they want.) The problem-solving and modeling process is exemplified by Rosemary's situation.

*Rosemary:* I was speaking with my mother the other day and was upset with what she said. You should know that we don't see eye to eye on many things, particularly child rearing. I wonder if you could tell me what I could do to get my mother to stop telling me how to raise my children?

*Group Leader:* Does anyone have any questions that might help us see the situation more clearly?

*Jerry:* What did your mother say exactly?

*Rosemary:* We were talking on the telephone, and out of the clear blue sky (can you imagine?) she said it was wrong that I allowed the children to eat their meals while they watched television.

*Ellen:* What did you say to your mother after her advice?

*Rosemary:* I told her that things have changed since she raised me and that she doesn't understand. That always seems to stop her advice, but then she sounds angry and I end up feeling guilty. [Several other questions were asked: "How often do you talk to your mother?" "Is this a common exchange?" "Do others in your family have the same difficulty?" These resulted in greater specification of the problem.]

*Susan:* Rosemary, I wonder if you could tell us when the "critical moment" occurred.

*Group Leader (noting that Rosemary looks confused):* Why doesn't someone explain what the critical moment is? Some people may have forgotten.

*Susan:* Isn't it the point in time when you are faced with a situation and have a choice of how to respond?

*Janet:* Yeah, the point at which you wished you had done something different.

*Rosemary:* I remember now. I guess my critical moment was after she said, "You shouldn't allow your children to eat their meals while watching television. I never did."

## THE MULTIMETHOD APPROACH IN ACTION

Now that Rosemary, with the help of the group, had identified the concrete situation, the response, and the critical moment, the next step was goal setting.

*Susan:* Rosemary, could you tell us what you would like to have achieved in this situation?

*Rosemary:* I want to get my mother to stop telling me what to do about my kids.

*Group Leader:* Who is this a goal for, I wonder?

*Ellen:* I think it's a goal for Rosemary's mother. I do that all the time. I want everyone else to change when it's me that has to do the work.

*Rosemary:* You're right. I guess my goal for myself is to let my mother know how I feel on this issue. Can you believe it, I've never told her?

Note that in the preceding dialogue, the group leader guided the discussion while maximizing member participation by asking questions rather than providing answers. Once the goal had been established and accepted by Rosemary, she was then encouraged to state specifically what she could do or say differently to achieve that goal.

*Susan:* Rosemary, what do you want to tell your mother? Use that phrase we were told to use, "State a feeling and make a request." [Note that Susan is beginning to assume a leadership role. The group leader usually encourages this unless the given member discourages active participation among others; however, if possible, the leader encourages more than one person to assume a variety of leadership functions.]

*Rosemary:* I want to tell my mother I am angry and ask her to not give me advice . . . that is, unless I ask for it [laughing].

The next step in the behavioral rehearsal process was for Rosemary to evaluate the risks involved in stating her feelings and making this request. The members then brainstormed alternative responses Rosemary could make to her mother.

*Jerry:* Maybe you could tell her that her advice pissed you off and that you really don't need it.

*Rosemary:* Oh, I could never say that to my mother.

*Group Leader:* Remember, group, we don't evaluate brainstorming ideas—any suggestion is valuable. Who hasn't given an alternative? How about you, Ellen? What would you say?

*Ellen:* I might tell her that she was a good mother and did a fine job raising me and that I had to do what worked for me.

After 2 minutes of brainstorming, Susan asked Rosemary to pick out something she could say to her mother that met her goal.

*Rosemary:* I think I could say, "Mom, sometimes I feel incompetent when you give me advice, especially since I usually have ideas of my own. It's important to me to stand on my own two feet and find my own way of doing things. I know this will be difficult for you, Mom, but I really don't want you to give me advice unless I ask for it, OK?"

Practicing the alternative response was the next step in the modeling sequence. Ellen volunteered to role play Rosemary's role, and Rosemary played her mother. When they finished, Lydia asked Rosemary if she wanted to repeat the statement in the way Ellen had said it. Rosemary responded that she liked it a lot and would be willing to try it out herself, with Ellen playing the role of the mother.

After Rosemary practiced the response in a role play, the group provided her with feedback on the performance.

*Susan:* What did you like about what you did in that role play?

*Rosemary:* Not much . . . well I guess I told her how I felt. That would be an improvement over how I usually handle it.

*Group Leader:* It's important that you see improvement, Rosemary, and I do, too. What did others like about Rosemary's role play?

*Jim:* Well, Rosemary looked directly into Ellen's, I mean her mother's, eyes.

*Janet:* She made a request for change.

*Group Leader:* Tell Rosemary what she specifically said that was a request. [The leader shapes more specific feedback while helping people give their feedback directly to the person involved.]

*Janet:* Rosemary, you told your mother to wait until you asked her to give advice, and I think you did it gently.

When the members had finished giving both positive and negative feedback, Lydia asked Rosemary to rehearse one more time.

Lydia complimented Rosemary on the quality of the role play and commented on Susan's and Ellen's active participation in the role playing. She also said that she was "impressed by the excellent comments" of the other members and noted how well they adhered to the feedback criteria. At the same meeting, Jim's and Janet's situations were handled. Because the time needed to get through all their situations was not available, Lydia asked if they could continue next week.

Lydia reviewed the problem-solving steps, in particular the modeling sequence. (The leader continues to teach the general principles after the group has had experience with the sequence, to enhance the generalization of change. The frequent use of review is an important leadership function.) She then ended session five in the same manner as the four previous sessions, with relaxation practice, group task negotiations, and completion of the postsession questionnaire. As their extragroup task, most members decided to see how many other stress situations they could come up with in addition to the one they were working on. Everyone committed themselves to practicing relaxation at least 10 minutes a day. Ellen, in addition, decided to role play her situation several times into a tape recorder to get it down perfectly.

After the meeting, because she had noted that Janet's evaluation of the group had gone down dramatically, Lydia called Janet. Janet said that she was thinking of not returning to the group. Lydia listened to her concerns. She wondered aloud whether Janet may have felt too much pressure after last week's role play. Janet admitted that the group was going too fast for her, and it was making her anxious; she had had the same trouble in another group she had been in. (The leader may have made a mistake in not using "warmups" before role playing to accustom members to role playing. Examples of warmups are role playing neutral situations, playing a game of charades, and so forth.)

Lydia noted that perhaps others were feeling the same way and suggested that this was a problem that could be talked about in general in the group. Janet thought this was a good idea and said she felt better about coming back to the group next week. She was glad Lydia had called. (The preferred procedure when identifying group problems is to present the problem to the entire group. In this case, the leader was concerned that Janet would drop out before the problem could be brought up in the group. However, after talking to Janet, the leader still had the option of bringing the problem to the group in the event that the concern was shared by more than one member.)

In the sixth session, after review of the extragroup tasks and evaluations, which had dropped slightly, Lydia stated that a few people were concerned that the group was going too fast or putting too much pressure on them to change. In the discussion several members agreed, although Jim noted that he needed pressure to change. Jerry laughed as he agreed with Jim, "I'm finally ready to talk about myself." After further discussion, the members agreed that everyone should go at his or her own pace without pressure from anyone. They also suggested that members could back off on any exercise that was too difficult for them to handle. Jim reminded the group that if they took too much pressure off themselves, "they probably wouldn't get much from the group." Janet listened intently to the discussion, occasionally nodding agreement but saying nothing. The rest of the session dealt with the stressful situations not discussed and rehearsed the previous week. Jim and Ellen had time to deal with a second situation. The evaluations were extremely high at the end of this session, and all comments were positive. (It is not uncommon for mere discussion of a group problem to result in an increase in group cohesion.)

During the seventh and eighth sessions members continued to handle stressful situations but added cognitive elements to the behavioral role plays. For example, Janet told of a situation in class where the instructor called on her and she panicked, telling herself "I'm too dumb to answer any question." The members suggested that because she usually knows the answers to questions in class and in this group, when called on, she might instruct herself to take a deep breath and relax and to repeat the question in her mind. Before class, she would prepare herself to say "I know the answers to almost all questions asked, and it's not so terrible to make a mistake." Jim then cognitively modeled what she had to say. This was followed by her own cognitive rehearsal (in a stage whisper), combined with an answer to the question aloud in a behavioral rehearsal. In the final practice, everyone in the group asked her one question as if she were in class. (Janet had provided the members with the questions.) She stood up and answered them while silently reassuring herself of her ability to answer. Her success was met with wild applause from the group.

These sessions also ended with extragroup task planning and session evaluations. In these extragroup tasks, the members actually tried out the behaviors and cognitions learned in the group much more frequently than in the earlier sessions. In addition, most members continued to practice relaxation and to note their successes and failures in handling stress.

### The Final Phase: Sessions Nine and Ten

During the final phase, the emphasis was placed on reviewing the skills that had been taught and planning for dealing with stress after the group ended. In session nine, Lydia suggested some extragroup tasks that would help members think of how they could maintain the skills they had learned during the previous 8 weeks. Lydia prepared them for the task of maintenance and generalization with the following presentation.

There are limits to how much people can change after 20 hours of stress management training. Although the extragroup tasks extend the power of the group during its 10-week course, without planning for the maintenance of skills after the group ends, any benefits of stress management training would greatly diminish over time.

The members discussed, one at a time, the principles of transfer and maintenance of change. Lydia suggested, as an extragroup task, that they use the principles to develop a personal maintenance plan that would be the focus of the last session. Everyone agreed to try it out.

At the beginning of the 10th session the members reviewed each other's plan. There were a variety of ideas. Jim planned to read several books on assertiveness and stress management; he had even purchased two the previous week. Ellen was going to maintain contact with Susan as well as keep a diary of stress situations and how she handled them. She was going to continue her new regimen of walking 2 miles a day, and Susan would accompany her. Susan had already joined a church group in which she planned to try out the assertive techniques she learned in the group. She was considering joining an assertiveness training group to bolster her newly learned skills. Rosemary decided together with her husband to enter marital counseling, something the members had suggested earlier. Janet was going to join a yoga class to improve her relaxation. Jim felt he should join another stress group. "I passed this one, but just barely," he joked.

Jerry asked whether any of the others might be interested in a booster session in 3 months. They could discuss how they had used their stress management skills, refresh any skills that had been forgotten, and do problem solving. Most of the members were willing to attend, and Lydia noted that she and the agency would be happy to cooperate with such a plan. Jerry and Ellen agreed to help organize it. The most important purpose of the booster session, they agreed, would be to see how well they were carrying out their maintenance plans (a focus on development of a maintenance plan, public commitment to the maintenance plan, and monitoring of the plan in a booster session contribute to implementation of the plan.)

Lydia commended the members for their hard work in developing these plans. She organized the following closing exercise. Each member distributed to every other member a note on which was written one positive comment. The members were not to read the notes until they went home. Thus, the group ended with the exchange of tangible positive feedback.

At the end of the 10th session, the members were asked to retake the three assessment tests from the pregroup interview, to assess individual gains in stress management skills. Lydia arranged to meet with the members individually during the week following the last session to inform them of the test results. At that postgroup meeting, members would be able to provide Lydia with feedback about the program.

## SUMMARY

In this 10-session group, the leader used a wide variety of assessment and intervention procedures, including the modeling sequence, reinforcement, cognitive restructuring, self-instructional training, and relaxation training. The leader dealt with group problems before they arose, for example, the negative subgrouping by Rosemary and Ellen, a drop in group cohesion, and low productivity. She encouraged broad participation through the formation of subgroups and the use of exercises and was careful to involve members wherever possible in leadership functions and decision

making. The leader brought her warmth, her interviewing skills, and her humor to the group. She encouraged self-disclosure but protected clients from too much too soon. She opened herself up to criticism and accepted it without becoming defensive. She acknowledged her mistakes. At the same time she kept the group moving and provided a flexible structure while the focus on improving coping skills was maintained. She recorded data and used them for evaluation and to improve practice.

This group is typical of the many multi-method groups we have dealt with through the years. No two groups are exactly the same even when they have the same general purpose. They vary with respect to specific purpose, composition, primary means of intervention, and assessment strategies and in every other aspect. They hold in common a focus on problem solving, goal orientation, cognitive-behavioral interventions, diverse approaches for diverse phases, and coping skill training. Of equal importance is the use of the group as a major tool of assessment, intervention, and generalization in the treatment process.

## References

Derogatis, L. R. (1983). *Administration, scoring, and procedures manual for the SCL-90-R.* Riderwood, Maryland: Clinical Psychometric Research.

McNair, D., Lorr, M., & Croppleman, L. (1971). *Profile of mood states.* San Diego: Educational and Industrial Testing Service.

Kanner, A. D., Coyne, J. C., Schaefer, C., & Lazarus, R. S. (1981). Comparison of two modes of stress measurement: Daily hassles and uplifts versus major life events. *Journal of Behavioral Medicine, 4,* 1–39.

# CASE STUDY 5.3

*Family caregivers are becoming a growing part of a response to our aging population. This case study illustrates the special problems caregivers face and how group work can help ease their burden.*

## Questions

1. In what ways can social group work respond to the needs of caregivers?
2. What difficulties and problems do caregivers confront when providing for their elderly relatives?
3. How was the problem-solving model used in the group sessions?
4. Does a group leader need the same or similar life experiences in order to work effectively with group members?

## FRIENDS DON'T REALLY UNDERSTAND: THE THERAPEUTIC BENEFIT OF SOCIAL GROUP WORK FOR CAREGIVERS OF OLDER PERSONS

*Terry Peak and Ronald W. Toseland*

This case study describes the therapeutic benefits of group intervention for caregivers of frail older persons.* Family caregiving to the elderly is a growing social problem, in part because the U.S. population as a whole is aging, older people are living longer, family groups are smaller than in previous generations, and more women are working than ever before. Most of the care provided to the elderly in the United States is given by family members, predominantly spouses, daughters, daughters-in-law, and sons. Family caregiving is preferred by the majority of care receivers. However, families are getting smaller, shrinking the pool of available helpers.

The aging of the population is also a concern. The proportion of older persons in the population is growing, and older persons need more care because they tend to have more chronic disabilities. Older care receivers tend to be provided for by older caregivers. As they age, diminished energy and chronic health problems limit the capacity of caregivers. Women, who are the majority of caregivers, are in the work force today in larger numbers than ever before. The economic necessity to work and competing demands from their own family place additional strain on them.

### CAREGIVING AS A SOCIAL PROBLEM

Although most caregivers report feeling satisfied by being able to provide care to family

* This research was supported by Grant #MH40129-02 from the Prevention Research Branch of the National Institute of Mental Health to Dr. Toseland.

147

members, it is also true that extensive, intensive, and extended need for care can have a negative effect on the physical and psychological well-being of the caregiver. In some cases, caregivers feel unprepared for their role. Acute illness or rapid degeneration of chronic illnesses make some caregiving situations unexpected. In others, there is an open-ended commitment by the caregiver to a situation that could change dramatically at any time. Disruption of normal daily routines and the addition of caregiving chores (toileting, lifting, feeding, and so on) can result in physical problems for the caregiver. Caregivers often feel isolated in their caregiving situations and abandoned by friends and family members. Feelings of guilt, depression, self-blame, stress, and anxiety are common and can have negative effects on the relationship between caregiver and care receiver.

## SOCIAL GROUP WORK

Social group work with caregivers of the elderly is designed to fill the need for emotional support and for improved coping skills brought about by stressful caregiving situations. Support groups can (1) provide a much needed respite from caregiving, (2) reduce isolation and loneliness, (3) provide an opportunity to share feelings and experiences in a supportive atmosphere, (4) affirm and validate feelings and thoughts about the caregiving situation, (5) instill hope, (6) educate caregivers about the effects of chronic disabilities and available community resources, (7) encourage a mutual sharing of information about effective coping strategies, (8) help caregivers to become motivated to identify and examine specific problems and concerns, and (9) help them to become motivated to use systematic problem-solving procedures and coping strategies to reduce or eliminate the stress they are experiencing (Toseland & Rossiter, 1989).

Practitioners can plan for a group and make contact with the family caregiving population through the formal and informal service system. County departments of social services, county offices of the aging, and home health agencies are frequently the first point of contact used by family caregivers when they seek assistance on behalf of the care receiver. Caregivers may also seek personal counseling for problems related to the caregiving situation. This could occur through an employee assistance program, a family service agency, or a community mental health center. Often an acute medical problem brings caregivers to the attention of hospital social workers. While making discharge plans, social workers assess the capacity and willingness of family members to provide supportive care at the time of discharge. Outside the formal service system, overwhelmed caregivers often turn to physicians and clergy for counseling and information.

## CAREGIVER SUPPORT PROGRAM

Members of the group described in this chapter were part of a larger Caregivers Support Project, a 3-year clinical intervention project funded by the Prevention Research Branch of the National Institute of Mental Health. The larger project was designed to assess the short-term and long-term effectiveness of lay-led and professionally led support groups for adult women who were experiencing high levels of stress from caring for a frail parent. To achieve this goal, an extensive personal interview was given to all 108 participants before their participation in a group or the control condition, within 2 weeks after their participation and then again at 6 months and 1 year. Nine-person groups met for eight, 2-hour, weekly sessions. All group sessions were audiotaped and analyzed by trained raters. Illustrated in the following case example are the beneficial effects of social group work on participants.

Both the professionally led and the lay-led groups relied heavily on supportive interventions. These included (1) ventilation of stressful experiences in an understanding and supportive environment, (2) validation and confirmation of similar caregiving experiences, (3) affirmation of members' ability to cope with their situation, (4) praise for providing care, and (5) support and understanding when struggling with difficult situations.

In addition to support, the professionally led groups used a semistructured approach that relied on education and problem solving. The lay-led groups were not as structured in their approach as the professional groups. They used a self-help approach that, in addition to support, emphasized a sharing of common concerns and a free exchange of information and coping mechanisms that members had found useful in their own caregiving situations.

In the professionally led groups, the educational component focused on a different topic each week: session one—introduction to the support group; session two—caregivers' emotions and feelings; session three—care receivers' reactions to illness; session four—taking care of oneself and doing positive things with the parent; session five—communication between the caregiver and care receiver and between the caregiver and other family members; session six—community resources; session seven—medical needs, pharmacology issues, and the nursing home placement process; and session eight—how to manage within the home and group termination. Participants were encouraged to ask questions and to share information pertinent to the weekly topic presented by the leader.

The problem-solving component of the professionally led groups was introduced during the first group session as a device to move members beyond ventilation of experiences and emotional reactions to methods for improving their coping skills. Each week participants were encouraged to work on their individual concerns using a six-step problem-solving model: (1) problems were identified by group members, (2) alternative action plans were developed through group discussion, (3) alternative action plans were assessed for their potential benefit and one was selected, (4) the action plan that was selected was discussed and cognitively rehearsed by the member who would implement it, (5) the action plan was carried out, and (6) the impact of the action plan was discussed in a subsequent group meeting, and any needed modifications were made. Careful analyses of audiotapes from the group sessions suggest that although the problem-solving model was not always carried out in a six-step linear fashion, the leader and the other group members were able to help many participants address problematic situations using the model.

## CASE DISCUSSION

To illustrate the therapeutic benefit of support groups for caregivers, a group led by a professional social worker who had over 5 years of clinical experience working with individuals and family members with chronic disabilities will be described.

During the first session, each member shared information about herself. The leader spoke first and modeled what was appropriate for a beginning discussion. She described her professional experience as well as her own caregiving experience with a parent. She decided to reveal her own caregiving experience because one of the basic premises of a support group is that no one can understand a situation as well as someone else who has experienced it.

Next, the group members introduced themselves.

Carm's mother, age 81, lives alone, has diabetes, is extremely overweight, has been widowed three times, and is extremely depressed. Carm, though married and working full-time, still manages to see her mother twice a day, does her mother's shopping, and supervises her mother's medication. Carm says "My mind is always with her."

Ethel cares for her mother-in-law, age 83, who came to live in Ethel's home 10 years ago after a small stroke. Three years ago Ethel's husband died, and since his death, her mother-in-law, who is also a diabetic, has been totally dependent on Ethel and is home alone all day while Ethel works as a legal secretary.

May is also caring for her mother-in-law who is bedridden. May's mother-in-law has Parkinson's disease and has lived with her for 5 years. An aide comes in three times a week for 4 hours a day, but the remaining burden of care is left to May.

Mary's mother, Beth, age 76, had lived alone and had not caused Mary undue stress until she suffered a stroke 6 months ago. At that time, Beth came to live with Mary. Because Mary was employed, Beth was left alone all day. After 3 months, she decided to live with her other daughter. Mary feels guilty about "driving her mother out."

Joan's mother, age 87, has lived with her for 10 years. Joan is an only child, divorced, with no children. Her mother has a heart condition and arthritis, wears a hearing aid, and is very argumentative. Joan finds it very difficult to live with her mother and wants to learn how to cope with her own impatience.

Kay's mother, age 93, has Alzheimer's disease and diabetes. Kay's husband resents his mother-in-law's presence and would like Kay to take steps to place her in a nursing home. Although Kay would like to accede to her husband's wishes, she loves her mother very much and finds it impossible to make the necessary arrangements.

Carol has been taking care of her mother for 25 years since her father died. Her mother, age 74, lives next door to Carol. Carol's sister and two brothers refuse to help, and Carol's own health is poor due to open-heart surgery 3 years ago and to arthritis in her legs. She feels unable to cope with the increasing physical demands of her mother's situation.

Betty's mother, age 77, lived alone until 4 years ago, when she had a series of strokes. Her physician did not think she should be home alone when released from the hospital, and she has been living in Betty's home ever since. Betty's husband is retired, they have a 10-year-old child, and Betty works full-time as a teacher. An aide comes every day for 3 hours a day, but Betty's husband feels his retirement is not turning out as he planned, and he is putting pressure on Betty to make alternative arrangements for her mother.

Rose is caring for her 71-year-old mother who is suffering from manic depression and high blood pressure. Rose is married, both she and her husband work, and they have two children who are away at college. Rose's mother, Anna, has been in this country for 35 years and has lived in Rose's home since Rose and her husband were married 25 years ago. Anna worked as a cleaning lady and is now retired and home alone all day. Anna has had several nervous breakdowns and has been in and out of the psychiatric units of local hospitals. She takes medication to control her psychiatric symptoms and high blood pressure. Rose's husband is fed up with the current caregiving situation and is exerting pressure on Rose to move Anna out of the home. Rose states frequently that she is not sure if her mother could live in another setting after living with Rose for 25 years.

After the introductions, norms for group participation were discussed and agreed to by the leader and the members. Emphasis was placed on the confidential nature of the group discussions. Because problem solving and stress reduction are the major foci of the group, skills for both are taught explicitly and modeled by the leader. Even when the stated topic is, for example, feelings of guilt or anger, the focus is not just on group sharing of these emotions but on reinforcing coping skills and problem-solving techniques that will help deal with these feelings outside of the group.

At the first session of the group, Rose shares basic facts about her family. She then launches into an emotion-laden description of her present unhappiness and the stress she is experiencing. She attributes her unhappiness to being overwhelmed by the demands of her family while responding to the increasing demands of her mother's worsening condition. Rose says her husband "has had it" with Anna but also says, "I'm the only daughter she has." This is the problem Rose would like to work on in the group.

The leader asks Rose to be more specific. Rose says "I want to address the problem of my mom (Anna) not taking her medication." Rose says "When Mom refuses to take her medication, her mood swings cause extreme disruption to all of us (the family). At this point I don't even like her anymore."

The leader tries to broaden the group perspective by suggesting that a possible motive for Anna's refusal to take her medication may be her anger toward Rose. Rose agrees and says Anna is "getting back at her" when Rose and her family go away for weekends. Rose says Anna "resents our having our freedom" and also shares with the group her feeling that "our problem is each other."

After gathering additional information, members suggest several possible solutions to the problem. One suggests putting the medication in Anna's favorite beverage. Rose doesn't see this as likely to be effective because Anna insists on supervising her own medication. Another member suggests sending Anna to adult day care. Rose insists "She (Anna) wouldn't go." The leader takes this opportunity to caution all members about making quick judgments before hearing what everyone has to say. A member continues by suggesting that Rose should tell her mother that she should move to an adult home where she would be able to have companionship during the day. The member states that this would enable Rose's family to increase their freedom. A member then suggests asking Anna's psychiatrist for his advice.

The leader recaps the suggestions. Rose thinks that the suggestion about discussing the matter with Anna's psychiatrist is the most appropriate and appealing at this time. Rose agrees to discuss the situation with the psychiatrist.

At each of the subsequent sessions, the leader tries to reinforce problem-solving skills and to focus group discussion in that direction. For example, at the next session, in response to the leader's query, Rose says she "feels better not because the situation has become any easier but because the group discussion of possibilities opened up my thinking about various alternatives." Also, Rose says she feels that group members "really understand my efforts to deal with Anna."

The following piece of dialogue may help to illustrate that it is possible for more than one person to derive benefit from group discussion of a particular topic.

*Leader:* Let's talk about manipulation. Do any of you feel manipulated in your caregiving situation?

*Joan:* I think manipulation gains advantage.

*Leader:* I don't understand quite what you mean; why don't you give an example?

*Joan:* When my mother says "I really don't feel well tonight," I feel she is telling me not to go out and leave her, and I feel manipulated and like I'm not in control. If I leave her and something happens while I'm out, I'll feel terribly guilty, but if I stay home I really resent having to give up my plans.

*Leader:* Maybe she needs to be reassured that she's still as important to you as you are to her.

*Rose:* Hey, you know this need for reassurance could be what's happening with my mother too.

*Leader:* Do you see a connection between your mother's medication problem and feeling manipulated?

*Rose:* Well yes; when she won't take her pills she becomes the center of attention, and she needs to be the center of attention when we go to our camp without her on weekends.

*Joan:* Are you saying that your mother won't take her pills because she wants to feel that you still love her even though you are going away for a few days?

*Rose:* It sounds as if it could be, don't you think? (to leader)

*Leader:* What do group members think?

*Kay:* Even if it's true, what should she do about it?

*Leader:* You know, it is possible to expose the manipulation to the person who is manipulating you. Sometimes if you lay your cards on the table you can be in a better position.

*Ethel:* That doesn't sound so easy to do. My mother-in-law would just say I was overreacting.

*Carol:* You have to remember that you have rights too; you have to stand up for yourself.

The leader asks Rose if she has any other thoughts. Rose brings up her worries about vacation plans for the upcoming summer season. "If I can't handle my mother about weekend trips, what will she do about longer vacations?" Rose says that mental illness is not like physical illness. "Mental illness makes it uncomfortable to invite visitors that other family members might enjoy seeing." Group members respond empathically to this statement and agree that it is potentially more embarrassing because of the unpredictable nature of some psychiatric symptoms. Rose says she is tired of hearing "I don't know how you do it" from visitors and friends and continues, "I'm not looking for meaningless praise." All the

group members agree, and several add that they would like to hear offers of help rather than praise.

At session six the leader brings up the issue of group termination. She mentions another group that has continued to meet. She also mentions that this group "would welcome new members." The leader also suggests that group members can be a resource to each other by phone. This leads to a general discussion by group members about the benefits of the support group.

*Carol:* On the way over here tonight I was worrying about what I would do when the group ended. You know, *friends don't really understand;* they mean well, but unless they are doing it too, they just don't know what it's like to be tied down like this and not know when it's going to end. Sometimes I think my mother will go on forever and I will die first.

*May:* You're right, with how many friends can you discuss the differences between Depends and Attends (different brands of adult diapers), which ones you use at different times, and which store has the best prices?

*Betty:* Yeah, even if you have a good friend, you think you'll drive her away if you talk about what's really on your mind. Can you tell your friend you think about what it would be like if your mother died? Your friend will think you're a monster and tell you "You should be grateful your mother is still alive." I don't know what I would do without the group.

*Rose:* You know, ever since I started coming here I've been much more patient with my mother because I know I can let it all out here. Now I have a place in which I can release my feelings of anger. I really look forward to coming here because I know you all understand what I'm going through.

*Leader:* I take it, then, from all your comments that you want to think about continuing the group when this one officially terminates. Let's think about how you want to do it, and we'll talk about it again at the last session.

When the leader goes around the group asking members about their past week, Rose shares her experience with Anna's psychiatrist. Rose had spoken to the doctor about her mother's medication as she had agreed to do. Rose says the doctor also suggested "placing Mom in an adult home or in a supported apartment program, a program run by the county mental health center." The doctor was very supportive of having Anna change living arrangements.

During the group discussion of this information, Rose admitted to still feeling manipulated by Anna: "I'm playing her game, playing into her hands, and I can't have my family disrupted anymore." The leader asks Rose how she feels about the suggestion from the doctor. Rose says "Terrible; I can't bring myself to dial the phone numbers that are necessary to make the arrangements." Carm and Joan tell Rose that even if she feels uncomfortable considering this move, she has still come a long way from the first session. However, other members confront Rose and remind her it takes two to continue this manipulative pattern.

*Ethel:* Nobody is going to treat you like a doormat unless you lay down.

*Betty:* That's right; it takes two you know. You must be cooperating with her or she wouldn't be able to do it.

*Leader:* Rose, by cooperating you give Anna a tremendous sense of power and control.

*Rose:* But even her psychiatrist says he never dealt with someone like her before.

*Leader:* Do you find that reassuring?

*Rose:* Yeah, wouldn't you?

*Leader:* Just remember, Rose, you are the one who is responsible for your own happiness, not Anna. It's up to you to take control of this situation, and you can do it.

*Rose:* I know I have to do it; I have to do something. Last week when we talked about community services and Carol told about Lifeline (an emergency button people wear around their necks that is connected to a 24-hour switchboard at a local hos-

pital and will summon aid if pushed), I thought that would be a big help to me knowing she could always push a button and get help in an emergency. She's just so used to me being there all the time.

*Leader:* I know it's hard for you trying to make all the changes that the doctor laid on you, but it will become more comfortable after you think about it for a while.

*Leader:* (speaking to the entire group) Remember the self-talk coping skills we learned earlier. Part of guilt is what you tell yourself. Give yourself credit for time served, and look at what you have done and have tried to do already.

During the eighth and last group session, nothing new is added from Rose. The group terminates but makes plans to meet informally once a month for lunch and to continue to share caregiving experiences with each other.

One of the drawbacks of time-limited support groups is that there may not be enough time to follow through completely on all the problematic issues that arise. It might be beneficial for follow-up meetings to be scheduled in order to resolve issues that were left without closure. Also, it is possible that short-term work may not be the most appropriate model for this population because caregiving is often a long-term proposition.

At a follow-up interview, Rose disclosed that Anna had finally moved out of Rose's home into her own "supported" apartment. So far Anna is managing to live independently, and Rose's family is much happier without Anna's constant disruptions. Rose also said that moving Anna was a very difficult process for her and that without the support and encouragement from group members, she would not have had the inner strength to follow through with her plan.

### Reference

Toseland, R., & Rossiter, C. (1989). Group interventions to support caregivers: A review and analysis. *The Gerontologist, 29,* 438–448.

# CASE STUDY 5.4

*Divorce mediation is being increasingly used as an alternative to judicial intervention. This case illustrates how the practice of divorce mediation requires the blending of law, social work, and counseling.*

## Questions

1. What is the role of the divorce mediator?
2. What social work skills are needed to facilitate mediation between two parties?
3. What are some similarities and differences between mediation and counseling?
4. What must be accomplished before the client can move to the resolution stage of the mediation process?

## DIVORCE MEDIATION: AN APPLICATION OF SOCIAL WORK SKILLS AND TECHNIQUES

*Ann L. Milne*

Susan and John Brown were married at ages 22 and 24, respectively. They had known each other and dated steadily for several years before marrying. They were well suited for each other. They were in love. The Browns have now been married 12 years. They have two children, ages 8 and 10, a house, and two cars, and both work outside the home. They're no longer in love.

To see them in court, one wonders how they could ever have cared for each other. Susan and John are fighting over everything—the children, the house, property, finances, even the bills. They've each hired attorneys who have pursued all legal avenues—depositions, interrogatories, multiple appraisals, private investigators, outside consultants, and witnesses—to protect the interests of their clients and to attempt to obtain the best deal. Susan and John have put their marriage on trial.

Each expects to be able to tell his or her own story to the judge, to be heard and understood, and to receive a fair settlement. Unbeknownst to the Browns, the rules of evidence do not permit them to tell all, and the judge finds that much of the story is irrelevant to the disposition of the case. The children are torn between taking sides and withdrawing from both parents. The lives of friends and family have been disrupted, and Susan and John have depleted their meager estate in litigation.

The Browns could spend the rest of their lives acting out of hurts, angers, and other emotions that occur before, during, and after the divorce. A judge's decision may not end the warfare. When a marriage dissolves, legal proceedings become entwined with the parties' emotions, making divorce-related decisions a matter of the heart and the law (Gold, 1981, p. 181).

Divorce mediation has evolved from a blending of the practices of law, social work, and counseling. Divorce mediation is an alternative to traditional judicial intervention and third-party decision making. A divorce mediator serves as a neutral who assists divorcing couples to develop their own parental, financial, and property agreements and promotes decision making within the family (Folberg & Milne, 1988).

The practice of divorce mediation has attracted a significant response from the field of social work. According to a survey of divorce mediators (Pearson, Ring, & Milne, 1983), approximately 42% of the mediators employed in private practice are social workers, and 72% of those employed by the public sector have a social work background.

## THE PROCESS OF MEDIATION

A description of the process of mediation will highlight the complementary relationship between mediation and social work. Several authors have described the mediation process as a linear series of stages (Brown, 1982; Folberg & Taylor, 1984; Gulliver, 1979; Kessler, 1978; Moore, 1983). Kessler (1978) describes mediation as a four-stage process: (1) setting the stage; (2) defining the issues; (3) processing the issues; and (4) resolving the issues. For the sake of simplicity, this four-stage approach will be used to describe the interventions and techniques of divorce mediation.

### Setting the Stage

The theater for mediation may be established long before the disputants enter the mediator's office. The initial phone contact provides an opportunity for both the parties and the mediator to gather limited data about each other, to explore individual expectations, and to formulate the beginning of the mediation relationship; that is, does this person sound like someone I can work with. This initial testing of the waters goes both ways—the client assessing the mediator and the mediator assessing the client. The agreement to set an appointment is preceded by a tacit agreement, an unsigned contract, that both the mediator and the parties are interested in further exploring the mediation process.

At the initial meeting between the couple and the mediator, the stage continues to be set as the mediator introduces himself/herself and asks the parties to tell something about themselves, what brought them to mediation, and what the issues are. Important here is the establishment of the relationship between the parties and the mediator based on a sense of trust, respect, empathy, and interest. As this is accomplished, the mediator builds credibility with the parties as he/she begins to explain the mediation process, what it can and cannot accomplish, and how it may or may not be of help to them based on their description of the issues in dispute.

By defining the mediator's role as that of a consultant, contracted by the parties to facilitate their communication and settlement process, the mediator marks his/her role as that of an expert in assisting them in reaching a resolution rather than determining a resolution for them. Most experienced mediators will emphasize that the final responsibility for settlement lies with the parties and that the job of the mediator is similar to that of a coach—calling on a particular set of plays and strategies that will assist the players on the field. The mediator further sets the stage by foreshadowing (Kessler, 1978) some of the elements of mediation—the need for flexibility, a willingness to negotiate and compromise, a willingness to settle the issues, and an acknowledgment of the typical stumbling blocks of mediation. This foreshadowing process furthers the definitional task of the mediator and assists the clients in committing themselves to the process (Kessler, 1978). As the parties become aware of their responsibility for the final outcome of mediation, they must confront the issues of trust and risk taking. How vulnerable are they willing to be with the other spouse?

This question is probably answered by most couples according to how much trust they are willing to invest in the mediator and their sense of his/her expertise and understanding of them.

As the parties and the mediator jointly assess the appropriateness of mediation, a "buy-in" process is initiated where the parties determine their commitment to the mediation process. When mediation is presented in such a voluntary fashion, the parties have the opportunity to discuss the various settlement processes available to them, that is, interpersonal negotiations, third-party negotiations, therapy, litigation, and adjudication. Those parties who choose mediation have already reached their first agreement—to resolve the issues privately and nonadversarily. Thus, the initial tasks in this preliminary stage of mediation are those that relate to the relationship between the mediator and the clients, the establishment of the limits of the mediation process, and the definition of the role of the mediator. Many of the aforementioned tasks in this stage of the mediation process are the same goals that a social worker hopes to initially accomplish—establishing trust, rapport, commitment to the process, and definition of the relationship between the social worker and the clients. The social worker may foreshadow the course of treatment by describing the general treatment plan and typical resistances to change that the client or family may encounter. Although the resolution of hurt, anger, fear, guilt, and rejection is not the purpose of divorce mediation as it is with counseling, these relationship issues are often germane to the mediation process. This then leads us to the next stage of mediation.

## Defining the Issues

When a mediator first asks the parties to define the issues in dispute, most parties do so by answering with their solution or with their final position. "Well Mr./Ms. Mediator, the dispute is about custody—I want custody and so does he/she"; or "I think I should have the house because . . . and he/she thinks he/she should have the house because . . ."

This positional bargaining (Fisher & Ury, 1981; Moore, 1983) is typically a dead end or at best leads the parties into a contest of wills to see who can convince and/or wear down the other.

The mediator's task is now twofold: (1) to move the parties from this positional posture to a discussion of basic needs and interests and (2) to surface any underlying conflicts that may inhibit the mediation process. This typically occurs through a questioning process such as "What is it that you are unhappy about?" and "What is it that you are really looking for?"

As this questioning process proceeds, the couple begins to surface a number of other issues, often of long-standing duration, related to the marital relationship and/or issues that are individual and specific to each spouse. Reflective of this will be the identification of conflicts of a personal and relational nature.

The task of the mediator is to assist the couple in cataloging the various kinds of conflicts. Kessler (1978) offers three categories: (1) topical issues, (2) personal issues, and (3) relational issues.

Topical issues may be described as the "point-at-ables" of divorce, that is, division of property, finances, how the children will spend time with each parent. They are issues that are often physical and observable and make up most divorce stipulations.

Personal issues may be described as those internal conflicts and concerns that each individual brings to mediation. These may be historical issues rooted in family of origin, such as self-esteem, power, anger, and loss of love objects. Mediation often opens the door to these personal issues of long-standing duration. These personal issues may also appear in the form of "new me," for example, "I was never able to assert myself in the marriage and I'm not going to let him/her walk all over me now." The need to turn over a new leaf and act differently is often observed in divorce mediation.

Relationship issues are the accumulated marital/divorce issues that were not resolved during the marriage and continue to be unresolved as the couple moves from being spouses to being former marital partners. The hurts, the angers, the unfulfilled expectations, and the unmet promises of the marriage are the substance of relationship conflicts and are often at the root of disputes brought to mediation.

The task of the mediator is to validate the topical, personal, and relationship issues as legitimate conflicts but to apprise the parties that mediation is a process that focuses on the topical issues. The goal is not the resolution of the personal and relationship issues but rather to manage these issues as they become road blocks to the resolution of the topical issues.

The issues presented in therapy are different from the issues presented in mediation. Clients typically contact a counselor because they are unhappy or are having problems coping with a life event or relationship issue. Therapy tends to focus on the personal and relationship issues as opposed to the topical issues. The therapist often takes a greater responsibility for defining the issues than does a mediator. As a therapy client presents the precipitating problem, the therapist is analyzing the psychological makeup of the issue and the underlying roots of the problem. The therapist's analysis of the problem is rooted in an understanding of psychodynamics, emotional needs, systems theory, and the communication process. The therapist will then present the issues to clients using this format and recommend a course of treatment on that basis.

The mediator on the other hand analyzes the presenting issues from a different perspective. Although not oblivious to the psychological nature of the dispute, the mediator assists the couple in defining conflicts based on mutual needs and interests and the need to separate psychological conflict from negotiations directed toward the resolution of the topical issues. The mediator's analysis of the problem focuses on the settlement of contractual issues and road blocks to the bargaining and mediation process.

It is this definitional process—defining the issues, cataloging them, and recombining them into needs and interests as opposed to positions—that brings the parties to the next stage of the mediation process.

**Processing the Issues**

The differences and similarities between mediation and counseling begin to emerge more clearly as we view the processing of the issues in mediation.

As the mediator assists the parties in focusing on the topical issues of the divorce and redefining them as interests or needs, the parties are able to move into the processing of the issues. This reframing process allows for a discussion of the issues in a manner conducive to settlement rather than the competitive push/pull routine that results from the taking of a position.

The mediator can now attend to the parties' communication/negotiation processes. Typical of most parties new to mediation is a communication process reflective of their behavior during the marriage. It didn't prove to be very workable then and probably is ineffective now too. The task of the mediator is to demonstrate this to the couple and provide them with more effective communication tools.

The mediator may point out patterns of rhetorical conflict (expanding conflict for its own sake) that result in an impasse and contrast this to such techniques as active listening, "I-statements," paraphrasing, modeling, and role reversal. By asking one party to take the other's position, the mediator reinforces an understanding of the other's needs and goals. Even a modicum of understanding and empathy begins to eat away at an adversarial, competitive relationship.

Blockages to communication typically result from the appearance of personal and relationship issues, as noted above. For some couples, mediation is a catch-22. It provides a means of continuing a relationship with one's spouse, while its goal is that of separating from the relationship. Some couples seem to relish the mediation process but avoid reaching any agreements. This is similar to the resistance to change that many clients experience in therapy.

The mediator must attend to relationship and individual issues as they become road blocks to settlement while processing the topical issues. Reestablishing the parties' commitment to the process of mediation and identifying the issues relevant to mediation and those more appropriate to therapy are ways of managing the emotional climate. Acknowledging the relationship issues and asking the parties to develop ways of dealing with these issues so that they do not inhibit the process of mediation is a management technique used in the mediation process. Unlike the therapist, the mediator will stop short of resolving these types of issues and instead will intervene with the couple to develop a means of managing these issues while focusing on the topical issues. A counselor may delve into the individual and relationship conflicts while the mediator and the couple will plan a means of detouring around these issues.

Often the mediator will be confronted with the relational issues of power and control. Power may lie with a party having a verbally aggressive style or a better ability to articulate or with a spouse who possesses more information about such things as finances or child development. Rarely are parties evenly matched in all areas. Often, though, this imbalance

provides a solution to the conflict—assisting parties in combining their assets (their power) in a cooperative decision-making process that can work to their mutual gain as opposed to the more destructive end of sole enhancement.

The counselor will attend to issues of power and control in a different fashion. Often these issues are related to family of origin, unmet psychological needs, and emotional well-being. Rather than accepting these differences between the couple, the counselor will work toward an understanding of these differences and a resolution of them. Therapists often find that they must become an advocate for a client in therapy and must then deal with the problem of triangulation. Inexperienced mediators may find themselves in the same position. More sophisticated mediators view themselves as an advocate of the settlement process and take less responsibility for the final resolution or agreement. In mediation, client advocacy is left to the parties' attorneys.

By reorienting the parties toward mutual goals and overlapping interests, the mediator moves the parties along the resolution continuum. Fisher and Ury (1981) analogize this reorienting process as one of having the parties move from sitting at opposite ends of the negotiation table to sitting at the same side of the table as though they were two judges faced with having to make a joint determination on a particular issue.

Moving the parties to the same side of the table allows for the continuation of the resolution process. This occurs by the mediator assisting the parties in developing a list of possible solutions and options that could potentially meet their identified needs and interests. This is done without evaluating any of the options on the table. This brainstorming process reinforces the mutuality of the problem and assists the parties in separating their interests from the solutions (Fisher & Ury, 1981).

It may become evident that the parties need more information to move to the resolution stage of the mediation process. Doing home-work, sharing information, and consulting with outside experts may help with this.

Once the options are generated and the parties have access to information pertinent to the issues, they will likely enter the resolution stage of mediation.

### Resolving the Issues

Once alternatives have been generated, the couple can begin the matching and mutual accommodation process inherent in resolving the issues. A building-block process begins when needs and interests are matched with solutions (Fisher & Ury, 1981; Moore, 1983). This building-block process is simplified when issues are dealt with in a singular fashion rather than allowing issues to be linked so that the resolution of one issue is dependent on the determination of a different issue. This is sometimes a luxury in divorce mediation, as plans for children and financial arrangements can be dependent on each other.

Often solutions are reached by parties combining proposals, reaching tentative agreements (eliminating the need to overcommit to something a party does not yet feel comfortable with), and agreeing to agree in principle. The combining of options is similar to a sounding-out process, where if we extend Fisher and Ury's (1981) analogy of the two judges, we find the parties working to fit pieces of the options together to fashion an agreement whose fabric will cover both their shared and separate interests.

As the agreement begins to take shape, the mediator helps the parties develop a plan for finalizing and implementing the agreement. This final stage in the mediation process is the culmination of a set of previously accomplished tasks that fall within the linear stages of mediation. The reliance on creativity and the generation of options in this final stage allows the parties to complete a means/end shift whereby the parties shift their focus from the desired end position to the means to that end (Moore, 1983). This shift breaks the deadlock that often occurs between parties who become enmeshed in the personal and relationship issues and who have positioned themselves in order to defend their separate stakes.

The counseling process also employs a means/end shift. Clients come to counseling seeking an end to emotional stress and a dysfunctional and unhappy relationship. The means to that end differentiates counseling from mediation. The counselor explores the precipitating factors or the means of psychological and relationship stress. Clients are helped to understand the cause of the conflict, which then allows them to change behaviors and approaches to troublesome situations. The cognitive understanding of the problem and the ability to satisfy underlying emotional needs based on a supportive relationship with the counselor allows the client to shift from the desire (the end) for well-being and happiness to the means to that end.

A redefinition of the presenting problem often occurs in both mediation and counseling. In mediation the redefinition process focuses on the isolation of topical issues from individual and relationship issues and the exploration of alternatives to settlement. In counseling, the nature of the presenting problem is redefined as an individual or interpersonal conflict. The resolution of the conflict in mediation is reached through the exploration of settlement alternatives—different ways of dividing the pie. The resolution of conflict in a clinical setting is effected through an understanding of the ingredients that make up the pie.

### CONCLUSION

Critics who state that mediation is only a whitewash of the more substantive interpersonal and psychological issues may have a point. Yet many couples do not wish to engage in a psychotherapeutic process and find that mediation is a means to an end that satisfies their interests in reaching a settlement. The resolution of the contractual issues provides the emotional distance and clarity that many couples need to separate physically and emotionally.

The blurring between mediation and counseling is attributable to the confusion between objectives and process. The objectives of counseling are not the objectives of mediation but may become the tools of the process.

Diagnosis of underlying issues, enhancement of self-esteem, facilitation of communication, reinforcement of autonomy, and extinction of dysfunctional behaviors are techniques used in mediation to facilitate the process. Diagnosis of underlying issues aids the definition of the conflict. The enhancement of self-esteem, the reinforcement of autonomy, and the extinction of dysfunctional behaviors aids the communication process and the ability of the couple to reach an agreement.

Mediation draws on the techniques of the more behavioral forms of therapy but differs from such forms of counseling because of the focus of the process. The relationship between the mediator and the client may include elements of a therapeutic relationship such as the establishment of trust, rapport, and identification, but the agreement-producing process does not rely on these elements to the same extent as occurs in therapy.

Mediation differs from counseling because of the issues addressed and the types of conflict that are resolved. The historical origin of the dispute is explored only when doing so is necessary to avoid an impasse and to move the mediation process along. The relationship between the mediator and the disputants is not dependent on elements of identification and individual support.

Mediation is an interpersonal dispute resolution process that focuses on the contractual issues of property, finances, and plans for the children. Mediation seeks to address and understand the future needs of the couple and their children. The resolution of past differences and the acquisition of insight into the dynamics of the conflict may occur as the result of mediation but are not goals of the process. Divorce mediation typically results in a written agreement that is incorporated into an order of the court at the time of judgment or postdivorce.

When behavioral change or emotional well-being are the predominant goals, the process is likely that of therapy. When the objective is that of resolving the topical and contractual issues of the divorce, the practice is that of mediation.

## References

Brown, D. (1982). Divorce and family mediation: History, review, future directions. *Conciliation Courts Review, 20,* 1–44.

Fisher, R., & Ury, W. (1981). *Getting to yes: Negotiating agreement without giving in.* Boston: Houghton Mifflin.

Folberg, H. J., & Milne, A. (Eds.). (1988). *Divorce mediation: Theory and practice.* New York: Guilford Press.

Folberg, H. J., & Taylor, A. (1984). *Mediation: A comprehensive guide to resolving conflicts without litigation.* San Francisco: Jossey-Bass.

Gold, L. (1981). Mediation in the dissolution of marriage. *The Arbitration Journal, 36,* 9–13.

Gulliver, P. (1979). *Disputes and negotiations: A cross cultural perspective.* New York: Academic Press.

Kessler, S. (1978). *Creative conflict resolution: Mediation.* Atlanta: National Institute for Professional Training.

Moore, C. W. (1983). *The mediation process: Practical strategies for resolving conflict.* San Francisco: Jossey-Bass.

Pearson, J., Ring, M., & Milne, A. (1983). A portrait of divorce mediation services in the public and private sector. *Conciliation Courts Review, 21,* 1–24.

# CASE STUDY 5.5

*Many cities are facing major problems that reflect growing crime, poverty, drug use, housing shortages, and racial and economic factions. Yonkers is one such city, and this case study aptly illustrates how community organizing can play a critical role in responding to such difficult challenges.*

## Questions

1. What factors led to the convergence of the problems described in the case study?
2. What skills are needed to be an effective community organizer?
3. How did the community organizer get the citizens involved in the organizing efforts?
4. What changes were brought about as a result of the organizing process?

## YONKERS: A NEW TALE OF TWO CITIES

*Jacqueline B. Mondros and Neil McGuffin*

In 1986 a group of Catholic clergy in the city of Yonkers received funding to hire a community organizer. Yonkers was a decaying town, fraught with problems of crime, poor city services, a failing school system, an expensive yet deteriorating housing stock, and racial and economic divisions. The organizer's task was to bring together Yonkers residents to begin to identify and work on city problems. During the organizing process, the organizer was compelled to respond to an unanticipated and nationally reported housing crisis.

This is the story of that initial organizing effort. We will first describe Yonkers and the ways in which Yonkers reflects the problems of other urban areas. We then explicate the assumptions and processes of community organizing and tell the story of how a community organization was built in Yonkers.

## THE CITY CONTEXT

The proud motto "City of Gracious Living" seems apt if you enter Yonkers from the north,

but driving into Getty Square (the traditional commercial, business, and municipal government area) from the south gives one an entirely different impression. Bordering on New York City, the bedroom community of Yonkers is actually two distinct communities—the urban area of southwest Yonkers, with all the signs of urban decay, and the suburban areas of northwest and east Yonkers, still neatly arrayed with large homes. The dichotomies and distinctions between these two communities constitute the motif, the underlying theme for housing, school, and related battles of the 1980s.

Yonkers is a city of 200,000, the fourth largest in New York state, and the largest city in affluent Westchester County. Built along the deep-gorged Hudson River, easily accessible by commuter railway, Yonkers is located equal distance from Manhattan and the wealthy Westchester villages of Scarsdale and Larchmont, directly in the path of New York's large urban sprawl. Yonkers' location makes it ripe for urban geopolitics. It is an attractive

161

community for many because of its decent housing stock and its proximity to Manhattan's diverse employment opportunities. The city is composed of 40% black and Hispanic families. The remaining 60% includes Italians, Germans, WASPs, Irish, Jews, Poles, Slovaks, Filipinos, Portuguese, and Arabs. According to the 1980 census, the median family income was $22,192, with 25% living below the poverty level. Median value of housing was $69,800, far less than surrounding communities. Housing stock is diverse: large single-family homes stand next to subsidized housing developments. At present, the southwest side of Yonkers is inhabited predominantly by white working poor and minority families—all the major public and subsidized housing was built in this area during the last three decades. The east, northeast, and northwest areas of Yonkers are home to largely white middle-class families.

The strong council form of government reinforces turf issues and struggles. Members of the city council are elected to represent wards. The only citywide elected official is the mayor, whose formal responsibilities are mostly ceremonial. The city manager, accountable to the city council, enjoys the stability of tenure comparable only to the manager of the New York Yankees. Elected officials have been so preoccupied with seemingly petty turf battles that they have not attended to the problems that have brought the city to the brink of bankruptcy several times in the last 15 years. Currently, all spending in the city is overseen by an Emergency Financial Control Board created by the state legislature.

In 1980, the United States Department of Justice filed suit against the city of Yonkers, charging it with intentionally segregating its schools and housing stock. The city was found guilty, and in 1984 a court order to remedy the segregation was issued. The order called for school busing and 200 units of public housing to be built on the east side. The suit

became a lightning rod for citywide anger, fears, and tensions. Politicians encouraged citizens to take sides in the controversy: one was either for the public housing or opposed to it. In the ensuing polarization, ugly epithets, not ideas or proposals, were exchanged as people argued, charged, and defended the extent to which differences were essentially racially or economically motivated or both. Other urban problems, serious problems like crime, drugs, unemployment, and plant closings, deserving to be in the forefront were pushed instead to the background. The controversy raged with hardly a hint of the deep moral issues implicit in the controversy. People seemed to have forgotten all the pertinent precepts they had learned in church.

While the attention was on the east side public housing storm, land on the west side along the Hudson River was being bought up for waterfront development, including luxury condominiums, fancy shops and boutiques, theaters, restaurants, and health clubs. Simultaneously, a wave of conversion to co-ops and condominiums was sweeping the west side, just as it had swept the east side 5 years earlier. To an experienced and analytic eye, the planned city changes were clear: tipping theory was at work. The current white and middle-income east side was slated to be tipped to a lower-income population, and the present low-income west side, located along the Hudson, would be tipped to attract a more affluent population. The script for the tale of two cities had been rewritten but not yet made public.

Citizens saw themselves, not unrealistically, as powerless to participate in these public decisions. In November 1987 the federal judge, as part of the penalty for the city's failure to comply with the public housing order, froze all development in the city, most of which was taking place in the poor area of southwest Yonkers. The councilman from the affected southwest ward of Yonkers was the only one on the council who had consistently voted to build the public housing, but it did not influence the decision of the judge to halt all development in his ward as well. The judge's good intentions notwithstanding, the needs of the residents of southwest Yonkers were put aside. To them it was again a clear indication that their franchise mattered little.

Federal judges (even well-intentioned ones), lawyers, and private developers were in charge of the future of Yonkers, while elected officials and the media fanned the fires of fears and the baser motives. Political campaigns were run on the single issue of opposition to public housing. The public record was not easily accessible to the average citizen, and so inaccurate media coverage went unchallenged. Media focused exclusively on the legality of the public housing suit, and their stories were about court documents, opinions, rumors, and the legal positionings of a slew of lawyers. The only accurate sources of information were the primary legal documents, located at the federal court in lower Manhattan—a brief journey as the crow flies but several hours as public transportation moves. To obtain the documents requires acuity in legal language and in research. They are in any case unintelligible to most laypersons, and even the most tireless public-spirited citizen would find it difficult to become and remain informed.

## YONKERS AND URBAN CHANGE

The emotions aroused by the Yonkers housing issue are not uncommon. The 1980s have produced clear evidence of a large-scale change taking place in our economy. As a recent study reported, the average American family was not "doing better" in the period from 1978 to 1988. Although wages have increased two and a half times, prices have increased three times. If more people work, it is because more families have two wage earners simply to stay in place. Prices have increased most in housing, and many families are unable to buy. This is occurring at the same time that housing subsidies have decreased by 50% since 1981 (*Low income needs,* 1987). For people in many communities, not just those in Yonkers, housing is an important concern, and buying a home is rapidly becoming an "impossible" American dream.

The city of Yonkers received national press attention and was depicted as "Mississippi on the Hudson." As Father John Duffell, pastor of St. Peter's Roman Catholic church, told the *Washington Post,* "Yonkers doesn't have any more racists than any other city in America." The resurgence of racism can be related to changing economic times and what has happened to the vaunted American middle class. Alinsky talked about the "haves," "the have nots," and the "have a little want some mores." Clearly, there are both more "haves" and "have nots," and those who "have a little want some more" are changing. For these Americans with two incomes, there is little hope that they can have more. The keys to American upward mobility—living in better neighborhoods, getting better educations, getting better-paying jobs, and pursuing better careers—has become virtually unattainable. The "have a little want some mores" have become "have a little want to keep its." When there is a belief that everyone can have more and that there are tried and true ways of getting more, the society has a common, if unrealistic, understanding: one can say that if others do as I do—that is, get an education, stay off drugs, and keep their house clean—they can have what I have. But when the belief is that one can't have any more and nothing one does will bring any more, keeping what one has becomes essential. People will fight any group that tries to take what they have. "Keeping it" becomes a defensive ethos, and you protect what you have with an angry, anxious defensiveness.

Changes in the culture and the economy have created a new and difficult environment for organizers. Economic divisions have intensified, and the belief in the chance for upward mobility has diminished. It is now clear to many middle- and working-class people that the prevailing ideology does not describe their reality. The major voice of our culture has enthroned self-interest and denigrated the public good; voices that counter the private-interest argument seem to be muted or rarely heard. A recent episode punctuating the Yonkers battle on public housing was the bombing of a group home for children in the New York City borough of Queens. Here, too, the people took positions based on "have a little want to keep it," unconcerned about the hopes of others to "have a little" as well. Here the language of narrow self-interest was palpable: my interests over your interests, and my power pitted against yours. The insistence on what is good for self against the possibly greater good for all is so consuming that people resort to violence and threats of violence rather than efforts to reconcile and accommodate to the needs and hopes of an adversary.

## THE WORK OF A COMMUNITY ORGANIZER

In direct contrast to this defensive ethos, community organizing is about participating, finding common ground, reconciling private needs with public issues, and giving everyone a stake in the American dream. Brager and Specht (1979) define community organization as:

> a method of intervention whereby individuals, groups, and organizations engage in planned action to influence social problems. It is concerned with the enrichment, development, and/or change of social institutions and involves two major related processes: planning (that is, identifying problem areas, diagnosing causes, and formulating solutions) and organizing (that is, developing the constituencies and devising the strategies necessary to effect action).

The organizer's task is to translate all this into action. Adherence to certain principles underlies and informs the organizer's behavior.

1. A community organizer has two purposes: (1) to empower people and (2) to redistribute existing power. To realize the first, the organizer validates people's perception of a shared problem, helps them identify their own important issues, and educates them about issues and how to proceed to resolve them. By working collectively and effectively on their own defined community issues, the organizer reinforces the competence of community people and shows them that they can, in fact, become powerful. To realize the second purpose, that is, power redistribution, the organizer offers and provides technical abilities in researching issues and designing strategy to help people achieve their goals. As victories accrue, power is taken from powerholders and brokers and given to the people.

2. The primary role of the community organizer is to help people do for themselves, which in current language is empowering people. In this sense, the organizer is an enabler, teacher, and resource provider, not essentially an administrator, planner, or manager who acts on behalf of or represents others. As people learn to act in their own behalf, they experience a sense of power, become more competent to act on their own, and see a need for an organization to represent them.

3. The organizer seeks to engage all interested people, recruiting from every existing and relevant segment and network, particularly those who have been previously excluded from the decision-making process. Community organizations are designed to include the broadest representation of people living within a community, and as many people as possible are encouraged to participate in every aspect and decision of the organization.

4. Because an organizer hopes to attract a large and diverse constituency, a variety of issues will arise that must somehow be addressed. Different groups of people bring with them different special interests, and if people are to have a stake in the organizing, their particular issues will have to be handled. The expertise of the organizer is not in single issue areas but in how to understand, do research, and plan for action on community issues.

5. Once people have understood the need to act collectively to achieve and use power, a structured and disciplined organization must be formed as a prerequisite to achieving its task. In this process, mutuality and accountability among members and with the organizer develops, and the organization becomes a countervailing force, able to negotiate with powerholders as equals.

## THE PARIS MINISTRY MODEL

In Yonkers, a city already in crisis and riven by racial tension, there was a very real question whether the establishment of a progressive, broad-based, multi-issue organization was possible.

If an organization was to have a chance of success in the turbulent environment of Yonkers, we felt it would have to be based on a Parish Ministry Model. Sometimes called congregational organizing, the model is animated by three ideas: (1) It calls for a federated structure based on area churches and synagogues. Religious institutions join the organization, pay substantial membership dues as an institution, and send delegates to the organization. (2) The organizations do a substantial amount of training of community leaders prior to working on common issues. The training is not about what to organize but how to organize, run meetings, select issues, and choose strategies. (3) Parish Ministry Model organizations ground their organizing

in scriptural teachings. Thus, the organizer encourages people to talk about and act as a "community of faith." Liturgy becomes part of the organization's private discussions and public face.

Federated structural arrangements are commonly used by grassroots organizers to tap into existing networks to recruit people. The superordinate strength of the parish model is that priests, ministers, and rabbis put their imprimatur on the organization and on the people in their congregations who are asked to become involved. This lends special legitimacy to the organization and a special sense of responsibility to the chosen representatives.

In organizing, training people before they are helped to take action on an issue is a relatively new idea. Organizers have thought that a classroom atmosphere is not conducive to leadership development; people learn best when they experience the organizing process. Training, however, is a way for new people to become involved in the organization slowly and cautiously, but an organizer must be aware that training doesn't compensate for acting on an issue.

The most innovative aspect of the Parish Ministry Model is the use of church doctrine as an ideology for organizing. It is, at least on the surface, a radical departure from Alinsky's admonition that people's organizations should carry no dogma. (Although he did write, "Do what you can with what you have and clothe it in moral garments.") In the Parish Ministry Model the use of religion is seen as a way to recruit and retain members, reward them, and reinforce group norms. It is a strategy that has been used to advantage by the far-right wing as well as by various groups in Latin America and other parts of the Third World to make organization-building more acceptable and powerful.

Our assessment in Yonkers was that a unified interfaith group of clergy and lay people could bring a moral voice, a calming effect, and political clout to bear on the city's crisis. Organizing in Yonkers, we knew, would require using basic organizing principles according to a Parish Ministry Model.

## THE ORGANIZING PROCESS IN YONKERS

In 1986, some religious and lay leaders obtained social ministry funds from two religious denominations to hire a community organizer. Initially the organizer set up meetings where residents of southwest Yonkers expressed and discussed their concerns and hopes for their neighborhood. It was not difficult for people to voice their problems and see commonalities. People chose to organize around their desire to renovate a park used by children and senior citizens. They wanted to add play equipment and benches. A small group of people met with the mayor and vice-mayor, who agreed to expend city funds and include the people in the planning of the improvements. Next, the organizer worked with two groups: a group of homeowners who wanted to have a vacant lot cleaned and fenced and a group of apartment dwellers who wanted building inspections to be done by the city and the establishment of a special fund to provide low-interest downpayments to purchase their apartments. The organizer worked with these tenants and homeowners jointly; each group supported the requests of the other. They met with the mayor, vice-mayor, and director of the Community Development Bureau, who agreed to meet their requests. Several other local issues were identified, developed, and successfully resolved. In each instance, the pastors from local churches and parishes were involved, and the group grew in numbers, influence, and diversity.

The wave of co-op conversions in west Yonkers led people to identify another problem. There was a need to protect tenants and buyers in buildings that had not been adequately maintained and were now being converted into cooperative residences. The organizer helped people collect data about how other cities handled co-op conversion. They decided that a co-op reserve fund should be established to require the building owner to set aside a percentage of the sales for necessary building improvements. The group then held a workshop to inform and get the support of residents throughout Yonkers, including tenants from both the east and west sides. A committee was organized to draft a city council ordinance mandating the establishment of the reserve fund. The ordinance was placed on the city council agenda and was unanimously approved. This victory was one of the first occasions when people from both sides of the city proposed a positive solution to a problem and found that indeed they could fight City Hall and even win.

The organizer now felt that the time was right to develop an organization. People throughout the city had been engaged in organizing around several issues. They came from different religious, racial, and class backgrounds. The organizer had been working to educate people about the organizing process and developing their leadership skills. A positive sense was growing among the people that they could induce change and gain power. All this indicated the desirability of a loose and flexible organizational structure, disciplined enough for further action and open enough to allow new people to join. In late 1987, a group of people met, elected four officers, and agreed to call the new organization Yonkers Interfaith Education and Leadership Development, or YIELD. The people chose the name to suggest the potential for power building that they hoped the organization would have.

Usually the organizing process continues with the organizer recruiting more and more people from different networks, identifying more issues, forming committees, studying the problems, and helping people shape demands to present to the more powerful. As the organization's victories grow, there is a concomitant growth in people's sense of dignity, competence, and power. But the organizer's analysis of the Yonkers form of government suggested that only the city council could make change, and this required a broad-based coalition of support from all geographic areas in the city. Because the economic and racial polarization in Yonkers was so great, such a coalition was virtually impossible at this time. The organizer asked a group of Catholic priests, who had been meeting on a regular basis, to sponsor a series of leadership development workshops for members of their parishes. In early 1988, a six-session organizing workshop was held for 120 Catholic lay people. The workshops included didactic and "hands-on" training on understanding power, selecting issues, designing strategy, doing action research, negotiating, and working with the media. The workshop leaders recognized the dilemma of training people about organizing without involving them in an organizing campaign on a specific issue. Theory has to be applied to be understood. The workshop organizers felt that people were anxious to *do something,* and if they did not do it soon, their motivation would wane. Each workshop series was designed to culminate in the formation of an issue committee, which would focus on a single issue and a proposed action strategy for it. The workshops were well received, and the Catholic priests then extended an invitation to repeat the workshops for the rest of the religious community. Additional sets of workshops were held involving Catholic, Protestant, and Jewish lay leaders and clergy.

A public safety/public housing committee was formed from the first workshop series; a public information committee was formed from the second workshop series; and people

were asked to join either or both. Enough people expressed concern about housing in Yonkers to warrant the establishment of a separate housing committee. The organizer worked with these three committees, all falling under the umbrella of YIELD. They began to meet, analyze problems, and develop action strategies. The Public Safety/Public Housing Committee designed a Police Anticrime Drug Control and Prevention Task Force, analyzed the city budget to determine where funds might come from for establishing a task force, and held numerous meetings with elected officials to present their idea, which was finally acted on by the police. The Public Information Committee discovered that the city did not have available in a central location the names, functions, and membership of the numerous appointed municipal boards. This lack of access to information was an obstacle to action and holding these boards accountable. The committee designed a form to solicit this data, met with public officials, and finally published and distributed through the churches and synagogues the city's first Public Information Handbook, which included data that had heretofore been unavailable. The Housing Committee developed a comprehensive strategy for housing in Yonkers, giving equal attention to the diversity of the housing stock— single-family units, subsidized and nonsubsidized multifamily units (co-op and condo conversions), luxury waterfront development, and court-ordered public and developer-assisted housing.

The courthouse activity during the summer of 1988 threatened to snap the delicate organizational ties the organizer had built. After years of negotiations, suits, and countersuits, the federal judge levied fines against the city and against the four out of seven councilmen who refused to vote to pass the ordinance required by the judge for building the public and developer-assisted housing. Fines doubled on a daily basis, threatening to bankrupt the city in less than 30 days. The State Emergency Financial Control Board asserted broader powers and began signing all checks for expenditures of more than a dollar. The board also ordered the city to draw up a "doomsday plan" for eliminating public services. New York's Governor Cuomo established a task force to study the Yonkers problem. As Yonkers teetered on the brink of financial disaster, antipathy among the various factions in the city heightened. A set of workshops given in August during the imposition of the fines were full of hot-tempered arguments. The organizer once again turned to the clergy, who wrote an open letter to their congregants and residents of Yonkers, urging people to accept the law and increase their pressure on the four noncomplying council members who were responsible for the imposition of the fines. In early September 1988, two council members changed their votes, and the fines were rescinded. The fragile organization had weathered its first crisis, and the organizing could continue.

In the fall of 1988, YIELD held its first community convention. The subject of the conference was the Housing Committee's investigation. Over 250 people met in workshops designed to inform and invite their participation in further elaboration of the comprehensive housing plan. These workshops were led by community people of different races, religions, and social backgrounds. Finally, the convention passed a series of resolutions covering single- and multifamily homes, the court ordered units of public low-income and developer-subsidized moderate income housing, stability pacts to prevent block busting by real estate agents, and low-income loans and grants. The conference was widely covered in the media. The *New York Times* noted YIELD's work as "the first comprehensive housing strategy for the city." Moreover, for the first time in recent memory, east siders and west siders; blacks, Hispanics, and whites; low-income, moderate, and middle-class professionals; and Catholics, Jews, and Protestants worked together to find common ground, to compose a new tale for one city.

The organizer has now decided that YIELD is ready for more structure. A steering committee to oversee the work of the issue committees has been formed and is composed of representatives from religious institutions and members of working committees. New and additional funds are being sought. The organizing also continues. Currently, the Safety Committee is meeting with the district attorney to encourage vigorous prosecution of drug dealers. The Housing Committee is aggressively pushing the city council to adopt YIELD's comprehensive housing strategy. The Public Information Committee is monitoring meetings of critical city boards. The possibility of establishing an Education Committee has been discussed. Another series of workshops for newly recruited people has begun.

Much has been accomplished in the last 2 years. The organization, by the use of parishes and congregations, has succeeded in bringing people together from all geographic areas of the city. Despite differences, people have been able to reach a working agreement about their needs and their hopes for Yonkers. Specific changes have occurred: The Police Task Force has been established, there is a new co-op conversion fund law, and public information is no longer inaccessible. Moreover, there have been indications that YIELD is being recognized as an organization to be taken seriously. Recently, representatives of the organization were asked to serve on the mayor's Advisory Commission on Housing. Although Yonkers may be posed at the threshold, it has by no means solved its numerous and complex problems. We believe that YIELD has added a new and moral voice to the discussion.

As we reflect on our organizing, we find it important that our own repugnance at the racism in Yonkers did not become an obstacle to helping the people hear the underlying messages in people's concerns and reinterpret what was being said. If we do not redefine the sense of hopelessness and loss of control, a vacuum may be left for a much more dangerous message. Ours was drawn from biblical and democratic traditions and was consciously developed to appeal to a common hope for a just and fair community. During the organizing we were shown a flyer circulating in Yonkers sent by the "Committee to Resurrect Yonkers," P.O. Box, Marietta, Georgia. Its message was to explain the imbroglio in Yonkers as a Black-Jewish conspiracy hell bent on profiteering from desegregation. That message may fill the vacuum, if organizers with a vision of the "common good" do not. The beginning of the organizing process may result in only small gains, but they are larger in their significance.

## References

Brager, G., & Specht, H. (1979). *Community organizing*. New York: Columbia University Press.

*Low income needs*. (1987). Reports of the National Low Income Housing Coalition.

# 6

CASE STUDIES

# IN GROUP WORK

GROUP WORK HAS BEEN A VALUED PART OF social work practice since the development of the profession. Mary Richmond, an early leader in the field of social work, recognized the need for social workers to understand small-group behavior.

Groups are designed to meet either socialization or resocialization objectives (Garvin, 1987). Socialization groups are used to help people who are unable to perform appropriate social roles. Clients join these groups on a voluntary basis to receive assistance from social workers with various life transitions. Examples of socialization groups include a group to help chronically mentally ill adults cope with the demands of having a job, a group for parents of children with cancer, and a group for patients coping with dialysis.

Resocialization groups respond to people with inadequate socialization skills and are often formed in response to a need for social control. Examples of resocialization groups include groups for men who batter, groups for children who have conduct disorders, and groups for parents who have abused their children.

Middleman and Goldberg (1987) present the essential elements of social work with groups. The first element is for the group to become a system of mutual aid. This means the group must develop the capacity to help its members both individually and collectively. The second element is to help group members make use of the group process. In order to achieve this group, workers must be skilled at facilitating the group members to share experiences, respond to each other empathically, confront appropriately, and achieve an atmosphere of working together toward goal-oriented change. The third essential element is to enable the group to function more autonomously—to become a mutual support group. This helps facilitate successful termination and generalization of learning experiences. A related element that Middleman and Goldberg (1987) discuss is helping members to recognize how the group experience can help them as they leave the group.

What is unique about group work is that more interpersonal interactions take place than in individual casework. Furthermore, many of the relevant and helpful interactions that take place occur between group members, not between the group members and the social worker. As a consequence many group workers stress the concept of the group as a mutual-aid system (Gitterman & Shulman, 1986). In the mutual-aid group, the group members are mobilized to help each other. The group leader has a mediating function to help the group members support and identify with each other, confront each other, and problem solve together. This results in a process whereby they help themselves as they help each other. Group leaders must be skilled in providing for this mutual aid as they work with the group to harness the healing power present in the group process. To do this, leaders facilitate the group to effectively share data about their experiences, experience the "all-in-the-same-boat" phenomenon, and explore mutual support and mutual demand, to name a few of the skills the group leader must possess (Gitterman & Shulman, 1986).

In addition to facilitating mutual aid, the group worker must also help group members achieve optimal social functioning (Garvin, 1987). This refers to helping individuals adapt and cope with their social situations by making changes within themselves, their environment, or both. In order to achieve effective social functioning, group workers may assist members to change their behavior, thoughts, or feelings as they respond to various environmental demands. Groups have been successful in helping clients with various social-functioning problems, such as seeking employment, getting along with peers, preventing pregnancy, and reducing social isolation. The group context may be the most effective format for helping clients change their social functioning (Rose, 1977).

The case studies by Shulman and by Berman-Rossi and Gitterman are excellent examples of groups that demonstrate the mutual-aid process. Shulman's group example focuses on single parents and emphasizes the process of developing support for parents who are struggling with their roles as single parents. Berman-Rossi and Gitterman present a case example of a group for relatives and friends of institutionalized elderly clients. It is a splendid example of how a social worker might go about planning for and establishing a group that fills a service gap. The case study by Le-Croy depicts a specific type of group, a social skills group for children. The contribution here is in a clear and detailed description of the process of teaching social skills in a group format. Tolman and Bennett describe a group for working with men who batter. This is a superb example of a resocialization group. The goal is to eliminate battering by men who are court ordered to receive treatment.

## References

Garvin, C. (1987). *Contemporary group work.* Englewood Cliffs, NJ: Prentice-Hall.

Gitterman, A., & Shulman, L. (1986). *Mutual aid groups and the life cycle.* Itasca, IL: F. E. Peacock.

Middleman, R. R., & Goldberg, G. (1987). Social work practice with groups. In the *Encyclopedia of social work* (18th ed., Vol. 2). Silver Spring, MD: National Association of Social Workers.

Rose, S. D. (1977). *Group therapy: A behavioral approach.* Englewood Cliffs, NJ: Prentice-Hall.

# CASE STUDY 6.1

*Single parents struggling with similar concerns can gain support and resources through mutual-aid groups. This case study illustrates the social worker's methods in enhancing mutual aid among participants in an intensive 2-day group.*

## Questions

1. What skills are evident in the group leader's approach to working with the group and the individuals in the group?
2. What types of follow-up services would be appropriate for clients completing the short-term group?
3. What did the group leader do to create a "demand for work" quickly in the group?
4. In what ways did the group leader help move the group from the beginning through ending and transition phases of group work?

## A SHORT-TERM SINGLE-PARENTS' GROUP

*Lawrence Shulman*

The explosive growth in single-parent families has caused us to rethink our view of the average family as consisting of two adult parents. Many forms of alternative parenting approaches—some voluntarily entered into, others the result of death, divorce, separation, and teenage pregnancy—have caused us to take a closer look at the special needs of this population (Shulman, 1986).

Although many of the issues facing single parents are common to all parents, there are often variations on the themes resulting from their raising children on their own. These common themes, illustrated in this case example, include the following: relationship with friends and family; relationship to the children; relationship to the former partner; socioeconomic stress; and intimacy issues.

This is a case illustration of social work practice with a small group of single-parent clients. The group is an example of short-term

work, taking place over 9 hours (an evening and the following day). The setting was a small rural town in the interior of the Province of British Columbia, Canada. I was the group leader, flown in to lead the group as part of an outreach program of the community psychiatry clinic at the University of British Columbia. Participants either responded from an ad placed by a local agency or were referred by workers. In addition to the clients, there were a number of community professionals sitting in to observe as well as to be available for ongoing services if needed.

The approach used in this case example focused on the development of a mutual-aid process in the group (Shulman, 1984). The underlying assumption was that these clients, struggling with similar concerns, could be helpful to each other. The task of the social worker was seen as to help the group members to help each other. In addition, as an example

175

of short-term group work, the impact of the time on the process is evident. Both the clients and I were conscious of the need to work directly and quickly in order to make the best use of the time available. As will be seen repeatedly in the case example, the clients are simply waiting for the signal from the group leader that he is ready and willing to work.

## THE FIRST SESSION

My goals in the beginning of the first session were to establish a clear sense of group purpose reflecting both the needs of the members and the service offered by the agency. I want the group members to get a sense of my role not as an expert on life but rather as someone who is there to help them to be experts for each other. In addition, I hope to set out the ground rules and to develop a beginning sense of trust in me as the leader, as well as in other group members. Also important is the need to convey what I call "the demand for work." I want the clients to get a quick sense that I mean business and that in this group, I am prepared to deal with tough and painful issues and emotions just as soon as they feel ready. My signal to them comes in my direct opening statement as well as my effort to reach for painful feelings in response to one member's early, joking comment.

I explained the purpose of the group as an opportunity for single parents to discuss with each other some of the special problems they faced because they were alone. I said that my role was not as an expert with answers for them but rather as someone who would try to help them help each other from their own experiences. In addition, I would throw in any ideas I had that might be helpful. I then offered a few examples of possible concerns (these were similar to those described earlier in this paper). There was much head nodding in agreement as I spoke. I completed my opening by describing some of the phases that both

parents and children go through after a separation. I invited the participants to share some of their own experiences, their concerns and problems, and suggested that we could use their issues as an agenda for our 2 days of discussion.

There was a brief silence, and then Irene asked how long it took to go through the phases. I asked her why she was asking, and she said it was 3 years since her separation, and she didn't think she had passed through all of them yet. The group members laughed, acknowledging their understanding of the comment. I said I thought there must have been a great deal of pain and sadness both at the time of the split and since then to cause it still to hurt after 3 years. I asked Irene if she could speak more about this.

Irene continued in a more serious tone by describing her ongoing depression. She described days in which she felt she was finally getting over things and picking herself up, followed by days when she felt right back to square one. Others in the group agreed and shared their own experiences when I encouraged them to respond to Irene's comments. I told them it might help just to know that they were "in the same boat" with their feelings.

My next effort was to encourage more specifics in this problem-swapping process. I wanted to help them develop an agenda, one with which they could all connect. Also, it is only in the specifics that real help can be given.

I then asked if the group members could be more specific about what made the breakup difficult. Members raised a number of areas, which I kept track of in my written notes. They included dealing with money and finances, problems with the ex-spouse, problems with the kids, and the strain in their relationships with friends and family. A great deal of emotion was expressed during discussion of this last area, with anger directed toward others who "didn't understand" and related to them in ways that hurt more than they helped.

Dick, a young man in his mid-20s, spoke with great agitation about his wife, who had left him with their 6-month-old baby only 6 weeks before. The group seemed to focus on Dick, who expressed a particularly strong sense of urgency and was clearly still in a state of shock and crisis. Dick had arrived early and had carried on a long and animated discussion with another member in the premeeting "chatter," listing all of the crises he had to get through in order to get to the session that evening. I pointed out to the group that it seemed like Dick was feeling this concern about friends and relatives rather strongly and, in fact, had a great deal of difficulty even getting here tonight. I asked if they would like to focus on friends and relatives first, perhaps using Dick's example to get us started. All agreed that would be helpful.

In this last excerpt I attempted to communicate my genuine empathy for the struggle Dick described. All of the clients would be watching me closely to see if I tried to understand and if I would be supportive. This is laying the groundwork for the support part of the working relationship. I will draw on this base later, when the need to confront clients is apparent. I encourage Dick to elaborate on his issues in the hope that as the group members focus on helping Dick, they will also be helping each other.

After Dick described the details of his separation and his current living situation with his 6-month-old child, he went on to describe the problems. He emphasized the difficulty of living in a small town and, in his particular case, being in a personal service occupation that put him in daily contact with many town residents. He said, "Sure I feel lousy, depressed, and alone. But some days I feel I'm getting over things a bit, feeling a little up, and everywhere I go people constantly stop me to tell me how terrible things are. If I didn't feel lousy before I went out, I sure do by the time I get home."

Dick added a further complication in that the baby had a serious case of colic and was crying all the time. He told the group that everyone was always criticizing how he handled the baby, and even his own mother was telling him he wasn't competent and should move back home with her. He continued by saying he was so depressed by this that he had taken to not talking to anyone anymore, avoiding his friends, and staying home alone at night, and he was going out of his mind. Others in the group shared similar versions of this experience. I said to Dick, "And that's the dilemma, isn't it? Just at the time you really need help the most, you feel you have to cut yourself off from it to maintain your sense of personal integrity and sanity. You would like some help because the going is rough, but you are not sure you want to have to depend on all of these people, and you are not sure you like the costs involved." Dick nodded, and the other group members agreed.

Conscious of the short-term nature of the work, I tried to move Dick quickly into an examination of his part in the problem. I encouraged him to share how he handled the specifics of his conversations with his mother or friends and asked the other group members to give Dick some feedback. When I and other group members pointed out that Dick was sending mixed messages to people, he became defensive saying "yes but . . ." frequently. In an interesting way, the process in the group was similar to how he handled his life. He also sent mixed messages to us, asking for help then resisting it when it was offered. I decided to confront the resistance directly. I tried to do it in a way that communicated my understanding of why he might feel defensive.

I pointed out what was happening. I said, "It seems to me that when I or a group member suggests that you (Dick) look at your part in the proceedings, you won't take in what we are saying. I have only a day and a half with this group, so I really can't pussyfoot around with you." I wondered if it was tough for Dick and the others to take responsibility for their part in their problems. Dick smiled and admitted that it was hard. He already felt lousy enough. Others joined in on how easy it was to blame everyone else and how hard it was to accept any blame themselves. I agreed that it was tough, but I didn't think I would be of any help to them if I just sat here for a day and a half agreeing about how tough things were for them. The group members laughed, and a number said they didn't want that.

At this point, Doris, one of the three workers participating in the group, surprised us all by saying that she had intended to listen and not talk during the session but that listening to Dick's problem made her want to share hers. She said she had come to the group as an observer; however, she was pregnant, unmarried, and about to become a single parent. She thought she was having the same problem in communicating with her mother as Dick was having with his. It was a classic example of a conflict between a mother who is hurt and embarrassed and a daughter who feels rejected at a critical moment in her life. At my suggestion, Rose offered to role play the mother as Doris tried to find a new way to talk to her mother. The group was supportive, but, at the same time, following my example, they confronted each other during the discussion in a healthy way. Dick listened and participated in the work on Doris's problem and, as is often the case, was able to learn something about his own situation as he watched someone else struggling with the same concerns. When I asked him later if he had taken something from it, he said it had helped him a lot to see how he was holding back his real feelings from friends and his own mother. I pointed out to all of the group members what a shock their situation was to their friends and close relatives and how at first contact they could not respond in a way that met their needs. I said, "This does not mean they don't love you. It just means that they have feelings and aren't always able to express them. Your mixed messages also make it difficult."

Cerrise, another worker/observer in the group, joined the discussion at this point and described how she had felt when close friends had separated. She realized now that it had taken her a couple of months to get over being so angry at them for ending their marriage because she loved them both. She hadn't been able to reach out to support them. They, however, had not given up on her, and she had been able to work it out. Dick said hearing that helped a lot. That is what was probably going on with some of his friends.

Carrie, who was both an unmarried parent and a worker in the community, described her own experiences with her mother when she split up. She shared how she had involved her mother in the process and had let her know her feelings. She wanted her mother's love and support but felt she had to handle the problems herself. Dick listened closely and said that this was probably what he had not been able to do. We role played how Dick could handle the conversation with his mother—how he could articulate his real feelings. The group was supportive.

When I asked the group how they felt about this discussion thus far, Doris said it was helpful because I kept stressing the positive aspect, the reaching out and caring between people. Most of them had been so upset they could only see the negatives.

The impact of time is once again illustrated in the following segment of the process. Just as the life of our work can be understood against the backdrop of time, each individual session has its own beginning, middle (work phase), and ending/transition. In this case, the ending of the first evening led to Dick raising a powerful theme. I believe he felt able to raise it, even in a first session, because of the way the group members and I had responded to his earlier productions.

The discussion turned to the question of how much they needed others to talk about what they were going through. Near the end of the session, in typical "door knob" fashion,

Dick revealed that a close friend of his, in a similar situation with a young child, had told him he was considering committing suicide. He went on to tell us, with tears in his eyes, that the friend had carried through with the threat and had just killed himself. I said, "It must have hit you very hard when it happened, and you must have wondered if you could have done something more to help." Dick agreed that was so, and the group members offered him support. After some time I asked Dick if he was worried about his own situation, since he had so many of the same feelings as his friend. He said he was worried, but that he thought he would be strong enough to keep going with the goal in his life to make it for his child. I told him he had shown a lot of strength just coming to the group and working so hard on his problem. Carrie said that he was not alone and that he could call her if he needed someone to talk to as a friend, or as a worker. Rose pointed out that there was a single-parent social group at the church, and Dick said he had not realized that. Others in the group also offered support. I asked Dick how he felt now, and he said, "I feel a lot better. I realize now that I'm not so alone." Irene, who had opened the discussion by saying she had not yet gone through all of the phases, summarized the evening's work when she said, "I guess we are all struggling to find ways of saying to friends and close relatives, please love me now. I need you." The discussion ended, and we agreed to pick up again in the morning.

## THE MIDDLE PHASE OF PRACTICE

The middle phase of practice actually began during the first evening meeting. If one considers the nature of the process, rather than simply the passage of time as the boundary of the phases, then when I confronted Dick and he responded by deepening the work, we had entered the middle phase of practice. Dick made what I call "the second decision." The

first decision was to show up and begin to participate. The second decision was to lower his defenses and to risk his real feelings, taking responsibility for his part in the problem. Dick went even further, probably because of the urgency created by the short-term nature of the work, and made the "third decision" when he opened up the theme of depression and suicide. The members have closely watched the proceedings of the beginning phase and the transition to the middle phase. Some trust has developed as evidenced by their moving directly into significant issues.

There were some new members in the morning, so I took some time to review the contract. The discussion picked up again with Irene raising the problem of dealing with the children. She described how tough it was on her when she asked her 11-year-old boy to babysit his 5-year-old brother. I asked if she could describe a specific incident, and she told us about the previous day. Her older son was about to go out to play when she asked him to cover for her, since she needed to take care of some business. His face dropped, but he did not say anything. I asked her if she could tell us how she felt when she saw his face drop. She said, "Miserable!" I asked her what she had said to him and she replied, "Nothing."

I pointed out how Irene had not leveled with her son and how she had avoided a frank discussion about her expectations of him and his feeling about having to carry some of the load. I asked if she had any ideas why it was so tough on her. She said he had not been getting along with his friends for a while after the split and in fact was moping around alone. Now that she saw him out and around, she hated to do anything that interfered. John, a new member, revealed that he had been a son in a single-parent family and that he felt the same way her son felt. He resented having to be responsible at such a young age. He said he would have very much appreciated it if his mom had talked directly to him about it and allowed him to get some of his feelings off his chest. I said, "I wonder if you parents really want to hear how your kids are feeling. I wonder if your kids' feelings are too close to your own."

As each problem emerges I try to reach for the commonality in feeling that is often just below the surface of the discussion. One of the most powerful forces for change can be generated by the mutual-aid process—in particular, the "all-in-the-same-boat phenomenon." Knowing that you are not alone can make a major difference. Each step, as evident in the following excerpt, is marked by ambivalence as group members appear to want to share and hold back at the same time. As each cue to resistance emerges, I try to explore the resistance by pointing out its existence and asking for its cause. In each case, it turns out that the reason for the resistance is a central issue for our work.

Gary said there was a lot of guilt in these situations. You feel responsible for your kid's problems because you've split up. He went on to say, "I'm also a little bit like a third-year medical student. Every time I see any sign of trouble with my kid, I'm sure it's going to be something really terrible."

I asked if a little role play might help here, and since John was a child in a family like this, maybe he could help by playing Irene's son. There was some hesitation by Irene, who said that was hard to do. When I asked about the hesitation, she said she was afraid she would make mistakes. Carrie pointed out they would be the same mistakes they all make, so she shouldn't worry about it. Irene responded by saying it was hard to role play. I agreed and then told her that I never said this work would be easy. She agreed to give it a try. The role play revealed how hard it was for them to reach the underlying feelings that they sensed were expressed indirectly by their children.

I introduced the skill of looking for trouble when everything is going your way as an active way of reaching for underlying feelings. I

illustrated how they could ask the child for negative feelings even when the child said everything was fine. There was a general recognition of how immobilized they often felt by their guilt. Irene tried again and this time was direct in opening up the question of mutual responsibility and her son's feelings. John told her that as her son he would be relieved to have it out in the open and would feel good that she respected him and needed him in this way. He still would not like to stay home and babysit, but talking about his feelings would make it easier. Irene said, "I guess if I get this off my chest, it will be a lot easier for me as well."

As is often the case, as members listen to the struggles of another member, their own issues are brought to the forefront. Once again, the issue of one member turns out to be the issue for all of them. The task of the group leader is to continually search out these connections as he or she, in implementing Schwartz's (1961) functional role of the social worker, "mediates the individual-social connection." The following excerpt illustrates how important it is to recognize that in group work, one always has "two clients": the individual raising the problem (in this case, Maureen) and the group as a whole. As the group responds to her powerful question, it is my role to tune in to the meaning of the group's behavior.

Maureen jumped in and asked how you handle it when your kid says, "Why can't we be a normal family?" This hit the group like a bomb, and they all jumped in with their versions of how they would answer the child's question. Most of the responses were variations of the defensive explanations, long analogies, or examples, all designed to provide the "good parent's answer." I intervened and said, "You know, you have jumped in to answer Maureen's child's question, but I wonder if we really know what the question is?" I explain that it often takes some time for others to tell us what they are really feeling and that a quick response may not be getting at the real feelings, particularly when a question hits us in our gut and touches our feelings. I asked, "What would happen if you asked your child what he or she meant by the question?" There was a thoughtful silence in the room, and then Rose said, "Then we might really find out, and I'm not sure I want to hear."

Although it is important to deal with the reactions of the group members, it would be a mistake to lose the individual in the process. I return to the specifics of Maureen's issues. Once again, I am pushing hard, making a "demand for work." It is important that I pay some attention to how this feels for the member.

I asked if we could get back to Maureen's example, and Maureen said, "Could we go on to someone else's example? I've been in the spotlight too long, and people are probably bored with my problem." I asked the group members if this was true. They vigorously shook their heads, indicating they were very interested. I said to Maureen, "Look, they are interested. Why is it you want to get off the spot?" Maureen replied, "It's hitting too close to home." The group members laughed in acknowledgment. I credited her for being honest and asked what she meant by "hitting close to home." She said, "I want to feel like I'm a good mother." There was silence in the room, and Lenore finally said, "I know what you mean. I feel I failed in my marriage, and now I'm desperate about not wanting to feel I have failed as a mother."

This was followed by a discussion of their sense of guilt, of how harsh they were on themselves, and how feelings of failure in their marriage and fear of failure as parents often translated into concern and overprotection in relation to their children, with a resulting fear of revealing the underlying painful feelings. We returned to Maureen's example. She role played a number of ways she might reach her

daughter's real feelings and the meaning of the question, "Why can't we be like a normal family?"

Because the process in the group is often a reflection of the problems the members are experiencing outside of the group, occasional reflections on the interaction can be an important source of learning for group members. It is important that reflection on process not become a substitute for the work on the content.

Before we broke for lunch, I asked the group members to reflect on what had just happened in our group. I thought in some ways our group was an illustration of some of the problems they faced. I pointed out how Maureen had said she wanted to be off the spot because others were bored. Instead of just accepting that, I reached for the feelings that might be behind her discomfort. It turned out that she was feeling many things, and her concerns were very much the concerns of the whole group. I wondered what they thought about my observation. Irene said that she could see what I meant. They had feelings they needed to talk about, and they would only get to them if I helped them. The same was probably true for their kids. I said, "Lecture's over; how about lunch?"

## THE ENDING AND TRANSITION PHASE

As the third and last segment of the work begins, the sense of urgency is heightened. The phenomenon called "door knob therapy" is evident as the ending of the group causes a number of members to move the group into the core issues of single parenting.

Ginette initiated this discussion by asking, "Is it always good to be honest?" When I asked why she raised that question, she described a situation in which her husband was rejecting their 5-year-old boy while at the same time caring for their youngest child. He had refused to visit or call this son, but promised to do so each time she raised the issue with him. When I asked her to describe her telephone conversations with the ex-spouse, it quickly became clear that she was pushing him and he was denying that any problem existed. When I asked her how all of this had made her feel, she replied, "I'm really tired of trying to get Dad to be Dad."

I told Ginette I thought this must have put her in an awful bind with the child when, for example, he asked her, "When is Daddy going to visit me?" I wondered how she dealt with it. Ginette described her conversation with her son, which indicated that she attempted to cover up the problem with "white lies" and to do whatever she could to avoid dealing with the child's feelings. I pointed this out to the group, acknowledging that I could appreciate the bind she felt.

June, a new member who had been listening quietly all morning, began to speak. She spoke with a low, soft voice and began to cry before she could complete her comments: "I have been sitting here listening to Ginette and thinking that she is describing my own problem exactly. And now, I think I realize . . . (crying softly) that I'm going to have to face my own rejection by my husband who walked out on me . . . before I can help my kids face their rejection."

The impact of the expression of emotion is felt by all of the members. The natural instinct of the members would be to reach out and comfort June. In part, this is hard because they have learned very different rules about behavior in social situations. When strong emotion is expressed, the norm is to ignore it and allow the other person to recover in privacy. This is often experienced by the other person as not hearing or caring. Once again the mediation function leads me to help the group reach out to the individual. If they could not respond, rather than being angry at them, the two-client idea would lead me to explore what it was about June's expression of feeling that

was hitting them so hard. If I can be "with" the group, my second client, it increases the possibility of members being with June.

We all felt very moved by June's words. I could see the group members were upset. Marie was sitting next to June, and I could tell she was very agitated—looking around the room, looking at June, and literally moving in her seat. I said, "I think June's feelings have hit all of us very hard. I have a feeling you would like to reach out to June, wouldn't you, Marie?" Marie said she really would. When I asked her why she didn't do it, she said, "Well, I'm afraid to." After a slight pause, she reached over and took June's hand, holding it tightly. June responded warmly to the gesture. I reassured her that it was OK to share her feelings with us and that her tears were an important part of how she felt. I told her that I felt she spoke for all the group members, and they quickly assured that I was correct.

We returned to Ginette at this point and the issues of being honest with her children and allowing them to express their own feelings. She said, "I want my son to share his feelings within certain guidelines." I responded, "You mean, you want him to share the feelings that are not too tough for you." The group members, including Ginette, laughed in recognition. Ginette said, "I realize I have to be straight with him. When I lied and tried to make it sound that his father loved him, it didn't make any sense, just like it wouldn't make any sense to make it sound like he didn't care at all." The group members agreed to role play the conversation, so that Ginette could find a helpful way to be honest and to recognize her child's feelings of rejection.

After a few difficult starts she finally decided on the following way of handling his questions: "Your Daddy does care about you, but right now he is having a hard time and feeling very upset and bad himself. That is why he hasn't visited you or invited you to stay with him. I know it must be very hard for you to understand why he doesn't spend more time with you if he really cares. It must make you feel very bad as well." As Ginette spoke these words, she was close to tears herself. I suggested that she might share with her child how hard this was for her. Then she and her son could cry together. Ginette said the discussion had helped, and she realized there was no easy way to handle this.

As the session moved into the final piece of work, Rose, a very supportive and level-headed member, who had offered helpful advice to all the other members, now sought her own help. Almost as if assigned the role by the group members, Rose took us into a central, core issue for all of the members: she raised the issue of loneliness.

I asked Rose if she could be specific about the loneliness: when did she feel it, and what was it like? She said the worst time was the emptiness in the house in the evenings. After a few more comments by other group members, the discussion shifted to the question of credit.

After some first offerings on the theme of loneliness, Rose switched the subject to another area of legitimate work—her unfair treatment as a woman by the financial institutions she must deal with. The group, and I the worker, accept her invitation to explore this important theme; however, in part, we are all probably avoiding her underlying pain.

The example picks up where I asked Rose how she felt after she described how her bank of 20 years had denied her credit because her credit rating went with her husband in the separation.

When I asked Rose how she felt about the whole experience, she replied, "Damned angry!" Carrie told her she had given up too soon. She said that Rose was going to have to assert herself if she wanted to obtain her rights. I asked Carrie how she thought Rose could do this, and she suggested the following plan. She advised Rose to visit the credit bureau and discuss her desire to establish a credit

rating. She pointed out that Rose was making monthly payments on a number of bills, for example, rent, telephone, utilities, and that she could use this to impress the credit bureau with her worthiness. She should also speak to the bank manager directly and point out that she had been part of the family that had given his bank the family business up to that point and that she would like his cooperation in developing a plan to establish a credit rating on her own.

The group members agreed that this might be her first step. They also felt that if she ran into difficulty with this approach, she should consider bringing this to the attention of the bank's head office by writing the president. She could also consider contacting the Human Rights Commission, since this actually constituted a form of discrimination. It was obvious that everyone was angry about her situation. Rose agreed she could do more on this than she had thus far. She said, "I guess I began to believe that they were right about me not having earned a credit rating. It never occurred to me to refuse to accept the decision." Carrie said, "The hard part is understanding that you're going to have to fight for your own rights because nobody else is going to do it for you."

Maureen said to Rose, "Maybe the problem is you've never been Rose. You've always been somebody's mother or somebody's wife."

Fortunately, I caught my mistake and pointed out how we had all moved off of the hot potato of loneliness. If one considers skillful practice as the ability to shorten the distance between when we make our mistakes and when we catch them, then I can be pleased with the result of the work. I was sending a message to the group members that we could even talk about this taboo issue.

I intervened at the end of the credit discussion and said, "You know, it seems you have all decided to drop the issue Rose raised at the beginning, that is, how to handle the terrible loneliness of the empty house." They all laughed, recognizing they had silently agreed to drop the hot potato. Brett spoke for the first time and said that when we figured out that answer, to let her know, since she had the same problem. I commented that probably they all did and that was why it was hard to help Rose.

Carrie wanted to know what Rose did about finding friends. I said I thought that was a good start in helping Rose. Rose described how she had been invited to a dance by a group of her friends, all couples, and then spent the whole night sitting there while no one asked her to dance. I said I could imagine how uncomfortable they might all have felt. Lenore said that when she goes to a dance and no one asks her, she asks them. Connie wondered if she couldn't find a female friend to go to dances with. A pattern started to emerge with Rose saying, "Yes, but . . ." to each suggestion. When I asked her if she had spoken to her friends about the discomfort directly, so they could better appreciate her feelings, it was obvious that she had not. Instead, she had been hurt and angry and had cut herself further off from her closest friends.

As her resistance stiffened, I finally confronted her and said it appeared as though she was not willing to work at maintaining her close relationships. She seemed to be saying that she wanted friends once again to "divine" her feelings, but she was not willing to take the risk and let them know what they were. At the same time she was complaining about being alone. There was a long silence, and then with great feeling she said, "I don't want anyone to ever get close to me again." The group was somewhat stunned at the force of her feelings, since she been speaking quietly and in control for most of the session. I asked her why she felt this so strongly. Rose went on to tell us that her husband had left her for her

best friend. I said, "So you really had two losses. You must have felt very betrayed and very bitter." She replied that she still felt that way, hurt and bitter. This initiated a powerful discussion by all group members of their feelings about intimacy. Their losses made them wonder if they should ever let themselves get close to anyone again. Irene said, "I think that's what I meant last night when I asked when you get over the last phase. I realize I have been depressed because I'm holding back. I'm not risking getting hurt again." The conversation dealt with their feelings about risking with friends of the same sex as well as with members of the opposite sex. Many of the women described men whom they had been afraid to get to know.

I tried to take us back to Rose by asking what she thought about this conversation. She shrugged her shoulders and said, "Well, maybe in a couple of years, it will get better." I said, "And maybe in a couple of years, it will get worse." I pointed out how all of them had been concerned that the kids come out of the situation whole, and yet their message to their kids appeared to be that when one gets hurt, it's better not to try again. Rose pointed out how much she had done about her life, even learning to drive a car so she could be a bit more independent. I agreed that she had shown a great deal of strength in tackling the strains of being alone and that was why I felt she had the strength to tackle this problem—perhaps the hardest one for all of them. Irene said, "You're right, you know. We complain about being alone, but we are afraid to let ourselves be vulnerable again, afraid to get hurt." I said, "And that's the real dilemma, isn't it? It hurt so much to lose what you've had, you're afraid to risk. And then you find it also hurts to be alone. The important point, right now, is that you are aware of the question of loneliness and what to do about it is really in your hands."

## CONCLUSION

With only a half hour left in the final session, I asked the group members to take some time to wrap up the work. I wanted to know what ideas they had found helpful and would take with them. I also asked them to comment on the group, my work with them and their work with each other. Participants thought it was helpful to hear other people with similar concerns. The problems did not seem so overwhelming when you broke them down and dealt with them one at a time. In addition, they found it helpful to see some specific next steps open to them. In particular, they felt they had learned how important it was for them to take some risks and to reach out to people who they needed. I pointed out that they had done just that during the three sessions of the group. Finally, they appreciated my understanding of their feelings but also my pushing them and not letting them off the hook when it came to painful and difficult discussions.

## References

Schwartz, W. (1961). The social worker in the group. In *New perspectives in services to groups*. New York: National Assoc. of Social Workers.

Shulman, L. (1984). *The skills of helping individuals and groups* (2nd ed.). Itasca, IL: F. E. Peacock.

Shulman, L. (1986). Healing the hurts: Single parents. In A. Gitterman & L. Shulman (Eds.), *Mutual aid groups and the life cycle*. Itasca, IL: F. E. Peacock.

# CASE STUDY 6.2

*Often it is necessary to develop new services when none exist and there is a need for them. In this case study, the social worker discovered the need for a mutual-aid or support group. The worker describes the process involved in developing and working with the group.*

## Questions

1. How did the structure of the group reflect the specific needs of the participants?
2. What barriers and obstacles need to be anticipated when attempting to develop a new service?
3. What factors do you think contributed to the group's success?
4. In what ways did the group leader influence the outcomes achieved in each of the group sessions?

---

## A GROUP FOR RELATIVES AND FRIENDS OF INSTITUTIONALIZED AGED

*Toby Berman-Rossi and Alex Gitterman*

Metro Home and Hospital for Aged (MHHA) is a 520-bed, nonprofit, long-term care facility with a 110-year history of serving older persons within the community and institution. Originally MHHA served the healthier aged who needed a residential facility. Over the years, as community services for older persons increased, and as funding priorities shifted, it has increasingly cared for the frail elderly. The average age of the MHHA resident is 86 years. As a facility, it has two central functions: (1) to provide a home for those for whom Metro is their last home and (2) to attend to the health care needs of residents. Conceiving of inhabitants as residents, rather than as patients, speaks to the home's belief that a sense of home and community, rather than hospital, should prevail. As a home it is organized to be responsive to the normative, recreational, educational, and social needs of older people as well as the additional needs engendered by institutionalization. As a medical facility it pro-

vides 24-hour medical care through a wide range of interdisciplinary departments. Balancing the competing pulls of "home and hospital" provides a challenge for residents, relatives, friends, and staff.

Social workers have been employed at MHHA for the last 40 years. Originally workers were assigned to individual residents on 15 individual floors. This arrangement was later changed whereby workers were assigned by floors and consequently to all residents, relatives, and friends on these floors. This structural shift was based on the belief that each floor constituted a small community within a larger community. Each floor was thought of as a block within a neighborhood and as such gave rise to an interdependence of need and resources, demands and opportunities. The development of the floor as a responsive community was thought of as a step toward counteracting the deleterious effects of institutionalization. Isolation, alienation, inequities in

186

power, and passivity, all negative features of institutional life, were to be minimized. A strong floor community would support residents' natural inclination toward mutual aid and communion with each other. Weekly floor group meetings with the social worker facilitated connections and provided a structured means for dialogue among floor members, between floor members and floor staff, and between floor members and the larger institution.

## DEVELOPING A GROUP FOR RELATIVES AND FRIENDS

Although weekly floor group meetings became an established part of offered social work services, similar services on a floor-by-floor basis had not been established for friends and relatives. Social work services to this population were provided through a monthly friends and relatives group and on an as-needed individual basis by the floor social worker. Through individual discussions, the floor social worker, Ms. Cara-Bruno, learned that many relatives and friends felt isolated from others and locked into their own individual experiences. Although some had been able to establish cordial or friendly relationships with others, many knew no one besides their resident. A casual nod on seeing a familiar face was often the extent of contact. These visitors subtly indicated that they would welcome contact with others. Some thought that a little friendliness could go a long way in decreasing tension for them when they visited; others stressed their interest in learning the various ways families and friends coped with the impact of institutionalizing a loved one; and still others wanted additional "muscle" in making service demands on MHHA. At the same time, some seemed not to want greater connections. They expressed that theirs was a private experience and not one about which they could tell strangers. They wanted to visit and leave.

As Ms. Cara-Bruno thought about her contact with families and friends, she became increasingly concerned about the sense of isolation many felt in their experience with MHHA. She noticed that her services more often concentrated on crises, and there were fewer contacts around less emergent situations. Although she felt good about her ability to respond to critical situations, she felt less good about providing services in relation to ongoing needs.

Ms. Cara-Bruno wondered whether a floor group for relatives and friends could serve the same purpose as the floor group served for residents. Similar concerns and a shared need to cope with an institutionalized loved one could represent a common ground from which to start (Schwartz, 1961). Relatives and friends could potentially help each other with the various issues and dilemmas they faced related to having an elderly loved one living in an institution. By sharing and helping each other with their common concerns, their sense of isolation could be lessened and replaced with a sense of greater strength and mastery. At the same time, a floor group for relatives and friends could also be taxing and induce further stress. For some, it wouldn't be easy to speak about how it felt to bring a relative to a nursing home or how it felt to be visiting an aging friend. Because relatives and friends were totally dependent on, and at the mercy of, the institution, some might be hesitant to make public complaints about the quality of its services. If individual concerns were raised at all, they usually were presented through a well thought out and carefully crafted approach. They feared reprisals and minimized risk. They, therefore, might be somewhat cautious and concerned about joining a group. With these anticipatory ideas, the floor social worker decided to discuss with prospective members the possibility of a relatives and friends group. She envisioned a series of four meetings to explore the possibility of such a group. At the end of the meetings, she and the group would determine whether it should be developed. She thought that a short-term commitment would be less threatening and more inviting to prospective members.

Before discussing the proposed group with members, the worker realized that she had to gain organizational supports and sanctions (Gitterman, 1986). She knew her department head would have confidence in her idea. To be successful, however, she would need tacit approval from others as well. Active rather than passive sanction would provide a strong base for the action to come. Strong vertical support from administration would be necessary to garner resources for the group (for example, worker time, space to hold the meetings, secretarial assistance, and money for refreshments). In addition, horizontal support from members of the floor team and their administrators would be essential, lest the service be undermined or sabotaged. Marshaling initial administrative and interdisciplinary support would pay off further along when and if group members brought matters to their attention.

To develop institutional sanctions and supports, the worker began by thinking through how the various organizational representatives might experience the service. She tried to imagine what institutional forces would support and constrain the creation of the service (Brager & Holloway, 1978). The worker's belief that those most affected by the group service would have a greater vested interest in, as well as be most threatened by, its creation prompted her to think about how it would be experienced by her team, and nursing staff in particular. She hoped that members would experience the relatives and friends floor group as a team effort, though she alone would be staffing it. Strengthened by her strong relationship with Ms. Wilson, the head nurse, the worker discussed the idea of the group with her and Ms. Schwartz, the nursing supervisor. Both were supportive. They said they knew they would get complaints from relatives, but they saw these complaints as opportunities to improve service or to clarify why things were done the way they were, for example, encouraging residents to push their own chairs. In addition, they immediately saw opportunities for their own self-interest. They thought about all the times they had said they wished they had an opportunity to raise certain issues with relatives and friends. They imagined that from time to time they could attend the group both to answer complaints and to raise their own matters, for example, when relatives give medication or alcohol without informing nursing staff. With this support behind her, the support of the rest of the team was easy to secure. In fact, team members began to imagine a range of things they could do together, for example, coffee hours, informational programs, seasonal parties. A potential common ground between the team and the relatives and friends emerged.

The group's purpose determined its composition. After the four sessions, the group might develop into an open-ended floor group designed to be responsive to ongoing needs of relatives and friends (all relatives and friends would have to be eligible). This broad designation would most likely result in four subgroups: children, siblings, more distant relatives, and friends. In some instances children, siblings, and friends were around the same age. Cultural, religious, and social class attributes of relatives and friends would reflect the character of the floor itself, where only 14% of residents were minority. Though the worker was concerned with difference, she believed that the common bond of shared concern about residents would provide the basis for a core stability of interest, energy, and affection (Hartford, 1972; Shalinsky, 1964).

The eventual time boundary would need to be thought about with group members, but the time structure of the initial meeting had to be determined by the worker. An hour and a half session would be offered as a starting point, with the worker open to members' ideas. It was anticipated that members would have a good deal to discuss and would have the energy, capacity, and skill to do so in a sustained manner. For the remaining three sessions, the worker preferred weekly sessions. This time arrangement would provide continuity, intensity, and a time-limited framework in which to arrive at a decision. The time of 5:30 P.M. was chosen to allow members to come after work but also to allow others to get home before dark. The worker understood that a middle ground would be necessary to attend to the diverse environmental needs of members. An ideal time in the winter months would be more difficult to determine, as it would get dark earlier in the day.

Group size was very difficult to anticipate. Potentially 5,075 people could attend, though the probability of this occurrence was low. For space, a meeting room off the unit and near the cafeteria was chosen to ensure privacy of discussion and privacy of attendance. Some relatives might not initially want to be seen either by staff or by their residents. Comfortable chairs were arranged in a circle designed to facilitate member-to-member interaction and mutual aid. Beverages, cookies, and fruit were provided.

Ms. Cara-Bruno was originally overwhelmed by the need to recruit and invite members to the meeting. Although it would have been easy enough to write a letter to all relatives and friends, she believed that personal contact would be more likely to ensure attendance. The expected hesitancy of members about involvement would best be responded to personally. Phone contact would allow her to deal with negative and ambivalent responses. Reassurance and discussion of issues could diminish uncertainty and mitigate against the buildup of additional fear. Two seemingly contradictory principles were established as criteria for recruitment: primary re-

sponsibility and inclusiveness. In each case situation, at the time of admission someone had been designated as the "next of kin," the person to be called in case of emergency. Most residents had either a family member or a friend. In a formal sense, this person was a primary person in the resident's life and therefore would be automatically invited. At the same time, the worker was concerned about limiting access to service and recognized that the residents' social supports were broader than the one person named as "next of kin." Recruiting only these "primary" people would exclude others who had frequent interaction with the MHHA and residents. What if the "next of kin" designee was "next of kin" in name only, for example, in making burial arrangements. The worker decided that with each primary person, she would discuss for whom else the group might be helpful. Reviewing each case record and recalling past contacts would help her to think of others for whom the group might be helpful. The worker and the "primary person" would decide together whom each called; for example, they might call siblings and she might call friends.

The worker made 37 calls within a 2-week period. About half of those called expressed interest. About a third indicated they would attend a series of meetings to explore whether the group could be of help. Others lived too far away, felt too frail to attend in the evening, had other obligations, or simply didn't think the group was necessary for them. Through these calls Ms. Cara-Bruno developed a better understanding of the nature of the residents' relationships with significant people in their lives.

## PHASES OF WORK AND PROBLEMS IN LIVING

Our presentation of the relatives and friends group is framed within a discussion of phases of work. Schwartz (1971) defines four phases of work: (1) tuning in, (2) beginnings, (3) on-going work, and (4) transitions and endings. These phases ebb and flow in response to the interplay of internal group processes as well as environmental forces. Although these phases are not always distinct in actual practice, they can be used to describe the work of a single group session as well as the work of a group of many sessions, over time. During each phase, worker and member tasks take on a distinctive character, which when considered together define the dominant nature and work demand of the phase. The manner in which these phases of work evolve is affected by the length of the group and by its open- or close-ended nature. In single-session and short-term groups they are truncated. If work is to occur and if the group is to develop, it must do so quickly, lest time elapse without much having occurred. In addition to thinking about the processes of helping (that is, how the worker helps), one also has to consider the types and content of the clients' problems (that is, with what the worker helps). Germain and Gitterman (1980) suggest that people experience problems in three interrelated areas: life transitions (for example, changes in life stages and situations), environmental pressures (for example, organizations, social networks), and maladaptive interpersonal processes (for example, scapegoating, testing worker's authority). We will further use the concepts of phases of work and problems in living to organize and develop a practice illustration.

The tuning-in phase concerns itself with the worker's initial preparation prior to each individual group session and prior to the group's first session. Through a process of understanding the ways in which members offer veiled communications, that is, anticipatory empathy, the social worker develops a state of readiness to receive the group and its members. Individuals often find it difficult to confide directly to a group of strangers about important thoughts, events, and feelings. In addition,

subtle aspects of experience are not necessarily clearly known or understood by members. The worker, therefore, preparatorily thinks about the ways in which members might express themselves in coded ways. Understanding these ways increases worker receptivity and can influence the development of increased responsiveness. As workers ready themselves, they actively use their knowledge about the particular client population before them, and the nature of the problems in living that bring individuals to the group. The development of preliminary empathy facilitates the work to come.

As Ms. Cara-Bruno prepared for her first group meeting, she tried to imagine what it would be like for relatives and friends to come together. About 18 people, representing 12 residents, said they would try to come. The overall response to the initial outreach phone calls was positive. Prospective members stated that it felt particularly good to have a social worker reach out to them rather than their reaching out at a point of crisis. Although the overall reaction was positive, the worker also heard hesitation and fear. Some felt embarrassed about talking in a group; that was new to them. Others worried that if they were really honest, administration and floor staff wouldn't like that. And still others couldn't envision how a group could help. They imagined that collective efforts might decrease continuance of individual arrangements already in existence. The worker was also aware of her own apprehension and excitement. First meetings always made her a little nervous. So much depended on her. She worried that the open-ended nature of the group would detract from continuity of work and hoped that a core membership would develop that would provide continuity from session to session. The worker understood that though she and group members had discussed these issues and she had offered reassurances, these issues would take center stage in the first session. During this first session she wanted to develop an agreement with the members as to whether they wanted to meet to discuss the possibility of establishing a relatives and friends group.

Beginnings, the second phase of work, points to the need for the worker and the group to arrive at a working agreement as to the nature of their work together, their respective role relationships, and the specific conditions related to their work. This contract is based on a marriage of members, perception of their needs, and the agency's perception of its service offering. This agreement, although still open to negotiation, sets the framework for the work to come. Boundaries, requirements, and demands for work between worker and members and among members receive their legitimacy from and are strengthened by this pact. A division of labor between members and worker can more readily be achieved when each is clear about their contribution to the joint venture. A structure for work is also required. In contrast, service and role ambiguity or a "hidden agenda" leads to anxiety, frustration, and disappointment. During this phase of work, the group as a whole is too fragile to offer much supportive sustenance to the members. Members experience each other as potential sources of satisfaction but currently as stress inducing. Mutual anxiety over the unknown predominates. Anxiety is perpetuated by the lack of structure and lack of norms for work and conduct. Introducing service and role clarity provides essential structure to engage members' attention and increases the potential for positive engagement. We turn to the record of the group's first meeting.

By 5:45 P.M., seven members, representing six residents, had arrived. After casual introductions and some small talk around refreshments, I suggested we begin.

The group began with another round of introductions, some initial talk of who each other's resident was, and how well they all knew each other. I then stated, "I asked you to this meeting to think with you about whether it would be helpful to establish a floor group. The social work department and the home itself are interested in knowing whether closer, more consistent, more ongoing social work services in the form of a group would be helpful to you in relation to the kinds of problems and concerns you experience as relatives and friends of residents." I added, "You all know the ways in which residents are helpful to each other in their floor group, and I thought that because many of you might be experiencing similar troubles and concerns, the group might enable you to be helpful to each other. For example, the group could help with any concerns you may have about the services your relatives are receiving and with issues more personal in nature such as the impact on you of having a relative or friend at MHHA."

A lively discussion ensued. Most of the initial concerns expressed were environmental in nature. Members brought up problems with laundry, lack of individualized programs for residents, residents not being taken off the floor frequently enough, irregularity of physical therapy, and aides not being involved enough with residents in the afternoon. As the issues were raised, I asked how widespread a concern these were and how members presently were handling their worries. There was a high degree of consensus with regard to ongoing concerns. Most members said they did very little with their concerns beyond suppressing them or raising the issue when and only when it became very pressing. I said, "It seems that you find it either difficult or not particularly useful to raise your concerns with staff." Mrs. Somers changed focus and voiced the first complaint about social workers. She said they simply praised the home or did very little with her complaints. I credited her strength in bringing forth her criticism and asked others for their experiences with social workers. The consensus was that social workers were helpful in crises but simply did not provide sufficient ongoing service. In addition, they did not feel they could bring problems to staff. In the main they felt isolated from others and left to solve their problems alone.

Having heard the members define ongoing problems for which they felt there was no available help, I asked whether they thought they might want to meet to work collectively on those problems they seemed to have in common. My question was met with silence. I waited, not being sure what was in the silence. I broke the silence with a smile saying, "Boy this is a change for me . . . usually relatives are busy chasing me, and here it seems like I'm chasing them." There was some laughter, and members spoke and said it felt too soon for them to commit themselves to the group. Several said they would like to have another meeting to think further about whether they wanted to continue. Several said they felt good that they shared similar concerns. That made them feel less alone. They agreed to meet the following week to discuss whether meeting in some ongoing way might be of help to them. The members left the meeting talking to each other.

Although members had clearly not resolved their hesitation by the end of the meeting, the connection they felt with each other appeared strong enough to encourage them to attend a second meeting. The worker understood that such uncertainty was natural after initial sessions. Experience within the group, rather than further discussion about the group, was key to its resolution.

As the members move into the initial period of the ongoing work phase they have, for the moment, "resolved" their ambivalence about the group and are readying themselves for the work ahead. To move forward they are particularly concerned with (1) developing a mutual-aid system that will support their use of each other in the service of work and (2) contending with the power and control of the worker. The substantive work of the group is obscured by the members' preoccupation with "the authority theme." The group as a whole must "solve" its relationship with the worker sufficiently before it can move on to fully developing its peer relationships. Criticism of the worker is at its greatest. We present practice excerpts from the group's second meeting.

I felt good approaching this meeting. I had a positive sense from last week's meeting. I had met several relatives during the week, and they said they were looking forward to another meeting. A few others said they were coming. I recalled that I had prematurely asked whether they wanted to formalize as a group. This time I really wanted to listen rather than push for a premature decision. I was somewhat uncertain how new members would be received.

After introductions I recalled last week's meeting and said that they had agreed to meet today to consider whether they would like to continue working as a group and, if so, in relation to what issues and what concerns. Mrs. Elgin began with a concern of hers. She said that she found the floor unattractive and wondered if they couldn't spruce up the bulletin boards and add some plants. Others nodded. In an effort to make the covert overt and to help determine the degree of consensus about the physical environment, I said, "I notice you seem to be nodding in agreement and wonder if you feel the floor is not a very attractive place." Everyone agreed.

Mrs. Gladstein said that the types of residents on the floor, in addition to how the floor looked, bothered her. Others said they too were disturbed. Miss Wallace and Mrs. Velez were particularly expressive. They said that they thought these "disruptive" residents didn't belong on the floor. I said, "I think you are identifying an important concern; let's spend a little time on this." Miss Wallace and Mrs. Bailey shifted focus and began to talk about residents not being taken frequently enough to the bathroom. Though I noticed the shift away from the more difficult topic of residents with Alzheimer's, I followed their lead. I knew that two group members had relatives with Alzheimer's and thought this would be a very difficult discussion for them at this point. The consensus of relatives was that not only is toileting a problem, but alienation exists between residents and floor staff. Mrs. Sherman offered the first comment of personal pain. She said that she thought she could understand how the aides feel. Sometimes she has to withdraw also.

Others returned the discussion to environmental troubles, steering away from the pain of their life transitional experience. They said they thought it was a matter of caring; if the aides cared, they would do more. A very lively discussion ensued. I acted on my hunch that members were afraid to mention names and asked whether this was difficult to discuss. Silence. I continued, saying "I wonder whether you are concerned about how I might use the information. Are you wondering about the issue of confidentiality and possible repercussion as a result of the meeting?" Members denied any concern about the worker and jumped immediately to an aide of whom they were critical.

Before I could return to the question of confidentiality, Mrs. Somers said she wanted to talk about what happened when someone died on the floor. She confided how awful she felt when she saw a body being wheeled off the floor. I felt the power of the experience and encouraged discussion of this painful life transitional concern. The members discussed this for a short period, and for the next 10 minutes continued to raise problems. As the end of the meeting was approaching, I asked them about their reactions to forming a group. They found it difficult to commit themselves. I said that they had now, for two meetings, touched on a wide range of concerns, from those involving the securing of concrete services to those involving the quality of life on the floor. Mrs. Somers thought the group could address both kinds of concerns if they wanted.

In a surprising shift, all but Mrs. Velez said they thought such a group could be helpful in the future and would like to continue to meet for a few more sessions. Mrs. Velez said that her sister felt she should be able to handle all issues by herself and didn't really want Mrs. Velez involved. She said she would talk with her sister. I asked if I and the group could help at all. She said no. They agreed to meet the following week.

As the members develop greater comfort and confidence in the worker, they can more assuredly move forward toward the issues for which the group was formed and to becoming more fully involved with each other. Themes, problems, and concerns, which were previously only identified, become fleshed out as members gain strength in working on their troubles. The knowledge that members must work for what they get propels involvement. There is a growing sense that the group is satisfying. Intimacy becomes greater. This is even more evident in the third meeting.

I thought the group had taken a step forward in declaring its interest in continuing. Though for most of the group there was little commitment, to my surprise at the end of the group, all but Mrs. Velez said they would want to continue. I noticed that the group had worked particularly hard in identifying environmental problems but had developed an approach-avoidance pattern on any criticisms of me (that is, interpersonal concerns) and any themes that spoke to the pain of their experience (that is, life transitional concerns). A core membership, however, was developing, which provided leadership from week to week.

At the beginning of the meeting only four members were present. Over refreshments, the members expressed disappointment and anger about low attendance. Two members challenged me and asked if I had really done enough to get members. This led to a discussion of shared perceptions of why people were not attending. I inquired whether there were aspects of the group that might have been experienced negatively. The members were steadfast in their praise. They said that they couldn't speak for those absent; they themselves felt positive and appreciated the chance to work on their problems with the home and with their family members. I then asked "If you are pleased with the group, I am puzzled by what your disappointment is all about." There was consensus that six was a better number than four. At that exact moment, Mrs. Anderson and Bailey walked in. The timing was perfect, and everyone began to laugh.

Mrs. Gladstein pursued the group's strongest challenge to me and asked me again to share my outreach efforts. I once again detailed my efforts. Mrs. Sherman stated that having more outreach wasn't so important to her because she was getting a lot out of the group as it was and she wanted to move on to their work for today. At this time, we filled in Mrs. Anderson, who was there for the first time, about the group's purpose. Mrs. Bailey and Miss Fields moved on to a sensitive environmental issue by raising how they believed that the head nurse didn't really like family members to help on the floor. They felt pushed away. I asked for examples and many came forth. Mrs. Gladstein said she had made peace with herself—she is now pleasant but not too demanding unless there is something seriously wrong. I asked what Mrs. Gladstein felt about our nudging—was she concerned that the group might disturb that peace?

With Mrs. Gladstein answering yes, the group members moved to a new level of honesty and authenticity. Many spoke about the toughness of the group because in some ways they were no longer as complacent. Individual and group complacency seemed to dissolve in the face of the possibility of change. They said

it meant a lot to them to have a place to talk, and yet they were also scared. I tried to sustain the discussion of the negatives of the group. The members went back to the discussion of wanting to help on the floor but feeling cut off. I asked them to elaborate on their feeling cut off. The members spoke about their fear of retaliation: physical harm and withdrawal of services and emotion. I asked for details and they came forth easily. They said that incidents where they thought their relatives and friends were mishandled physically were the hardest to take. No one wanted to pursue a complaint. The tone was somber. The theme of discussion changed, and more environmental troubles were raised. Mrs. Gladstein said she thought a dying resident should not be kept on the floor—that has a negative effect on everyone else. The pros and cons were discussed. And then, for the first time, the group asked the worker to actively help them negotiate their environment by passing on their desire for dying residents to be placed on another floor. I stated that I would be willing to act in their behalf but wanted to get a better understanding of their concerns. Mrs. Bailey said that for her, the mentally incompetent residents proved to be even more distressing. She thought we didn't place residents well. The others energetically agreed. I precipitated discussion of ways they might become involved in these decisions, and there was an emotion-filled discussion of how they felt MHHA kept tight control over their lives.

The time watcher announced that they had been working for 2 hours. I asked about having another meeting, stating that I would be available for two more, or we could quickly sum up and then plan to meet again after the summer. Miss Wallace, feeling the emotional weight of the discussion, asked whether they hadn't discussed enough already. I invited elaboration, and Miss Wallace simply stated that she would come if others did. It was clear that the intimacy level comfortable for most was uncomfortable for her. I suggested that they use the next 2 weeks to further discuss this last question of the emotional life on the floor and their relationships with the home and then evaluate the experience in the last meeting. They agreed.

It seemed clear that the group had moved fully into the middle of the work phase. Perhaps the members' challenge of the worker's competence at outreach had cleared the air, and members were more actively able to pursue issues of importance to them. Perhaps also they were more trusting of each other. The group had become important to the members. This is poignantly evident in the fourth meeting. We turn to the worker's recording:

In the next to the last session, the group had one last major chance to raise and work on matters of concern. They had agreed to pursue discussion of the emotional life of the floor and their relationships with the home. I wanted to monitor the intimacy issue in an effort to ensure, if possible, a workable comfort level for Miss Wallace. All members arrived early, and after refreshments and small talk, the group began. Mrs. Sherman started with an environmental problem. After everyone agreed about the problem, Mrs. Elgin shifted the discussion by saying that she was beginning to feel better when she went on the floor. This led to a discussion of how the group members felt a greater sense of communion with each other and with each other's residents, when they went on the floor. Mrs. Elgin said that her mother felt that the floor was beginning to feel like a family to her. Members pursued discussion about what they had done with each other's relatives. Mrs. Somers spoke of the social support she received from the group and credited the group with lessening her sense of isolation. She felt an interest in her and her mother. I wondered what they actually found different. They offered examples and noted how beautifully the aides cared for Mrs. Velez's sister's roommate.

The news that this roommate had died stunned the group. The main conversation of the evening shifted to a discussion of death, illness, and dying (the members' shift from environmental to life transitional concerns was evident). Mrs. Somers began to cry. I touched her arm and said, "It's OK to cry here." She said she felt awful and was pleased that she could show how she felt. Others said the same. (Clearly the norms of the group had changed, and they had achieved a high level of intimacy with each other.) Others cried and shared various experiences with death. Mrs. Elgin's pained story of her sister's death 20 years earlier was particularly poignant. Miss Wallace said she found this discussion hard to take. She was 83 and only had her sister; everyone else had someone. Others suggested that although that was true, the loss of a loved one was hard for all of them. Miss Wallace persisted and said she felt they were dwelling on the pain too much. She asked "Why is it necessary?" She said she thought the group should focus on topics where change was possible. They were all going to die, and no one could change that. The room was silent. Members looked at me. I said that I was a little confused because Miss Wallace had said that she had no friends to help her when she felt blue, and I had thought that meant she welcomed the chance to talk. Miss Wallace went on to describe herself as a private person and that when she went home she was more upset than when she came. The support from the group came forth immediately. Mrs. Elgin said that if Miss Wallace wanted, she would drive her home, or they could go get something to eat together. (The mutual aid in the group was strong.) Mrs. Sherman expressed her sentiment by stating that part of the group was for them to help each other. She spoke of how she had things locked up in her and maybe in the future she could talk about these things, for example, the guilt she felt for bringing her sister here. Others agreed and reaffirmed that they thought the group could help with that. I stated that the group was there to help them in this way too—they were in charge of what they would talk about, how much they would talk about, and how they would use each other.

After some additional outreach to Miss Wallace, members changed focus and brought up environmental problems: laundry, dentures, getting information. They explored ways of going directly to nursing staff, as I would have to do just that to find out what they wanted. Mrs. Sherman said she felt our work was so important and wondered if there was a way to get it to the other families, "Could they write a newsletter?" They all agreed that this was a wonderful idea and strategized about the division of labor between them and me. It was agreed that they would think over the summer, and it would take more final form in the fall.

Our time keeper signaled that it was time to end. I mentioned that we had decided to have one more meeting and that they had agreed to evaluate their experience and to discuss plans for the fall. They agreed to have this be our focus next week. The mood was quiet as they acknowledged the work for the last session.

The members worked very hard during this meeting, fulfilling the potential of the final work phase. Their shift to the *life transitional* issues of death, dying, and loss seemed fitting for this fourth meeting, when mutual aid and intimacy among members were at their strongest. The quiet manner in which they acknowledged the forthcoming final meeting suggested they were already dealing with the loss of the group.

In the transition and ending phase, the impending demise of the group and separation of group members from each other and the worker provides the final momentum for participants to work on remaining issues. All energy shifts toward disbanding the group, which members labored to create. The stronger the connection, the more difficult the process of separation. The tasks of evaluating the group's work and defining and completing remaining work—if possible, while contending with feelings of loss—become the major work of the group.

In the fifth and final meeting the members' ambivalence about the ending of the group was clear. On the one hand they understood the need to evaluate the group and project to the future, and on the other hand they used the meeting to attend to unmet needs. In an important way, they used this last session to develop coping strategies, over the summer, in the absence of the worker and the group. They noted ways they could approach staff directly and how they could continue to use each other to think through problems. They were particularly excited by Mrs. Gladstein's suggestion that from time to time they approach staff together. Although as part of the evaluation process the worker encouraged discussion of negatives as well as positives, primarily positives were forthcoming.

Members agreed that the decrease in isolation they felt with each other and the greater receptivity they experienced from floor staff far outweighed any negatives. There was strong positive sentiment expressed about meeting in the fall. Members agreed to talk to relatives and friends over the summer, thereby keeping the group alive. Much physical affection was expressed as members and the worker left the room.

## CONCLUSION

Including relatives and friends in making the decision about whether group services would be helpful to them proved to be an important element in the creation of the group service itself. A partnership relationship between worker and members made it possible for participants to advance at their own pace. Because the members were allowed to make their own decisions, the development of the group as a whole was encouraged and strengthened. Phases of work were clearly apparent to the worker, despite the short-term nature of the group. Equally apparent and interesting was the manner in which the members moved from their initial preoccupation with environmental obstacles to their more painful life transitional struggles.

## References

Brager, G., & Holloway, S. (1978). *Changing human service organizations: Politics and practice.* New York: The Free Press.

Germain, C. B., & Gitterman, A. (1980). *The life model of social work practice.* New York: Columbia University Press.

Gitterman, A. (1986). Developing a new group service: Strategies and skills. In A. Gitterman & L. Shulman (Eds.), *Mutual aid groups and the life cycle* (pp. 53–71). Itasca, Il: F. E. Peacock.

Hartford, M. (1972). *Groups in social work.* New York: Columbia University Press.

Schwartz, W. (1961). The social worker in the group. In *New perspectives on services to groups: Theory, organization and practice* (pp. 7–34). New York: National Association of Social Workers; and *Social Welfare Forum (1961)* (pp. 146–177). New York: Columbia University Press.

Schwartz, W. (1971). On the use of groups in social work practice. In W. Schwartz & S. R. Zalba (Eds.), *The practice of group work.* New York: Columbia University Press.

Shalinsky, W. (1964). Group composition as an element of social group work practice. *Social Service Review, 43,* 4249.

# CASE STUDY 6.3

*Group approaches can be an efficient and effective way of working with children who have various social difficulties. This case describes a structured approach to teaching children specific skills to help them address various situational difficulties.*

## Questions

1. What types of difficulties would be best suited to this model of treatment?
2. How are group members involved in the teaching of social skills?
3. How was role playing used to teach social skills?
4. How can the group leader evaluate whether the skills are learned?

## A SOCIAL SKILLS GROUP FOR CHILDREN

*Craig Winston LeCroy*

Ms. Thompson called the social services office of the school district for the third time. Her student Kevin had caused so much disruption that she lost complete control of her class. It was the end of an exhausting day that was beginning to become too familiar.

I met with Ms. Thompson and other teachers about important concerns with their various students. "Kerry is so insecure and withdrawn—I'm concerned about how her brother teases her." Another teacher exclaimed, "Tom can't control his anger; when he gets mad he lets the other kids have it!" Ms. Thompson spoke mainly of Kevin: "I can't keep him in his seat and under control."

I listened to the complaints, feeling, as I had in the past, disappointed that the children could not get the individual time and attention they needed. It became clear that the children had a less than promising year ahead if they weren't able to gain some control or comfort in the classroom and with their peers.

Teacher concerns such as these frequently lead to the beginning of groups designed to respond to the various needs of troubled children. Groups that focus on social skills do well in addressing the various difficulties such children face in their day-to-day lives. The purpose of social skills groups is to teach children new ways of responding to their problematic situations.

A skills-based approach has become increasingly popular as we learn more about the relationship between poor peer relationships and subsequent social difficulties. Child developmentalists stress the importance of children learning necessary peer relationship skills because without such skills children are more easily beset with friendship difficulties, inappropriately expressed emotion, inability to resist peer pressure, and so on. Within a social skills framework, problem behaviors, such as the child behavior problems presented by the teachers, are viewed as deficits in appropriate skills. This suggests the need to teach children prosocial responses or social skills as opposed to an exclusive focus on the elimination of problem behaviors.

## TEACHING SOCIAL SKILLS

The logic behind teaching social skills is based primarily on social learning theory. Social situations are presented, and then children are taught to implement skills in responding to the various social situations. The process begins with the social situation and the social skill being taught. The group discusses the use of the social skill, the rationale for the skill, and the steps used to implement the skill. Next, the stage is set for learning the skill through role playing. The leader or group member models the skill, which is followed by feedback from the group members as to whether the criteria for successful demonstration of the skill were achieved. The group members take turns rehearsing the social skill in various role-play enactments. Following the acquisition of the basic skill, the group then works on more complex skill situations. Successful use of the skill requires the use and practice of the skill in the natural environment. Many variations of this basic format are used.

## STARTING THE GROUP

As I reviewed the theory and rationale underlying social skills groups, the concerned teachers began to identify skills they would like to see their students learn. I try to encourage teachers to think in terms of desired outcomes they would like to see students develop rather than focusing on problems they want eliminated. Having teachers focus on outcomes brings them one step closer to specifying what objectives they believe are important for the children to acquire. I find that asking, "What would the child need to do differently to be less of a problem?" is helpful in moving the discussion to desired outcomes that are more specific and positive. When I asked this of Ms. Thompson, she began to express hope for Kevin: "Well, Kevin's a natural leader—but

he needs to learn to ask for things politely and resist peer pressure to disrupt the class."

Together, we identified six children, 9 to 11 years old, who would benefit from a social skills group. The tasks of recruiting and scheduling the children, notifying and informing parents about the group, and arranging logistical details were shared by Ms. Thompson and myself. We agreed the group would run for 10 weeks, which would give me adequate time to teach the children some specific skills, encourage application of the new skills to classroom and home situations, and teach problem-solving skills for difficult and complex situations.

## AN EXAMINATION OF THE TRAINING PROCESS

The skills training process proceeds in a fairly straightforward, structured way. The following sections describe the key leadership skills and procedures in a social skills group. A brief process recording from a group session follows.

### Selecting Skills and Situations

When I decided to conduct the social skills group for the school, the first step was to decide what basic skills I was going to focus on. Given the identified needs of the children, I decided to focus on the skills of giving and receiving feedback, making friends, and resisting peer pressure. Other social skills programs might choose a variety of skills to teach, such as negotiating, making requests of others, being assertive, handling encounters with police, practicing pregnancy prevention skills (for example, discussing birth control, asking for information), getting a job, using independent living skills (for example, using community resources), and practicing anger control skills (see LeCroy, 1986).

When broad social skills are selected, as in our example with resisting peer pressure, then the micro skills that constitute resisting peer pressure must be identified. For example, the micro skills of resisting peer pressure include speaking slowly and calmly, saying no clearly and as soon as possible, continuing to refuse pressure, and suggesting another activity or leaving the situation. One of the critical and valuable aspects of social skills training is the discrete level at which the social skills are taught and learned. Breaking the skill down into small components facilitates learning and provides for an increased sense of control for the group members. As the children learn small steps they master new ways of responding to situations and gain greater self-confidence in their abilities.

Another consideration that is important in planning a social skills group is the type of problem situations that are used in the group. It is important in a social skills group to provide the group members with situational problems that demand the use of the skill. Problematic situations need to be devised that reflect a realistic situation where the social skills can be practiced. For example, with resisting peer pressure, situations could be constructed around pressure to steal, pressure to cheat, pressure to have sex, and pressure to take drugs.

## Discussing the Social Skill

To begin the process of teaching a social skill, I start with a discussion about the use of the social skills. The purpose of the discussion is to provide reasons for learning the skills and to give examples of where the skill might be used. I asked the group, "Why is it important to learn how to resist peer pressure?" If children understand the reason behind why they should use the skill, then they are more motivated to learn the skill. Furthermore, if children are given examples of how the skill can be used, then they will be motivated by understanding how to apply the skill in their day-to-day life. I also ask, "What examples can you

think of where you used or could have used the skill of resisting peer pressure?"

In discussing the skill with the group, it is important to describe the skill steps needed to operationalize the skill. It is critical to break down the skill and provide the group members with a clear understanding of how the skill steps compose the overall application of the skill. I list the skill steps on the board, and I often tell the students that they must remember them. Together the group works out games or acronyms to facilitate retention of the steps. In teaching the children the skill of resisting peer pressure, I listed five skill steps I wanted them to learn:

1. Look the person in the eye; be serious.
2. Say no, clearly and quickly.
3. Continue to say no if you get repeated pressure.
4. Suggest an alternative activity.
5. If pressure is continued, leave the situation.

These skill steps break down the skill of resisting peer pressure and give group members a clear idea of how to respond to peer pressure effectively. We spend some time discussing what each step means in the children's own words.

## Set Up the Role Play

Next I must set up the role play for the group members. There are several critical decisions in composing the role plays. For instance, I usually select a protagonist who I think can do a good job as a model for the other group members. I get the group involved in setting up a realistic role play by asking the group, "What is the situation?" "Where is this taking place?" "Who would be there?"

It is important to prepare the group members to participate in and observe the role play. I structure the group so that the group members are actively involved and listening to the role play rather than sitting back passively, uninvolved in what is going on. I encourage the group members to define some of the characters in the role plays. For example, I ask "What is this person like?" or "What kind of character should we give this person?" "What does this person sound or look like?" I ask the students who play the roles to pay attention to their nonverbal as well as verbal behavior in the role play.

I also instruct the group members to be observers by giving them observer tasks. I have the observers choose a name like *Detectives* or *Watchers,* and I say, "Make sure the skill steps are followed" or "Someone watch the nonverbal behavior," or I ask a more general question like, "Do you think this is similar to situations you know about?" By assigning the group or specific members observation tasks, they become more actively involved in the role play and therefore acquire the skills more readily. At this time I also discuss with group members how to give and receive feedback. I always have the children practice giving feedback prior to starting role plays.

## Modeling of the Skill

For each new skill, I either model the skill or select a group member to model the skill. I model the skill so that I can carefully follow the skill steps. When a group member is used to model the skill, it is important to ensure good modeling. This can be facilitated by reviewing the skill steps with the protagonist immediately prior to the role play. It is important to go briefly over the plan of what the role players are going to say in the role-play enactment. I then review the skill steps for the group members who are responsible for giving the protagonist feedback on his or her performance.

## Role Play and Rehearsal of the Skill

The role play is enacted, and the role players do a live demonstration of the problem situation. Although the situation is contrived, the role plays frequently become spontaneous, and each role player must act accordingly. Following the role play, the group members are ready to respond with their feedback. I take an active role in soliciting positive feedback first by asking the group what the protagonist did well. I encourage and often require the protagonist to also state his or her self-evaluation. This is followed by a careful critique of the skill steps. "Were the skill steps followed?" "Which steps could have been performed better?" and "How would you do it differently?" The leader must structure the feedback and keep the group focused on learning the discrete skill steps.

The feedback is then incorporated into another role play. Here the protagonist must concentrate on changing his or her performance to meet the demands of the feedback. It is critical for me to help facilitate this by asking, "What are you going to do differently this time to use the group's feedback?" The process is continued until the protagonist has performed all the skill steps. For every skill, I provide an opportunity for each member to be the protagonist so that each member learns the skills proficiently.

## Practice Complex Situations

As the group members became skilled in the basic skills of giving and receiving feedback, making friends, and resisting peer pressure, I introduced increasingly complex situations. The use of more extended role plays was one way I accomplished this. I also asked the group members to bring in their own social skill situations so that the group can help them work out new responses to problematic encounters. After the group had acquired many of the basic skills, I taught the group accessory skills in dealing with problematic situations. For example, we began to focus on using problem-solving skills in addition to practicing social skills. During one of the later sessions, Kevin brought up a situation where he had successfully resisted his friend's pressure to skip school, but his friend said he would no longer be his friend. We worked on generating different alternatives for solving Kevin's new dilemma. In addition, I encourage the development of role taking by having the members play different roles in various social situations. In this way I can encourage the members to experience the role. I often ask, "What does it feel like to be _____?" In Kevin's situation, I helped him develop some perspective-taking or empathy skills when I asked him to play the role of his friend. When he did this he was able to discover some new ways to try talking with his friend.

As a leader I try to think about what the goal is I am trying to achieve with the group. If the goal is skill training, then I will focus the group on the acquisition of the skill. "What would you do in that situation?" If the goal is role taking or empathy, I will focus on feelings by helping the children experience different feelings and roles. "How does this person feel?" or "Why does he feel this way?" If the goal is to encourage problem solving, I will focus on alternative ways of solving problematic situations and various consequences for different alternatives. "What are some other alternatives?" "What would happen if you choose that solution?"

## GROUP PROCESS ILLUSTRATED

The transcript below from the group's fourth session will demonstrate the techniques and procedures used in leading a social skills group.

---

**Group Process**

*Leader:* Today we are going to practice our social skills. One skill that we have talked about is learning to resist peer pressure. What does it mean to resist peer pressure?

*Beth:* It's when your friends try to force you into things.

*Mark:* It's when other kids get you into trouble and it's not your fault.

*Leader:* That's right, Beth and Mark; resisting peer pressure means other people are trying to get you to do something you don't want to do. So when you are in a situation where you don't want to do something that your friends want you to do, you need to be able to say no and do it in a way that your friends will leave you alone. What reasons can you think of for learning how to resist peer pressure? I'll start—you resist peer pressure so that you'll feel better about yourself because you didn't get talked into doing something you might feel bad about later.

*Kevin:* So you don't get into trouble with your parents.

*Explanation of group leader's behavior*

*The leader begins by soliciting an explanation of the skill.*

*Encouraging and reinforcing the group members to share.*

*Summarizing the skill.*

*The leader points out the influence of peers and stresses the need to learn the skill. Providing rationales for the skill. The leader begins by modeling the first response, and the group members follow in a similar fashion.*

*Leader:* Good, Kevin.

*Wendy:* So you don't get talked into using drugs.

*Tommy:* Your friends will listen to you and know you're not just saying things.

*Leader:* Great, Wendy and Tommy. As a number of you have pointed out, there are a lot of good reasons to resist peer pressure. I think you have also talked about how hard it is to do. That's why we need to practice the skill. Let's go over the steps in how to resist peer pressure. Remember, practice good nonverbal skills and start by saying no as soon as possible, stick to your no, and if necessary leave the situation or suggest something different. Here's a situation we can use: two friends come up to you at recess and ask you to steal someone's homework as a joke. This is a person that gets picked on a lot, and he will probably feel picked on if you do it. Wendy, pick two people to do a role play of this situation. OK, role players take a minute to think of what you want to say. Everyone else can watch to see if Wendy follows the skill steps. Kevin will you also see if she uses good nonverbal behavior? OK, let's start.

*Tom:* Hey, Wendy, go get Todd's homework; it's sitting right there (points to a chair).

*Kerry:* Yeah, he'll never know you did it.

*Wendy:* Uh . . . I . . . Uhmmm . . . I don't think I better.

*Tom:* Come on Wendy, just do it.

*Wendy:* No, I can't—you do it if you want Todd's homework.

*Leader:* OK, break. Let's give Wendy some feedback. Kevin, let's start with you; what nonverbal behavior did you observe?

*Kevin:* Well, she spoke up and looked Tom in the eye.

*Leader:* OK, good, what do you think she could have done better?

*Kevin:* She tripped over her words at the beginning.

*Provides reinforcement for group member participation.*

*Summarizes and emphasizes the difficulty in resisting peer pressure.*

*Reviews the skill steps that identify a sequence that the members should follow in learning how to resist peer pressure. The leader puts these on the board or provides students with a handout.*
*The leader provides a situation for the group. This is provided to assure that the skills are understood and learned. Later, members can bring in their own situations to practice.*

*The leader chooses a member who can do a good job with the role play (that is, modeling the skill) since this is the first time through.*

*Preparing the group members to listen and observe so that they can observe the model and give feedback. One member is singled out for a special task to help ensure he pays attention. The leader must be responsible for getting everyone in the group involved in the role play.*

*The leader begins the process of feedback by asking group members to comment on Wendy's performance. The group members have been taught to use positive feedback at first before being critical, although here they too quickly move to the critical.*
*The leader encourages students to share observations and then asks for specific critical feedback.*

*Continues*

*Beth:* Yeah, she could have said no better at the beginning, but the second time was better.

*Leader:* Beth, what do you think would be a better response when Tom asked her to take the homework?

*Beth:* She could have said, no, I don't think that is right.

*Leader:* Why isn't it right?

*Beth:* Because it would hurt his feelings.

*Leader:* Yes, I think it would. OK, any other feedback for Wendy? Well I have some. I think Wendy did a good job of being serious. I think the second time she spoke she could have suggested another activity like we learned. Any ideas on what she could have suggested?

*Tom:* You mean she should have said let's go play outside?

*Leader:* Yeah, she could have suggested they go outside and forget about taking Todd's homework. OK, we've got a good start; let's redo the role play, and Wendy, try to use the suggestions for improvements the group gave you. For example, how could you say "no" right away after Tom and Kerry put pressure on you?

*Wendy:* I could say, "No, I think that's mean and I don't want to do it."

*Leader:* Good. That's better. Let's go ahead and try it out again. Remember to say no early on, be forceful, and suggest an alternative activity.

*The leader gets other group members to model better responses to the situation.*

*Encouraging the members to think about what it is like when someone hurts your feelings.*

*The leader gives his feedback, making sure that the role play incorporates the skills needed to resist peer pressure.*

*The leader summarizes the suggestions and then prepares the group to redo the role play and incorporate the ideas suggested by the group. Here it is important to make sure the role players understand how to incorporate the feedback for an improved performance.*

*The remainder of the session is devoted to continued practice and feedback. The leader helps students to identify situations outside the group where they can practice skills in the upcoming week and assigns homework practice using the "buddy system." The group closes with a brief fun game to increase social connections among the children and to keep the group interesting and fun.*

## PRACTICING SOCIAL SKILLS IN THE NATURAL ENVIRONMENT

A primary goal in teaching social skills is that the skills learned will be used in the child's natural environment. Throughout the 10-week sequence I encouraged the children to practice the skills outside of the group. This was accomplished by giving and monitoring homework assignments. At times all group members were working on the same skill—for example, after the session where we worked on resisting peer pressure. At other times during the 10 weeks, group members would work on different skills; for example, Wendy would focus on starting a conversation (a discrete friendship skill), while Kevin focused on generating alternatives to peer pressure situations. Group members were given assignments to use the skill and record the outcome in a journal. The journals were helpful and were used by half of the group members; the other three members typically forgot or lost their journals. For those that used them, I reviewed the journals in the group and used them to reinforce the members' practice outside the group. I also encouraged the use of the skills outside the group by having the group members practice the skills with their "buddy" as a homework assignment. "Buddies" were rotated to promote increased social interaction among all group members and to provide a variety of peer role models for each member. As much as possible I consulted with teachers to monitor the group members' interpersonal interactions so that examples of when and where to use the skills could be incorporated into the group procedures.

## CONCLUSION

Promoting competence in children and adolescents is a fundamental strategy for helping young people confront stressful situations and avoid problem behaviors. It has been effectively used to help children develop new patterns of interpersonal relationships, confront new social situations, gain membership in new social groups, and learn new behavioral responses. Without adequate social skills, such experiences can become avenues to pregnancy, delinquency, drug use, and social isolation.

Social skills training is perhaps the most promising new treatment model developed for working with young people. It approaches treatment by building on the positive aspects of functioning—building needed skills for youth. Children and adolescents must adapt and cope with an increasingly complex society. As a normal part of growing up, young people must confront the developmental task of dealing with such issues as drugs, sex, and alcohol. To be successful, we must teach our children social skills so that they can respond to difficult social circumstances and do so with self-confidence and competence.

## Reference

LeCroy, C. W. (1986). Social competence training. In A. R. Stiffman & R. Feldman (Eds.), *Advances in adolescent mental health* (vol. 2, pp. 101–114). Greenwich, CT: JAI Press.

# CASE STUDY 6.4

*Social workers often work with nonvoluntary clients. This case study describes a group model of working with such clients because of battering behavior.*

## Questions

1.  How can social workers respond to denial when working with nonvoluntary clients?
2.  How did the social worker use confrontation in working with the resistant client?
3.  What interventions contributed to the changes described in the client?
4.  How does group treatment address the special circumstances of men who batter?

---

## GROUP WORK WITH MEN WHO BATTER

### Richard M. Tolman and Larry Bennett

Sam, a white 26-year-old laborer who lives in a working-class suburb, was referred by the court to a group program for men who batter. He is employed full-time, earning about $20,000 annually. Sam has been arrested three times. His most recent arrest was for the battery of his wife. He received 6 months probation and was mandated to attend domestic violence counseling. He had two previous arrests, one for auto theft when he was a teenager and one 2 years ago for disorderly conduct.

At the initial intake interview Sam was secretive, and it seemed that he did not want the worker to know much about him. His flat affect and deceptive manner made it appear that he thought the agency was out to get him rather than help him. This type of presentation was not unusual for a court-ordered client. For the most part, men who batter do not come to treatment voluntarily. They are generally either court-mandated or "wife-mandated"; that is, their partners left or threatened to leave the relationship unless they receive counseling. Our experience is that de-

spite the men's nonvoluntary status they may be helped and that a court order can actually facilitate progress when they might otherwise drop out. In fact, evidence suggests that batterers' contact with the criminal justice system in itself is effective in reducing violence (Sherman & Berk, 1984).

To enter the program, men must minimally be willing to admit that they have battered and to verbalize a willingness to take responsibility for change. Ongoing denial of battering and responsibility for it is common and expected and must be confronted throughout the treatment process.

An important step in the intake process is taking a history of past and current abuse. The history taking may be facilitated by using structured interview protocols and checklists. In this case, the use of such checklists revealed that Sam had a significant history of both psychological and physical maltreatment of his partner, including interrupting her eating and sleeping; refusing to let her see people; frequently insulting, swearing, and screaming at her; threatening to hit her; pushing, grabbing, and restraining her; slapping her; driving recklessly to frighten her; throwing objects at her; hitting her with his fists; throwing her bodily; and hitting her with an object.

Generally, men who batter will minimize or deny their violent behavior. In addition, they may attempt to use the treatment program manipulatively, perhaps to convince their partners not to leave them or to drop charges in the court system. Treatment for the men can be stressful and can inadvertently increase the risk of abuse. Therefore, contact with the men's partners is crucial in delivering safe services. When Debbie was interviewed she corroborated Sam's account of the violence. The fact that Sam accurately described his violent behavior was a good sign that he could come to take responsibility for his behavior.

At intake, Sam was asked about his own alcohol and drug use, and his perception of the role of drugs in his violence. This is important because untreated substance problems make progress in treatment for violence unlikely. Many clients attribute their violent behavior to the effects of the substance. It is important to uncover and challenge such a defense in treatment. In this case, Sam attributed none of his violence to alcohol or drugs. He has been abstinent for 5 years. His family history (ACOA, brother with drinking problem) and his own history suggest that he is an alcoholic (he reports blackouts, drinking-related amnesia, friends and family expressing concern about his drinking, and trying to cut down unsuccessfully). He has, however, maintained his abstinence without involvement in any treatment program or attendance of Alcoholics Anonymous.

Sam grew up in an alcoholic, violent family. His father and stepmother are active alcoholics. Sam's brother is currently facing a prison sentence for a felony. Sam witnessed physical abuse of his mother, and he himself was physically abused. As Straus, Gelles, and Steinmetz (1980) report, both witnessing and being a victim of abuse in one's family of origin are predictors of subsequent abusive behavior.

Sam met his wife, Debbie, when he was 21, five years ago. At that time she was 15 and working as a waitress. He was attracted to her because she was "cute." He had been dating her for one week when he was kicked out of his home. Debbie's mother invited him to move in with their family. He never moved out. The first year of their relationship was stormy because of "forced closeness." Sam felt he was underemployed. He blamed money for the arguments between he and his wife. He described his in-laws' household as very stressful.

Following intake Sam was placed in an ongoing group. The group approach is preferred over couples or individual treatment for several reasons. Despite obvious problems in Sam and Debbie's relationship that would warrant couples counseling, conjoint sessions are dangerous if undertaken prior to a man successfully stopping his violent behavior. The safety necessary to foster cooperation and adequate self-disclosure cannot be assured while men are actively violent toward their partners. Conjoint therapy may compromise the goal of changing violence because of its emphasis on strengthening or healing the existing relationship. Some men won't change until threatened with loss of their partners and, in the couples treatment context, a woman may not be able to safely explore her ambivalent wishes to leave the relationship. Further, counseling in a couples context may be implicitly victim-blaming. Men have frequently told their partners that the battering would stop if she only changed her behavior. Bograd (1984) points out that there is a subtle but crucial difference between suggesting that the wife modify her behavior to protect herself and suggesting that she initiate events so that she can control him. As a result, even couples counseling that explicitly focuses on a woman's safety may reinforce a man's projections of blame on his partner. Although conjoint work to deal with marital discord can be very useful, it should not occur until the primary problem of violence has been addressed successfully and the woman feels safe when participating in the sessions.

A group format offers the men a variety of models and sources of feedback for learning to self-observe, change cognitions, and interact differently. Although many men who batter express regret about their behavior, they are given mixed messages by those around them. The importance of having other men in the same situation saying, "I don't like what I am doing and I want to stop," supports a commitment to nonviolent behavior. In a follow-up study of a program for men who batter, Gondolf (1984) found that men ranked the group support as the most important element in helping them to stop their violence.

Sam's group treatment had several goals. First, Sam had to take responsibility for his violent behavior. This required confronting his denial. Second, he needed to learn skills to help maintain nonviolence. The necessary skills include self-observation, time-out, cognitive restructuring, and interpersonal skills training. They will be described in more detail below. Third, Sam needed to examine and adjust his attitudes and expectations that encouraged his violence. Fourth, it was hoped that Sam would begin to explore his family of origin and other personal issues that may be related to his violence.

The main ingredients of the group experience are the support and confrontation of the men by other group members and the leaders, education-practice in group, and homework assignments. Each group session is relatively structured and begins with a check-in. At check-in the men report if they have been violent and if they have used any of the techniques they have learned in group. Problem-

atic situations are then discussed in group in detail, and various techniques are practiced further. This work with the problematic situations the men describe is followed by discussions of specific themes, such as men's control of women or sexually abusive behavior.

In the first sessions with Sam, the primary focus was on helping him take responsibility for his violent behavior, to begin to observe the behavioral chain that leads to violent behavior, and to practice time-outs. Initial training in self-observation begins at intake. The use of a contract for nonviolence encourages men to identify physical, cognitive, affective, and situational cues for violence. Once these cues are identified, a plan for using alternative coping behaviors can be formulated. The metaphor of an early-awareness system is used: intervention is easier when the cues are identified at more subtle, earlier points in the chain of events.

Time-out is a crisis intervention technique that a man can use to take a break from conflict when he feels himself becoming extremely tense in a conflict. Men can use time-out to short-circuit what might become an abusive act. Time-out may include leaving the house or closing oneself in a room alone. Time-outs give men the time to use relaxation techniques, to problem-solve solutions to the conflict, or to reach out for support from others. The skill is often taught quite early in treatment, at intake, and may be incorporated into a no-violence contract, in which a man identifies high-risk situations and agrees to use a time-out or other skill rather than become abusive. When men first join the group, the leaders assign practice time-outs to help the men learn the technique and to troubleshoot problems in the men's application of time-out. Noncompliance with the assignment often becomes a point of confrontation.

For Sam, one problem in using time-out was that Debbie at times tried to block his leaving the house. This problem actually occurs frequently. Partners may perceive time-outs as an attempt to avoid discussing an issue or an attempt to punish her by withdrawing. Indeed, many men do abuse time-out in these ways. For Sam, the group helped him problem-solve ways of getting out of the house or taking a time-out when he needed to without using physical aggression toward Debbie.

At first, Sam disclosed relatively little in group. He seemed to have very little ability to be introspective. As he began to discuss details of his life, it was clear that the conflicts he faced with his wife were totally her fault.

Although the leaders and group members could empathize with Sam's pain in the relationship, these descriptions were not accepted at face value, and limits were set on Sam's use of the group to complain about his wife. The importance of keeping men focused on themselves rather than on their partners cannot be emphasized enough. If unchecked, the group sessions could easily become exclusively focused on how badly treated the men are by their partners. It is critical for the group leader to listen empathically to the men's complaints and the pain that underlies them but to appropriately refocus the group discussion on the men's responsibility for change. When modeled appropriately in the group, the other members begin to take over the function of confrontation from the leader. Such peer confrontation is more powerful, as it is perceived as coming from someone else who knows what it is like to be in the group member's place.

At first Sam was not confronted very directly in the group. His denial was addressed, however, in several ways. First, as mentioned, limits were placed on his complaining about his wife. Second, other members modeled taking responsibility for their own behavior. Gradually, the confrontation became more direct.

In the 10th session, Sam discussed an argument he had with Debbie:

*Sam:* I work two jobs and she just lays around. She's lazy, she doesn't work, and she doesn't even keep the house clean—her mother does all that. She's like a teenager. And then she goes out and bangs up my car.

*Co-Leader:* You're blaming your wife for everything that's wrong in your relationship. What can you do to improve the situation?

*Member 1:* Yeah, you need to take more responsibility for problems at home. You're just trying to make it seem like your abuse is her fault.

*Member 2:* You don't even face the real problems. You just give us your "magic fairy" report every week. You have a big blowup, and then the next day everything is fine. You don't talk over the issues with her; you don't tell her the feelings that were underneath your anger—a magic fairy just comes and takes the problem away.

*Member 3:* That's stuffing—just like it talks about in the manual.

*Member 2:* Yeah, you're "saving stamps," man. If you don't work on the real issues and tell her how you feel, you are just going to store up those resentments and blow up again. We don't want to see that happen to you. You've got to get your head out of your ass and start to take care of yourself.

A group discussion of how to deal with resentments followed. The group leader followed up and asked Sam to focus concretely on what he could do between sessions to improve the situation. The plan was for Sam to praise his wife for doing the bills. By framing the general discussion of the group into a specific homework assignment for Sam, the worker extended the work of the group into the week. Behavioral change was promoted by giving a concrete task and holding Sam accountable for accomplishing it. This particular directive had several purposes. First, in asking Sam to praise his wife for her help, Sam had to take responsibility for using positive reinforcement rather than coercion in dealing with the issues he has with his wife. Second, focusing on praising his wife for her help got at the issue of entitlement that Sam felt in regard to his wife's labor. Frequently, men assume that they deserve their wife's labor and that she simply must comply with his requests for what she must do in the home. In this case, Sam was getting the message that labor in a relationship is negotiated and that he is responsible for showing his wife that he appreciates those things she does for him in the relationship. Thus the group challenges a sexist attitude that contributes to violence against women because that attitude diminishes the status and value of women.

This directive also illustrates an initial application of interpersonal skills training. Men who batter are often limited in their ability to resolve conflicts with others assertively rather than passively or aggressively (Rosenbaum & O'Leary, 1981). An important component of group treatment for men who batter therefore involves teaching the man new interpersonal skills for conflict resolution. Applying skills training procedures with men who batter requires that a specific set of skills be identified and then taught to men, using situations that are personally relevant to them. Training in nonviolent conflict resolution often focuses on the man's ability to identify and express his own feelings about what is happening, identify and state his partner's point of view, offer solutions from which both he and his partner will benefit, and negotiate a final compromise.

It should be noted that although completion of the assignment might have led to improvements in Sam's relationship, that was not the purpose per se. The function was to teach Sam noncoercive means for dealing with conflict and with his feelings. It is possible that Debbie will not fulfill Sam's expectations for her behavior, despite Sam's attempts to change himself in a positive manner. In such a case, Sam would be reminded that his responsibility is to act noncoercively, despite her

actions. Abusive behavior is never justified, however uncooperative she may be.

At the next session, Sam reported that the arguments with his wife had continued and that he did not complete his assignment. Interpersonal skills training continued. Training often begins as it did with Sam, by identifying interpersonal situations in which the man has experienced difficulties. Various ways of achieving a more positive outcome are explored in the group. After sifting through the alternatives, the man chooses one that is most likely to increase the chances of a positive resolution. This alternative can be demonstrated by the leader or a group member. After observing the modeling, the man rehearses the new skill, with someone else playing the role of his partner. Group members then offer feedback on the man's performance, and he may optionally rehearse the new skills a second time to incorporate the feedback. The skills training usually culminates with an agreement to use the new skills in an upcoming situation and report back on the effect.

In this session the leader spent 10 minutes of rehearsal with Sam on how to praise his wife. During this discussion several men praised Sam's empathic presentation of his wife's chronic unemployment problem. The evidence for Sam's progress in this session is mixed. His empathy indicated a willingness to view his wife as a person rather than as an object. This empathy reduces the probability of violence and suggests that Sam was internalizing the group content. However, his issues of control appeared to be surfacing around homework completion. In regard to the noncompletion of his previous assignment, the leader reinforced the importance of assignment completion by confronting his noncompliance and dealing with it in a concrete manner. He was reassigned the same homework.

The following session demonstrated Sam's progress vividly. His adoption of new prosocial behavior is mirrored in his group behavior as well as reports of behavior outside the group. Sam collected the group members' fees, a shared group responsibility, for the first time. He reported that he completed his assignment, to tell his wife that he appreciated her doing the bills. She blushed and felt good. Sam also reported a surprising improvement in the home situation—Debbie got a job.

During the next group session, Sam was discussing his relationship with his wife and frequently remarked, "I'm just stupid." The group leader pointed out how easily Sam slipped into such negative self-talk; this was an opportunity to apply some cognitive-restructuring techniques with Sam. Cognitive-restructuring techniques teach individuals to analyze and modify maladaptive thinking patterns. A man's rigid beliefs about how he and his partner should behave in a relationship increase the probability that he will be violent. Several interlocking steps are involved in the application of cognitive restructuring in groups. In discussing situations the men have encountered during the week, the following steps may be used: (1) elicit internal dialogue; (2) identify underlying irrational beliefs and faulty assumptions; (3) challenge irrational or faulty beliefs; (4) replace irrational or faulty beliefs with more realistic appraisals; (5) generate self-instructions for using nonviolent coping behavior.

Much of Sam's negative self-talk in this case was self-referent; that is, he was making unrealistically negative appraisals of himself and his abilities. He had difficulty generating positive self-appraisals, so the leader asked if Sam would listen while the group made positive statements about him. Sam said he would listen because nobody ever made positive statements about him. The depth of his problems with self-esteem and the role of his family of origin in the genesis of those problems was then revealed in his apparent off-task comments about his brother's impending prison

sentence, and how his father's long drinking binge put his family deep in debt.

The leader refocused the group on giving Sam positive feedback and then asked the group to proceed. About half the group was able to give him positive comments. Sam was pleased with the feedback from the group members. Following the feedback Sam commented that he wanted his brother-in-law to come to the group: "I didn't realize the different types of abuse there are — my brother-in-law is emotionally abusive."

Sam's comment illustrated that progress had been made on several important treatment goals. His recognition of his brother-in-law's emotional abusiveness demonstrated that Sam had come to redefine abusive behavior more broadly. He no longer limited his definition of abuse to physical aggression. Of course, it is critical that Sam recognize his own use of such behaviors and not focus only on others' behavior.

This session also illustrates how the group itself becomes an instrument of social change. Frequently, group members begin to reach out to their own social networks, and the abusive men that they know, to bring them to group. Such action can be seen as a demonstration that an individual man has internalized the need for change—confronting another man about his abuse takes a degree of courage and self-disclosure. In doing so, the man has begun to exercise an influence on his environment. One of the most important maintaining causes of violence against women is the lack of negative social sanctions and the sometimes overt social support for abusive behavior that men receive from other men around them. When men begin to confront other men, they are removing some of that social support.

The need for Sam to focus on his own non-physical abusive behavior was apparent at the next session. Sam did not come to the group. He had called the crisis line earlier, saying he had gone to his wife's workplace and been told by her boss that it didn't matter if she came in or not because she was always late and a poor worker. This checking-up behavior was illustrative of his need to control and infantilize his partner.

At the next session, Sam demonstrated that he continued to redefine abuse for himself and was beginning to address his responsibility for behavior change. During the group, Sam described as abusive his breaking of a mirror while talking on the phone. He recognized this behavior as indicating that he was at risk of using direct aggression toward his partner and that breaking a mirror could imply a physical threat to Debbie. The group confronted him on his checking up on his wife at work, and Sam was able to see how such behavior illustrated his need to control Debbie.

Some of the core cognitions that support Sam's abusive behavior were also identified and challenged in this session. Sam began to discuss his belief that he was worthless without his partner. Such beliefs may lead men to extreme behaviors to control their partner. A plan was developed for how Sam can directly enact behavior that further challenges this irrational belief. He was to attend groups for adult children of alcoholics, to spend some time by himself away from his wife, and to monitor his feelings of worth while with these people.

This session also began a direct focus for Sam on his family of origin. He began to be in touch with his own victimization as a child. Focusing on family of origin issues can be a tricky process. On the one hand, it is helpful because it can help Sam begin to empathize with his wife and what his victimization of her feels like. He can begin to understand the role of his early learning in a way that can lead to healthier coping behaviors, that is, caring for himself rather than coercing his wife into fulfilling his needs. However, a focus on family of origin issues can be counterproductive if it deflects responsibility and defocuses Sam and

the group off of the primary issue of his current abusive behavior.

In the next session, men's control of women was the theme. Sam was quiet during most of the group. In commenting on another member's attempt to control his wife, Sam compared the man to his own father —"I was scared of him all the time. . . . If I would have stood up to him we would be talking today—but we aren't." Sam revealed that he recently told his father that he was coming to the group and that he wanted to live his life differently. His father was scornful. Despite the unsupportive response of his father, his self-disclosure to his father illustrated that Sam was actively integrating the work of the group into his life.

As it turned out, this session was Sam's last mandated session. His court supervision ended the following week. Through the period of his mandated treatment Sam progressed steadily. He moved from blaming his partner for his abusive behavior to a sense of responsibility for his own behavior. He expanded his definition of abuse beyond direct physical aggression and began to modify his other abusive behavior, actively applying the skills taught in the group. He made linkages between his current problems and the problems in his own family of origin. He applied this connection positively; that is, he began to challenge family members to accept his new definition of himself as someone who was attempting to live nonviolently. He had initiated linkages with other services. The challenge for Sam in participating in the group following his completion of the court mandate is to maintain these changes and to progress.

Although this case focused primarily on intervention with one man in a group setting, it is important to recognize that the intervention did not occur in isolation. Treatment of men who batter needs to be part of a comprehensive, multisystems approach to ending violence. At a minimum, intervention in any community should include (1) immediate protection, support, and advocacy for battered women and their children; (2) intervention for the abusive men; (3) on-going support and education for battered women and their children; and (4) coordinated intervention in social institutional responses to battering (Brygger & Edleson, 1987). When services are provided for men, they must be coordinated with intervention with other family members. If these services do not occur within the same agency, practitioners working with men must work to establish and maintain good working relationships with shelters and other agencies working with battered women.

A final point to be made here is that Sam's treatment was facilitated by being mandated by the court. However, the justice system has traditionally been unresponsive to the issue of domestic violence. Therefore, it is important for programs working with men who batter to coordinate closely with institutions that provide social sanctions for violent behavior. When working with criminal justice systems, social workers need to provide pressure for the courts to impose meaningful sanctions if the man is not successfully complying with program requirements. A court-mandated client for whom no sanctions are delivered upon failure in treatment will soon learn that police, court, and social service actions are not credible. The resulting message will be that he can continue his behavior without serious consequences. The message to his partner will be that his abusive behavior is not to be taken seriously. Social workers must be proactive in working for change in larger systems so that they may provide effective direct service to men who batter.

## References

Bograd, M. (1984). Family systems approaches to wife battering: A feminist critique. *American Journal Orthopsychiatry, 54,* 558–568.

Brygger, M. P., & Edleson, J. L. (1987). The Domestic Abuse Project: A multisystems intervention in woman battering. *Journal of Interpersonal Violence, 2,* 324–337.

Gondolf, E. (August 1984). *Men who batter: How they stop their abuse.* Paper presented at the Second National Conference for Family Violence Researchers, Durham, NH.

Rosenbaum, A., & O'Leary, K. D. (1981). Marital violence: Characteristics of abusive couples. *Journal of Clinical and Consulting Psychology, 49,* 63–71.

Sherman, L. W., & Berk, R. A. (1984). The specific deterrent effects of arrest for domestic assault. *American Sociological Review, 49,* 261–272.

Straus, M. A., Gelles, R. J., & Steinmetz, S. (1980). *Behind closed doors: Violence in the American family.* New York: Doubleday & Co.

# 7

CASE STUDIES

# IN CROSS-CULTURAL
# SOCIAL WORK

SOCIAL WORKERS HAVE HAD A LONG-STAND-ing commitment in their work with socially and economically oppressed people. However, often there is a great deal of difference between the social work practitioner and the client. Such differences include gender, sexual orientation, and socioeconomic, cultural, and racial differences. It is not surprising that these differences may become barriers to understanding and providing effective social work services. Social workers must continually attempt to reduce the barriers that interfere with their helping someone in the most effective manner possible.

Social workers must recognize that each individual comes from a group with a specific cultural background. Group members want social workers to be aware of their existence and to know something about their group—its characteristics, values, beliefs, attitudes, and goals. Although such group members want you to know about them as a group, you

must not forget that each person is very unique and should be viewed in light of their uniqueness. Often knowing something about a group helps you identify what is unique for each person. Practice procedures should be varied depending on the client's ethnic, sex, and age group but need to be assessed for each individual.

It is important to note that one of the most important factors in successful cross-cultural work is your attitude. Social workers communicate a lot through reactions to clients. If clients perceive the worker as not having a positive attitude, they will not be encouraged to continue working. Shulman (1979) has recommended "preparatory empathy," or having a helping frame of mind prior to meeting with a client, as a needed skill.

Cross-cultural social work emphasizes the importance of the client's world view or how the client perceives his or her relationship to the world. This culturally based variable has an important influence on the interaction between the social worker and the client. This is particularly true when social workers have a different world view than their clients. This difference can sometimes lead to negative judgments about the client's attitude, values, or behaviors.

Often this is discussed within the context of a "dual perspective" (Norton, 1978). The dual perspective is understanding the values, attitudes, and behaviors of the larger dominant society and those of the client's immediate family and community. Clients are seen as part of two systems—the dominant system, composed of power and economic resources, and the nurturing system, composed of the family and community.

A major goal for social work is to develop ethnic-sensitive practice principles. In order to accomplish this it is important that you understand the client's world view within an ethnic or cultural context. Gordon (1964) believes that ethnic group (race, religion, or national origin), social class, rural-urban residence, and regional residence determine a particular subculture within society. In analyzing ethnic variables, Garvin and Seabury (1984) suggest a framework that consists of six dimensions: communications, habitat, social structure, socialization, economics, and beliefs and sentiments. This type of framework helps the social worker understand the behavior of the members of various ethnic groups, since this behavior is affected by group membership. Ibrahim (1985) would add variables that represent more universal factors: the modality of human nature, the modality of human relationships, the relation of people to nature, the temporal focus of human life, and the modality of human activity.

Given the above considerations, it is critical for the social worker to understand the client's world view, the relationship of the client's world view to the client's primary subculture, and how the majority or dominant culture affects the client's values and behavior. For example, the social worker receives a referral to help a Native American woman. First, the social worker must try to understand the client's subculture or group. General knowledge about Native Americans is helpful. The worker can attempt to understand the subculture by analyzing the various ethnic variables—socialization, economics, modality of human relationships, and so on. This is helpful but limited because it does not take into consideration the client's subjective reality. How does this client perceive her relationship to the world? What is the relationship between the client's world view and the client's subculture? These questions focus on an understanding of the context of the client's perceptions and behaviors. Also, what is the relationship between the client's perceptions, the client's subculture, and the majority or dominant culture? It may be important to know the extent to which the client is bicultural or experiencing cultural contradictions. Is the client in conflict with either majority values or those of the client's culture of origin?

Green (1982) believes that social work services must be offered in a manner that enhances the client's sense of ethnic group participation and sense of power. In order to accomplish this, he suggests that agencies respond to the client "not only in terms of the specific problem presented but in terms of the client's cultural and community background" (Green, 1982, p. 4). Green encourages social workers to develop "ethnic competence." He defines ethnic competence as the ability to "conduct one's professional work in a way that is congruent with the behavior and expectations that members of distinctive culture recognize as appropriate among themselves" (Green, 1982, p. 52). Critical to ethnic competence is cultural awareness that "represents a depth of comprehension of others that surpasses the usual injunction about patience, genuineness and honesty in client-worker relationships" (Green, 1982, p. 52).

The client's experience is one of the most important sources of information. It is critical to discover how the client represents the world. The process of change begins in helping the client integrate various aspects of the client's world view to maximize the client's effectiveness (Sue, 1981). Ethnic competence can be determined by how well the social worker is aware of and can understand and accept the client's world view. Devore and Schlesinger (1988) offer a means by which to become ethnically competent: be aware of your cultural limitations, be open to cultural differences, possess a client-oriented learning style, make use of the client's cultural resources, and acknowledge the client's cultural integrity.

This section begins with a case study by Patton, who describes his work with a gay couple where one partner is dying from AIDS. His sensitive analysis examines the couple's relationship, the potential for social workers to develop homophobic attitudes in their work with gay couples, and the cultural context that is needed to better understand gay men. He presents a very difficult case where the worker is simultaneously addressing such factors as death, the couple's relationship, and the family's reaction to their son's death and their difficulty in accepting their son's homosexuality. Social workers must confront homophobia, the fear and dislike of homosexuals, which is pervasive in the dominant heterosexual society.

Ho presents a case study that focuses on the difficulties an interracial couple experiences. He describes in a clear and straightforward manner how to engage the couple into counseling and then sets forth to help them build a better relationship. A major part of the treatment focuses on helping the couple understand and resolve their cultural differences.

The case studies by Freud and Woodman address social work practice with women. Freud outlines a feminist approach, and Woodman presents a case study of working with lesbian women. Gender is an important variable that must not be overlooked in providing social work services. Although gender is not directly addressed in the above discussion, most of the content previously discussed is relevant. Men and women create different subcultures that consist of different values, attitudes, behaviors, and ways of coping. You must attempt to understand your client within this context. Some would argue that only female social workers should help women—in order to truly understand experiences and behavior that are unique to women. Whatever the perspective, it is critical that social workers be aware of and analyze the barriers that may interfere with effective social work practice because of gender.

Parnell and VanderKloot present one of the most important case studies in this book: social work practice with the urban poor. Social work has a special commitment to serve the socially and economically oppressed. These authors present the special skills and knowledge needed to work in this important arena. Their case is complex, and they refer to their difficulties as working with chaos—taking into consideration the poverty, the drug use, and the community. Their case study suggests that a different perspective and a different approach to intervention is needed when working with the urban poor.

## References

Devore, W., & Schlesinger, E. G. (1988). Ethnic sensitive practice. In *Encyclopedia of social work.* Silver Spring, MD: National Association of Social Workers.

Garvin, C. D., & Seabury, B. A. (1984). *Interpersonal practice in social work: Process and procedures.* Englewood Cliffs, NJ: Prentice-Hall.

Gordon, M. M. (1964). *Assimilation in American life.* New York: Oxford University Press.

Green, J. W. (1982). *Cultural awareness in human services.* Englewood Cliffs, NJ: Prentice-Hall.

Ibrahim, F. A. (1985). Effective cross-cultural counseling and psychotherapy: A framework. *The Counseling Psychologist, 13,* 625–638.

Norton, D. G. (1978). *The dual perspective: Inclusion of ethnic minority content in social work.* New York: Council on Social Work Education.

Shulman, L. (1979). *The skills of helping individuals and groups.* Itasca, IL: F. E. Peacock.

Sue, D. W. (1981). *Counseling the culturally different.* New York: John Wiley.

# CASE STUDY 7.1

*This case study challenges stereotypes of gay relationships and illustrates the importance of examining the intricacies of each couple's relationship regardless of sexual orientation. When a client is diagnosed with AIDS, it presents a complex set of problems for the individual, couple, and families of origin. The case study illustrates these complexities by describing a gay couple confronting AIDS.*

## Questions

1. How can social workers address homophobia?
2. What are the social work tasks once an AIDS diagnosis has been confirmed?
3. What types of interventions might be appropriate with families of persons with AIDS?
4. What are some of the issues the social worker will have to address with the couple in the later phases of treatment in this case?

## AIDS AND THE GAY COUPLE

*John Patten**

Charles was 21 when he moved with his family from the south side of Chicago to a small country town near Madison, Wisconsin. There he met Clayton. With his flamboyant clothes and theatrical manner, Clayton was hard to miss in the conservative little town, and the two young men were immediately drawn to each other. Charles, already recognizing that he was gay, had had several homosexual relationships. Clayton, however, had struggled with his sexuality. He had tried dating girls and fitting into the straight world but suspected—to his horror—that he was "different."

Charles and Clayton eventually became intimate. In their small town it was difficult to keep their relationship a secret from their families and neighbors. One refuge was the drive-in movie. As Charles told me, "I used to put a kerchief around Clayton's head so I could kiss him." After several years, the hiding and clandestine meetings began to take too much of a toll. The two lovers decided it was time to leave.

Charles's family somberly accepted the news that he was moving with Clayton to New York City. Even though the word *homosexual* had never been uttered in their household, they knew. Clayton's parents reacted more explosively. Although long critical of their son's flamboyance and his indifference to sports and school, they had always vicariously enjoyed his flouting of conventions. But Clayton's sudden announcement of his plan to move away with Charles drew forth their full fury. The forbidden topics of Clayton's homosexuality and covert relationship with Charles became the target of his parents' outrage. Fi-

* Reprinted from the *Family Therapy Networker*, January–February, 1988. Reprinted by permission of the author.

nally Clayton's father told him, "If you leave, don't you ever come back."

Four years later in New York City, Charles and Clayton were a picture of the stylish, successful gay couple. They had a beautiful West Side apartment, complete with maid, shiatsu, and private gym off the mirrored bathroom. Clayton worked as a fabric designer, and Charles traded in future's options on the stock market and, on the side, worked on the great Harlequin novel. Charles stayed in regular contact with his parents, who even visited once. Clayton's father reneged on his original threat, and Clayton returned home to visit several times, growing used to his parents' pleas to come home and give up his hedonistic life-style.

Meanwhile, Charles and Clayton's relationship withstood the challenge of being transplanted into the giddy excitement of New York City. It also withstood the occasional affairs each man engaged in. Their understanding was that neither would try to hide his infidelities and that theirs was a permanent commitment. They took some pride in their ability to talk openly about their attraction to other people and accepted the periodic fits of jealousy that were the price of such openness.

Then, one day, Clayton, who had previously been in excellent health, came down with a bad case of pneumonia and had to be taken to the hospital. There he learned that he had AIDS.

The story of Charles and Clayton—or variations on it—will be one that many more therapists will be hearing about in the years to come as we all feel the impact of the AIDS plague. This is not to say, of course, that AIDS is exclusively a gay problem. Actually, studies indicate that, as homosexuals have become increasingly educated about AIDS and safer sex procedures, there has been a dramatic reduction in HIV transmission among them. Still, AIDS continues to cast its shadow over the gay community. Unfortunately, many therapists—like so many people in the population at large—harbor attitudes that make it difficult for them to respond to the needs of gay clients.

The most extreme of these attitudes is homophobia—the total rejection of homosexuality as a normal and acceptable human choice about one's sexual preference. Homophobic attitudes can be very subtle, and we continually find them even among professionals who are presumably attempting to help their clients. One therapist, while showing a videotaped interview with a gay couple at a recent workshop, warned the audience that they should be a little skeptical of the men's statements about their relationship since the couple knew they were on camera and "gay men like to exhibit themselves."

Perhaps more common than outright homophobia in these presumably enlightened times is an attitude one might call homonegativism. Such attitudes don't lead people to actively discriminate against or condemn homosexuals but do prevent them from truly accepting someone in their family having a gay relationship. "What my son does in the bedroom is truly his own business," a mother once said to me. "But I just can't see myself accepting the image of him sleeping with another man or my inviting him with his lover to Thanksgiving. I just couldn't do it—I'm sorry."

Finally, there is a group—probably much larger than the first two—that I call homoconfused. They don't have any strongly held views against homosexuality but are confused by all the conflicting information they get from the media and other sources. As one female therapist told me, "I would very much like to work with gays with AIDS, but I just don't know anything." Such therapists, given some education and some positive interaction with gays, can learn to move past their hesitancy and awkwardness in working with people whose sexual orientation they do not share.

What homoconfused clinicians need to recognize is that the differences between gay and straight relationships have been enormously exaggerated. My own work has taught me that, from a systems perspective, homosexual and heterosexual relationships share more similarities than differences. My operating assumption is that, whether gay or straight, we are all looking for understanding, tenderness, and love. We fall in love with a person, not a sexual organ.

Straight therapists, uncertain how to work with gay couples, might consider approaching them as they would a couple from another culture whose relationship departs from mainstream American patterns. With a Japanese couple, for example, it would be easy to become fixated on the way their relationship rules and beliefs differ from middle-class America. But, although therapists may need to appreciate these differences and enlist their clients' help in learning about them, their basic task remains one of helping two human beings struggling with closeness, conflict, family legacies, and life's unpredictable crises.

## THE CULTURAL CONTEXT

The prevailing view of gay men is that they are promiscuous and obsessed with sex. To understand the role of sexuality in gay men's lives it is important to understand the cultural context in which they grow up. Most gays aren't permitted the usual adolescent rehearsal for relationship that occurs naturally in the heterosexual world. Given the lack of role models and places to socialize openly, it is hard to find validation for gayness as an acceptable identity. Even more than the straight teenager, the world of the gay adolescent is filled with the sense of being strange and different, of powerful feelings that must be kept hidden. One gay client put it this way: "As a teenager, none of my friends seemed to even remotely share my sexual interests. I soon saw myself as a freak, 'mentally ill,' a woman hater. Since there was no peer or adult whom I perceived as experiencing life as I did, I isolated myself more and flinched every time I heard one of those adolescent faggot jokes. For years I was preoccupied with how different and aberrant I was."

Both straight and gay adolescents are obsessed with masculine symbols; both show off sexually, exhibiting themselves directly or indirectly. "The Hunt," the male search for sex conquests, is a universal adolescent experience. But because of cultural, religious, and familial constraints, many gays either deny this developmental phase or delay it into adulthood. As a result, the primacy of the physical experience of sex rather than relationship and intimacy can continue to dominate some gay men's lives way beyond the period of adolescence.

Nevertheless, in his book *Man to Man*, Charles Silverstein asserts that "excitement seekers," those who maintain an adolescent preoccupation with novelty and change rather than stability and longevity in a relationship, are only one group within the gay community. Silverstein contrasts excitement seekers with "home builders," homosexuals who look for permanence in a relationship and want to plan for the future with another man. A home builder judges a relationship by the degree of intimacy achieved rather than the level of sexual excitement.

Silverstein's work can be useful in helping move beyond the simplistic stereotypes that most gays have strange sexual habits and prefer transient relationships based on sexual performance. He also addresses an especially common misconception, one that we confronted early on in our AIDS project, that one member of a gay couple always plays the female, passive, one-down role and the other partner is more masculine and active. As one member of a homosexual couple we saw in the project put it, "Gays are a lot more creative than straights in that regard." Understanding the intricacy of gay couples was central to our work with Charles and Clayton.

## BEGINNING TREATMENT

Typically, the gay couples in our project come in angry and depressed after one or both have been diagnosed with AIDS, often fighting about where the infection came from. Charles came into the first session furious and in a panic about losing Clayton. As soon as I asked what brought the two of them in for therapy, the room exploded, "Surely you must know, Doctor," said Charles, who was certain that Clayton had contracted AIDS in a brief affair he had had with a Frenchman. "Clayton's been given a death sentence by that --- Frenchman and he will do nothing to help himself. He has isolated himself, stopped work, and won't talk to me or our friends. He won't even look at any of the information about AIDS treatments I've gotten for him."

My first goal was to address the panic and provide some medical information. I told both of them, "No one is dying right now. Your fighting is just a way of staying close while expressing your fear of being separated." I reassured them that AIDS is a very episodic illness and they had a lot of living to do. When Clayton expressed his fear that he would get PCP (pneumonia) again, I tried to allay his anxiety by emphasizing that his being on antibiotic prophylaxis made a relapse virtually impossible. By the end of the session both men were calmer.

When they returned the next week, there was even a little humor in the room. Clayton observed, "The best thing about having AIDS is that you don't have to worry about getting

it any more." Because they knew that I am a physician, both men had lots of medical questions for me. We talked about the pros and cons of Charles getting testing and discussed the various AIDS treatments. In general, family therapists who are working with AIDS should not get involved in answering such medical questions unless they know what they are talking about. However, the more you do know, the more clients will feel that you care enough to be thoroughly informed.

By the next session, Clayton had returned to work and begun treatment for his illness. The focus was on Charles's concern that Clayton's family, who were coming to New York to visit their sick son (who by now was basically healthy), would take him back to the Midwest. Both men agreed to invite Clayton's family to the next session to discuss openly how Clayton's medical treatment would be handled and how future decisions about it would be made.

Clayton's parents quickly made it plain that they wanted their son to return home with them and had already contacted "the best hospitals and doctors" in anticipation of his return. I gently coached Clayton into getting his parents to understand and acknowledge the permanent commitment he and Charles had to each other. "The best way you can help me now and in the future," Clayton said to them tearfully, "is to respect that Charles and I can handle this situation. I know we have excluded you from our life in the past, but trust that we will not exclude you from here on."

The session had the effect of finally validating and legitimizing Clayton's relationship with Charles in the eyes of his family. Often, of course, the conflicts between lovers and their families of origin are not addressed this directly, but, when possible, we try to deal with systemic issues in clients' extended families and help them clearly define boundaries around their relationships with their lovers.

Our work with Clayton and Charles continues. In later phases of treatment with this couple, there will inevitably be other issues. But they have begun to do what they need to in order to live their lives more fully and prepare themselves to handle the crises that lie ahead.

## Reference

Silverstein, C. (1981). *Man to man: Gay couples in America*. New York: William Morrow.

*This case study identifies critical issues facing interracial couples and highlights characteristics of one Asian culture that may influence the counseling relationship.*

## Questions

1. How was the social worker able to engage the husband in the counseling process?
2. What developmental changes were challenging the couple in this case?
3. What kinds of tasks could the social worker assign this couple to enhance intimacy in their relationship?
4. What can social workers do to help interracial couples recognize and value each person's culture and improve communication skills?

## COUNSELING AN INTERRACIAL COUPLE

*Man-Keung Ho*

Mrs. I, a 45-year-old Filipino-American, was referred to the Transcultural Family Institute by her family physician, who diagnosed the patient's affective disorder as "psychosomatic" and "neurotic." In addition to periodic depression, Mrs. I had a minor heart problem. Her depression and family-related problems caused her to occasionally "forget" to take medication for high blood pressure. Mrs. I frequently complained that she had no desire to live any more.

In the initial interview, Mrs. I impressed me as a neat, well-dressed, and well-groomed individual who appeared outwardly friendly and sociable but inwardly withdrawn and suspicious. Although she seemed to be relieved when she noticed my Asian physical appearance, Mrs. I avoided direct eye contact with me when I first greeted her. *[Asian way of conveying respect and interest]* To ease her discomfort and curiosity about my nationality and occupation, I volunteered that I am a naturalized American citizen from Hong Kong

and that I help individuals and families with their problems. *[To return respect and collect data]* Mrs. I responded immediately that she too is a naturalized Asian-American from the Philippines. As I nodded my head to establish communication with her, she explained that she had immigrated to the United States 20 years ago with her Anglo-American husband. *[Empathizing]* He had been in the military in the Philippines. Mrs. I then asked me about my immediate and extended family. I thanked her for her interest. When I told her about my family, I noticed that she began to relax. I then took the opportunity to inquire about her family. *[Client self-determination]* Mrs. I sighed, slumped down, and appeared to be teary. I responded immediately that she must have thought a lot about her family and that if talking about her family upset her, she could choose to change the topic. *[Relationship building]* Mrs. I apologized for becoming a "crybaby" and said "getting emotional has always been my problem." I responded by granting her permission to cry if she felt like it. "Family is a vital part of one's life," I empathized.

Mrs. I continued that she and her husband have two grown daughters. The older daughter resides in California with her husband and two young children. Her younger daughter, whom Mrs. I called "baby," married 5 months ago. She and her husband moved to a neighboring state after marriage. I complimented her on raising two responsible daughters. *[Show of respect and courtesy]* Mrs. I sighed again, saying, "It was not easy." Mrs. I continued that she missed her daughters very much. *[Adjustment in family life-style]* As a way to "fill up her lost feeling for her daughters" and to occupy her time, Mrs. I began babysitting in her own home. "I enjoy taking care of babies, but—they are not mine," Mrs. I said regretfully. *[Empty nest syndrome]*

I took the opportunity to assess her relationship with her husband by asking her how her husband had adjusted to their second daughter's departure. Mrs. I shook her head and responded, "It didn't bother him; nothing bothers him." I detected some anger in Mrs. I's voice, and I provided her a general lead by commenting, "Your husband reacted differently than you did." Mrs. I explained that her husband is an "easy-go-lucky" type of person. "He works long hours as a maintenance person for two elementary schools. Between work and after work, he drinks with his buddies and visits with his mother who lives in the same town as we do," continued Mrs. I. *[Enmeshment and family of origin issues]* I then asked her how she felt about her husband's activities. *[Assessing the couple's relationship]* Mrs. I said angrily, "It doesn't bother me." I clarified by reflecting that her husband's working long hours, drinking with his friends, and spending time with his mother did not bother her. Mrs. I commented, "What is the use!" "It seems to me that you must have let him know how you feel about this, but that

nothing has changed," I empathized. Mrs. I then burst into tears saying, "My husband and I have had nothing to do with each other for quite some time. *[Dysfunctional couple relationship]* When I had my daughters with me, I was able to cope with it. Now my daughters are gone; I guess I just go crazy." Mrs. I also volunteered that lately she really did not care about living or dying (which explained why she often "forgot" to take her blood pressure medicine). *[Emotionally cut off]* "If my parents were still alive, I would have packed up and gone back to the Philippines by myself a long time ago," said Mrs. I.

As a means to combat Mrs. I's depression and her low emotional, mental, and physical state, I requested to see her husband as a first step toward improving the marital relationship. *[Ecological approach for helping]* Mrs. I agreed to ask her husband to contact me. Three days after my first interview with Mrs. I, Mr. I telephoned me to request a counseling session for the couple. I offered him an individual session. Mr. I rejected and said it was not needed. I interviewed the couple conjointly 3 days later.

Mr. I appeared very anxious and eager for the interview to start. He is a physically big, tall man. He spoke loudly and seemed to intimidate his wife. After a few sociable exchanges, Mr. I commented that he was glad to see an Asian therapist who he believed could potentially help his wife with her problem. I asked Mr. I how he felt about an Asian therapist, and he replied abruptly, "Okay." *[To clarify Mr. I's potential doubt and discomfort]*

I then asked Mr. I his impression of his wife's situation. *[To clarify]* Mr. I's immediate response was, "It blows my mind." I asked him if he would elaborate on what he meant by "it." Mr. I said that he did not understand why his wife did not want to do anything, including taking medication to save her life. I inquired if Mr. I understood why his wife did not seem to enjoy living. *[To assess empathic ability]* Mr. I responded quickly with a low voice and head down: "I wish I knew." To minimize Mr. I's anxiety and potential feelings of threat and guilt, I nurtured him by stating that he must care about his wife, since he made an early appointment to see me. *[To strengthen marital bond]* Mr. I spoke with a low but calm voice, "How can you not care about a person you have spent more than 20 years with?"

To accentuate the couple's marital bonding, I encouraged them to reminisce about some memorable moments in their marriage. *[Accentuate the positive to counter present conflicts]* Mrs. I assumed a less active verbal part in reminiscing, but she smiled and nodded to show her approval of her husband's stories about their relationship. To focus on the presenting problem, I asked about the couple's present relationship. *[Refocusing on the problem]* Mr. I responded defensively, "What relationship?" I empathized by stating how much both of them were hurting. Mr. I commented on his understanding of his wife's present predicament and social isolation. "I understand," whispered Mr. I with his head down again, "but I do not know what to do."

I turned to Mrs. I for suggestions. *[To help the couple reconnect]* After a long pause, Mrs. I admitted that she had not been "much of a wife" to her husband. She then complained that she and her husband had nothing in common. *[Common in interracial marriages]* They had different interracial interests, and they never saw things the same. Because Mr. I is a Protestant, she had ceased to attend the Catholic church a long time ago. "Since I don't go to a Catholic church, I have no contact at all with my close Filipino friends who are Catholics," complained Mrs. I. "Just because I do not think the way you do and do not do the same things you and your American friends do does not mean that my way is wrong. I hate it when you use stereotypes to put me down simply because of my Asian ancestry," continued

Mrs. I. *[Characteristic of dysfunctional intermarriage]* Mr. I sat up straight and appeared to be startled. "This is exactly how I feel too. You think your Asian way is superior to the American way. I cannot stand it when you call me a big-mouthed American."

I explained to the couple the dynamics and inherent cultural value conflicts intermarried couples usually experience. *[To shift from the personal to the cultural]* In addition, I shared with them the potential richness in mutual sharing between interracial couples (Ho, 1988) who experience cultural transition. I challenged the couple to stop widening the cultural gap and emphasizing value differences but instead to find commonalities that could repair and solidify their marital bond. *[To narrow cultural and emotional differences]* Mrs. I responded by saying, "Since we have never established a solid marital bond, I really do not know where and how to repair it." Mr. I appeared to be offended by Mrs. I's statement, and he stated that as far as he was concerned, they got along fine when they were first married. Mrs. I responded that during the initial period of their marriage, they tried their best to minimize their differences. "Besides, I didn't want my parents and relatives to think that I had made a mistake by marrying an American instead of a Filipino," added Mrs. I. *[Characteristic of initial phase of intermarriage]*

Before the session ended, I encouraged the couple to recapitulate the parts of our discussion that had special meaning for them. Both partners agreed that although they felt uncomfortable and apprehensive, they were pleased to have an opportunity to ventilate their feelings. Mrs. I expressed surprise to learn about her husband's emotional hurt and feelings of isolation. Mr. I indicated that this was the longest and most helpful talk they had had with each other for quite some time. He also expressed hope that his relationship with his wife would improve and that his wife's depression would be lifted. The couple agreed to return for four more sessions aiming to improve their marital relationship.

The next three sessions with this couple were devoted to engaging them in communicating effectively with each other. Essential communication styles and skills for conflict resolution were taught. Assignments were given so that the couple could practice these skills at home. Despite the couple's strong motivation to learn about new communication skills, occasionally their interaction ran into barricades. The couple's old hurt and resentment erupted when they focused on personality deficits instead of cultural differences. The couple's newly learned problem-solving skills gradually helped them to disagree agreeably. As a result, they began to enjoy spending time together at home. *[Importance of social network to systematic change]* Mr. I also encouraged his wife to rejoin the Catholic church to resume her fellowship with several Filipino families and interracial families. As the couple began to reconcile and find companionship with each other, Mr. I drastically reduced the time he spent with his friends. Mr. I's mother was somewhat puzzled and upset with her son's infrequent visits, but she later learned to accept her daughter-in-law as a means to entice her son to visit her. Two months after the last counseling session, Mrs. I paid me a surprise visit. She brought me freshly cooked banana dumplings. *[Use of a ritual for termination]* She informed me that she felt much better and that her physician had decided that she no longer needed medication for high blood pressure.

### Reference

Ho, M. K. (1988). *Family therapy with ethnic minorities*. Newbury Park, CA: Sage.

# CASE STUDY 7.3

*In this case study, a college student faces difficult decisions about her future. A short interview illustrates how feminist counseling was used with this client.*

## Questions

1. If the social worker were to continue beyond one session with this client, what issues, from a feminist counseling perspective, might they pursue together?

2. What are some of the values and cautions in defining a client's problems as "purposeful and adaptive choice" (feminist perspective) versus "symptoms" of dysfunction (traditional perspective)?

3. If the social worker were to focus primarily on the sociopolitical context of the client's concerns, what would she target as areas to change?

4. How can you apply feminist counseling principles to your work regardless of your therapeutic orientation?

## DROPPING OUT: A FEMINIST APPROACH

*Sophie Freud*

The idea of feminist therapy—or feminist counseling, since the word *therapy* comes from the medical model that is being opposed—developed as one aspect of the women's movement. Criticism against traditional psychodynamic counseling was directed primarily against the following aspects: its theoretical structure, which views women as defective men and which has no understanding or respect for the unique nature of female experience (Miller, 1973; Strouse, 1974); its emphasis on inner-space pathology rather than the constraining socioeconomic political setting in which women have to function and survive (Greenspan, 1983; Loewenstein, 1983); its being conducted in a power framework in which women end up having one-down positions similar to those they usually have in their lives (Chesler, 1971); its emphasis on unhappy love relationships with men

rather than self-development, career goals, and friendships with other women; and its interest in diagnosing pathology rather than seeking strengths (Berlin, 1976; Freud, 1988; Marecek & Kravetz, 1977; Radov, Masnick, & Hauser, 1977; Russell, 1984; Thomas, 1977; Williams, 1976).

The most "radical" feminist counselors might insist that their goal is to help clients with preparation for political action and social change (Greenspan, 1983). Other counselors who also define themselves as "feminist" view certain values and attitudes as the essence of feminist counseling, believing that it could be compatible with any other kind of therapy, even psychoanalysis, as long as it is conducted in a nonsexist, humanistically oriented manner (Krause, 1971; Menaker, 1974). We are thus not talking about a monolithic belief system, and it might be useful to distinguish feminist counseling that has a strong political component from counseling that is gender sensitive.

After outlining the highlights of the following consultation, which took 3 hours, I will explore to what extent I used the principles of feminist counseling outlined by the feminist literature.

A young woman we will call Elsa called me rather boldly at home to ask me for a consultation. She attends a prestigious school in a neighboring state and comes from a country abroad where I was once most graciously received. Her mother, whose friend was my gracious host abroad, told her that she should call me for help.

Elsa was more than willing to travel to Boston to see me, and we made an appointment. It was my opportunity to pay back an old debt to my former host. The situation was thus not a purely professional one. We did not exchange money, and I made things as informal as possible, inviting her to come with me to the kitchen to get her a cup of coffee. I would not have done that with a "real" client. (I discuss the reason for this later.)

Let us call these two people counselor and client, for simplicity's sake. Feminist counseling calls for complete equality between client and counselor. It is questionable whether such equality is really possible. In this case, for example, the age difference was considerable, the young woman being 27 years old and I more than twice her age. She had traveled some distance to see a "famous" woman therapist, and the power constellation was there, as it often is. It can be questioned to what extent power differential should be avoided or whether it might be a useful bit of additional magic that enhances any change effort.

One would not "feed" (coffee) a client in traditional therapy because that would promote dependency and create a social situation out of a professional situation—at least so the theory goes, and it might be right. I once did a survey of what people thought was the most important incident in their therapy, and one respondent reported that it was a cup of coffee that her therapist gave her on a rainy day when she came in all wet and bedraggled. This does not mean that one should always offer coffee. Things become dramatic and eventful when they are unusual, for example when they are considered to be against the rules. Bateson (1972) would say we notice only differences. If we had no therapeutic rules, they could not be broken, and our clients could not be happy when they are broken. I am thus given a small boost to traditional rules, for the paradoxical reason that they can be broken.

There has also been much controversy about whether counselors should be warm or neutral. Traditional psychoanalytic teaching has emphasized therapeutic neutrality, whereas recent feminist literature has promoted warmth. I take a somewhat in-between position. Although I was feeding Elsa coffee and being friendly, I was careful not to be too sympathetic, and by insisting on her strengths, rather than accepting her weaknesses, I was also somewhat provocative. I prefer to focus on attentiveness and wish to understand rather than provide warmth.

Elsa told me that she was about to drop out of her studies in her sophomore year because her classes had become boring, constraining, and technical, and she was made to conform to some old-fashioned, useless educational ideas. She was older than most of her classmates, but her teachers treated her just like any other student. She had enjoyed her freshman year, when there had been opportunity to develop and demonstrate one's individual creativity, and her talents had been noticed by all her teachers. She also complained that she was much too shy and could not really function in a large class. She could not speak up and just "disappeared" in the classroom.

We can quickly tell that Elsa has a common female conflict between her intense need to be noticed and special and her fear of being seen. Psychiatrists have called such needs narcissistic exhibitionism because traditional theory emphasizes pathology. Feminist counseling emphasizes strength rather than pathology. Feminist counseling, in deliberate contrast to the medical model, deemphasizes diagnostic labels and focuses instead on the extent to which the client's behavior furthers or defeats her own goals. I commented on and applauded her wish to be seen and to be special and unique.

Elsa continued to protest against being treated like a young student when she was already 27 years old. She was not willing to sit endlessly in class and perform boring technical procedures. Her way of learning was different from how her teachers wanted her to learn. She then discussed some of her teachers and her power struggles with them, and I commented on her fierce resolution not to be coerced and pushed around. She definitely felt that I understood. In one situation she was defeated in her struggle not to attend classes, but at the end the teacher had expressed respect for her. She said she had lost that fight. I responded that it looked as if they had both won: the teacher had won her attendance, but she had won his respect. She accepted this reframing of the situation—after all, victories and defeats are mere constructions of reality.

Elsa talked in the language of "I can't." She had to go to bed and sleep; she could not get herself to go to classes any longer; she could not find the energy to do the homework; she could not get herself to say a single word when she was out with her friends the other evening. She wondered what her friends had thought, because usually she was the one who comforted them. I insisted that she substitute *want*, for *can't*. Every time I corrected her, she laughed a little. I pointed out that by not going to class and by not speaking to her friends she had achieved several goals: she had made herself visible in class by disappearing, since her teachers had started to worry about her. By

being conspicuously silent she had reminded her friends that they should stop dumping on her and that it was her turn to have problems. Moreover, she effectively resisted all forms of coercion by going to bed.

It is definitely a feminist technique, which is gradually becoming more generally accepted in all counseling, to understand how a person's symptoms may be a purposeful and adaptive choice. Miriam Greenspan (1983), for example, views typical feminine symptoms, such as depression, as unconscious strategies of adaptation and rebellion, however self-defeating they turn out to be. She looks for the seeds of strengths behind every symptom. This rule was easy to apply to Elsa's behavior. She had dropped out once before from another field of study because she had felt too coerced. I had the feeling that Elsa was perhaps an overloved, "spoiled" child who had to feed her parents' narcissism and punished them by repeated failures. But on further questioning, it turned out that her father had not really respected her last course of study, and so we decided that she had done him a favor by dropping out. This led her to talking about her struggle between being an obedient daughter or a disobedient daughter, very much a woman's theme. Her father had been very understanding about her present condition, had labeled it a depression, and assumed that it would take her a while to recover. It was after she had talked to him (long-distance) that she had taken to bed in the middle of the morning. I asked her whether it would be fun to prove her father wrong, and she laughed again. By now she did a lot of laughing, considering that she had defined herself as severely depressed.

Yet, she actually enjoyed this particular school and thought these studies were for her rather than for her parents. She then outlined a plan that she had made with the head of the department to speak to her teachers and tell them that she was not up to continuing her studies at this point. Above all she wanted their respect and did not want them to think that she was a nonserious person with emotional problems.

I asked her with some surprise how else she hoped that her teachers would define her and how she would define herself. She was taken aback. It seemed a turning point in the interview.

She did not want her teachers to think she could not do the work. The work was actually easy and potentially enjoyable, if she could only do it her own way and not her teachers' way. I said that by now she was a month behind, and so she would have to face the challenge of making up a great deal of work. She might do this in her own way, perhaps accomplishing twice as much as she really had to, and surprise everyone. No matter what, by now she was going to achieve special status, either by going to bed, by dropping out, or by demonstrating her special talents. She had the choice of how she wanted to become visible and special. The challenge of doing extra work on her own suddenly captured Elsa's imagination, and her eyes started to sparkle. She also asked me how I had reacted to her nerve of calling me up and daring to impose on me for my time. I said her calling me and her making an appointment with the head of the department reassured me that she was a person who could take initiative on her own behalf, so I had never really been too worried about her.

By the end of the morning Elsa could hardly bear the thought of the Columbus Day holiday, because she was in such a hurry to get back to school and get started on all these projects.

Although this is a somewhat lighthearted case, it demonstrates typical feminist issues, such as a struggle about autonomy, obedience, taking care of others or being taken care of, and being visible or invisible. The case also demonstrates the counselor's efforts to empower the client to find some creative solution in which these struggles could be played out

without self-defeating results. It also demonstrates the thin line between feminist counseling and any other approach.

I have commented on my strategy in the course of my "story," and I will now match my interventions more systematically against the principles of feminist counseling outlined succinctly and methodically by Mary Russell, a Canadian social worker, in her book *Skills in Counseling Women* (1984). She convincingly demonstrates her viewpoint that feminist counseling is not just psychodynamic counseling purged of its sexist elements but that it is a distinct new counseling method arising out of feminist theory. Russell avoids the medical implications of the word *therapy*, and uses *counseling*, a word that has educational and developmental implications, as well as being less exclusively intrapsychic. The difference between *counseling* versus *treating* is important. Language is the epistemological knife that creates distinctions in our lives, and we need to be attentive to the language and words that are being used.

Russell suggests that all counseling processes are based on such basic skills as communicating accurate empathy, positive regard, and warmth; questioning; listening; paraphrasing; clarifying; and contracting for goals. Beyond these basic counseling techniques, Russell distinguishes five counseling skills that she considers the core of a feminist counseling approach. I will enumerate them and then give you my own associations and their use in Elsa's case.

1. Positive evaluation of women
2. Social analysis
3. Encouragement of total development
4. Behavioral feedback
5. Self-disclosure of counselor

In one form or another, similar points are mentioned in all articles on feminist counseling, although the actual wording may be different.

## POSITIVE EVALUATION OF WOMEN

I believe this refers to the particular client and women in general and is meant to counteract the existing negative stereotypes that, I suggested above, were at least partially introduced by psychoanalytic theory. Most women in this culture have internalized negative stereotypes and tend to feel deficient, inadequate, uniquely responsible for not measuring up to various cultural ideals, and even responsible for the misfortunes that have befallen them. It is likely that men have similar feelings. What is perhaps unique to women, however, is their internalized prohibition against "selfishness," which interferes with their ability to become self-loving and self-nurturing. Self-love is of primary importance for all human beings, yet it becomes confused with selfishness, which women consider a sin to be avoided at all costs. Besides, for most of us, our self-doubts interfere with our capacity to be self-loving. I tell my women students that we need to pretend to love ourselves better than we really do. A pretense at more power, more self-confidence, and more control over our lives than we really feel or can realistically assume may serve us well enough. An attitude of affirmation emphasizes strengths and capacities of a particular client and women in general.

I practiced this first therapeutic principle with Elsa and showed her the respect that she deserved.

## SOCIAL ANALYSIS

This is a central feminist principle, and I have mentioned that some theorists would confine their feminist counseling to that dimension. It places a woman's problem and its roots in a sociopolitical context, making the personal into the political and mobilizing feelings of anger and rage to be expressed in common social action. Many feminist counselors think that change must be both individual and collective.

The counselor also tries to highlight female socialization patterns that may be self-defeating. This could include compulsive caretaking, or overloving patterns, or self-sacrificing martyrdom patterns. A victim position is tempting and morally superior but ultimately self-defeating. I think it also includes paying attention to feminist language, both in content and in style. I try to discourage my female students, for example, from starting out a comment with a disqualifying introduction.

I am not sure whether I worked on this principle with Elsa. Perhaps our discussion about whether she wanted to be a good or a bad person or a spoiled little girl belongs here.

## ENCOURAGEMENT OF TOTAL DEVELOPMENT

Counselors must identify sources of strength, talent, power, and self-development. Work is considered a natural aspect of living, and a woman is encouraged to discard stereotypical notions of women's work when she thinks about a career. She is also encouraged to find some balance between work and interpersonal commitment in her life. Emphasis is on expanded options and opportunities. I certainly did that with Elsa, since the whole interview was about how she viewed her own development as a responsible working person.

## BEHAVIORAL FEEDBACK

Russell (1984) distinguishes behavioral feedback from insight into unconscious motivations, childhood experiences, or the impact of the past on the present. I am not sure why a consideration of the past would have nonfeminist connotations, but she is worried about the therapeutic mystique and one-upmanship. I imagine, however, that behavioral feedback might lead to examination of certain dysfunctional patterns, trying to understand where one has acquired them and whom one needs to please. I cannot imagine a meaningful counseling experience without some mention of parental expectations and the form that the usual struggles with each parent has taken for a particular woman. I would also think it important to understand what kinds of models a woman has been exposed to. Behavioral feedback may also be problematic, in that it may be more relevant to the counselor's preferences and idiosyncratic reactions than to the client's life problems. Some writers have suggested that behavioral feedback may be misinterpreted as a call for compliance: I will like you only if you behave in certain ways.

A word should be said about insight-promoting techniques, foremost of which are interpretations. You may have noticed that I did a lot of that with Elsa, perhaps because it was a one-time consultation or perhaps because she was so sophisticated and quite in tune with what I was telling her. We need some caution with interpretations, however, since process can become more important than the content. An interpretation could be seen as a gift, or a one-down gesture, or an invasion into the person's inner space by an all-knowing counselor who knows one better than one knows oneself. I thus suggest that we need to evaluate the total context in which an interpretation is given and received rather than just examine its truthfulness. Generally it can be said that feminist counseling is more compatible with a Sullivanian model than with a Freudian model. In that former model of "participant observation" (Havens, 1976), the counselor and client look together at the world. The counselor's affirmation gives the client the courage to examine herself. Such a stance is more compatible with feminist counseling than transference, resistance, and interpretations.

## SELF-DISCLOSURE OF COUNSELOR

Russell recommends this in order to promote identification and minimizing hierarchical differences. Feminists have called for a symmetrical relationship between counselor and client. They think it is important in order to set a model of equality for the client's other important relationships. There is actually a stress between feminism and professionalism that derives from a certain feminist mistrust of experts in general. I think it is a stress that must be faced, because many professional relationships, such as the student–teacher relationship, carry some degree of asymmetry, at least within the professional encounter. The power distribution is not one-sided. Clients and students could look for a different counselor or a different teacher and thus threaten us with unpopularity or even unemployment. On the other hand, a counselor or teacher has certain kinds of expertise and knowledge and is looked up to for that reason, a different source of power. I think it is therefore more desirable to see the counseling relationship as complementary, rather than symmetrical, with two partners who have different but matching needs and responsibilities. I suggested earlier that "therapeutic magic," consisting of the expectation that help will be received, could become a self-fulfilling prophecy. It might have been an ingredient in Elsa's situation.

I am not sure whether specific self-disclosure is very useful, since this could be easily misused in the hands of an inexperienced counselor, with the client feeling that she must take care of the counselor rather than vice versa. Yet, I have also heard it being used with great success. If a counselor, for example, mentions that she has or once had similar difficulties, the client might be relieved of her shame. One-upwomanship can be minimized through the use of clear contracts and emphasis on the commonality of the female experience.

I have a bias toward symmetry in how client and counselor address each other, both using either first or last name.

I am also not sure whether promoting identification of the client with the counselor is a fair goal. It strikes me as quite presumptuous.

I used self-disclosure with Elsa, when I told her how students who did not talk in class, who skipped classes, or who were late with their homework affected me and what I did about it. I don't know whether this was relevant or useful to her.

It is possible that you as a reader might see the above example as a traditional therapeutic session or as simply a session of friendly informal advice between an older woman and a younger one. I hope that it demonstrates the compatibility between feminist counseling, humanistic values, and psychodynamic understanding.

The women's movement has helped women to define and validate their own experiences and their own identity as women. Such clearer differentiation may lead to a new coming together of women and men, with increased mutual understanding and respect for their similarities and differences. Many of the principles of feminist counseling are in the process of becoming absorbed in all counseling for both women and men. Feminist counseling has strengthened and clarified the theory and practice of the counseling process.

## POSTSCRIPT

Because the young woman described in this chapter is the daughter of a friend of a friend, I received an informal follow-up about 3 years later. Here is what was said:

> You may remember a young woman, _____, who came to see you a few years ago, whose mother is my friend. You saw her once, but that meeting had a tremendous impact on her. She is finishing college now with honors. She was moved by your discussion with her and also by the fact that you picked her up at the train (another of the human unprofessional acts we don't talk about). And her parents are forever grateful to you. That morning you spent with her did make a difference.

## References

Bateson, G. (1972). *Steps to an ecology of mind.* New York: Ballantine Books.

Berlin, S. (1976). Better work with women clients. *Social Work, 21*(6), 492–497.

Chesler, P. (1971). Women and psychiatric and psychotherapeutic patients. *Journal of Marriage and the Family, 33,* 746–759.

Freud, S. (1988). *My three mothers and other passions.* New York: New York University Press.

Greenspan, M. (1983). *A new approach to women and therapy.* New York: McGraw-Hill.

Havens, L. (1976). *Participant observation.* New York: Jason Aronson.

Krause, C. (1971). The femininity complex and women therapists. *Journal of Marriage and the Family, 33*(3), 476–482.

Loewenstein, S. F. (1983). Feminist perspective. In A. Rosenblatt & D. Waldfogel (Eds.), *Handbook of clinical social work.* San Francisco: Jossey-Bass.

Marecek, J., & Kravetz, D. (1977). Women and mental health: A review of feminist change efforts. *Psychiatry, 40,* 323–329.

Menaker, E. (1974). The therapy of women in the light of psychoanalytic theory and the emergence of a new view. In V. Franks & V. Burtle (Eds.), *Women in therapy.* New York: Brunner/Mazel.

Miller, J. B. (Ed.). (1973). *Psychoanalysis and women.* New York: Brunner/Mazel.

Radov, C. G., Masnick, B., & Hauser, B. (1977). Issues in feminist therapy: The work of a women's study group. *Social Work, 22*(6), 507–511.

Russell, M. N. (1984). *Skills in counseling women.* Springfield, IL: Charles.

Strouse, J. (Ed.). (1974). *Women and analysis.* New York: Grossman.

Thomas, S. A. (1977). Theory and practice in feminist therapy. *Social Work, 22*(6), 447–454.

Williams, E. F. (1976). *Notes of a feminist therapist.* New York: Dell.

# CASE STUDY 7.4

*The urban poor face serious difficulties in their day-to-day lives. This case describes the complexity of working in an environment characterized by poverty, drug abuse, poor parenting, child abuse, and general chaos.*

## Questions

1. How did the social worker engage the client to become involved in treatment?
2. What specific barriers were present in attempting to deliver services to the client?
3. How did drug use affect the progress made by the social worker and the client?
4. How can an ecological perspective help in understanding the complex set of factors affecting this case?

---

## WORKING WITH THE URBAN POOR

*Myrtle Parnell and Jo VanderKloot*

Anyone who has worked with the urban poor is aware of the chaos in their lives as well as in the communities in which they live. Social work journals describe these families as multi-problem, disorganized, underorganized, crisis prone, enmeshed, and disengaged.

In the process of the usual intake, procedures and forms are used to provide order, which enables the clinician to then fit the client into the traditional psychiatric categories. However, this process of creating order leaves out crucial information about the client's life. The piece that is omitted is, in fact, vital to the clinician's understanding of and ability to connect to the client's reality. What seems to the clinician to be chaotic is rather a different way of being in the world—a way of being that is in large measure determined by the decisions of the dominant culture, which are often at odds with the needs and realities of the poor.

Just as the urban poor do not understand or know how to function in the mainstream, so too most middle-class clinicians must ac-knowledge that they do not understand or know the world in which the poor client lives. The need to create a knowable order on the part of the clinician is understandable but if not resisted will yield information that does not provide the framework in which change can take place.

We suggest that the clinician must recognize chaos and learn to see the patterns within it in the interests of helping the client. In order to recognize and use the chaos, one needs to put aside the usual traditional theoretical structures—the reductionistic, linear way of viewing the client, often in isolation from his or her context. We make little or no attempt to structure the client but observe the patterns as they unfold. This leads to an understanding of the patterns and how they repeat across the different levels in the client's life—individual, couple, family, community, and society. We can then choose a level in which to intervene that will trigger change across all systems.

The following statement is from the Family

Networker Symposium 1988:

> We knew the frame had to be drawn differently and on a much larger scale than was originally conceived. What existed as a body of knowledge for working with the poor appeared to be a caricature in relation to the realities encountered in the field. Poor people did not believe in the models which were provided to be helpful to them. These were the theoretical constructs from the dominant culture which we attempted to impose on a different reality. This often resulted inadvertently in a negation of the world that the poor person knew to be true. What often followed was a negative experience for client and clinician which often led to a clinical picture of lack of motivation, resistance, etc.

The following case illustrates a way of using the theory of chaos when working with a client who would normally be described as extremely "resistant" to treatment.

Dorothea is a 27-year-old, black, single parent of five children. She is a tall, wraithlike woman, attractive even though some of her front teeth are missing. For the first 2 years she presented sporadically at the clinic and appeared like a frightened little bird, sad and noncommunicative. She saw no need for therapy or counseling and did not even know what that meant. What she was sure of was that she would not be seen in a positive light.

The presenting problem was that the childcare agency responsible for her three children in placement had mandated psychotherapy as a prerequisite for return of the children. The oldest child had been given to Dorothea's sister at birth because Dorothea's mother did not think she was mature enough to care for him. The sister refused to return the child. Three children were in placement for neglect and abandonment; a fifth child was born after the others were placed and remained in Dorothea's custody. A sixth child was stillborn, and two more, born during treatment, remained in her custody.

Dorothea and the children's father, Ken, were known drug abusers who frequently left the children alone. On one of these occasions a neighbor reported her to the child protective agency. The daughter, age 4, had been staying with a woman friend and had been sexually abused by the babysitter's boyfriend. It took several days to locate the child because Dorothea did not know where she had been taken.

Dorothea remained in a relationship with Ken, who was diagnosed as paranoid schizophrenic with a secondary diagnosis of polysubstance abuse. His initial psychotic episodes followed PCP abuse. Ken's most significant achievement and the one he spoke of proudly was that he had used the $12,000 he received at age 18 (from a childhood accident) for PCP. At age 22 he had had four psychiatric hospitalizations, and, according to him, every psychiatrist who had treated him had been amazed he could function at all considering the amount of drugs he used daily over an extended period of time. This led to Ken's belief that he is invulnerable.

Dorothea is the seventh of 11 children. Very little is known about her family except that her mother married or remarried when Dorothea was 5 years old. The family had been on welfare but now were supported by the stepfather, Henry, who worked steadily. He was very strict and acted as if he did not particularly care for children. Her mother was so pleased to be married and off welfare that she required that the children accommodate Henry's every need.

Dorothea's view was that her mother definitely put her husband ahead of the children. She had personal evidence to corroborate this. When Dorothea was around age 12, Henry had begun sexually abusing her, as he had an older sister before her. At age 14, she told her mother about the ongoing abuse. Her mother was furious, denied that this had happened to her, and demanded that Dorothea leave the house. She left and never returned. She first lived with acquaintances and then began prostituting. At 16 she married and had her first child. After the separation from her husband (late adolescence), she began using drugs and continued until the placement of her three children into foster care, at which point Dorothea stopped using all drugs.

Dorothea was a street person with many superficial friends whom she saw episodically and who could not be counted on in times of trouble. With the exception of one older woman in her building, Dorothea had no kin or friendship networks in the traditional as well as the ghetto sense. The extreme degree of social disconnectedness made it very difficult for her to function in a community where most rely on kin and friendship to survive economically and emotionally.

Dorothea lived in a "crack building" (cocaine dealing) in a neighborhood where drugs were the major business. Parents had to worry about drug pushers on the street as well as the possibility that their child might be molested in one of the many abandoned buildings along the way to school. It is not uncommon in these areas for children to be escorted to school by parents until age 10, or for some even longer. Needless to say, this poses a hardship for the children's growing need for autonomy. Most of the preceding information was not known until 2 years had elapsed in the treatment process.

Once the building was taken over by drug pushers, the landlord ceased all services and repairs. By the time Dorothea managed to leave the building, she had no working stove, refrigerator, or toilet and no lock on her apartment door. The lock on the main door to the building had been removed several years earlier. The family used to take turns leaving the apartment so that someone would always be left behind to protect their belongings.

However, prior to Dorothea's leaving, all of her furniture was stolen.

At this time in the South Bronx, finding a new place to live for someone on welfare was all but impossible. The shelters were full, and the homeless were increasing in numbers. This particular community consisted of those for whom the larger society had no place: no jobs, inadequate education, little or no recreation, and inadequate public services. The small churches that remained struggled to provide support with clothing and food for emergencies as well as spiritual comfort. The community needs were so great that the churches hardly made a dent.

Dorothea's strongest connection was her identity as a female and as a mother. She was so disconnected to everything else that she did not even appear to have a clear tie to her own racial group. Her only connections with the dominant culture were through its institutions. The two connections she did have were abusive ones: she abused her body, and she abused her children through neglect.

Clearly, with these kinds of cases the ordinary rules and techniques of traditional modalities are inadequate in the face of the enormity of the problems. It is not surprising that most agencies would tend to document the "resistance" and close the case.

We have found that if the client is not doing what we think he or she should be doing at a given time, it is usually not because the person is willfully defying the norms. It is because that person lives with a different reality, one in which the treating person possibly could not survive. Just as the urban poor do not know how to function in the mainstream, so too the middle-class clinician does not know the rules of the world in which the client lives (Parnell & VanderKloot, 1989).

When one is working with chaos (chaos theory as presented at Family Therapy Networker Symposium 1988 by authors), namely in a domestic war zone, one must learn to extrapolate the pattern that runs across all the possible levels of intervention rather than get lost in the myriad of presenting fragments.

Any of Dorothea's problems, taken one by one, posed a formidable challenge. Without attention to the overriding pattern of disconnection, one would be unable to help with the smallest fragment—that is, that Dorothea was unable to keep appointments. By permitting this woman to show up at will, we hypothesized that a pattern would emerge.

There was only one logical intervention to make, and that was on the level of the pattern of disconnection. Engagement would be a lengthy and difficult process without which there would be no treatment. To Dorothea, being a mother was a major value and the only thing that mattered to her. She lived from one visit with her children to the next. It was the only thing that organized her life and was the only therapeutic hook. If the clinicians could not help the client with parenting, they could not help the client.

For the first year and a half, Dorothea dropped by sporadically—one month she might drop in twice and then disappear for several months. The sessions lasted as long as she needed. She would sit with her head down, looking more frightened than depressed. It was obvious she was there because she was sent. She spoke as little as possible, but after a while she could be engaged on issues concerning the children. In addition, there was a steady flow of complaints about the foster care agency, which she felt treated her with contempt. The clinical intervention during this phase consisted of persistence without pressure with the hope of gaining the client's trust.

Telephone contact with the foster care agency bore out the client's complaints. The caseworker's tone was one of contempt, with an openly stated determination that this woman would never get her children back.

Therapy has been extremely difficult because Dorothea cannot maintain regular, consistent contacts. Fortunately, each time she came to the clinic she was able to see one of the authors, even though a long time had elapsed between visits. In most clinics administrative rules would have required that the case be closed. It was important for Dorothea that she be accepted and worked with on her own terms. Her inability to connect emotionally prevented her from learning enough about people to assess who would and could be helpful and who was simply taking advantage of her. She came across as unbelievably naive and childlike for someone who had been in the streets since age 14. She was unable to deal with any large system because she projected all problems, concluding that her situation, whatever it was, would not work out because "they" were not doing their job.

Dorothea began to drop in more frequently without a sense of being "sent." She gradually began to talk more about what was going on in her life. Given her experience growing up and afterward, Dorothea's evasiveness was largely due to her inability to cope with what she expected from others, which was severe and unrelenting criticism. She was not used to being accepted for herself, and she tested at every juncture.

When she finally began to talk, she gave the authors a chance to focus on her strengths and how she might harness them. At first we used her visits with her children, praising her for the amount of time and effort she spent planning every detail of the time she was to be with them. She would save her money to buy a special something for each one.

During this time, the child-care agency moved to sever her parental rights to the youngest child in placement. She immediately became pregnant again and became more involved in treatment. It was not possible to prevent the loss of that child to adoption, but from that time on the focus of treatment was on helping Dorothea regain the custody of her other two children in placement. She brought them to the office on several occasions, and it appeared that there was enough positive feeling and competence on the mother's part to give the situation a chance. The children seemed to adore her and talked mostly about returning home.

In order to help Dorothea connect to peers and build a social network, she was urged to join a mothers' group in the clinic. This was in addition to individual weekly sessions. She gradually felt comfortable, learned a lot about children and parenting, and did connect to several women in the group. Unfortunately, the group was disbanded after 2 years, and there was not another group available appropriate to her needs. The experience helped somewhat in her relationships with acquaintances and neighbors, but the damage of her early life could not be significantly ameliorated in 2 years.

At the time, a decision had to be made regarding discharge of the children. One of the authors went to court and testified on her behalf. The children were discharged in Dorothea's custody. This occurred at a time when services in general had been severely cut back and finding decent housing required a miracle. She was unable to find a decent apartment for the amount of money allowed by welfare, so she, Ken, and by that time five children were crowded into a dark, very dreary three-room apartment. The children's discharge coincided with a flooding of crack (cocaine) into the area in which they lived. Within a year there was hardly a family in her 60-unit building that was not either using or dealing in drugs.

Numerous home visits were made throughout the treatment process. Because the neighborhoods the clinic served were often dangerous, we made visits accompanied by whomever we felt would be most helpful at a given time—sometimes a mental health assistant, sometimes a psychiatrist or other clinician. In this case a mental health assistant was closely involved in working with the concrete service problems and accompanied the author(s) on each visit.

The 10-year-old son, Donald, and 8-year-old daughter, Olga, were overjoyed to be home, and all went well for a short while. As soon as it was clear that Ken was making a commitment to Dorothea and the children, his mother stopped paying her rent, was evicted, and moved together with a younger son into the three-room apartment with Ken, Dorothea, and the children. Despite the overcrowded conditions and the tension between Dorothea and Ken's relatives, the children made a good adjustment to school and seemed to be doing well at home. The major problem seemed to be Dorothea's difficulty with disciplining the children in a consistent way. Her rules seemed arbitrary and therefore confusing. The children began making their own rules, and Donald was becoming the parental child. At age 10, he could not handle this, and it was certainly not good for the three preschool children.

In cases of child abuse and neglect, the children's well-being is monitored both directly in sessions and through school contacts and observations and informal involvement with the children. Parents are encouraged to bring their children to appointments whether the children are to be formally seen or not. Other staff in the waiting area also help by keeping us informed of any changes they observe in the children or the mother–child interaction. Parents who are overwhelmed with daily survival issues may not be aware of the early signs of a child getting into difficulty.

Joint sessions with Dorothea and Ken helped somewhat because Ken had the ability to be more consistent. The situation stabilized temporarily. We had six family sessions in which the parents practiced jointly taking charge of the children and setting up reasonable rules.

The situation just described highlights the complexity of working with one of the difficult cases of the urban poor. Interventions were made to connect to Dorothea and help her connect to her children and a meaningful social network. As these interventions took hold, new problems emerged in force: first, her neighborhood was one of the early ones to be overrun by crack; second, Ken's mother accelerated her hold on her son as he moved dangerously close to Dorothea and the children. Another complicating variable was Ken's Social Security Disability check, which he had previously shared with his mother and now committed to the care of his children.

Although we were clear that family intervention should include Ken's mother and brother, they were definitely unavailable, despite many efforts to engage them. Mother had been on welfare all of her life and was extremely distrustful of any agency contact. His brother, also a poly-substance abuser, functioned at a considerably lower level than Ken. A home visit was not made during this time because of the description of the brother's potential for violence toward any agency representative. The mother and son's distrust bordered on paranoia. The children were not affected directly by these attitudes. They seemed to have good interactions with their uncle and spoke fondly of him.

The couple's situation began to deteriorate because of the tension in the home and community. For two people who found it hard to connect, the pull of drugs in the community and the mother's hold on Ken undermined their fragile connection.

Ken was able to get his family other housing, but by this time he had returned to drug abuse and stopped going to the clinic for his prolixin injections. He became abusive to Dorothea and no longer contributed to the children's support. Then came the violence, followed by his attempt to take her money for drugs. The police were called for these incidents but took no action, although Dorothea requested that he be removed. When it was clear that she could not, on her own, get a reasonable response from the police, we helped her contact a District Attorney who was known to be effective in helping women get a fair deal in cases of domestic violence. The District Attorney informed Dorothea of her rights and of the procedures to remove Ken from the home. Once it was clear that he could legally be removed, the authors accompanied Dorothea to the police precinct with the request that he be removed. The police did not understand why we would bother with this woman and her problems. Their attitude was very judgmental, and they conveyed the feeling that they considered us naive in our efforts to help her. We contacted the District Attorney, who advised the police to remove the man from the home so as to protect the rights of this woman and her children. Still they refused to act. Fortunately, one of the officers we know from the local delicatessen came into the office at this time. After a prolonged discussion, the detective explained the legal difficulty that this type of case presents for the police. The issue was resolved when the detective agreed that because the man in question was a psychiatric patient, known to have discontinued his neuroleptic medication and also known to be on crack, they could, on that basis, remove him from the home. They accompanied Dorothea home and removed Ken.

By this time the children had been subjected to too much chaos, tension, and violence. Dorothea's pressures were also too great. The basic appliances in her apartment were no longer working, and we had been unsuccessful in getting the landlord to make repairs either by working with him directly or by working through the welfare system to bring pressure on him. Shortly after Ken began using drugs,

Dorothea joined him after what had been a 6-year hiatus. The five children were placed in foster homes, and Dorothea went voluntarily to a detox program, followed by a long-term drug rehabilitation program.

In this case, despite all attempts to help Dorothea parent, the combination of her own deprivation in childhood and the present unending series of problems in her environment and family made growth and change very difficult. Dorothea has, however, made personal gains. She is more available to people in general. She is beginning to understand her participation in what is happening to her children and to her. There is less projection and more responsibility. However, it is probably too late to get her children back; termination of her parental rights was being considered as the authors were leaving the agency.

When last seen, Dorothea had completed the drug rehabilitation program and was living in a shelter but was expecting to be relocated within the month. She proudly announced that she has a full-time job, which she likes, at a large department store in the area.

In retrospect we were bothered over the outcome of the children again being removed, and we questioned our decision and persistence in helping Dorothea get the children back initially. There were seven compelling reasons for this intervention. First, Dorothea's only connection was to her children; without them, if she were unable to become pregnant she was at risk for suicide; second, the children's verbal and nonverbal behavior showed a strong desire to be with their mother; third, Dorothea cooperated fully with all that she needed to do to retain custody; fourth, we had a strong impression that the foster care agency was sabotaging the mother's efforts to regain custody. For example, at the very time that Dorothea was working the hardest and was most cooperative, the agency informed the

children that they were to be adopted by the foster parent. When Dennis began running away from his foster home, the agency said it did not know where he was and could do nothing about it. They also did not file a "missing child" report with the police.

The fifth reason was the awareness that Dorothea would continue to have more children with each threat of the loss of a child. At age 33 she had had 10 children. The sixth reason was based on the fact that Dorothea discontinued all drug use on her own when the children went into placement and remained drug free for 6 years. This seemed to indicate a very powerful motivation to be a mother. The seventh reason had to do with our own personal bias of "when in doubt, try the parent."

In summary, we have illustrated a model for working with the chaos in the life of the urban poor. Intervention in the pattern of disconnection did not magically cure Dorothea and her family, but it enabled her to connect and thereby opened up new possibilities for her. She would probably never become middle class economically or in terms of values. The purposes of the treatment of the urban poor in difficult cases such as this one are amelioration of the presenting conditions and development of new skills that will enhance the client's overall functioning.

Interventions with this client included an extensive engagement process followed by interventions with the individual and in the family system by the school, police, courts, drug programs, and medical system.

The initial pattern of disconnection was disrupted and the client had a different experience. She connected to the clinicians, the agency, her children, and, for a while, her husband. This was a new pattern of connection in which she could receive feedback from others that was useful to her. This shift made new inputs, skills, and values available to Dorothea which she could then build on. Although Dorothea's ability to remain connected to her husband and children was disrupted, her connection to herself was solidified.

## Reference

Parnell, M., & VanderKloot, J. (1989). Ghetto child. In L. Combrinck-Graham (Ed.), *Children in family therapy*. New York: The Guilford Press.

# CASE STUDY 7.5

*The impact of oppression on lesbians and gays results in a variety of feelings and behaviors that may cause difficulties for clients. This case study illustrates the attitudes, skills, and resources exhibited by effective social workers working with lesbian couples.*

## Questions

1.  What social work skills best demonstrate respect for a client's sexual preference?

2.  What are the similarities and differences in counseling lesbian couples and heterosexual couples?

3.  What are the primary goals of couple counseling in this case?

4.  What personal and professional experiences or factors do you recognize in yourself that might influence your comfort and skills in working with couples with sexual orientations different than yours?

## COUPLE COUNSELING WITH LESBIAN WOMEN

*Natalie Jane Woodman*

In case consultation with professionals in various agencies, the role of non-gay/lesbian social workers working with lesbian clients usually arises. The following case example will demonstrate that sexual orientation need not be an impediment to service with this client population. Examples of social work principles and issues as well as some of the dynamics involved in similar situations are interspersed within the excerpts from selected interviews. These examples are identified in brackets and set in italics. Additionally, it should be noted that although much of the casework process is similar for clients in general, there are unique dimensions to working with the lesbian or gay client. Of primary importance is the need for the social worker to be comfortable with his/her own orientation *and* with difference. Also, the counselor must be aware of the impact of oppression on lesbians/gays. Fear and secrecy about a lesbian life-style are not unusual, nor

are the results of those feelings and behaviors. With lesbian and gay clients, we are dealing with a "hidden minority" group in that there are no overt identifying characteristics nor physical manifestations of sexual orientation. The situation of Sue and her partner, Nancy, is one that those who work with lesbian clients see with regularity.

Sue Smith called the Employee Assistance Program (EAP) of the Hightech Corporation and requested an appointment. Sue stated that she felt she needed help because she was having trouble concentrating on doing her job as well as she knows it should be done. Andrea Jones, the social worker at EAP, learned from the employment records that Sue was 25 years old and single and had been employed as a computer programmer for the past 6 years. During that time, she had completed college on a company scholarship, going evenings and summers while working full-time. All of Sue's evaluations were glowing, with special note of her initiative and ability to get along with supervisors and co-workers.

In the first interview, Andrea began by asking Sue to explain a bit more about her situation, as this might be affecting her ability to concentrate. [*Of particular note is that the social worker began by focusing on the first part of Sue's presenting problem, using this to gain additional information. Also, the open-ended question allowed for further exploration of Sue as a biopsychosocial person.*] Sue clarified that for the past 6 months she has been constantly worried about her home situation and her relationship with her parents. These worries keep nagging her all day long, and she feels as if she is at the end of her rope. When Andrea asked if Sue would explain what she meant by her "home situation," Sue hemmed and hawed and then said that she thought maybe asking for help wasn't such a good idea after all. She could probably work out her own problems herself. After learning that Sue just didn't feel comfortable with EAP, Andrea explained that using this service would in no way go on Sue's records or be reported to anyone, and anything they talked about would remain strictly confidential. Because Sue had called for help after wrestling with her problems for 6 months without success, maybe she could give counseling a try, and at any time she didn't feel it was helping, she could look at other alternatives.

Andrea then explored whether Sue felt discomfort with Andrea as a person. The response was "Well I did see that you're wearing a wedding ring, and I'm not sure you can understand my problems. Maybe I should find someone else." [*By asking directly about client—worker rapport, Andrea was demonstrating sensitivity to Sue's right to find a helping person who would be best for her. Andrea also used her knowledge of the fact that clients often feel hesitant to confront a worker with concerns about cultural or life-style differences.*] Sue's ability to identify the "barrier" enabled Andrea to clarify that because of her ethics, values, and training, she considered personal life-styles to be an individual's own and that the important thing was to be sure of being secure in that life-style. If Sue still felt this to be an issue now, then together they could find someone else with whom Sue would be more comfortable.

[*By identifying the need for comfort within one's life, Andrea displayed acceptance of differences and understanding that such differences can create discomfort for which help is warranted. Also, just as with clients of other minority groups, the social worker can indicate his/her background and comfort level, while being prepared to make an appropriate referral. This last point means that the worker must be knowledgeable about alternative resources in the minority community. Additionally, Andrea acknowledged Sue's right to make the final decision.*]

Sue stated that she did feel a bit more comfortable now and was willing to give EAP a try. She went on to say that she has been living with Nancy for the past 5 years and that, while Nancy insists on identifying their relationship as a lesbian one, Sue can't accept this. Things had been just fine until Nancy met two lesbian women on her job and began insisting that she and Sue socialize with them.

[*This author has interviewed numerous women who considered their relationship to be "just a phase," or "a deep friendship," or "a loving relationship nothing like that lesbian stuff" for any number of years. The denial of identification with sexual orientation takes various forms and may continue until some event, crisis, or other person brings one or the other partner out of their mutual closet. The social worker obviously does not begin by tearing down this well-entrenched defense. This process of coping has been necessary for survival in the face of both internalized and external evidences of homophobia. The fear of*] *anything connected with homosexuality is rampant in our society, and most persons are socialized with racist, sexist, and homophobic stereotypes and bias—including members of groups most affected by such oppression.*]

Andrea asked Sue to tell her about herself and Nancy and learned that the couple has had a very sharing, egalitarian, and supportive relationship for 4 years. They have enjoyed similar recreational activities, have helped each other to progress in their jobs, and have two cats that they both love dearly. As she talked, Sue became more and more animated and commented that it really was neat to tell someone about her life with Nancy. On the job, she pretends that she is dating men and makes up all sorts of stories about her weekends with them. In fact, this has been the big problem with her parents. They too hear about the "dates" and think that, although Nancy is a very nice person, she may be preventing their daughter from marrying. Mr. and Mrs. O'Brien keep pressuring their daughter to date more and get married. The entire family is extremely religious (Roman Catholic) and believe that homosexuality is sinful. "But then, that's another whole issue with Nancy too," Sue added.

[*Andrea's accepting demeanor and nonjudgmental questioning have enabled Sue to reveal more about herself and her problems. The social worker now is able to see that Sue's problems are not as much intrapersonal as they are intersystemic. Also, Sue's strengths had been notable in her personnel record, and the couple's strengths have been identified in this interview.*]

Andrea concluded this intake interview by listing the various problems she thought Sue had identified:

1. Problems in concentrating because of worrying about relationship problems—which in turn were related to life-style definition and self-perception.

2. Not feeling comfortable with Nancy's recent coming out to others and wanting Sue to also self-identify with other lesbian women. This would also relate to Sue's own lack of comfort with their life-style.

3. Discomfort with having to pretend to be some other person on the job and with parents.

4. Conflict with her parents over Nancy's presence in Sue's life.

5. Religious conflict that involved Nancy's attitudes.

6. Not doing her job as well as *she* thought it should be done. Andrea added that although they hadn't discussed this, it had been part of Sue's opening request for help and might be something she would want to talk about more.

Sue commented that this pretty well summed things up, and Andrea then listed strengths that Sue had indicated existed for her as an individual and in her relationship with Nancy. Andrea stated that she thought that she could be of help, but she wanted Sue's opinion about continuation. In the decision-making process, Andrea offered Sue some options for future appointments. If Sue felt any discomfort about continuing with EAP, Andrea would try to help her find a more comfortable setting. Sue immediately discounted this, so Andrea continued by suggesting that, since four of the six problem areas involved Nancy, perhaps Sue would like to talk with Nancy about both of them coming in together. On the other hand, Sue had some issues of her own (such as the job situation and her own feelings about lesbian relationships) on which she might want to focus. When Sue expressed surprise at the idea of including Nancy, Andrea explained about couple counseling. She stated that sometimes by talking with a social worker together, couples found that they were able to gain new perspectives about each other and their interaction. This was partly a result of the impartiality of the caseworker and partly because each person found it somewhat safer to explore hitherto unexpressed feelings on "neutral" territory. Sue responded that she'd like to talk with Nancy about this. She thought Nancy would jump at the idea because Nancy had actually been suggesting something like this for months. Andrea then asked that the couple discuss this further and then call to set an appointment convenient for both.

[*During this conclusion, the social worker provided effective feedback by identifying both problems for solution and strengths that could be used in the problem-solving process. Andrea also indicated that she thought there was hope for problem resolution. Ripple (1964), in a rigorous research project, examined the degree to which clients' motivation, capacity, supportive environment, or feelings of hope provided by the intake social worker mitigated most favorably for continuation with counseling. Hope was THE most influential factor in preventing "dropouts." Andrea offered Sue options for intervention, thereby involving Sue in decision making rather than the social worker presenting herself as omniscient. She next synthesized some problem areas (interpersonal and intersystemic as well as interpersonal), which further served to separate the problems on which Sue would be working. These basic principles apply to all clients but are identified here because of the clarity with which they were applied. The caseworker also used the opportunity to define her role in couple counseling so that Sue would have some knowledge that this was not a means for having her own ally in the disagreements with Nancy. By having both women talk about an appointment time, Andrea did not assume that Nancy would be willing to come in to see her just because Sue said so.*]

Two weeks later, Sue and Nancy came in for a joint interview. After introductions and clarification of her role, Andrea asked Sue and Nancy where they would like to start. Nancy jumped in and said that one incident this past weekend really pointed up the big difference she and Sue were facing. Nancy explained that she worked as a copy editor for a small women's magazine where everyone was comfortable with everyone else's life situations. She had been invited to a staff party and wanted Sue to go with her so that they could meet the other lesbian couples who would be there. Sue had reacted with alarm because nongay couples would be present, and "who knew who else would be there." She also argued that she was *not* going to be "labeled" as "one of them" because she didn't feel that she really was "lesbian." Nancy said that she had become furious and issued an ultimatum that either Sue face facts or get out so that Nancy could go on with her life knowing who she was and feeling comfortable with that. After a lot of tears and pleading, Sue said that she couldn't visualize life without Nancy, but she didn't want to go to the party.

Andrea asked Sue if she could clarify how she perceived her relationship with Nancy. Once again, various descriptions of the meaning, interactions, and behaviors in their lives were given. In response to a question from Andrea, Sue stated that she really loved living with Nancy and couldn't imagine any other life. Andrea then noted that Sue had not said anything about sexuality. She wondered if this, too, was important to each of them. Nancy unhesitatingly described how this "was just great" and sometimes got in the way of resolving basic issues. Sue appeared distinctly uncomfortable with the discussion, and Andrea acknowledged this impression, asking Sue if she was able to talk about sex at all with anyone other than Nancy. After a negative reply and an explanation of how her parents considered sex "an off-limits topic," Andrea grinned and stated that she'd be willing to bet that lesbian sex was totally taboo. [*The social worker demonstrated that she was not afraid of the topic and was accepting of lesbian sex, thereby providing a new role model for Sue.*]

Andrea then went on to explain that from what she had heard, it seemed as though Sue and Nancy did have a committed relationship and that it might be that "labels" and fear of others labeling them was getting in the way of "rounding out" their lives. Andrea asked each of them how they had felt not having anyone else with whom they could interact. Both young women gave examples that basically described months of feeling that they were "the only ones like us" and that they couldn't identify with the militant lesbians they had seen on television. Sue then added that *maybe* if she could know that there were other couples like herself, she could figure out where she "fit." However, she absolutely couldn't jeopardize her job at Hightech by letting anyone there know about her relationship with Nancy.

Andrea agreed that "labels" could be destructive or limiting and also acknowledged the realities of Sue's fears of homophobia. The social worker additionally provided some educative counseling about the fact that living "in a cocoon" led to either atrophy and death of the relationship or "becoming butterflies." Sue and Nancy seemed to be at a critical point in this metamorphosis. She wondered if Sue would feel less discomfort and be willing to consider inviting Nancy's new friends for brunch as a way of learning about some other couples and their life-styles. She also asked how much reading they had done about variations in lesbian life-styles and, on learning that this was minimal, prepared a reading list of recent novels and autobiographies depicting positive pictures of lesbian couples of various ages and sociocultural backgrounds.

Andrea asked if there were other areas with which they could deal in the remaining time, and Sue raised the question about how religion could be dealt with. After some discus-

sion, it transpired that there frequently were times when Sue became very depressed. She felt that she couldn't be true to her religion and still be with Nancy, yet she *knew* inside herself that this relationship was not sinful. Andrea found that Nancy understood little of this conflict, since she had been raised in a home that stressed values and consideration for others but that had minimal ties to organized religion. Both responded favorably to the idea of reading in this area, and Andrea added that she knew of a lesbian/gay Catholic group in town that might provide support. She added that confidentiality was a part of group membership and that Sue might want to call one of the women in Dignity to talk about the group in order to regain an affiliation with Catholicism that might feel more integrated and less guilt producing.

In concluding, Nancy and Sue said that it looked as if they had some thinking and work that they had to do before the next interview. Together with Andrea, they summarized that they could:

1. Consider some new ways to admit others they could trust into their private life and assess the pros and cons of private versus "public" self;
2. Explore some of the reading suggested and, from this, discuss the implications for them;
3. Reexamine the meaning of religion, for Sue especially, and see how new knowledge and understanding could help this to fit into their lives.

[*During this interview, various factors affecting lesbian/gay clients were evident. Also, it is apparent that the social worker needs additional knowledge. Sue particularly was affected by the aforementioned internalized homophobia, which restricted her from gaining new knowledge about diversity in lesbian/gay life-styles. Andrea did not reinforce the ho-*

*mophobia by avoiding words like* lesbian *and* gay. *Simply by the social worker's acceptance, affirming statements, and focus on work to strengthen the relationship, Sue became able to state with positiveness that she knew this relationship was all right. Her fears of homophobia in the job situation were probably very reality based and were not discounted by the caseworker, who suggested other areas for socializing that might feel safer. The social worker must beware of forcing clients "out of closets" but must also deal with the hazards to self and the relationship resulting from isolation. Lowenstein (1980) speaks to the issue of achieving an integrated identity in the face of conflict between public and private selves. Although a dichotomy may be necessary for economic survival throughout life, attaining comfort within those separate "lives" can eliminate conflict. Helping the client to learn survival skills in a homophobic society can be part of the casework process.*

*By suggesting an alternative means to involve others, the social worker reinforced the need to expand Nancy and Sue's social sphere by increasing the "comfort level" of locating such first meetings on Sue's own territory. Many writers in this area (Grace, in press; Lewis, 1984; Moses & Hawkins, 1982; Woodman & Lenna, 1980) indicate that the process of coming out to others reinforces the process of coming out to self and helps in establishing a lesbian/gay identity. "Bibliotherapy" can also be an invaluable tool for the worker. The* Annotated Bibliography of Lesbian and Gay Readings *(Council on Social Work Education, 1983) and* Lesbian and Gay Issues: A Resource Manual *(Hidalgo, Peterson, & Woodman, 1985) can provide a starting point. However, the worker also should be aware of lesbian/gay book stores and mail order resources for up-to-date materials.*

*Finally, with regard to religion, the social worker must recognize that a lesbian/gay lifestyle is not one that revolves only around sexuality and intimacy. Clark (1977) reminds us that the involvement includes social, spiritual, and intellectual dimensions as well. Therefore, the process of resolving the values dilemma that may exist between earlier socialization and current realities can be dealt with in the context of religious affiliations with which the client is comfortable. There are gay groups throughout the country of almost all religious denominations. Again, the* NASW *Resource* Manual *is a help in locating such resources as is a local lesbian/gay hot line.]*

Five weeks later, Nancy and Sue came in for their sixth interview. They spent the first part of this hour recounting how well things were going in various dimensions of their lives, particularly at home and with newfound friends. Sue said that she thought she still had one issue she wanted to address—her parents. Nancy's birthday had been last week, and Mr. and Mrs. O'Brien had really gone all out for the occasion but then once again brought up the subject of "you girls getting out and getting married." Sue thought she just had to let them know what was going on but didn't know what to do. Nancy was all in favor of just laying it on the line as she had with her parents, but Sue was terrified of the reaction she'd get. Andrea began by exploring the reasons for coming out to parents, learning that Sue had a very close and loving relationship with them and couldn't keep this newly integrated part of herself a secret any longer. Furthermore, she was just sure her family would guess sooner or later, and she thought it might be better if she talked about it now rather than "later."

The next step was to explore the possible reactions—both positive and "worst scenario," examining with each the consequences and how Sue could live with those. After considerable discussion, Sue considered that the love her parents had for her would outweigh their negative feelings about homosexuality. This consideration became the basis from which to proceed to the actual coming-out process. Andrea reminded Sue how long she herself had struggled to accept the lesbian dimension of her identity and emphasized that she could expect a need for her parents to have time to absorb this also. Role playing was used in arriving at how to go about the coming out, with Nancy helping with comments about what might work best, based on her insights of the family. Andrea concluded by also giving Sue some resources for Mr. and Mrs. O'Brien such as Parents and Friends of Lesbians and Gays and another reading suggestion (Borhek, 1983).

[*Again, the social worker involved the clients in a well-considered process of further coming out. Using the strength and insights of one partner to help the other might make this next step easier. Additionally, Nancy was helped to be aware of the emotional turmoil that Sue felt and with the fact that this probably wouldn't be a "one shot" miracle, thereby increasing empathy within the relationship. Parents and Friends can also be a resource for a lesbian/gay person considering such a step and/or in helping with the aftermath of the coming-out discussion.*]

During the eighth interview, Nancy said she would like to conclude with just one more issue—Sue and her job. Sue was working increased hours, which took away time from socializing and doing chores that were necessary. Sue explained that she had to work longer and harder to do better than anyone to prove that she should have her job. Andrea then explored with them how much of this was related to Sue's self-image and residual guilt about identity and how much to reality needs.

During the course of discussion, Sue said she still was afraid that if anyone "found out," she'd be fired. Andrea, Sue, and Nancy then reworked the implications of private and public selves and how to deal with these. They next examined the realities of choices in job environments. Using basic problem solving and weighing pros and cons, Nancy realized that Sue's job was not only important to her self-esteem but necessary to their life-style. Given such considerations, she thought she might help Sue more to figure what was essential at work and what they needed to retain their well-being.

Andrea explained that research (Woodman, 1988) did indicate that many women feel the pressures of sexism and homophobia on their jobs and emphasized the need for stress management in such situations. She also wondered if it would help if Sue sought more support from a new group of professional women who also felt the strain of having to be highly confidential about their life-styles. Nancy leaped at the idea, but Sue said that she'd think about it, although it felt good to know there was a recourse. Meanwhile, she would try to work more with using Nancy's support to be less afraid.

[*In concluding, Andrea helped the couple to use their own capabilities at problem solving and dealing with reality-based homophobia. She neither discounted this oppression nor left the couple with hopelessness. By suggesting another group, both Sue and Nancy were left with a widening potential for social supports. Such supports are vital for lesbian/gay clients and couples (Woodman, 1988; Woodman & Lenna, 1980).*]

This article has demonstrated that basic problem solving is applicable regardless of sexual orientation, as are role playing, bibliotherapy, and couple counseling. What is important is that the social worker must have:

• A firm sense of the need to recognize variation in forms of oppression;
• A value stance that accepts diversity in life-styles;
• A body of knowledge relative to lesbian/gay issues and resources;
• The skill to use all of these.

The social worker also should endeavor to end such oppression. It is hoped that Andrea will proceed to work within Hightech to gain Affirmative Action policies that protect employees regardless of sexual orientation. Finally, the social worker must continue to recognize the multiple oppression faced by many clients. Racism, sexism, ageism, "lookism," and homophobia are rampant in our society, and many of our clients encounter more than one form of such discrimination.

## References

Borhek, M. V. (1983). *Coming out to parents: A two-way survival guide for lesbians and gay men and their parents.* New York: Pilgrim Press.

Clark, D. (1977). *Loving someone gay.* Millbrae, CA: Celestial Arts.

Council on Social Work Education. (1983). *An annotated bibliography of lesbian and gay resources.* Washington, DC: Council on Social Work Education.

Grace, J. (in press). Affirming lesbian and gay adulthood. In N. J. Woodman (Ed.), *Lesbian and gay life-styles: A guide for counseling and education.* New York: Irvington.

Hidalgo, H., Peterson, T., & Woodman, N. J. (1985). *Lesbian and gay issues: A resource manual.* Silver Spring, MD: National Association of Social Workers.

Lewis, L. A. (1984). The coming-out process for lesbians: Integrating a stable identity. *Social Work, 29,* 464–469.

Lowenstein, S. (1980). Understanding lesbian women. *Social Casework, 61,* 29–38.

Moses, A. E., & Hawkins, R. (1978). *Counseling lesbian women and gay men.* St. Louis: Mosby.

Ripple, L. (1964). *Motivation, capacity and opportunity: Studies in casework theory and practice.* Chicago: University of Chicago.

Woodman, N. J. (1988). Lesbian women in their mid-years: Implications for practice. Manuscript submitted for publication.

Woodman, N. J., & Lenna, H. R. (1980). *Counseling with gay men and women.* San Francisco: Jossey-Bass.

# 8

CASE STUDIES

# IN USING PRACTICE EVALUATION

ALTHOUGH RESEARCH AND EVALUATION HAVE been a part of social work since its inception, there has been increasing interest in the role of research and evaluation in contemporary social work practice. In fact, schools of social work are now required to present information on how social workers are to evaluate their own practice. This emphasis on practice evaluation, often referred to as empirical clinical practice, has been advocated because of several recent changes.

Social work practice has been increasingly under pressure concerning its accountability. For example, funding sources want to know if social work makes a difference for the clients it serves. Social workers became increasingly concerned about effectiveness following Fischer's (1973) review of research that concluded that social work was not effective. Also influential in the empirical clinical practice movement were early efforts by social work

researchers to specify their interventions and evaluate the effectiveness of the interventions.

The social work profession has moved beyond the early concerns regarding effectiveness and is now concerned with harnessing the technology, knowledge, and skills to promote effective practice. Thus, the question is no longer, Is social work effective? Instead, the emphasis is on more specific questions such as, What type of social work intervention is most effective with what type of client group or problem? In addition to this emphasis on knowledge building, a major trend has been teaching social workers to use single-system designs to evaluate their practice. The idea is to teach a scientific approach to practice so that it can be used to enhance the performance of social work practice.

The central idea in single-subject designs is the ongoing monitoring and evaluation of the client. These designs are simply methods to collect ongoing data about a client and use that information to examine whether the intervention being offered is helpful. Therefore, the key steps include defining the problem in measurable terms; measuring the problem in an ongoing manner; evaluating the result; and making decisions based on the information being received. Practice evaluation focuses on questions such as, What intervention should I use? How long should I continue the intervention? Is my intervention effective in helping the client? Should I try something different?

For example, if you were working with a depressed client, you could measure the client's depression prior to any intervention. To measure the depression you choose the Beck Depression Inventory, a standardized measure. You administer this 2 weeks prior to beginning your intervention—once at intake and once prior to your first session. The intervention consists of cognitive therapy. Each week the client completes the Beck Depression Inventory. The weekly data give you an idea of whether your intervention is working. Has the cognitive therapy led to a lower depression score compared with the first 2 weeks prior to the intervention? The answer to the question has important implications for what you plan to do to help this client. But what if you didn't have this information? The client could be getting worse, and you might not know it.

Social workers have always been interested in assessing whether they are helping their clients change. However, in the past the focus was on social workers' qualitative judgment of whether they were helping the client. Such judgments are usually subjective and unreliable. What was the level of the problem prior to the social worker's intervention? The answer to such questions is not known, and this makes it difficult to determine the true impact of the intervention. Social workers need to be concerned about whether they are offering effective services, to know whether their clients are improving or deteriorating. Practice evaluation has as a primary concern the monitoring of client progress.

Five case studies are presented in this chapter. The first three focus on practice evaluation. Blythe presents an example of practice evaluation with a difficult case of sexual assault. She was successful in helping the client clearly define the problems that resulted from the assault—flashbacks and accompanying depression. Also, her case study shows how the practitioner must individualize the methods for collecting data. Corcoran's case study presents the evaluation of family therapy with an acting out adolescent. His case study is an example of how to use multiple measures to evaluate progress. He uses several assessment checklists and a measure of school absenteeism. This case is also intriguing because initially the intervention in this case was not successful and the data that were collected suggested a need to redirect the treatment. The case study by Nurius demonstrates that with some creativity, practice evaluation can be useful across a variety of human service settings. She shows how practice evaluation was helpful with a client in an inpatient hospital setting, with a limited contact intervention, and in a health setting where the focus is on high-risk clients.

The case study by LeCroy and Ismail does not conduct an evaluation of practice but instead uses the scientific method to understand the dynamics of the case. Referred to as an intensive case analysis, the goal is to apply the rules of scientific thinking in order to understand the individual and respond in an effective manner. It is basically an exercise in problem solving rather than an evaluation of a case. The last case study by Schinke et al. presents a model for how to develop a re-search-based program and rigorously evaluate its effectiveness. Social workers have an important role to play in the development of new programs and in assessing the effectiveness of such programs.

## Reference

Fischer, J. (1973). Is casework effective? *Social Work, 18,* 5–20.

# CASE STUDY 8.1

*Sexual assault is a devastating experience. This case describes the impact of sexual assault on a young adolescent and how the social worker designed and evaluated her treatment efforts.*

**Questions**

1. What problems developed as a result of the sexual assault?

2. How did the social worker get the client to collect data that would be useful in evaluating treatment progress in this case?

3. How was the plan for treatment influenced by the results of the data collected about the client's problem?

4. How did the worker reduce the self-blame that is common among victims of sexual assault?

## EVALUATING THE TREATMENT OF A SEXUALLY ASSAULTED CHILD

*Betty J. Blythe*

This case study describes the treatment of a young boy who was sexually assaulted. Services were delivered by a social worker in a sexual assault treatment program. As with all of her cases, the worker used measurement and research tools to define the target problems, specify indicators of these problems, and routinely monitor the client's progress throughout and following treatment. This paper describes the treatment and evaluation of this case.

The client, a 12-year-old boy named Gary, was sexually molested by an adult man. The boy was returning from softball practice when the man, who was dressed as a utility meter reader, enticed him into a wooded area. The man performed oral sodomy on Gary and forced the boy to fellate him. Before allowing him to leave, the man threatened to harm Gary and his family if he told anyone about the episode.

On returning home, Gary immediately told his older brother about the attack, and his brother called their parents. Gary's parents took him to the local hospital emergency room, where he was examined. The hospital social worker referred Gary to the sexual abuse treatment program at the local community mental health center.

As is typical at this agency, the intake was conducted over the telephone by the social worker who would continue to see the client. At the time of the intake, Gary was still extremely upset by the incident. He was afraid to leave home and walk anywhere by himself. He refused to attend softball practice, even if his parents drove him there. Most upsetting to Gary were frequent flashbacks in which he recalled the attack. Like many victims of sexual assault, he felt both depressed and guilty. Gary indicated that he feared that his assailant might carry out his threats to hurt Gary or his family.

The social worker told Gary that his feelings and the flashbacks were common responses by people who have been sexually assaulted. She also said that, working together, they could try to reduce the frequency of the flashbacks and improve his mood so that he was less depressed. Gary said he was willing to come for counseling and that he wanted to work on these areas.

The worker next began to further specify the two target problems, flashbacks and depression. She asked Gary to describe in detail the flashbacks. He said that a flashback was like seeing and feeling the experience again, as if he were back in it. The worker also learned that reliving the attack through the flashback was accompanied by a strong sense of fear, increased heartbeat, sweating, fear for his life, and feelings of helplessness and rage. There did not seem to be any pattern that might predict when the flashbacks would occur. They happened throughout the day and evening, regardless of whether he was alone or with someone, and in any setting. Gary reported that a flashback lasted 4 or 5 minutes and that they all were of equal severity. After a flashback episode, Gary typically anguished about how he might have avoided the attack. He experienced strong feelings of sadness and guilt. This information helped the worker better understand the nature of the flashbacks and determine what interventions would likely be helpful or not helpful.

The worker told Gary that she wanted him to begin keeping a record of how often he had flashbacks each day. She explained that this information would help her determine if she was helping Gary reduce the frequency of the flashbacks. If they did not occur less frequently after a few sessions, she said she would change what she was doing in some way. In addition, information collected about what Gary was doing at the time of a flashback would confirm or disconfirm their conclusion that there was not any pattern associated with the flashbacks. The worker asked him to get some 3 x 5″ index cards and make two columns with one labeled "day" and the

other labeled "flashbacks." She also told him to fill in the days and dates in the first column. In the second column, Gary was to record what he was doing when the flashback occurred and any other information he wanted to provide about the flashback itself. At the end of the telephone intake, the worker went over the request to collect information about flashbacks with Gary's mother, explaining how the cards should be completed and the purpose for doing so. She asked his mother to help him prepare the cards immediately and to remind him to carry a card with him and to fill it out.

To establish the level of the problem before Gary talked to her (the baseline), the worker questioned Gary carefully to determine how many flashbacks he had experienced over the past several days. She did this by having Gary describe his routine on the previous day and then indicate if he had had any flashbacks. The worker was able to get Gary to go back over the day of the intake and the 2 days since the attack in this manner. If, at any point, the worker had felt that Gary was not able to provide accurate information about the frequency of the episodes, she would have abandoned the questioning. This type of baseline is called a reconstructed baseline.

The worker then explained to Gary that she wanted him to complete a questionnaire when he came to the office. She said that the questions did not have right or wrong answers and that they would help her better understand his feelings of sadness and depression. She also told him that she would go over the questionnaire with him, and that he would complete it occasionally to help them determine if he was getting less depressed. Gary agreed to fill out the questionnaire. The questionnaire actually was a standardized measure, the Generalized Contentment Scale (Hudson, 1982). It is relatively short (25 items) and uses simple, understandable language to assess the level of depression. As with the self-report measure of flashbacks, the worker also described this measure and its application in the treatment to Gary's mother and gave her an opportunity to ask any questions.

Gary came in for his first session 4 days later. Before he saw the worker, the receptionist gave him the standardized measure to complete in the waiting room. When the worker saw Gary, she asked how he was doing. Gary soon volunteered the information he had collected about flashbacks. The social worker added these data to a graph she had started with the reconstructed baseline. She told Gary that they would add his information to the graph each time he came to a session, and she repeated that the information would help them determine if she was helping him. The information about what Gary was doing at the time a flashback occurred validated their suspicions that there was no discernible pattern associated with the flashbacks. The flashbacks apparently occurred in numerous settings and when Gary was alone and with others. The worker and Gary agreed that there was no need to continue collecting additional information about the antecedents of each flashback. The worker asked if Gary had any difficulty in collecting the information, and he said that he was embarrassed to get the card out when he was around other people. The worker asked Gary if it would be easier to carry some small beads in his pocket and move a bead from one pocket to another each time he had a flashback. At the end of each day, Gary could count the beads and put this information on the index card. Gary responded that he would prefer to use that method, and the worker gave him 10 beads.

At this point, she also scored the Generalized Contentment Scale. Gary's score of 54 indicated that he indeed was depressed. The scale has a clinical cutting score of 30, which means that clients scoring above this level have a "clinically significant problem." The worker relayed this information to Gary in a matter-of-fact fashion and tried not to alarm him or otherwise lead him to worry unnecessarily about being depressed.

## INTERVENTION

Having achieved some understanding of the baseline level of the problem, the worker was ready to begin intervention. The intervention was actually a package of several different techniques.

### Psychoeducation

The worker gave Gary information about sexual assault and how people typically respond after being assaulted or experiencing other crisis situations. She emphasized that these feelings would not last forever. She also underscored that Gary was not to blame for the attack but rather that the assailant had committed a crime against Gary. The actual attack was always portrayed as a violent act rather than as a sexual act.

### Environmental Manipulation

With the approval of Gary and his mother, the worker contacted Gary's school and arranged for Gary to ride a bus to and from school (previously he had walked). She also involved Gary's family in the intervention by having a family member stand at the bus stop with Gary in the morning and meet his returning bus in the afternoon. Gary's mother was responsible for organizing this schedule to ensure that a family member was available to help Gary.

### Empathic Listening and Normalizing Feelings

Gary was encouraged to express his feelings about being attacked. As noted in the intake, these feelings included fear, anger, sadness, and guilt. Later, Gary began to express a desire to gain revenge. The worker helped Gary "name" and recognize these feelings, as he did not always have words to describe them. She also attempted to normalize the feelings so that Gary realized that these feelings were not unusual or inappropriate.

## Relaxation and Calming Self-Talk

Gary was taught deep-breathing exercises to help him calm himself when he felt a flashback coming or when he began to feel uncomfortable or fearful. The worker and Gary developed a set of self-statements that Gary could also use at these times. The worker stressed the importance of making accurate statements to help Gary regain a realistic sense of security. Examples of calming self-statements were "Nobody will attack me here in the classroom" and "Try to stay calm. I am in a safe place now." By recording the flashbacks, Gary had become aware of his early feelings when a flashback was developing. Thus, he was often able to use relaxation and calming self-talk to interrupt a flashback before it fully developed. Over time, as Gary ventured out alone, these statements were revised to include messages reminding Gary that he knew how to respond if he saw a suspicious person or if someone approached him.

## Reframing Gary's Role
## During the Attack

The worker repeatedly pointed out that Gary had demonstrated courage, intelligence, and fast thinking when he was attacked. He had managed to get and remember a clear description of the assailant. When the assailant asked his name, Gary gave a phony name. Moreover, he had managed to tell his brother about the attack and to talk about it with the hospital staff, the police, and the social worker, all of which were stressful and difficult interactions. The worker also emphasized that Gary was a survivor rather than a victim.

These interventions were delivered over the course of five weekly sessions in the worker's office. The environmental manipulations were instituted immediately, followed by the educational intervention. The relaxation and calming self-talk were introduced during the third week. The other interventions were used as needed in each session. Because it was so difficult to track exactly when some of these interventions were used or if they were used at "full strength" during each week of the intervention, no attempt was made to specify the intervention beyond calling it a package consisting of the above five components.

## RESULTS

Each week, Gary brought in his information on flashbacks. He completed the Generalized Contentment Scale before two additional office visits and when it was mailed to him 3 months after treatment was terminated.

As depicted in Figure 1, the baseline data indicate that Gary was having an average of 8.42 flashbacks per day. Although the actual daily number varied from 7 to 10 flashbacks, the range was not too great and the worker felt that she had a good idea of the general level of the problem. Also, the number of flashbacks was increasing somewhat before intervention, so it does not appear that the problem was being resolved without intervention. Over the course of intervention, the frequency of the flashbacks generally decreased, with a striking exception on Day 16. When Gary brought in these data, the worker asked about that day in particular. Gary told her that he had had to give the police additional information about the attack and examine some photographs of suspects. Talking about the incident in this way made him quite uneasy and brought the whole incident back. Note that the trend did not continue to go downward for a few days after Day 16, as it

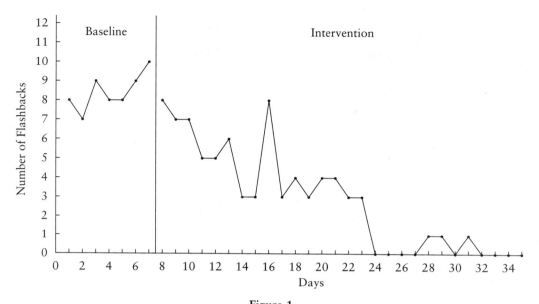

**Figure 1**

Number of flashbacks per day during baseline and intervention phases

had before that time. By the last week, however, the flashbacks had sufficiently reduced such that the worker felt she could terminate treatment.

At this last session, the social worker explained to Gary that she would contact him by telephone at a later date to see how he was doing. Accordingly, she called him 3 months after termination. The worker asked Gary if he would collect data on flashbacks for 1 week. He said he would do so but that he was no longer having any flashbacks. When the worker contacted Gary a week later, he indicated that he had not experienced any flashbacks.

Figure 2 depicts Gary's scores on the Generalized Contentment Scale. As can be seen, his scores dropped to just under 30, the clinical cutting score. Hudson (1982) indicates that such borderline scores must be interpreted cautiously. The worker observed, however, that Gary's mood seemed to have im-

proved. He was involved in more activities again and generally showed more enthusiasm for whatever he was doing. His mother confirmed these observations. Thus, the worker decided it was safe to close the case.

At the 3-month follow-up, the social worker also sent a copy of the depression inventory to Gary and asked him to complete and return it. His score, also depicted in Figure 2, was 23 and suggests he was continuing to be less depressed. During the telephone call to set up the follow-up data collection, the worker also asked Gary some general questions about how he was doing. This anecdotal information served to confirm the quantitative information, all of which suggested that Gary was continuing to improve.

## DISCUSSION

The data Gary and the worker gathered portray continued improvement in terms of the

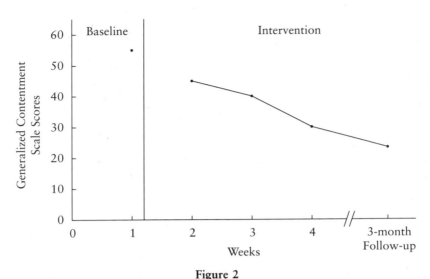

**Figure 2**

Generalized contentment scores during baseline and intervention phases

frequency of flashbacks Gary experienced and the severity of his depression. Although in no way do they "prove" that the interventive package led to Gary's improvement, the data provided ongoing, routine information about the two problems being dealt with in treatment, flashbacks and depression. Had the trends not been in the direction of improvement, the worker could have quickly revised the treatment plan.

Defining the exact nature of a flashback so that it could be measured through self-report by the client yielded information for practice, as well as evaluation, purposes. The worker learned that there were no apparent precipitants of the flashbacks, so the intervention package did not need to focus on particular events that might be leading Gary to experience the flashbacks. Information about the intensity and nature of the flashbacks suggested that certain components of the treatment package might be helpful, particularly using relaxation and coping self-statements, normalizing feelings, and reframing his role in the assault. Because the baseline could be recon-

structed in part and then continued after the telephone intake, the worker was able to get an idea of the level of the target problems without withholding intervention. If the baseline had not been stable (that is, had it fluctuated widely so that it was difficult to know what the "average" level of the problem was), the worker probably would have initiated intervention anyway, since her goal in collecting data was to measure client progress rather than to determine if her intervention was responsible for the progress.

The treatment plan itself was allowed to unfold in the manner the worker thought was best for Gary, without being modified in any way because the case was being evaluated. The intake process could have had certain interventive qualities, thereby affecting the baseline levels recorded by Gary, but the worker did not worry about this. In fact, the data suggest that the client experienced flashbacks with approximately the same frequency both before and after the telephone intake. Further, the intervention did not have to be artificially carved up with certain components being delivered in certain sessions, because the worker was not interested in determining what were the more or less effective ingredients of the intervention.

At the close of treatment, the termination date was set when the social worker thought that Gary had made sufficient progress, based on both the data and her clinical impressions, including interviews with Gary and his mother. Termination was not artificially delayed to allow more data to be collected. Moreover, the follow-up point provided an opportunity for the worker to determine if the client was maintaining his gains.

In short, the evaluation of this case did not needlessly consume the client's or worker's time. The information gathered through data collection was helpful to the client and to the worker. As the data began to suggest improve-ment, Gary felt both relief and increased motivation to continue practicing the relaxation exercises and calming self-talk. The data informed the worker as she made certain clinical decisions. Although it did not lead to tremendous clinical revelations, the monitoring helped the worker and client stay focused on the treatment goals, readily see that the client was making some improvement, and eventually realize that the case could be closed. Obviously, adjunct information collected in the sessions and through interactions with Gary's mother also were helpful in the clinical decision-making process.

## Reference

Hudson, W. W. (1982). *The clinical measurement package: A field manual.* Homewood, IL: Dorsey Press.

*Family problems are a typical concern for the clinical social worker. This case discusses the use of family therapy and demonstrates how it can be evaluated.*

## Questions

1. What were the major treatment strategies used to help change family patterns?
2. How did the social worker respond to the lack of progress in treatment?
3. How did the measures chosen to evaluate this case reflect the problems being addressed in the treatment?
4. What are some other ways that the presenting problems in this case could be measured?

## DOING FAMILY THERAPY WITH AN ACTING-OUT ADOLESCENT: APPLYING THE EMPIRICAL CLINICAL PRACTICE MODEL

*Kevin Corcoran*

Few clients enter treatment with a single problem; most, in fact, present multiple clinical issues. This is especially true for casework with families where the number of people alone makes for more complexity. The following case study—fictitiously called the Olivetti family—will demonstrate the complexity of family problems. The case also displays the importance of assessment in determining whether an intervention is a success or a failure by illustrating both failure and success. In other words, the case will illustrate how the assessment initially led the clinician in the wrong direction and to a lack of effectiveness. This type of problem further supports the call for accountability in monitoring and evaluating one's treatment (Briar, 1973). By using the empirical clinical practice model to monitor the case, the clinician was able to see the need to change interventions in order to effectively help the Olivetti family.

## THE FAMILY AND THE FAMILY'S PROBLEMS

Genny Olivetti was referred to treatment subsequent to her discharge from a psychiatric hospital after reaching the limits of her parents' insurance coverage. Genny's admitting and discharge diagnosis was dysthymic disorder, a mental disorder similar to "neurotic depression" (American Psychiatric Association, 1987). The discharge summary recommended group and individual therapy. No mention was made of family problems or the need for family therapy. The psychosocial assessment was based on a 45-minute telephone conversation with Genny's mother, a 2½ hour family interview and home visit, an individual interview with Genny, and her responses to the Multimodal Life History Questionnaire (Lazarus, 1981).

Genny is a 16-year-old white female who

appears her stated age and is slightly over-weight. She reports having few, if any, close friends. She is very intelligent and was refusing to attend school. Genny complained of "being depressed" for over 2 years. She seemed overwhelmed by her emotions and unable to express them verbally; consequently, she acts them out. Her parents, Curtis and Lane, complained of family conflict with frequent—often daily—arguments, which twice included physical altercations between Lane and Genny; these fights resulted in Genny's hospitalization. All the family members agreed with Lane, who stated "We have problems in communication."

In summary, the identified client appeared depressed, with a flat affect and inability to understand and express her emotions. She seemed to have a low self-esteem and lacked a sense of control over her life. Consequently, the client was perceived as acting out her feelings instead of verbally communicating them. The acting-out behavior was considered an effort to exert control over her life by forcing her parents to establish strict limits on her behavior. Essentially, the client seemed to be trying to have her parents provide the control she could not; for many adolescents, a controlled environment provides a sense of security and psychological safety. Curtis and Lane, on the other hand, seemed intimidated by Genny and allowed her to run the family. Finally, Genny's lack of intrapersonal emotional control and her parents' inability to set limits seemed to exacerbate her depression.

As a consequence of this assessment, two general goals were established: one, to improve the communication between the family members, and two, to establish more appropriate family roles between Genny and her parents. Communication skills training and structural family therapy, respectively, were used. The clinician also used homework assignments to further the change that occurred during the therapy sessions.

## OVERVIEW OF TREATMENT TECHNIQUES

### Communication Skills Training

This behavior therapy is part of social skills training designed to systematically train effective communication skills in human relations. Theoretically, social skill deficits are considered a cause of interpersonal dysfunctioning (Kazdin, 1978). The therapy is based on the clinician modeling effective behaviors, the client's behavioral rehearsal, and positive reinforcement in the form of feedback from family members and the clinician. The Olivetti family had several communication skills deficits, including the lack of expression of content and affect between Genny and her mother, "mind reading" where one member would speak for another, and a lack of active listening.

### Structural Family Therapy

Unlike many therapies, which begin with the middle and upper class, this therapy originated from work with the poor (Minuchin et al., 1967). It focuses on the functioning of families as determined by their structure, namely the social organization. Structure essentially refers to the relationships, codes, rules, and norms that regulate the way members relate to each other. The transactions are determined by the boundaries between family members, their alignment with each other, and each member's power (Aponte, 1981). Briefly, boundaries refer to the rules that define "who participates and how" (Minuchin, 1974) in terms of the degree of enmeshment and disengagement; alignment refers, in part, to the coalitions and alliance of family members; and power describes the amount of influence each family member has in determining the outcome of transactions. In general, the goal of structural family therapy is to reorganize the family. To these ends, the clinician assumes a very active role by creating, joining, or restructuring transactions.

## Homework Assignments

The treatment also used homework assignments. This approach is designed to use the natural environment to initiate change and to generalize the change from clinical sessions to the natural environment. When possible, the homework assignments followed Reid's (1975) five-step format: (1) discussing the assignment's benefits in order to enhance compliance, (2) planning the task implementation, (3) evaluating obstacles to completing the task, (4) conducting a behavioral rehearsal, and (5) summarizing the homework task.

## THE TREATMENT PROCESS

The clinician approached the case from the empirical clinical practice model, which uses rapid assessment tools to monitor a client's progress and evaluates one's effectiveness (Corcoran & Fischer, 1987; Jayaratne & Levy, 1979). Genny was instructed to complete the Child's Attitude Toward Mother (CAM) scale, which assessed her discord with her mother. Lane completed the Index of Parental Attitudes (IPA), which assessed her discord with her daughter, and Curtis completed the Index of Family Relation (IFR), which was used as a measure of intrafamilial stress. These scales have excellent reliability and validity data and have cutting scores of 30 (plus or minus five points), where scores below the cutting score suggest the absence of a clinical problem (Hudson, 1982). The assessments were taken weekly. One retrospective assessment was made of the problem "in general over the past year" during the home visit. Additionally, a pretreatment assessment was also taken during this interview. These two data points served as the baseline data. Additionally, the school registrar reported Genny's weekly absenteeism rate, which served as an unobtrusive measure of the child's progress.

These data were plotted on graphs on a weekly basis (see Figure 1). Curtis's IFR scores are plotted against the left axis of the upper portion of the figure, and school absenteeism is plotted against the right axis. Genny's and Lane's scores are in the lower portion of the figure.

Over weeks two through four, the clinician systematically trained the family in communication skills. The sessions consisted of modeling, behavioral rehearsal between Genny and Lane, and positive reinforcement with feedback. Training included use of "I"-statements where each would be responsible for their communication; having members "ask for what they wanted"; confrontation and correction on "mind reading"; and attentive listening, which included having members "check out" what another said and asking for clarification. During session three, Lane and Curtis reported feeling frustrated over Genny's single-sentence correspondence at home, where she would talk by only saying "yes," "no," or "I don't know." Consequently, they were taught to use open-ended questions in response to this passive-aggressive behavior. Between each weekly session, the clinician gave the family homework assignments to further their communication skills. One assignment, for example, was for the family to review Genny's application to college and develop a contingency plan should she not get admitted.

During the fifth week the parents said they thought "things were better around the house." However, little change was occurring on the rapid assessment instruments, and Genny's school absenteeism rate remained unacceptable. This troubled the clinician, who brought it up during the fifth session. Curtis and Lane acknowledged that they tried to have "good" conversations with Genny and not those that would be confrontational or disputatious—such as whether or not she was going to school. They admitted they felt manipulated by Genny.

The next day Curtis telephoned to report that "all hell broke loose." The parents re-

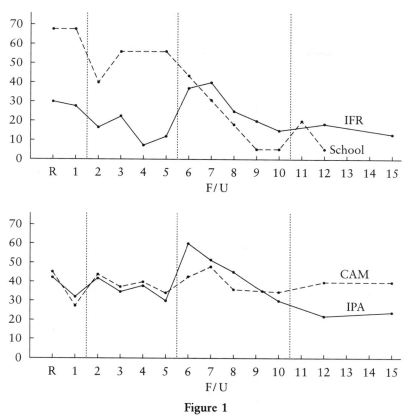

**Figure 1**

Index of family relations, number of school absences, child's attitude toward mother, and index of parental attitudes during the 15 weeks of treatment

portedly confronted Genny about "just playing games with us" and had "put our foot down about school." An argument ensued, and Genny assaulted her mother and then barricaded herself in her bedroom. For the next week she refused to talk with her parents or to eat dinner with them. This discord is clearly reflected on all three rapid assessments scores for week six (Figure 1).

Because of the lack of noticeable progress on the rapid assessment tools and because of the current crisis, during the sixth session treatment moved immediately to the goal of restructuring the family. This was to be ac-

complished through a variety of subtle and direct techniques aimed at emphasizing the difference between Curtis and Lane's role as parent and Genny's role as child, as well as blocking inappropriate transactions when Genny attempted to be in control. To illustrate, the clinician's office had two large leather wing-backed chairs and a Chesterfield. The chairs were rather massive and powerful, whereas the Chesterfield sat lower to the floor. The clinician had the parents sit in the chairs that directly faced Genny in the Chesterfield. Additionally, the clinician structured questions that empowered the parents, whereas those directed to Genny could be answered only in submissive ways. For example, during the crisis phone call, Curtis stated that he did not think Genny would come to the next session; thus the clinician stated "I see you got your child to come today. How did you make her do that?" Genny, on the other hand, was asked questions demanding more conciliatory answers, like "Do you understand what your mother is telling you?"

The structural family therapy used more direct techniques as well. For example, during session six Genny was dismissed from the office and told to wait in the car, while the parents discussed how to respond if she was to hit her mother again. They also discussed how to manage Genny's school absenteeism. Lane later told Genny that if she missed school once again during the next 2 weeks, they would sell her car. Part of the success of restructuring is a consequence of the power it bestowed on the parents. This, however, requires that the parents be sincere on their positions and carry through with threats if necessary. To the reassurance of the clinician and the dismay of Genny, some lucky soul purchased a used car in good condition during week seven. Genny was told she would be using the school bus for the rest of the year and the money would be used to pay the family therapy bill.

The structural family therapy also included homework assignments. Many of these assignments focused on the symptoms by exaggerating, deemphasizing, or relabeling them. For example, during the seventh week, when Genny refused to eat with her parents and was eating in her bedroom, Curtis and Lane were instructed to move the entire dinner—table, chairs, dishes, and all the food—into the bedroom with her. From the next evening on, Genny joined her parents in the dining room.

Over the course of the next three sessions, additional efforts to reorganize the family structure occurred. Curtis and Lane reported that although Genny did not seem to like it

and remained rather taciturn, she was participating in family responsibilities more. This progress was also reflected in the scores on Curtis and Lane's IFR and IPA scores for weeks 6 through 10. While Genny's CAM scores were not significantly improving, which isn't too surprising, her school absenteeism had.

Additional homework assignments were given to restructure the family. For example, before session 10, Lane and Genny were instructed to play an hour of miniature golf, a game they both hated. They were told that Genny had to pay for one half of the game and Lane the other half; that one was to drive to the golf course and one was to drive home, and that they were to play to win. Most important, they were told they could not talk for the entire assignment. Reportedly, on the way home one of them said "I beat you," and both broke into laughter.

## TERMINATION AND FOLLOW-UP

Treatment—totaling 11 sessions—terminated after week 12 because the family was relocating. A follow-up visit was scheduled for the 15th week. As displayed in Figure 1, progress was noted during the structural family therapy sessions (weeks 6 through 10), with gradual decreases in scores on familial stress (IFR) and Lane's discord with Genny (IPA). Additionally, Genny was going to school, in spite of having to take the bus. The only time she skipped school was during week 11, which was "senior skip day." The clinician was not too troubled by this because Genny was out with a group of newly formed friends; alternatively, the behavior simply may have been an effort by Genny to "test the limits" the week before the follow-up session.

Subsequent to the relocation, the clinician had a final telephone follow-up with the family. Curtis and Lane both reported the family was doing well. Genny had not graduated but was completing school over the summer and had enrolled in a local college for the fall semester. Genny stated "I still don't like my mom much, but I guess I'm not supposed to; I'm a teenager, you know."

## References

American Psychiatric Association. (1987). *Diagnostic and statistical manual of mental disorder* (3rd ed. revised). Washington, DC.

Aponte, J. J. (1981). Structural family therapy. In A. S. Gurman & D. P. Kniskern (Eds.), *Handbook of family therapy* (pp. 310–360). New York: Brunner/Mazel.

Briar, S. (1973). The age of accountability. *Social Work, 18,* 14.

Corcoran, K., & Fischer, J. (1987). *Measures for clinical practice: A sourcebook.* New York: The Free Press.

Hudson, W. W. (1982). *The clinical measurement package: A field manual.* Homewood, IL: Dorsey Press.

Jayaratne, S., & Levy, R. L. (1979). *Empirical clinical practice.* New York: Columbia University Press.

Kazdin, A. E. (1978). Sociopsychological factors in psychopathology. In A. S. Belleck & M. Hersen (Eds.), *Research and practice in social skills training.* New York: Plenum.

Lazarus, A. A. (1981). *The practice of multimodal therapy.* New York: McGraw-Hill.

Minuchin, S. (1974). *Families and family therapy.* Cambridge, MA: Harvard Press.

Minuchin, S., Montalvo, B., Guerney, B., Rosman, B., & Schuner, F. (1967). *Families of the slums.* New York: Basic Books.

Reid, W. J. (1975). A test of the task-centered approach. *Social Work, 22,* 3–9.

# CASE STUDY 8.3

*Three case examples are provided to suggest the diversity and flexibility in which practice evaluation tools can be applied. The examples, purposefully not ideal, reflect the realities of integrating evaluation methods with practice.*

## Questions

1.  What difficulties were evident in applying practice evaluation methods to each of the cases?
2.  When is it necessary to devise your own measure rather than rely on a previously developed and standardized measure?
3.  What conclusions can be drawn from the social work interventions in each of the examples?
4.  What skills and knowledge were evident in the implementation of the practice evaluation techniques?

## PRACTICE EVALUATION METHODS: PRACTICAL VARIATIONS ON A THEME

*Paula S. Nurius*

". . . there is a sense in which investigation continues as long as does treatment" (Richmond, 1917, p. 363).

A little more than a decade ago, the presence of a chapter on practice evaluation methods in a casebook for social work practice would have struck many as curious. Today, the absence of such a chapter would seem peculiar. Such is the nature of our constantly evolving profession, reflecting and responding to an ever-changing array of needs and realities.

Practice evaluation is itself in the midst of evolution. As the quote above suggests, social work has a historic commitment to systematic inquiry as a fundamental component of its in-

The author would like to acknowledge the very useful input and stimulation from a host of students and practitioners over the years, and Donna Linz, Murray McCord, Jani Semke, and Misty Cleman in particular.

terpersonal practice. What changes with each passing decade are the tools with which to pursue this mission and the organizational context within which that mission must be pragmatically fashioned. It is toward this fitting of tools to setting that the present case studies will speak.

Specifically, this series of case studies advocates a creative and credible approach to employing various aspects of practice evaluation across the spectrum of human service settings. Three case examples of very different types of social work intervention will be used to illustrate the diversity and utility of practice evaluation tools flexibly and practically employed. Each case example will be followed by discussion of how features of this particular application could generalize to other interventions or services.

Because the focus of this chapter is on practice evaluation methods and because space is limited, information on the clients, treatments, and settings are necessarily abbreviated. Moreover, no attempt was made to locate "textbook perfect" examples. Rather, the goal was to offer cases where compromises had to be struck, constraints balanced, and creative alternatives generated. This reflects both the blessing and the bane of social work—its enormous diversity of service and thus the need for diverse and flexible means of depicting, tracking, and evaluating that service.

## SCENARIO 1: ONGOING TREATMENT AND CASE MANAGEMENT

A host of case examples are presently available in the literature of longitudinal single-system designs with individuals, families, and even groups. For this reason, emphasis will be placed here on less "conventional" applications—those that do not lend themselves quite so readily to standard counseling models. The first example will come closest to this standard in that ongoing therapeutic client contact is involved. Features that complicate evaluation efforts include client limitations as a collaborator in monitoring, use of interdisciplinary team approaches that tend to cloud the social worker's unique input, and the rapidly growing emphasis on types of casework whose outcomes are difficult to measure (for example, prevention, case management). The case example described here involves an inpatient psychiatric setting followed by case management and monitoring through an outpatient setting.

### Case Example

The client is a 32-year-old female of Mexican descent, married and the mother of two young children. She was admitted to an inpatient psychiatric center following increasing disorientation, delusional ideation, depression, and sleep and appetite disturbance. The worker

established target problem areas for this client to be psychosis—as evidenced by auditory hallucinations, confusion, and delusional thinking—and depression—as evidenced by agitation, inability to concentrate, latency, tearfulness and depressed affect, and sleep and appetite disturbance.

For purposes of monitoring and evaluation, the worker selected three primary indicants—auditory hallucinations, confusion, and depressed affect. Rationale for selection of these indicants included (1) they were viewed either by the worker as both observable and representative or by the client and her family as most debilitating; (2) they were reflective of the treatment goals, that is, reducing or eliminating psychotic and depressive symptoms and enhancing the client's self-management abilities; and (3) they were able, with a reasonable degree of accuracy, to be operationalized and monitored by family members and, to a more limited extent, by the client and by human service workers.

The worker then devised a series of rating scales to tap key dimensions of target symptoms. A 1–5 rating was assigned to varying degrees of auditory hallucinations, confusion, and depressed affect, with each rating level operationalized for each indicant. For example, 1–5 ratings for confusion included:

1 = No confusion noted or reported, processing information well

2 = Mild confusion, some periods of clear cognitive functioning, minimal latency

3 = Moderate impairment, moderately confused, distracted about half the time, some latency

4 = Very confused but still attempting to function and process information, very marked latency

5 = Extremely confused, disorganized thinking, unable to function or process information

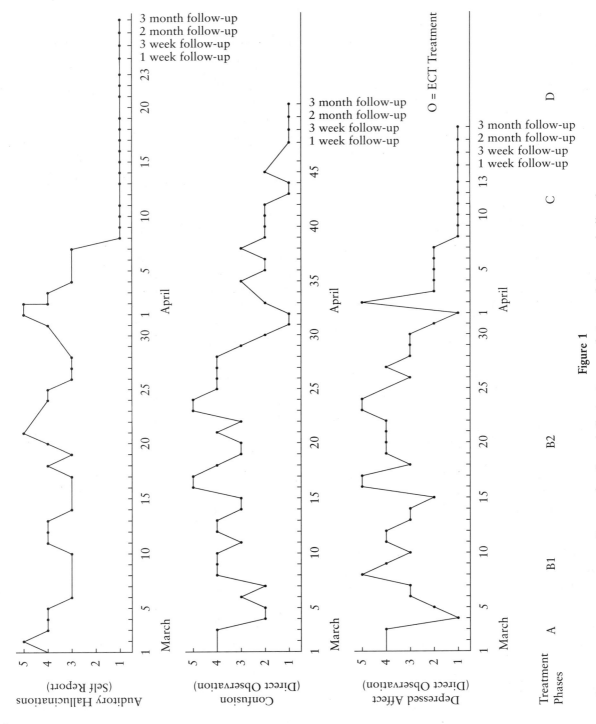

**Figure 1**

Degree of auditory hallucinations, confusion, and depressed affect during phases of the treatment

For auditory hallucinations, the worker drew on client self-report, whereas for confusion and depressed affect, direct observations by treatment team members were used.

The profiles of these indicators over the course of treatment are depicted in Figure 1. As is evident, stable positive change was not achieved with the first two treatment components—that of antidepressants (B1) followed by use of antidepressants and antipsychotic medications (B2). Rapid and sustained change was evident on use of electroconvulsive therapy alone (C); no medications were given during this period. The final phase (D) represents outpatient case management. This phase of treatment included a maintenance dose of antidepressants, daily attendance at a day treatment program, and periodic follow-up contact with a staff psychiatrist and case manager.

As in most cases, compromises between research and service delivery agendas were necessary. Specifically, decisions based on clinical and organizational factors qualify and constrain data-based interpretations. For example, the course of treatment (that is, "design") renders inferences of causality tentative due to lack of controls. On the other hand (1) the immediate, consistent (across three measures), and stable change in indicators with the onset of electroconvulsive treatment, (2) the lack of prior consistent change, and (3) an existing empirical literature base supporting the efficacy of this treatment with patients who present with this diagnostic profile combine to suggest the likelihood of causality. Practical significance was achieved in that treatment outcome goals were met and the client's improved functioning areas stabilized, permitting return home.

The case manager who was assigned to the case continued to monitor maintenance as reflected by these indicators and added additional indicators appropriate to her specific work with the client (not depicted here). Notably, the client and her husband were also able to monitor her functioning and adjust as needed as a result of learning the early indicators of slippage, the ways in which this could be distinguished from normal variations (for example, mood, stress), and options for adjustment. The combination of observational monitoring (by workers, family members) and self-monitoring (often entailing client education) holds utility across a broad spectrum of case management and maintenance and prevention-oriented interventions.

## SCENARIO 2: LIMITED CONTACT INTERVENTION

In some settings, use of practice evaluation methods has been seen as untenable because of the nature of the services (for example, discharge planning) or of the circumstances (for example, very limited client contact). In addition, practice evaluation has tended to be portrayed in terms of ongoing care, thus involving longitudinal designs, individualized goals, and measures of incremental progress toward goals. Yet in an increasing proportion of human services, this evaluative model is not well suited to setting realities. One case in point is that of discharge planning.

The case example described here involves an injured adult in a hospital setting. The issues encountered are broadly generalized across a variety of populations (for example, those in correctional settings, frail elderly, the acutely or chronically mentally ill, individuals with terminal illnesses) and across residential, long-term care, or transitional settings where discharge planning and preparation are needed. In spite of its prevalence, guidelines for distilling and evaluating the relative *effectiveness* of discharge planning have thus far not been adequately addressed. The following scenario will present several creative applications of practice evaluation methods tailored to the needs and constraints of the case and setting. As noted earlier, the following illustrations are not intended as templates of "correct" evaluative approaches but rather of viable examples generated by busy practitioners on the job.

## Case Example

The client is a 43-year-old black male referred to a spinal cord injury unit for treatment and rehabilitation of spinal cord lesions. The client's injuries, sustained through an accident, left him a complete paraplegic and a partial quadriplegic. The client is a Vietnam veteran, has limited financial resources, has not worked for several years because of a prior injury, and lists only a sister living in another state as a family member with whom he has contact.

The client was referred to the hospital's social services department by the medical staff for discharge planning and assistance in obtaining community resources. The client's presenting problems were consistent with this referral agenda, with clear preference to live by himself and be as independent as possible.

The worker used a two-pronged approach to outcome evaluation. First, a standardized inventory of criteria constituting an effective discharge plan was developed. In circumstances such as discharge planning involving high frequency, limited client contact, and similarity across cases, repeated use of standardized as opposed to individually developed instruments tends to be most viable. An attractive alternative is the ability to individually tailor, on a manageable scale, a standardized format.

Figure 2 details one such approach used here. The social service department staff had previously constructed a listing of various goals practitioners typically consider or strive toward accomplishing in discharge planning. The extent to which each of these is attained, as applicable, is indicated on a 0–3 scale: 0 = not at all, 1 = a little, 2 = moderately, 3 = substantially or completely. In addition, spaces are available to write in individualized goals for each client and to rate their degree of attainment on the same four-point scale.

In the present case, the worker used this latter option to detail specific factors related to this client obtaining and sustaining his independent living goals. These included his knowledge of independent living/housing options, the level of personal control (locus of control) the client assumed toward establishing and maintaining an independent life plan (ILP), and the extent to which the client had peer and professional supports in the community that would facilitate maintenance of his independent living.

To enhance its validity and reliability of use across cases and raters, it is optional that each level for each criterion be operationalized or "anchored." As an illustration, the locus of control ratings were operationalized as:

0 = client does not take any responsibility for establishing his ILP

1 = client is minimally involved in establishing his ILP

2 = client is moderately participating in establishing his ILP

3 = client is actively involved in establishing his ILP

This charting format has proven useful in a variety of ways. First, it provides a multidimensional approach to assessing client outcome vis a vis the discharge process with more interventionally relevant detail than typically afforded (see Zilligen, 1985 for background). This is of value to the practitioner, the supervisor, and the manager alike. It can be an efficient communication aid among staff involved with a case, particularly in those circumstances where several caseworkers may be coordinating the discharge plan or sharing discharge duties for a given case, some of whom may be less familiar with the client. It also provides valuable data at the point of referral

| | |
|---|---|
| 3 | 1. Planning process started early |
| 2 | 2. Comprehensive assessment completed |
| 3 | 3. Problem list established and prioritized |
| 3 | 4. Problem-specific goals with action plans developed |
| 2 | 5. Patient involved in planning process |
| NA | 6. Family/significant others involved in planning process |
| 3 | 7. Action plans adjusted as needed to fulfill goals (i.e., problems resolved) |
| 2 | 8. Planning goals achieved (prior to discharge) |
| 3 | 9. Follow-up arranged (care and/or contact) |
| 3 | 10. Patient discharged by scheduled date |
| 1 | 11. Patient satisfied |
| NA | 12. Family/significant others satisfied |
| 2 | 13. Initial evidence of discharge follow-through (e.g., patient received in new health care site) |
| 2 | 14. Patient thriving in new setting |
| NA | 15. Patient readmitted within one month of discharge |
| 2 | 16. *Other: Knowledge of IL / housing options |
| 2 | 17. *Other: Patient locus of control |
| 1 | 18. *Other: Social support network |
| | 19. *Other: |
| | 20. *Other: |

**Key**

0 Not At All
1 A Little
2 Moderately
3 Substantially
NA Not Applicable

* Anchors for each rating level need to be specified on back of form.

**Figure 2**

Discharge planning criteria and outcome evaluation

to community service agencies as to the status of the patient (for example, relatively low level of social supports and moderate degree of engagement in independent plan maintenance).

A variety of other limited contact situations may be aided in practice evaluation efforts by this type of pool. Among others this could include a variety of crisis interventive circumstances, information and referral, and short-term education, mediation, and brokerage services.

## SCENARIO 3: CASE ACUITY AND HIGH-RISK ASSESSMENT

Primary prevention, long a concern of the social work profession, has been growing as a service objective across a wide spectrum of client populations and problems in living. The following case example will illustrate one health care center's efforts to identify and operationalize factors constituting high risk for a given client group and then to systematically assess, be guided by, and monitor these factors over the course of client contact. For purposes of brevity, only the assessment and risk classification steps will be illustrated. Monitoring of stability or change in risk factors over time and outcome evaluation based on these trends can, however, readily be pursued by recording client status on these factors over time.

## Case Example

The client population involves pregnant women receiving prenatal care at a county health care setting. High-risk factors with respect to pregnancy resulting in both a healthy full-term birth and satisfactory mother–infant bonding were targeted by the women's clinic staff.

The staff had been discussing and employing "mental checklists" regarding factors each had come to see associated with problematic pregnancies, births, or bonding. Over time, this informal and somewhat idiosyncratic method proved inadequate (for example, clinic staffing became less stable, the proportion of complex cases began rising, hospital administration was considering cutting funding of the social work component in the clinic), motivating staff to develop more formal assessment instruments and monitoring procedures.

Figure 3 presents the high-risk profile of a sample of clinic patients. The ten targeted factors by no means represent an exhaustive list. They were, however, viewed as adequate

| Weight | Risk Factors | A | B | C | D | E | F | G | H | I | J | K | L | M | N | O |
|---|---|---|---|---|---|---|---|---|---|---|---|---|---|---|---|---|
| 1 | 1. History of Sexual Abuse | | | | • | | | | | | | | | | | |
| 3 | 2. History of Drug and/or Alcohol Misuse | • | | | • | | • | | • | | | | • | • | • | • |
| 1 | 3. History of Depression/Psychiatric | | | | | • | • | • | | | | | • | | • | • |
| 1 | 4. History of Runaway/Street Life | • | • | | • | | | • | • | | | | | | | |
| 1 | 5. History of Physical Abuse | | | | • | | | • | | | | | • | • | | |
| 2 | 6. Under Age 18 | • | • | • | • | | | • | • | | • | | | | | |
| 1 | 7. No Stable Partner | | | | • | | | • | • | | | | • | | | |
| 2 | 8. First Prenatal Visit ≥ 20 Weeks | • | • | | | • | | | | • | | | • | | | |
| 1 | 9. Education < 12th Grade | • | • | • | | | • | • | • | | • | • | | | | |
| 1 | 10. Low Income (AFDC, WIC, Etc.) | | • | • | | | • | | | • | | • | | • | • | • |

N = 15

↑ (arrow pointing to column G)

**Figure 3**
Sample patient profiles of pregnancy high-risk factors

given the delimited goals and intervention options the clinic was in a position to pursue with respect to their clients. Note also that weights were assigned to each factor such that youth, lack of early prenatal care, and a history of drug or alcohol misuses carried greater risk relative to other factors.

Figure 4 presents the high-risk classifications of these women. This classification provides one indicator of the acuity of each case and thus the need for more immediate and/or intensive services. It does not, of course, suggest that the same interventions will be designated within each set. For example, clients D and E are both classified at the same level of risk, but their risk profiles are quite different and will require intervention plans tailored to those differences. This underscores the importance of using both sets of information in relation to each other. Also important in weighing

the various factors and alternatives are the client's priorities and perceptions of need.

A third step taken was to develop clusters of interventions that generally correspond to level of risk and, thus, need. This treatment planning aid was necessarily viewed as suggestive rather than directive for many of the same reasons noted above. For example, because of her history of drug/alcohol use, medical and counseling services targeting this factor would be provided to client E immediately.

The majority of clinic services are more brokerage related than therapeutic oriented. The overarching goal is to get the client through the pregnancy safely and to increase the likelihood of adequate mother–infant bonding and parenting ability. Therefore, specific goals and progress indicators established for individual clients tend to be operationalized vis a vis those outcomes. Broadly general-

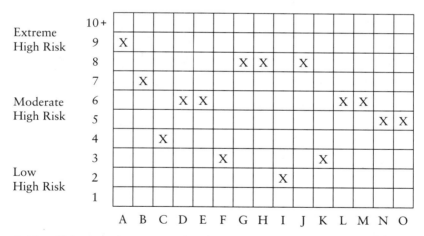

8–10+: University alert, PHN referral, possible CPS referral on basis of noncompliant patient plus 1–7 as needed

4–7: Prenatal/parenting classes, referrals for housing, employment, teen alternative schooling, PHN plus 1–3 and 8–10 as needed

1–3: Emergency funds, food bank tickets, bus tokens, short-term therapy/counseling referrals, plus 4–10 as needed

**Figure 4**

Service provision priorities based on high-risk profiles

izable outcome indicators, useful for both clinical and quality assurance purposes, include the term delivery of a healthy infant, good health of the mother, and satisfactory indicators of preparedness to parent and to maintain the health of mother and infant.

## CONCLUSION

There has been a long-standing dialogue regarding the means, utility, and appropriateness of practice evaluation. Proponents have tended to view single-case research methods as a means to address questions regarding the effectiveness of social casework and have formulated how these methods can and should be used in practice (for example, Bloom & Fischer, 1982; Fischer, 1978; Gambrill, 1983; Hudson, 1982; Jayaratne & Levy, 1979; Reid, 1980). Others have argued that attempts to merge service and (empirically based) research questions and methods are untenable, inherently conflictual, and fundamentally inappropriate (for example, Heineman, 1981; Ruckdeschel & Farris, 1981; Thomas, 1978). And, there have been an increasing number seeking some practical and viable approaches between these two poles (for example, Berlin, 1983; Gambrill & Barth, 1980; Gottlieb, 1987).

Recently, another factor has begun to figure into this discourse. This has to do with the rapidly developing role of computers in social agencies, particularly with respect to administrative information management and decision support and the subsequent implications for evaluation paradigms and pressures. The need for integrated systems that require and use interventionally relevant information as well as traditional management indicators (for example, productivity, efficiency) has been advocated (Grasso & Epstein, 1987; Johnson, Williams, Klingler, & Giannetti, 1977; Mutschler & Hasenfeld, 1986)—although as yet not as a majority sentiment. Similarly, calls for shifts

in traditional evaluation paradigms to embrace service effectiveness as a central and equal concern of management have emerged (Patti, 1985; Patti, 1987; Poertner, 1986)— although again not yet a majority perspective.

Social work has historically sought and grappled with bridging needs such as these. Questions regarding whether to employ practice evaluation methods, how, under what circumstances, and to what end are legitimate questions that can and need to be continually examined and flexibly dealt with. It is a joint mission for the social caseworker, administrator, and academician, and one in which an informed and active contribution by the direct practitioner plays a vital role.

## References

Berlin, S. B. (1983). Single-case evaluation: Another version. *Social Work Research and Abstracts, 19,* 3–11.

Bloom, M., & Fischer, J. (1982). *Evaluating practice: Guidelines for the accountable professional.* Englewood Cliffs, NJ: Prentice-Hall.

Fischer, J. (1978). *Effective casework practice: An eclectic approach.* New York: McGraw-Hill.

Gambrill, E. (1983). *Casework: A competency-based approach.* Englewood Cliffs, NJ: Prentice-Hall.

Gambrill, E., & Barth, R. P. (1980). Single-case designs revisited. *Social Work Research and Abstracts, 16,* 15–29.

Gottlieb, N. (1987). *Perspectives of direct practice evaluation.* Seattle, WA: University of Washington School of Social Work.

Grasso, A. J., & Epstein, L. (1987). Management by measurement: Organizational dilemmas and opportunities. *Administration in Social Work, 11,* 89–100.

Heineman, M. B. (1981). The obsolete scientific imperative in social work research. *Social Service Review, 55,* 371–397.

Hudson, W. W. (1982). *The clinical measurement*

*package: A field manual.* Homewood, IL: Dorsey Press.

Jayaratne, S., & Levy, R. (1979). *Empirical clinical practice.* New York: Columbia University Press.

Johnson, J. H., Williams, T. A., Klingler, D. E., & Giannetti, R. A. (1977). Interventional relevance and retrofit programming: Concepts for the improvement of clinician acceptance of computer-generated assessment reports. *Behavior Research Methods and Instrumentation, 9,* 123–132.

Mutschler, E., & Hasenfeld, Y. (1986). Integrated information systems for social work practice. *Social Work, 31,* 345–349.

Patti, R. (1985). In search of purpose for social welfare administration. *Administration in Social Work, 9,* 1–14.

Patti, R. (1987). Managing for service effectiveness in social welfare: Toward a performance model. *Administration in Social Work, 11,* 7–22.

Poertner, J. (1986). The use of client feedback to improve practice: Defining the supervisor's role. *The Clinical Supervisor, 4,* 57–66.

Reid, W. J. (1980). Research strategies for improving individualized services. In D. Fanshel (Ed.), *Future of social work research.* Washington, DC: NASW.

Richmond, M. (1917). *Social diagnosis.* New York: Sage.

Ruckdeschel, R. A., & Farris, B. E. (1981). Assessing practice: A critical look at the single case design. *Social Casework, 62,* 413–419.

Thomas, E. J. (1978). Research and service in single-case experimentation: Conflicts and choices. *Social Work Research and Abstracts, 14,* 20–31.

Zilligen, R. S. (1985). Quality assurance for basic discharge planning. *Continuing Care Coordinator, 4,* 24–26.

# CASE STUDY 8.4

*This case study applies an "intensive" methodology in order to scientifically examine the facts and events that have a bearing on a person's functioning. By systematically evaluating a large range of information and data, an overall understanding of the case can be developed and supported with rationales.*

## Questions

1. In what ways is the method presented a "scientific" approach to practice?
2. How does this method promote a problem-solving approach to practice?
3. What theories were used to help develop an understanding of the client's problems?
4. How could this approach be used in supervision or case staffings?

## AN INTENSIVE CASE ANALYSIS: APPLICATION OF THE QUASI-JUDICIAL METHOD

*Craig Winston LeCroy and Bian Ismail*

JB is a 15-year-old adolescent who lives in a residential treatment center. He comes from a troubled family. He was abused as a child, has had numerous foster home placements, and is diagnosed as having attention deficit disorder with hyperactivity. He has a history of being abusive and displaying aggressive behavior toward others. There are indications that he is self-destructive, having attempted suicide when quite young, taking dangerous risks, and abusing drugs. He has not made much progress since being placed in a residential treatment center.

- What facts do we have about this individual?
- Are situational aspects of JB's difficulties receiving proper consideration?
- What explanations are useful in attempting to understand JB's functioning?
- What is the validity of this account?
- Is there additional evidence about the nature of JB's difficulties that would better explain things?
- What professional explanations, as opposed to lay explanations, are being used to understand JB's behavior?
- What general conclusions about JB have the most evidence for them?

The purpose of this case study is to present an intensive case analysis of a child in a residential treatment center. It is an *intensive* case analysis because the attempt is to piece together a comprehensive and complete account of the significant events that influence the current functioning of this child. Of course, practitioners are quite familiar with the idea of a case study or case presentation. However, the intensive case study includes both this familiar narrative style and an explanation of the facts and events that help explain the person's functioning.

The intensive aspect of the case is equivalent to the process of doing research. However, in this circumstance the research process is most similar to the quasi-judicial method and was recognized by Richmond (1917) over 60 years ago as an important aspect of social diagnosis (Bromley, 1986). Unfortunately, the early attempts to use the case study method were not completely explored, and the scientific aspects of this method have yet to be realized.

The unfortunate history of the case study method in social work is that it frequently has represented a narrative account in support of one central idea or theory about why a person is functioning in certain ways. In contrast, an intensive case study is more of an exercise in problem solving (Bromley, 1986). It is an application of the rules of systematic thinking, that is, logic, in order to understand and respond in an effective manner. The benefit in doing a case study is in the resulting thoroughness in which one attempts to gather data and make conclusions about individuals and about what might be helpful to them. Bromley (1986, p. 37) summarizes the scientific aspects of a case study:

> The basic aim of a quasi-judicial case-study is to formulate a cogent argument, i.e., a rational and empirical argument, which explains the behavior of the person under investigation. Such an argument is, in effect, a *theory* or *explanation* about that person's adjustment, and is therefore open to question and subject to continual revision in the light of the fresh evidence and new ideas. Ideally, the case-study eventually reaches a stage at which it makes good sense: it is internally coherent; it corresponds with the empirical evidence; it successfully predicts how the individual will behave; and it is accepted by competent investigators working independently of one another.

This chapter will apply the case study method as suggested by Bromley (1986) to a subject who is currently in a residential treatment center receiving services. The case study method begins with the following steps: narrative or case description, listing of the problems, grouping of the problems, reasons for the groupings, diagrams of events and relationships, and final narrative understanding and conclusions.

## ABBREVIATED CASE DESCRIPTION

JB's mother, Ms. M, was pregnant with him in 1971. She was using both LSD and speed while pregnant. She was not married at the time but was living with JB's father, Mr. T. Shortly after her pregnancy, Ms. M discovered that Mr. T had been involved with another woman. As a result she threw him out of the house and had no further contact with him. JB was born in 1972, and shortly thereafter Ms. M married Mr. E, who then adopted JB. Mr. E was physically and emotionally abusive with JB. In 1974 JB was diagnosed as hyperactive and placed on Ritalin. During this time JB's mother describes him as uncontrollable. Records indicate that at the age of 4, JB attempted to hang both himself and his sister and began self-abusive behavior such as throwing himself against walls. He remained in the home only until 1976, when he was placed in foster care. In 1977, Mr. E (who had adopted JB in 1972) died of cancer. JB was returned to his family the day of Mr. E's funeral. During the next 3 years JB was hospitalized twice in a children's psychiatric program. JB's behavior continued to be abusive toward his siblings and mother. He became so uncontrollable that JB's mother brought him to Child Protective Services. She stated that if he was returned home she would end up killing him. Child Protective Services placed JB in several foster homes, but he remained uncontrollable, often hitting the younger children in the families. In 1986 he was placed in a residential treatment center. At the center JB is reported to be impulsive and in need of constant attention, demonstrating little social maturity or sense of responsibility. He has had difficulty relating to peers and authority figures. There have been numerous incidents of his abusive behavior and sexual misconduct.

The second step is to take the information available and begin to develop a listing of the problems. At this stage the emphasis is on laying out all the problems—later the list can be reexamined to eliminate problems that do not have supporting evidence. This process helps in identifying and clarifying the problem. It should facilitate the process of further inquiry—what needs to be looked into further, what connections begin to emerge between the problems, what problems are the most salient, and so on. Listing the problems also begins the process of rearranging the information, and such rearrangements encourage new and alternative viewpoints about the problem. Table 1 presents a list of JB's problems.

The next step is to study the list of problems and begin to organize the data. In order to obtain a better understanding of the client, the procedure of structuring and restructuring can be used. This facilitates a better description and interpretation of the data and is similar to exploratory data analysis. Table 2 presents one way of structuring data using the case example. The table shows some initial ideas about how to understand JB's functioning within a life history perspective. It also presents data on the sequencing of events that led up to JB's current status as a client in long-term residential treatment. At this point we have little empirical understanding of JB's functioning. There are vague and general terms being used, and their empirical basis still needs to be established.

Another procedure for organizing the data is to sort the problems into categories that fit together conceptually. This process should be a result of both inductive and deductive approaches to the problem. As Bromley (1986) points out, the empirical approach classifies the information without much concern for meaning, and the rational approach attempts to look for patterns of meaning from the data. Table 3 uses the case description and other data and begins the process of sorting problems into categories.

Table 3 presents the mechanism by which the data begin to acquire meaning. Patterns of meaning or theories begin to come into play as one attempts to group problems into conceptual categories. In order to begin scrutinizing the data and interpretations of the data, it is useful to make explicit the reasons for the conceptual groupings. At this level of analysis one examines his or her beliefs, judgments, and inferences in a more explicit manner. By making statements explicit we are more compelled to justify our actions.

**Table 1**
**List of Problems**

| | |
|---|---|
| Asthma | Limited impulse control |
| Hyperactivity | Poor peer relation |
| Oppositional to authority figures | Attention deficit disorder |
| Grand mal seizures | Provokes others |
| Poor self-concept | Sees world as against him |
| Aggressive behavior | Compulsive liar |
| Manipulates others | Substance abuser |
| Low trust level | Inappropriate sexual behavior |
| Poorly developed conscience | Difficulty completing tasks |

**Table 2**
**Structuring the Data**

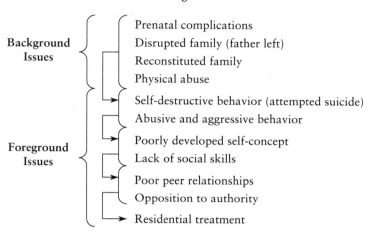

Background Issues
- Prenatal complications
- Disrupted family (father left)
- Reconstituted family
- Physical abuse

Foreground Issues
- Self-destructive behavior (attempted suicide)
- Abusive and aggressive behavior
- Poorly developed self-concept
- Lack of social skills
- Poor peer relationships
- Opposition to authority
- Residential treatment

**Table 3**
**Problems Sorted into Categories**

A. *Physical Problems*
Hyperactivity
Asthma
Seizures

B. *Poorly Developed Conscience*
Compulsive liar
Provokes others without cause
Sees nothing wrong with antiso-
cial behaviors
Poor concept of women

C. *Poor Self-Concept*
Lack of identity
Sees world as against him
Substance abuse
Takes risks
Aggressive behavior to protect

D. *Lack of Self-Control*
Little impulse control
Oppositional to authority figures
Aggressive behavior
Difficulty completing tasks

E. *Relationship Problems*
Manipulates others
Low trust level
Provokes others
Oppositional behavior
Poor peer relationships

# REASONS FOR GROUPINGS

## Group A: Physical Problems

This relates to physical problems that JB may or may not have created. Grand mal seizures are organic in nature and can be treated through medication. JB's asthma problem may have environmental causes; however, this can also be maintained through medication.

## Group B: Poorly Developed Conscience

Several factors indicate that JB has a poorly developed conscience: he lies for no apparent reasons. He lies even to his closest friends. When confronted by someone who knows he's lying he will not admit to lying.

JB antagonizes others, especially younger children who are defenseless. He sets up people and seems to enjoy seeing them take the fall. He spares almost no one except if he feels he cannot be successful.

JB feels no remorse after lying or provoking others physically or verbally. He rarely says "I'm sorry." He has a hard time distinguishing right from wrong with his behaviors.

JB has a poor concept of women. He often makes derogatory remarks to women. He also buys pornographic materials whenever possible. He does not respect women and will not accept authority from women.

## Group C: Poor Self-Concept

JB sees the whole world as out to get him. Whenever he is criticized he feels that everyone is against him.

JB also has a poor self-image, and this can be observed by his lack of self-care and his inability to accept any positive feedback. He is definitely afraid of any rejection.

JB takes life-threatening risks and engages in behaviors that are harmful to himself. JB also engages in substance abuse whenever he gets a chance. Alcohol and pot have thus far seemed his major sources.

JB is developing aggressive tendencies and is involved in physical assaults.

## Group D: Lack of Self-Control

JB has a lack of self-control; this is suggested by his diagnosis of attention deficit disorder with hyperactivity. JB shows little impulse control; when agitated he will hit someone without thinking. He often blurts out things that are inappropriate or harmful or that seem unrelated to anything.

JB also lacks the ability to follow directions by parents, teachers, or other authority figures. JB cannot complete tasks. He cannot sit down and finish something without constant prompting.

## Group E: Relationship Problems

JB has had a long history of relationship problems. Many of his early behavior problems revolved around abusive behavior toward others.

He never established a good relationship with his mother, and there is not much affection between them. His mother reports not wanting him back in the home.

JB has had numerous incidents of aggressive behavior with other residents at the residential treatment center, and he has had numerous incidents of inappropriate sexual behavior.

JB is described by staff at the residential center as someone that manipulates others and who will provoke others for no reason.

Five problem areas have been grouped together in this case analysis. The assumption is that these five areas fit together in some functional sense; that is, there are some causal factors suggesting the groupings. The reasons for the groupings need to be made clear. The supporting evidence for each grouping needs to be rigorously evaluated and reviewed; therefore, the next step is to examine closely the possible reasons for each of the groupings.

This process is facilitated by the use of diagrams. Each grouping is diagramed in order to examine the nature of the relatedness of the problems. This diagraming process is similar to that used in path analysis. The attempt is to explore the causality—the exact manner in which problems may be related to one another. Figure 1 presents a series of diagrams that look at causality for each of the different problem groupings.

The information in this case study consists of narrative, statements, test results, and dia-

**Group A: Physical Problems**

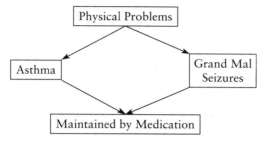

Commonality = maintained by medication

**Group B: Lack of Conscience**

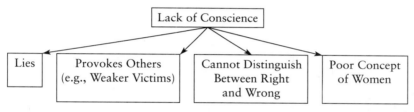

Commonality = sees little value in others

**Group C: Poor Self-Concept**

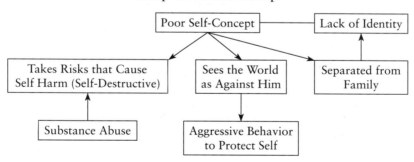

Commonality = does not see himself as valuable

**Figure 1**
Diagram analysis of client's problems according to problem groupings

**Group D: Poor Self-Control**

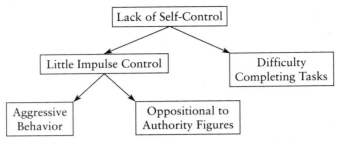

Commonality = cannot control impulsive tendencies

**Group E: Relationship Problems**

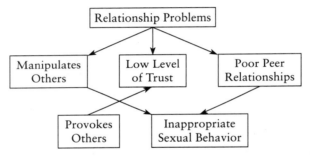

Commonality = has not established meaningful and
satisfactory relationships with others

**Figure 1** (*Continued*)

grams organized in certain ways. It is important to point out that this information is composed of various facts, assertions, suppositions, inferences, and judgments. These data have been taken from numerous sources and organized in different ways.

The *intensive* case analysis examines the data carefully. What is based on fact and what is based on opinion? What interpretations are being made from the data? What judgments are lacking empirical support? Validity is of concern in the case analysis. For example, we have independent correspondence substantiating JB's aggressive tendencies. There are self-reports (he will talk about being "mean"),

staff reports of aggressive behavior, family reports of aggressive behavior, and psychological evaluations suggesting an overly aggressive disposition. The reliability of the data is also of interest; do observers report behavior in an internally consistent manner? The scientific method in an *intensive* case analysis is critical; "a case-study is to be judged by its internal coherence, by the extent to which its empirical content can be independently and objectively verified, and by the validity of its conceptual framework" (Bromley, 1986, p. 95).

In order to make the knowledge, assumptions, and arguments understood, it is important to write out the reasons for the problem groups. This step brings us closer to putting together the pattern. At this point the major issues are refined and a justification of the person's functioning is beginning to develop substance. The following section demonstrates this process with JB.

*Group B Category*—Poorly developed conscience system; possible reasons:

Mrs. M was a poor role model. She frequently abused substances, moved from relationship to relationship, and lied to JB on several occasions.

There is a lack of positive relationships in JB's life. JB has a poor relationship with his family. He does not get along with siblings or parents. There has not been much nurturing, caring, or love in his family.

That JB cannot see right from wrong may stem from his experience of child abuse. JB often got hit for no apparent reason. As a result, consistency of punishment vs. rewarding are not related in his mind. Inappropriate parenting may have led to a low level of moral development.

The problem of JB provoking others without cause could result because JB may want rejection to maintain a negative outlook of himself.

*Group C Category*—Poor self-concept; possible reasons:

JB feels unwanted by his mother. This may be due in part to her not protecting him from his stepfather's abusive behavior. JB was removed from the home and has experienced much rejection from home. Also, constantly being taken out of foster homes may lead to a feeling of constant rejection.

Constant abuse for no reason is likely to lead to a poor self-concept. The abuse also relates to JB seeing the world as being against him. JB was taken out of the home because of his acting out; however, his stepfather, who was abusing him, remained in the home. Also, constant relocation may have made JB think the whole world was out to get him.

Substance abuse may have been a way to take risks, to deal with anger, or to rebel. The child abuse and lack of nurturing may have caused this.

JB's risk-taking behavior can be seen as a result of a poor self-concept resulting from the above factors. His self-abusive behaviors early on in life have translated to risk taking in early adolescence. Also, this self-destructive behavior could be a way of punishing himself because his stepfather died as soon as JB was placed in foster care. JB may feel responsible for his stepfather's death. Self-abuse may occur as a means to punish himself.

*Group D Category*—Lack of self-control; possible reasons:

This may have been caused by an unstructured, abusive home environment and by a lack of positive and consistent discipline. JB's stepfather hit him whenever he felt like it.

The parents showed little impulse control and therefore provided a role model for a lack of self-control. JB may be defiant as a result of his parents' abusive nature. His opposition to authority figures may have resulted from this. Also his inability to complete tasks may be related to his oppositional state. Clinicians also see this as lack of impulse control.

*Group E Category*—Relationship problems; possible reasons:

JB developed a basic lack of trust early in his life. Because of an abusive home environment, he did not receive appropriate nurturing or attachment. He began life unwanted and without a father. Because few people in his life have given him love, he may believe he can only get attention through provoking others. Also the many disruptions have not allowed him to become attached to any adult figures and explain some of his lack of self-control. JB's early tendencies toward aggressive behaviors have also contributed to general poor peer relationships. Inappropriate sexual behavior is suggested by the lifelong lack of attachment and the tendency to manipulate others.

## PUTTING IT ALL TOGETHER

The final step in an *intensive* case study is to put together a final understanding of the person. Figure 2 presents an overall understanding of the events and relationships for JB. This

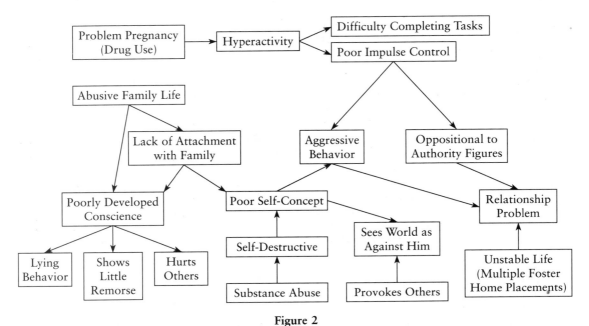

**Figure 2**

Overall understanding of events and relationships

is best done in a diagram or graph form that shows the theoretical or supposed relationships between causes and effects. The graph should represent a functional analysis (Bromley, 1986) of the events and relationships. The strength and direction of the factors and their relationships should be shown. The procedure of making a diagram of the relationships forces one to grapple with important assumptions about the case. It can be an aid to forestalling premature problem solving and can help get a broader perspective. This final diagram should represent the visible end-product of a long process of thinking about the case

(Bromley, 1986). As the figure demonstrates in the case of JB, a complex set of events are described and linked together based on the existing evidence available for understanding his particular life situation.

## References

Bromley, D. B. (1986). *The case study method in psychology and related disciplines.* New York: John Wiley and Sons.

Richmond, M. (1917). *Social diagnosis.* New York: Russell Sage Foundation.

# CASE STUDY 8.5

*Many agencies and programs are actively involved in research. This case study presents an example of how to design and implement an applied research program among Native American youth.*

## Questions

1. What special considerations are needed when designing and conducting research programs?
2. How were the interventions designed to reflect cultural values?
3. How was research integrated with practice in the design of this program?
4. How can other similar programs be more systematically evaluated in order to assess the impact of social services?

## PREVENTING SUBSTANCE ABUSE AMONG NATIVE AMERICAN YOUTH

*Steven P. Schinke, Michael S. Moncher, Gary Holden,*
*Mario A. Orlandi, and Gilbert J. Botvin*

Kristin and Mary played quietly in the abandoned lot near their reservation home. As Gordon Adams, a recently graduated M.S.W. watched the two Native American girls at play, he wondered if the substance abuse prevention program he was planning for youth on the small coastal reservation was a good idea. After all, the major problems with substance use and abuse for residents of the reservation occurred among adults. Moreover, most of the children and young people on the reservation appeared happy, secure, and untroubled by conventional substance abuse. In fact, the only substances that were truly "abused," according to Adams's observations, were snuff and chewing tobacco. And those

tobacco products could hardly harm the children, Adams thought to himself.

Adams knew that he faced many challenges in the execution of this applied prevention project. He not only was confronted with the exigencies of prevention program delivery and evaluation that attend any such project but also was challenged by the special circumstances of working cross-culturally with members of a population who differed in many ways from himself. Adams was not an Indian.* He was a child of the American middle class and thus was born into the lap of luxury, relative to most members of the tidy but poor reservation where he now worked. Adams's charge, therefore, was not unlike that confronted by increasing numbers of social workers who—by choice or by chance—find them-

Funding for the preparation of this chapter was provided by research grants from the National Institute on Drug Abuse (5 ROl DA03277) and the National Cancer Institute (1 ROl CA44903).

* For ease of presentation, the terms *Indian, American Indian,* and *Native American* are used interchangeably throughout this chapter.

selves serving members of at-risk populations who differ culturally, socially, and often economically from the workers' own backgrounds.

In the service of advancing clinical and research knowledge and in the spirit of sharing with other social worker clinicians and social work clinical researchers the processes of developing and implementing an applied substance abuse prevention program, this chapter presents case material on the study that Adams directed. Specifically, the chapter focuses on the primary prevention of tobacco use, alcohol, and drug abuse among adolescents from empirically designated at-risk populations of Native Americans. The authors begin the chapter by reviewing briefly the health and behavioral risks associated with smoked and smokeless forms of tobacco use, alcohol use, and drug use.

Next, the authors note theoretically and empirically supported explanations for substance abuse among youth. On that foundation, the chapter then details procedures and gives illustrative case material for the design of preventive interventions that respond to the needs of high-risk adolescents from Native American groups. Throughout the chapter's presentation, we draw from the experiences of Gordon Adams, an empirically grounded social worker who we believe represents the forefront of today's clinicians and applied program evaluators.

## SUBSTANCE ABUSE RISKS

Tobacco use poses clear health and behavioral risks for adults and, perhaps more urgently, for young people. More than their adult counterparts, children and adolescents have the potential to altogether avoid the problems of smoked and smokeless tobacco use by never taking up the habit.

Of all the popularly abused substances, alcohol remains the most common and devas-

tating for many groups of Indians (Schinke et al., 1985a; Schinke et al., 1985b; Schinke et al., 1986a). Despite a concerted effort by health professionals over the past two decades, the use of these substances remains at an unacceptably high level. Not only does the use of alcohol and tobacco—together or separately—pose immediate problems to the health, educational development, and social functioning of adolescents, but also the early use of these substances has been linked with later problems throughout adulthood. A large literature supports the known dangers and probable risks of alcohol use among children, adolescents, and adults. Consequently, these dangers and risks do not require a detailed exposition within this proposal. However, it is appropriate to highlight a few of these in order to underscore the seriousness of the problems of alcohol and drug use in Native American society.

First, the use of alcohol and drugs has been associated with a number of chronic diseases and health problems, separately and in combination. Second, the use of alcohol and drugs has been associated with an increased risk of injury and death resulting from accidents among Native Americans. Alcohol use has been found in numerous studies to be a major contributory factor in traffic accidents, falls, fires and burns, and drownings. The relationship between substance use and accidents is a major source of concern, since accidents are the leading cause of death among American Indian youth between the ages of 15 and 24.

Third, alcohol and drug use have not only been associated with the use of a variety of illicit substances among adolescents and adults but have been identified as "gateway" behaviors for many adolescents, leading to other forms of substance abuse. Data from a number of sources indicate that experimentation with one substance frequently leads to experimentation with others in a logical and generally predictable progression, as already detailed. Most individuals typically begin by using alcohol and tobacco, progressing later on to the use of marijuana. For some individuals, this progression may eventuate in the use of depressants, stimulants, and psychedelics. The use of opiates and cocaine typically does not occur until the end of this progression.

Finally, to some extent the use of alcohol and drugs increases the risk of becoming an IV drug user. In the case of both types of substances, where the likelihood of engaging in unprotected sexual activity might be increased while the individual is intoxicated, new urgency now exists for the development of effective prevention strategies because of the potential for contracting AIDS.

## EXPLANATIONS FOR SUBSTANCE ABUSE

A number of nonexclusive explanations exist for smoked and smokeless tobacco use, alcohol use, and drug use among Indian and non-Indian young people and adults. Peer pressure is a frequent explanation for tobacco use among Indian youth. Often, American Indian adolescents appear to consider smoking and smokeless tobacco use rites of passage (Carpenter, Lyons, & Miller, 1985). Moves toward smokeless product use may further be explained by smokeless tobacco industry advertising, new and easily used snuff and rolled leaf products, the absence of laws governing the sale and labeling of smokeless tobacco, and antismoking campaigns (Gritz, Ksir, & McCarthy, 1985; Lichtenstein, Severson, Friedman, & Ary, 1984; Severson, Lichtenstein, & Gallison, 1985). Smokeless tobacco use deceptively offers American adolescents and adults a "benign" alternative to cigarette smoking.

The impact of adult tobacco users as negative behavioral role models for Indian children and adolescents cannot be denied. Added explanations for tobacco use among American

Indians come from data on gender differential use rates and patterns. American adolescents frequently evidence gender-specific styles of smoked and smokeless tobacco use, alcohol use, and drug use (Brunswick & Messeri, 1984; Dembroski, 1984; Gritz, 1982; Hunter, Croft, Burke, Webber, & Berenson, 1986). Like their adult counterparts, adolescent females may use tobacco and other substances to control their weight. Young men may regard substance use as a sign of masculinity (Beauvais & LaBoueff, 1985). Although causal linkages remain elusive, empirically described explanations for tobacco, alcohol, and drug use can direct efforts to prevent substance use and abuse among American Indian youth.

## PREVENTION

Prevention efforts offer a cost-effective and promising approach to reducing health problem risks from smoking and smokeless tobacco use. Besides reducing health risks, efforts to prevent smokeless and smoked tobacco use could lower adolescents' and adults' risk of other substance use, as suggested earlier in data on the progression of tobacco, alcohol, and licit and illicit drug use (Yamaguchi & Kandel, 1984b). Furthermore, as Jessor (1982) observed:

> Adolescence is a pivotal stage in the life span for the development of health-related behavior. Not only is it a period of heightened health risk, but what happens in adolescence is consequential for health in later life (p. 297).

For many American children and adolescents, interventions to prevent tobacco use could bring lasting returns.

Given the available explanations of why people adopt and continue tobacco use, scientists agree that the onset and maintenance of cigarette smoking and of smokeless tobacco use are preventable behaviors through psychosocial and life-style changes. The wisdom of preventing tobacco use notwithstanding, sensitive and empirically tested preventive interventions do not exist for the highest-risk groups of Americans. Particularly underresearched are preventive interventions for young Americans, who by virtue of their membership in empirically documented risk groups, have much to gain from early life-style changes. In the present context, positive lifestyle changes through behavioral means not only could enable high-risk adolescents to prevent their own and others' tobacco use but also could promote their physical and mental health by exploring alternative recreations and adaptive coping and interpersonal skills.

## INTERVENTIONS FOR HIGH-RISK YOUTH

As a first step toward producing tobacco use prevention strategies for high-risk youth, social work researchers can develop and test theory-based interventions drawn from previous empirical studies. Those studies offer modest support to the efficacy of skills-based interventions for preventing tobacco use among adolescents who are at least at average risk for future smoking and smokeless tobacco use. Derived from social learning theory, skills interventions help adolescents prevent problems and promote their health through problem solving, coping, and communication skills (Schinke & Gilchrist, 1986). To date, skills interventions have largely been tested with middle-class, nonminority youth (Biglan & Ary, 1985; Jason & Glenwick, 1984; Johnson & Solis, 1983; McAlister, Puska, Salonen, Tuomilehto, & Koskela, 1982; Pentz, 1983).

Among the reasons for this limited testing are research designs that favor studies with stable, compliant, homogeneous populations. Suburban school-based studies, the venue for most skills intervention research, are apt to overlook ethnic-racial minority group youth.

Sporadic attendance patterns and high rates of dropout and absenteeism bode ill for outcome research in such nonschool, neighborhood settings as youth clubs, churches, and recreation facilities. New and innovatively designed and executed studies, planned and carried out collaboratively by social work clinicians and investigators and by school district administrators and line staff, could overcome these impediments.

## PREVENTION PROGRAMMING FOR INDIAN YOUTH: CASE STUDY

To continue our case study of Gordon Adams's experiences in the development, implementation, and evaluation of an intervention program to reduce substance abuse risks among Indian youth, the remaining sections of this chapter describe steps we have employed in our past clinical research. These steps, moreover, can easily serve the needs of other social work clinicians and investigators in the design and execution of applied substance abuse prevention programs with youth and young adult members of high-risk populations.

The steps that we will detail and illustrate by Adams's experiences in conducting a substance abuse prevention program for Indian youth are (1) base-rate data gathering and (2) constructing intervention curricula for high-risk youth. Elsewhere, we have presented guidelines on the processes of executing prevention research studies conducted by clinical social workers in school environments (Schinke, Gilchrist, Lodish, & Bobo, 1983). Though not repeated here, those guidelines also have currency for the present material and setting.

In particular, the means and ends of social work services and research protocols in nontraditional human services and social agency settings—including schools and reservations—must conform to the norms and prerogatives of the host environment. Specific examples of that conformity appear in subsequent sections of this chapter. In the next section we describe and illustrate the first step of our prevention programming approach for developing preventive interventions for Native American adolescents and other youth from high-risk backgrounds.

## Base-Rate Data Gathering

To prepare for a study of substance abuse prevention among Indian and other high-risk youth, social workers must first accurately determine the current rates of smoked and smokeless tobacco use, alcohol use, and drug use among the youth sample. This step requires the development and administration of assessment measurement instruments and the subsequent analysis of the collected data. Conventionally, substance abuse prevention investigators have adapted a battery of psychosocial and physiological measures that have proven helpful for this task. These measures seek to validly quantify youths' tobacco, alcohol, and drug use and to assess psychological and behavioral correlates of future substance use.

To obtain valid, if not reliable, estimates of youths' tobacco use, investigators largely rely on a combination of self-report and biochemical sampling procedures. Self-report procedures simply ask youths to note, along quantitative parameters, their recent use of smoked and smokeless tobacco products. Typically, such questions cover the most recent past day and week of youths' substance use. Youths' reported substance use, in turn, is usually measured by multiple-choice questions about the incidence and number of cigarettes, smokeless tobacco products, alcohol, and drugs consumed during the index reporting period.

Gordon Adams, for example, collected base-rate information on the 117 Indian children and adolescents involved in the prevention program he was coordinating through several measurement instruments. For his purposes, Adams drew on a series of measurements developed and tested in the authors' and others' past research with Native American adolescents (Cvetkovich, Earle, Schinke, Gilchrist, & Trimble, 1987; Gilchrist, Schinke, Trimble, & Cvetkovich, 1987; Oetting, Beauvais, Edwards, Waters, Velarde, & Goldstein, 1983; Schinke, Orlandi, Botvin, Gilchrist, Trimble, & Locklear, 1988; Schinke, Schilling, & Gilchrist, 1986b). From these measures, Adams and his associates compiled a list of items that covered substance use self-reports, knowledge, attitudes, and beliefs about various substances, and a host of parameters related to youths' identification with Indian culture and the Indian way of life.

These latter items about Indian culture were included in the battery because of our interest in empirically ascertaining the extent to which Indian youths' substance use and their success in the prevention program were explained by youths' identification or lack of identification with their historical roots. For example, a growing body of research suggests that Indian youths who are aware of the benefits of Indian culture and of non-Indian culture for their everyday lives (often called a bicultural orientation) are better able to resist substance use pressures than youths who closely align themselves either with Indian culture or with non-Indian culture (LaFramboise, 1982; LaFramboise & Rowe, 1983; Oetting, Goldstein, Beauvais, Edwards, Goldstein, & Velarde, 1980).

Drawing on his base-rate data, Adams was able to profile current substance use rates among the target population of American Indian adolescents on the reservation slated for the preventive intervention program. Further, Adams could empirically learn about the levels of selected correlates and associated variables relative to substance use and abuse. By descriptively analyzing these findings, Adams and the social work researchers who were in charge of the study could better focus the resulting prevention program.

For example, because of youths' reported use of certain substances and their low use rates and nonuse of other substances, Adams and his colleagues could aim the intervention at those substances that posed greatest problems and risks for the target adolescents. Data on youths' knowledge, attitudes, and beliefs about substance use and abuse also gave direction to the program by guiding the level and complexity of instruction for beginning intervention. Last, Adams used information about youths' orientation to the Indian way to shape the amount and nature of cultural information included in the planned preventive intervention program. With these base-rate data, Adams and his social worker colleagues were ready to construct a responsive intervention curricula for preventing substance abuse among American Indian youth on the index reservation.

## Constructing Preventive Intervention Curricula

Admittedly, curriculum construction and the design of preventive interventions are complex processes. These curricula development processes lend themselves neither to hastily fashioned programs nor to facile guidelines for others. Still, most principles for constructing preventive interventions aimed at tobacco, alcohol, and drug abuse among high-risk children and youth, including American Indian youngsters, are within the ken of many social work clinicians and clinical investigators. Thus, those principles are suitable for coverage in the present chapter. Illustrated by Adams's experiences with the design of curricula to prevent tobacco, alcohol, and drug use among American Indian youth, these principles begin with a careful quantitative and qualitative analysis and a subsequent interpretation of base-rate data, as briefly noted above.

Adams and his colleagues thus posed several nonexclusive and nonexhaustive questions of the data to start building the foundation for their substance abuse prevention curriculum. Illustrative of these questions were: Do the data show patterns of tobacco use, alcohol use, and drug use among certain age groups, reservation neighborhoods, and areas of the community in the sample? What correlates exist between biochemical and self-report measures of substance use? Do various psychosocial measures of tobacco, alcohol, and drug use correlates point up any trends or indicators of knowledge, attitudes, beliefs, or preferences that suggest prevention strategies?

By asking and answering these and related questions, Adams can empirically portray the nature and scope of substance use among the target children or youth—American Indian children and youth who live on a reservation, in the present example. Further, such questions may reveal information that identifies deficits in youths' abilities to avoid substance use or that identifies strengths for prevention programming.

Adams's efforts to create a curriculum that was responsive to the needs and preferences of American Indian youth followed a three-phase sequence of intervention, development, and pilot testing. First, Adams and his associates reviewed past prevention research, as found in the retrievable scientific and social work practice literature, to locate intervention content and procedures that had application for their planned curricula for Indian youth at risk for substance use and abuse.

Second, Adams and other members of the clinical research team focused on groups of adolescents from the target population of Indian youths to identify areas of emphasis and to screen the preventive intervention plans thus far. Third, Adams and his colleagues pilot tested the resulting intervention with Indian children and adolescents to determine the levels of acceptance, responsiveness, and salience of curricula developed through the preceding steps.

Against this backdrop, the following sections provide an overview of the preventive intervention efforts of Adams and colleagues intended for delivery with American Indian youths at high risk for future and serious tobacco, alcohol, and drug use.

*Illustrative Preventive Intervention Curricula.* Depending on the venue for intervention, our preventive intervention curriculum is suitable for delivery by graduate level social worker staff. These staff are found and recruited from the ranks of existing professionals or qualified paraprofessionals or students undergoing training. In some instances, workers with less than graduate degrees can deliver preventive intervention curricula, as long as these workers are directly supervised by M.S.W. or similarly advanced clinicians. For example, community-based intervention on an Indian reservation can be delivered by paraprofessionals from human services agencies or by undergraduate or graduate assistants from a college or university, providing that these workers receive the appropriate levels of supervision.

Whoever delivers it, preventive intervention aimed at tobacco, alcohol, and drug use among American Indian adolescents occupies fifteen 50-minute biweekly group sessions. Harmonious with youths' cultural values, intervention integrates normative and learning theory components. As an example, intervention group leaders can help Indian adolescents use traditional folk tales, legends, and myths to promote their healthy development and to prevent smoking, excessive drinking, and drug taking.

Additional steps to infuse cultural values into preventive intervention are exercises for youths to observe and report on instances where American Indian values did or could beneficially serve them in everyday tasks. By the infusion of ethnic pride, intervention encourages Indian adolescents to apply their cultural heritage along with prevention skills to promote their lives and avoid tobacco, alcohol, and drug-related problems.

Problem solving for substance abuse prevention can be depicted on posters that show Indian children and youths engaging in steps for defining problems, generating solutions to them, evaluating the solutions, selecting the most meritorious ones, and planning to implement the solutions. Youths can practice the steps in age- and culture-relevant vignettes.

Finally, communication skills can be introduced by videotapes of American Indian youths who clumsily, then competently, interact with peers. Group members can model for one another effective use of eye contact, posture, gestures, intonation, and words. Youths can break into dyads for experiential practice while group leaders offer feedback and coaching. Scripted interactions ease subjects into these practices. Because prevention learning, not unlike much knowledge acquisition among adolescents, is subject to decay over time, booster sessions can aid youths' retention and use of intervention content, procedures, and skills. Every 3 months, Indian youths in the program conducted by Adams thereby receive two booster sessions one week apart. Intervention group leaders start the first booster session of each pair by asking youths to review their past learning. Youths then share instances where their prevention knowledge and skills paid off.

Next, Indian youths relate their prior experiences to future applications of substance abuse prevention methods. Toward this end, youths receive timelines to project the next 3 months of their lives. The timelines help youths identify recurring and special events that could lead to tobacco use, alcohol use, or drug taking. Youths specify how they will avoid problem situations. After they describe their plans in writing, Indian youths are subsequently paired as buddies. Buddies review each other's plans and will arrange for progress reports outside of group sessions.

In the midst of implementing their preventive intervention program with American Indian children and adolescents in a reservation-based setting, Adams and his associates cannot empirically gauge the success of the prevention effort. Definitive data on Indian youths' substance use rates and other relevant outcomes are unavailable and will not be forthcoming until after a long follow-up period. Preventive intervention efforts, because they seek to reduce the risks of future problem behavior, must await evaluation until a sufficient amount of time has passed between intervention delivery and target youths' eligibility to engage in the behaviors of interest to the program—use of smoked and smokeless tobacco, early and problem drinking, and non-recreational drug use, in this example.

The lack of such outcome data notwithstanding, Adams's program offers fresh and empirically derived hope for Kristin, Mary, and the scores of other American Indian youths who live on the reservation where the program is occurring and who are at inordinately high risk for future habitual and serious problems with substance use and abuse.

## DISCUSSION

In this chapter, we have described and illustrated through a clinical case study how social work practitioners and investigators can analyze a health behavior problem among high-risk adolescents and can then use the results of that analysis to construct a preventive intervention strategy. With a target population of American Indian children and youth and a target problem of substance use, the authors outlined and demonstrated major steps in the construction of a culturally responsive, sensi-

tive, and needed preventive intervention program.

Prevention as a treatment or intervention modality has several advantages for social work practice. These advantages are pronounced in the development of social work services with children and adolescents. In the present illustration, we described how interventions for Native American adolescents who are at high risk for tobacco use, alcohol use, and drug use were developed through a two-sequence approach. That approach involves base-rate data gathering and curriculum construction.

By outlining methods for reducing the incidence of tobacco use among Indian adolescents, the illustration demonstrated several features of the advocated approach to preventive intervention development. These features included an intervention developed with equal attention to theoretical fealty and to empirically derived explanations for the phenomenon under consideration. Finally, our intervention development approach attended to cultural sensitivity and to the need for empirically testable intervention components.

Despite the positive inroads described and illustrated by Gordon Adams's experiences as recounted in this chapter, more research is needed by social work clinicians and clinical investigators on preventive intervention strategies for problem behaviors among members of high-risk populations. Of all the behavioral and social sciences, social work is in closest contact with its practice and clinical roots. This contact will serve well the means and ends of intervention development and research efforts.

What is more, social work's long-standing expertise in person—environment issues adds credence to our special ability to research problems that increasingly manifest discord between these two essential elements of human functioning. Perhaps the present discussion and illustration offers ideas and will provoke additional investigations on the development and testing of preventive interventions for high-risk youth.

## References

Beauvais, F., & LaBoueff, S. (1985). Drug and alcohol abuse intervention in American Indian communities. *The International Journal of the Addictions, 20*(1), 139–171.

Biglan, A., & Ary, D. V. (1985). Current methodological issues in research on smoking prevention. In E. S. Bell & R. Battjes (Eds.), *Prevention research on deterring drug abuse among children and adolescents* (NIDA Research Monograph Series). Washington, DC: U.S. Government Printing Office.

Brunswick, A. G., & Messeri, P. (1984). Gender differences in the processes leading to cigarette smoking. *Journal of Psychosocial Oncology, 2,* 49–69.

Carpenter, R. A., Lyons, C. A., & Miller, W. R. (1985). Peer-managed self-control program for prevention of alcohol abuse in American Indian high school students. *The International Journal of the Addictions, 20,* 299–310.

Cvetkovich, G., Earle, T. C., Schinke, S. P., Gilchrist, L. D., & Trimble, J. E. (1987). Child and adolescent drug use: A judgment and information processing perspective to health-behavior interventions. *Journal of Drug Education, 17,* 295–313.

Dembroski, T. M. (1984). Stress and substance interaction effects on risk factors and reactivity. *Behavioral Medicine Undated, 6*(3), 16–20.

Gilchrist, L. D., Schinke, S. P., Trimble, J. E., & Cvetkovich, G. T. (1987). Skills enhancement to prevent substance abuse among American Indian adolescents. *International Journal of the Addictions, 22,* 869–879.

Gritz, E. R. (1982). The female smoker: Research and intervention targets. In J. Cohen, J. W. Cullen, & L. R. Martin (Eds.), *Psychosocial aspects of cancer* (pp. 39–49). New York: Raven.

Gritz, E. R., Ksir, C., & McCarthy, W. J. (1985). Smokeless tobacco use in the United States: Present and future trends. *Annals of Behavior Medicine, 7,* 34–61.

Hunter, S. M., Croft, J. B., Burke, G. L., Webber, L. S., & Berenson, G. S. (1986). Longitudinal patterns of cigarette smoking and smokeless tobacco use in youth: The Bogalusa Heart Study. *American Journal of Public Health, 76,* 193–195.

Jason, L. A., & Glenwick, D. S. (1984). Behavioral community psychology: A review of recent research and applications. In M. Hersen, R. M. Eisler, & P. M. Miller (Eds.), *Progress in behavior modification* (Vol. 18, pp. 85–161). New York: Academic.

Jessor, R. (1982). Problem behavior and developmental transition in adolescence. *The Journal of School Health, 53,* 295–300.

Johnson, E. A., & Solis, J. (1983). Comprehensive community programs for drug abuse prevention: Implications of the community heart disease prevention programs for future research. In T. J. Glynn, E. G. Leukefeld, & J. P. Ludford (Eds.), *Preventing adolescent drug abuse: Intervention strategies* (pp. 76–114). Rockville, MD: National Institute on Drug Abuse.

LaFramboise, T. D. (1982). *Assertion training with American Indians: Cultural/behavioral issues for trainers.* Las Cruces: New Mexico State University, Educational Resources Information Center Clearinghouse on Rural Education and Small Schools.

LaFramboise, T. D., & Rowe, W. (1983). Skills training for bicultural competence: Rationale and application. *Journal of Counseling Psychology, 30,* 589–595.

Lichtenstein, E., Severson, H. H., Friedman, L. S., & Ary, D. V. (1984). Chewing tobacco use by adolescents: Prevalence and relation to cigarette smoking. *Addictive Behaviors, 9,* 351–355.

McAlister, A., Puska, P., Salonen, J. T., Tuomilehto, J., & Koskela, K. (1982). Theory and action for health promotion: Illustrations from the North Karelia Project. *American Journal of Public Health, 72,* 43–50.

Oetting, E. R., Beauvais, F., Edwards, R., Waters, M. R., Velarde, J., & Goldstein, G. S. (1983). *Drug use among Native American youth: Summary of findings (1975–1981).* Fort Collins, CO: Colorado State University.

Oetting, E. R., Goldstein, G. S., Beauvais, F.,

Edwards, R., Goldstein, L., & Velarde, J. (1980). *Drug abuse among Indian children*. Fort Collins, CO: Colorado State University.

Pentz, M. A. (1983). Prevention of adolescent substance abuse through social skill development. In T. J. Glynn, E. G. Leukefeld, & J. P. Ludford (Eds.), *Preventing adolescent drug abuse: Intervention strategies* (NIDA Research Monograph No. 47, pp. 195–232). Washington, DC: U.S. Government Printing Office.

Schinke, S. P., & Gilchrist, L. D. (1986). Preventing tobacco use among young people. *Health and Social Work, 11*, 59–65.

Schinke, S. P., Gilchrist, L. D., Lodish, D., & Bobo, J. K. (1983). Strategies for prevention research in service environments. *Evaluation Review, 7*, 126–136.

Schinke, S. P., Gilchrist, L. D., Schilling, R. F., Walker, R. D., Kirkham, M. A., Bobo, J. K., Trimble, J. E., Cvetkovich, G. T., & Richardson, S. S. (1985a). Strategies for preventing substance abuse with American Indian youth. *White Cloud Journal, 3*(4), 12.

Schinke, S. P., Gilchrist, L. D., Schilling, R. F., Walker, R. D., Locklear, V. S., Bobo, J. K., Maxwell, J. S., Trimble, J. E., & Cvetkovich, G. T. (1986a). Preventing substance abuse among Ameri-can Indian and Alaska Native youth: Research issues and strategies. *Journal of Social Service Research, 9*, 53–67.

Schinke, S. P., Orlandi, M. A., Botvin, G. J., Gilchrist, L. D., Trimble, J. E., & Locklear, V. S. (1988). Preventing substance abuse among Ameri-can Indian adolescents: A bicultural competence skills approach. *Journal of Counseling Psychology, 35*, 87–90.

Schinke, S. P., Schilling, R. F., & Gilchrist, L. D. (1986b). Prevention of drug and alcohol abuse in American Indian youths. *Social Work Research and Abstracts. 22*(4), 18–19.

Schinke, S. P., Schilling, R. F., Gilchrist, L. D., Barth, R. P., Bobo, J. K., Trimble, J. E., & Cvetkovich, G. T. (1985b). Preventing substance abuse with American Indian youth. *Social Casework, 66*, 213–217.

Severson, H., Lichtenstein, E., & Gallison, C. (1985). A pinch or a pouch instead of a puff? Implications of chewing tobacco for addictive processes. *Bulletin of the Society of Psychologists in Addictive Behaviors, 4*, 85–92.

Yamaguchi, K., & Kandel, D. B. (1984b). Patterns of drug use from adolescence to young adulthood: III. Predictors of progression. *American Journal of Public Health, 74*, 673–681.